EMPIRICAL THEOLOGY: A HANDBOOK

Contributors
Randolph Crump Miller
Tyron Inbody
Nancy Frankenberry
Karl E. Peters
Marjorie Hewitt Suchocki
William Dean
Bernard J. Lee
Gerard S. Sloyan
William C. Tremmel
Robert S. Corrington
Frederick Ferré
John B. Cobb Jr.

Empirical Theology: A Handbook

Edited by
RANDOLPH CRUMP MILLER

Religious Education Press
Birmingham, Alabama

Library of Congress Cataloging-in-Publication Data

Empirical theology: a handbook / edited by Randolph Crump Miller.
   Includes bibliographical references and index.
   ISBN 0-89135-088-8
   1. Empirical theology.   I. Miller, Randolph Crump, 1910-
BT83.53.E57   1992
230'.046—dc20   92-33139
                                                                      CIP

Religious Education Press
5316 Meadow Brook Road
Birmingham, Alabama 35242
10 9 8 7 6 5 4 3 2

Religious Education Press publishes books exclusively in religious education
and in areas closely related to religious education. It is committed to enhancing and professionalizing religious education through the publication of
serious, significant, and scholarly works.

PUBLISHER TO THE PROFESSION

Contents

Preface

When James Michael Lee wrote to ask if I would be interested in editing a volume on empirical theology, my immediate reply was "yes." Beginning when I was a college student, empirical theology has been a major interest. At Yale I studied under Douglas Clyde Macintosh, and the chief topic of my dissertation was the thought of Henry Nelson Wieman. So Lee's inquiry was just what I wanted.

We selected the outlines and possible contributors. Most of the requests to the writers were immediately answered in the affirmative. Nine of them are members of the Highlands Institute for American Religious Thought, and the other three writers agree with them on the significance of empirical and process theology.

The working paper suggested that the book be an overall resource and permanent reference book. The chapters are to be a summary of what has taken place, with some room for personal and original interpretations and advances in thought. It was suggested also that much use should be made of the empirical theologians of the first part of this century along with the thinking of younger scholars, including developments in process thinking. The book was to be aimed at professionals in the fields of both theology and pastoral ministry, at students in college and seminary, and at educated lay persons.

The working paper also stated that empirical theology begins with observation, experimental behavior, and reason. It makes use of the data of direct experience, experimental testing and analysis, imaginative construction of hypotheses and concepts, pragmatic testing, and rational inferences. Experience includes sense experience, experience of relations, a sense of the whole, and appreciative consciousness. There is a "vague affective tone" (Whitehead) as the basis of experience. This leads to theological concepts formulated within a historical and metaphysical perspective and makes use of models that are consistent with a modern worldview, leading to what is called naturalistic theism.

1

This has significance for religious education, because theology and educational theory need to be participants in dialogue if we are to have effective religious education. Thus we can have adequate guidance for Bible study, teaching beliefs that can withstand today's cultural assumptions, participation in the life of the church, and an ethical approach to daily living and a public theology for acting to achieve a just society.

The writers were free to make use of these suggestions and the chapter outlines in any way that suited their own expertise. The exchange of chapters among the writers in the early drafts helped to clarify some points. Because of the cooperation of all the writers, the publisher's deadline has been met. The editor is grateful for all of the writers for their participation in what has been a creative and satisfying project.

RANDOLPH CRUMP MILLER
Editor

PART ONE

"Let empiricism once become associated with religion, as hitherto, through some strange misunderstanding, it has been associated with irreligion, and I believe that a new era of religion as well as of philosophy will be ready to begin."

William James

Randolph Crump Miller

The spirit of American theology, insofar as its primary interests are consistent with American culture, makes use of radical empiricism, pragmatism, and pluralism. It is an open-ended theology, based on a naturalistic view of the world. It is usually consistent with the major insights of Christianity but is free from the authority of so-called revelation and takes the developments of history seriously. It leads to an understanding of religious experience and points toward social and ecological issues. Usually it moves toward a philosophy of organism or process.

Forms of empiricism have been around for many years, but there are indications that a revival of empiricist theology is occurring. It is occasioned not only by the empirical plausibility of that theology but by new methodological openings provided by postmodern interests in pragmatism, pluralism, history, and local experience within the American idiom.

Therefore, empirical theology is important. It provides a degree of verification for concepts that are significant for everyday living in a world of science, secularism, and deeply rooted evils. It is a theology of hope grounded in realism. In some forms it is so rooted in human experience that it deals only with human relationships. In other forms, especially when it develops a rational view of the world, God is understood as a deity at work in history and nature as well as in human beings. In some of its forms, it works well in local congregations, but in other forms it may reject the church and end in a kind of spirituality that is free from institutional controls and therefore is restricted to an individualism that lacks communal relationships and social or political force.

Empirical theology had its beginnings with John Locke and early empirical philosophy. Tyron Inbody, in the opening chapter, traces its history from Locke through Schleiermacher to the modern period. His description of empirical theology makes clear the naturalism that it takes for granted and describes the method of inquiry that makes it empirical. All theology reflects experience, even the most orthodox and traditional ones, and the difference is found in the way in which experience is evaluated. In the U.S.A., beginning with the twentieth century, Inbody looks first at John Dewey and William James and then at the developments of the Chicago School, leading to the emergence of process theology. He brings the story up to date with the current emphasis on radical empiricism, history, and pragmatism as represented by the current Highlands Institute for American Religious Thought.

Nancy Frankenberry enlarges on this topic by listing the major themes of empirical theology. She does not deal with particular writers as much as give a composite view of what the major writers have established. She reasserts the naturalistic principles in which energy-events, happenings, and processes are the major constituents. She lists the ten major elements of this vision. She then turns to the claims of radical empiricism and pragmatism and establishes ten epistemological themes. But there is no claim that one can identify the human ideas of the divine with the reality of the divine. She quotes Bernard Meland: "We live more deeply than we can think." A theology of ambiguity, freedom, and creative advance leads to belief in God, and here there are serious differences between some empirical and process theologians. She concludes by looking at the inadequacies of the English language and the need for better ways of expressing empirical concepts.

Empirical theologians have had a close connection with scientific method. In 1919, Douglas Clyde Macintosh wrote *Theology as an Empirical Science* and in 1926 Henry Nelson Wieman wrote *Religious Experience and Scientific Method*. Already William James and John Dewey had worked toward a scientific pragmatism and the Chicago School had established scientific research in the work of Edward Scribner Ames, Shailer Mathews, and Gerald Birney Smith. But today both science and empirical theology have moved beyond these early conclusions. Karl Peters has provided a study of the similarities and differences in a comparison of empirical theology and science. Peters deals with the purposes and methods of empirical theology and science, distinguishing between knowledge and human fulfillment and showing how these purposes overlap. He quotes Einstein: "You will hardly find one among the profounder sort of scientific minds without a peculiar religious feeling of his own." Both empirical theologians and scientists realize that there are many barriers to knowledge, yet they both find that experiences are value-laden. He compares the two approaches to concept formation and justification. He concludes by proposing a research program for empirical theology.

Many people, including those in the church, live in a world that is constantly moving, filled with ambiguity, and open to new interpretations coming primarily from modern science. When these people try to fit classical theology into their thinking they either become confused or reject traditional concepts. This was the basis for the "God is dead" movement of the 1960s. Marjorie Suchocki faces this problem with her comparison of classical theology, especially as found in Augustine and Aquinas, with the thinking of

Alfred North Whitehead with his picture of a dynamic universe in process. She begins with the interpretation of revelation and its relation to reason and the authority of the church, including the recovery of Greek thinking and the philosophy of Aristotle. This is compared with the relational world of Whitehead and his use of prehension as a key to knowledge on the basis of radical empiricism. She then explains the doctrine of God in the thought of Augustine, who interpreted the Trinity in terms of will and love, and Aquinas who saw the Trinity in terms of intellect and knowledge of God as the end of religion. With the emphasis on human sin, God in Christ is the reconciler. In facing the evil in the world, empiricists do not emphasize human sin and supernatural salvation, yet they do not belittle the horrors of human evil. Suchocki turns to the more radical empiricists, including Bernard Loomer, with suggestions for the next steps in which she sees that Christian theology continues to be creative.

Part II turns from the comparisons and contrasts and examines the beliefs about God, Jesus, humanity, the church, the good, and the integrity of creation. William Dean begins his chapter by looking at the American perspective and its history. This partial historicism is essential to understanding the God of American empirical theology. Dean writes, "Empirical theologians moved God from beyond history to a particular position within history—just that position at which God's power is limited by history's power while God's character is protected from history's moral and spiritual ambiguities." Dean upholds this position by referring to four theologians who illustrate the problem and the possible solutions: Douglas Clyde Macintosh of Yale and three of the Chicago School, Henry Nelson Wieman, Bernard Eugene Meland, and Bernard Loomer. Macintosh tended to defend a Western, Christianized concept of God. Wieman shared this view, but in not nearly as orthodox a manner as Macintosh. Meland was much more aware of other religions; he concluded that there are forces toward good that are universal, but God is known through local symbols and cults. With Loomer, the concept of God moved from unambiguous good toward a more aesthetic form of beauty that could encompass ambiguity. Against the challenge of Loomer, the empirical theologians assert the goodness of God who has limited power, who is at work in history, and in human hearts. For Dean, the question of whether God must be more completely historicized or not remains. The question needs to be left open.

In the next chapter, Bernard Lee approaches the problem of God from the standpoint of Spirit as established in biblical sources. This is also an empirical approach. Lee begins by concentrating on two key words: *Ruach*, and *Dabhar*, Spirit and Word, pointing out that these are metaphors. *Ruach* is a metaphor for breath, wind, or what Lee calls the "Who" of God. *Ruach* is related to justice and righteousness as they come into the world. *Dabhar* emphasizes the power of speech. It is the active, dynamic, effective presence of deity as a pressure on historical existence. Lee then offers some conclusions on God as Spirit. At the end of his chapter, he ties in this understanding with the process theology of Whitehead, with the resemblances of the primordial and consequent natures of God with Spirit and Word.

Central to Christian beliefs is Jesus of Nazareth, the Christ or Messiah. Empirical theologians recognize that Jesus was active in history and made a profound impact, but they often fail to establish or even ignore the claim that Jesus was the Christ. Gerard Sloyan deals with the difficulty of interpreting the flimsy historical evidence, chiefly found in the canonical gospels. None of the gospels is interested in what Jesus was like before his death and resurrection, for the latter was the point of the early preaching. Sloyan traces the search for the "real" Jesus from the nineteenth century on. There was a basic distrust of the church on these matters. Ultimately, however, the gospels do not provide a biography of Jesus but a story of those who attempted to live with that life. There was a creative fidelity until the gospels were canonized. Today Jesus is known primarily through the church. Sloyan turns to the meaning of empiricism as it relates to history and concludes that indeed we have empirical knowledge of Jesus.

We then turn attention to humankind. William Tremmel takes us back to how it all started with an explosion which was followed by a greenhouse effect and in turn by the development of the atmosphere that protects the earth. As we reconstruct this story, we may ask why humanity is the only type to seek out answers to these questions. We are the product of this process and we ask, "Why?" Tremmel then takes us into the development of human beings and the social relations between them, emphasizing the place of language and communication. Human beings are nonprogramed animals. Using insights from George Herbert Mead and William H. Bernhardt, he discusses the search for a workable definition of religion and how people do religion. Human beings are religious animals and religion happens to them.

Bernard Lee, in his second contribution, discusses the nature of the church, interpreting the early church as community. He makes clear his perspective on his approach to experience. He interprets *communitas* and *societas*, suggests that the church is a hybrid, and then looks at the early church. He reinterprets Pharasaism and Jesus' relation to the emerging community. He clarifies the concept of the fatherhood of God and sees the church as a society of equals. He then turns to the emergence of basic Christian communities in the current scene, comparing them with the house churches of the first centuries. He seeks to retrieve *communitas* as the basic unit of the church in the public, political life of the church and the need to convert the systems of secular society. There is hope if the basic communities survive.

We normally expect that the religious life is a moral life. Within empiricism and naturalism, we find that the study of the good leads to ethics and concern for the good of all. Robert Corrington describes the nature of naturalism as it moves through four stages with ecstatic naturalism as the culmination. Each form of naturalism has its own type of empirical method. Charles

Sanders Peirce comes into the picture as Corrington interprets the meaning and use of musement as a key method. The emergence of the good leads to the recognition that the supposed separation of the "ought" and the "is" is overcome by the lure of given goods and the sense of obligation that accompanies them. It is a more complicated process than this, and Corrington deals helpfully with the solution for humankind. He brings in the concept of the "not yet" as an emergent force. Dynamic goods, which live in the not yet of the spirit, are the gifts of nature's spirit. To be adopted by the spirit is to go beyond ethics to a realm of empowerment.

Frederick Ferré looks at empirical theology from a new dimension by starting with the Boston personalists, who do not accept naturalism as basic. He compares and contrasts personalism, naturalism, and organicism. Personalism ties experience to mind and whatever is real is to some extent mental. Wieman's naturalism, in contrast, begins with interpersonal transactions of human social life. Whitehead's organicism uses a broader and vaguer empiricism. Ferré then compares the concepts of God in the three traditions, leading to their approach to the meaning of creation, which really means the "sub-human" element of the world. The personalists have difficulty with nature and seek its meaning in terms of mind or personality. Wieman took the sub-human level more seriously, but in his later thinking he concentrated on God as the source of *human* good. Ferré concludes that only organicism has a suitable theology for dealing with the integrity of nature, an ecological model developed by Charles Birch and John Cobb Jr. The ethics for a just and sustainable world is most likely to come from organicism. But nature demands its price in terms of suffering, sacrifice, and the elimination of the weak, and a purely formed organicism is not the final answer. Ferré develops the significance of environmental ethics by using insights from all three forms of empirical theology.

In Part III we turn to the living of empirical theology, with primary concern for pastoral care and the life of the local congregation. It would have been possible also to look at political theology, economic theory, and minority issues, but the decision was to stay within primary religious circles.

John Cobb looks at pastoral theology, beginning with a helpful listing of writings by Daniel Day Williams, Norman Pittenger, Bernard Lee, and others. Empirical theology is an aid in shifting the basis of pastoral care from the medical to the growth model, from one's functioning in society to the attainment of personal wholeness, and centering of life in a social and even an ecological context. Cobb mentions twelve points on which empirical theology and pastoral care coalesce. He then turns to the concept of grace, quoting Wieman: "The 'grace of God' would then be creative transformation becoming dominant in the life of" human beings. Daniel Day Williams develops this concept in more theological language and extends it to include its metaphysical background. Grace also includes the working of forgiveness and divine acceptance. This does not eliminate the seriousness of suffering and sin but asserts that God shares our experiences. Cobb then outlines ways in which the pastor can use pastoral and practical theology. The aim of the church in this endeavor is the creative transformation of the church and its people and the testing of empirical theology against case material that exposes the actual situation and its transformation.

In the final chapter, I attempt to show how empirical theology works in a local congregation. John Cobb has faced the problem of pastoral care and practical theology in the previous chapter. In my *The Theory of Christian Education Practice*, the first four chapters dealt with "God Is What God Does," "Process Thinking," "Nature and God," and "Empirical Method in Theology," thus anticipating some of the insights of this chapter. The ultimate pragmatic test of empirical theology is how it works in the local congregation. Beginning with a description of a local congregation in action, it moves to a statement of the basic nature of commitment, as expressed by Bernard Meland. One reaches what Meland calls "the appreciative level" of the "more-then-self." Tradition is important, as it helps to provide the language by which it operates. The church is related to the world through the work of its laity. Worship is at the heart of the life of a congregation; and thus worship becomes the empirical anchor. Empirical theology lacks an adequate vocabulary for worship, and new models and symbols need to be developed. Empirical theology results in changes in models for God and for the language of the liturgy. Worship reinforces the sense of worth and still deals with the sense of sin and provides a basis for hope. Preaching would be similarly affected. Religious education would help persons make sense of the modern world, develop a sense of community, link together human experience and the church tradition, and link the pupils to ultimate realities. Seen in this light, it is possible for most empiricists to be Christian and for Christians to be empiricists.

There is a certain logic in reading this book from beginning to end, but it is also convenient for some readers to start wherever their interest lies and to work forward or backward. The constant theme is empirical theology, often with added treatments of naturalism and process theology. The end result is to commend to the readers a reality that checks with their own experience or to encourage such experiences.

So read on!

CHAPTER ONE

History of Empirical Theology

TYRON INBODY

INTRODUCTION

Empirical theology is a type of modern liberal theology. Its historical roots are embedded in the Protestant revolt against tradition and institutional authority and the effort to establish other grounds of authority for theology. Its impetus is the Enlightenment search for a reliable methodology. Its agenda is the liberal project to ground theology in human experience and to use reason to understand experience.

All empirical theologians are naturalists in the sense that they believe this world alone is the locus of purpose and value. They relinquish any world of transcendental causes or principles. Reality is the processes and relationships of this world; all theological meaning and truth lies within the natural world.

Empirical theologians, also, are rational in the sense that they appeal to autonomous individual or social experience in contrast to the formal external authority of tradition, magisterium, or scripture as the source for theology; they appeal to human understanding as the criteria for theological judgments; and they use speculative reason to create a framework for understanding value or what is implied metaphysically in a theology grounded in experience.

The term "empirical" is used in three ways in empirical theology.[1] First, it refers loosely to a general temperament or attitude of the thinker, viz., to tough-mindedness or a bias for the stubborn facts of experience. Empirical

---

1. Nancy Frankenberry, *Religion and Radical Empiricism* (Albany: State University of New York Press, 1987), pp. 1-4.

theology is an effort to develop in theology a spirit of total openness before the entire range of experiential evidence. Empiricism, then, is closely tied to experience. A theology is empirical if it acknowledges no other final basis for its claims than human experience. All theological knowledge is descriptive of the concrete character of observable data given in experience. Knowledge is ultimately tested for its truth in terms of the evidence supplied by experience.

Second, empirical refers to a method of inquiry, a way of getting at and organizing the data of experience that is instrumental, operational, or experimental. An appeal to experience in theology alone does not make one an empirical theologian. Empirical theology has to do with a method of empirical inquiry into the data of experience. Empirical theologians open all theological claims about the data to public inspection and correction. The experimental method of reflection upon the data of common experience designates a theology as empirical.

Third, empiricism is an appeal to common human experience in one form or another as the source and justification for their assertions. All knowledge is derived from a description of experience, either in the weaker sense that experience provides us with knowledge or the stronger sense that no source other than experience provides us with knowledge at all. All empirical theologies appeal to experience as the primary source and empirical method as the primary norm for justifying any theological claim whatsoever.

The key to understanding the variety of empirical theologies is to understand what in their view constitutes experience. There are two different ways the term experience can be understood. In classical empiricism, represented by John Locke and David Hume, experience was understood as the perception of ourselves and the world which takes place by means of the five senses, so that experience meant sense perception. All knowledge originates in and derives from the experience of the five senses.

No empirical theologian understands experience is this classical sense or its contemporary positivistic variants. Theological empiricism moves away from this picture of knowledge derived from and verified by sense experience toward a more inclusive view of experience. Experience is vastly richer and deeper than mere sensation. Sense perception is neither the only nor even the primary mode of experience but is derived from still more elemental awareness both of ourselves and the world around us. It adds to the five senses an affective or bodily sense of value within an environment. Before we employ the discrimination of our senses, we are already aware of ourselves and our environment as causally efficacious powers mutually interacting with one another.

This newer empiricism attempts to broaden the notion of experience beyond sense experience in two ways. One is to focus on wider modes of experience, such as emotional, volitional, evaluative, aesthetic, and social. The other is to stress the givenness and primacy of relations and bodily feelings from which sense experience itself is an abstraction. Experience is the felt, bodily, psycho-social, organic action of human beings within an environment.

Theological empiricism, then, is an effort to overcome the sensationalism and reductionism of the classical empirical tradition. This effort at revision has issued in two distinct ways of understanding experience within an empirical orientation. One is an appeal to the numinous, which stands at the center of Immanuel Kant's critique and informs Friedrich Schleiermacher, Albrecht Ritschl, and many of the liberal theologians in Europe and North America. Empiricism in the numinous tradition tends to refer more to mystical and religious experience than to general human experience. Empirical theologies with this understanding of experience draw primarily from the modern European philosophical tradition, including Kantianism, Ritschlianism, existentialism, and phenomenology.

The other is a radical view of common experience which informs the branch of twentieth-century North American empirical theologies shaped by Jamesian, Deweyan, pragmatic, and Whiteheadian understandings of experience. This stream of empiricism focuses not on numinous experience but on general experience and originates more in the Anglo-American philosophical tradition from Locke and Hume to radical empiricism. It culminates in a series of variants within theology designated as process thought and radical empiricism. Here empiricism attempts to work with experience as recorded in history or interpreted by the social sciences, to examine what in general experience is operational to transform human beings, or to explore the structure of experience.

THE ROOTS OF EMPIRICISM

Where do the roots of empiricism in theology lie? The pivotal point in modern empiricism was the English empiricist, John Locke (1632-1704). His central thesis was that we get all our ideas from experience; there are no innate ideas or innate principles stamped upon the mind. The senses furnish us with particular ideas, which the mind becomes familiar with, remembers, and names. All knowledge, however complex and sophisticated, must finally refer back to that from which it began, viz., experience and sensation. There are two sources of knowledge, then, sensation and reflection, but the source of all ideas is ultimately in experience.

This empirical bent of mind was to culminate with the classical empiricism of David Hume (1711-1776). His first rule was that all our simple ideas in their first appearance are derived from simple sense impressions, which are correspondent to them, and which they exactly represent. The content of the mind is impressions from sensations and ideas are copies or faint images of impressions. These impressions are atomistic and are associated only by habit or custom.

Hume's sensationalism led to skepticism both in science and in religion. Since there is no necessary connection between impressions, causal connections and all other qualities and features of experience were considered wholly to be subjective, residing in custom. Since our ideas reach no further than our experience, we have no way to hypothesize and characterize a being who is both nonhuman and superhuman. All Hume could do was to justify religion as a custom.

The European version of empirical theology was an effort to respond to the skepticism introduced by Hume. It consisted primarily of the "liberal empiricists" employing the strategy of Kant. Kant addressed himself to the empirical skepticism of Hume. With Hume, he asserts knowledge begins with sensory experience. But a science of nature is possible because the mind is not simply receptive of stimuli but active by imposing synthetic forms of categories of understanding on the data of the senses.

This saving of the appearances and assurance of objective knowledge of the phenomenal world through science, however, was not to be taken as the sole or total meaning of the world or human existence. The meaning of the "thing-in-itself" was not to be had by sensory grasp of events. Human beings could go beyond the scientific understanding of the world and penetrate the noumenal world, the transcendent order that is beyond the bounds of space and time but which nevertheless conditions the sensible world, through transcendental or regulative ideas, ideas which are necessary if the rationality of the phenomenal world is to be retained.

The core of Kant's religious philosophy is the practical reason of the moral law. The moral intuition of conscience is a moral fact, laying its claim upon one to do one's duty. It is reducible to two imperatives, viz., universalizable conduct and deal with persons as ends not means. So to act in regard to this moral law requires God, freedom, and immortality. His system is thus crowned by moral faith existence.

The grounding of religion in the practical reason of Kant took two forms in the German phenomenological emphasis on religious experience: the mystical and the moral. Schleiermacher represented the former, Ritschl the latter. From the former issues the numinal theology of Rudolf Otto, Samuel Taylor Coleridge, Søren Kierkegaard, and Paul Tillich; from the latter developed the thought of Wilhelm Herrmann, Julius Kaftan, and Adolf Harnack, and the practical reason for establishing faith in the dialectical theology of Karl Barth and Emil Brunner. Various combinations of these appeared most clearly in American "evangelical liberalism"[2] where the appeal was to experience as the internal judgment of values (Ritschlianism and personalism) or the Christ-like tendencies in thought and action (William Newton Clarke).

The inclusion of Kant, and the Kantians, in the history of empirical the-

2. Kenneth Cauthen, *The Impact of American Liberalism* (New York: Harper & Row, 1962), Part Two.

ology poses one of the most significant problems in defining empirical theology. Is empirical theology an appeal to experience in distinctly ethical
and religious forms along Kantian lines, or is empirical theology experimental inquiry into general experience along the lines initiated by Locke
and Hume and developed in the American pragmatic tradition? In the former,
the religious consciousness and religious experience of the numinous is the
source of data and the object of inquiry, whereas in the latter experience is the
felt, bodily, organic action of human beings in history, or lived experience,
or vital immediacy, or the givenness of relations and the primacy of bodily
feelings of causal efficacy. This radical form of empiricism distinguishes
empirical theology from Kantian forms of theology which focus on specific religious experience.

Schleiermacher is an empiricist in the sense that he moved away from
the authoritarian appeal to tradition and from a priori ideas to experience
as the data and resource for theology. The experience he appealed to was
the data of the religious consciousness, viz., the feeling of absolute dependence. That which is immediate to the self is simply and solely the self as
dependent, the way the underived self is present to itself as given.

Schleiermacher is more a phenomenologist than an empiricist. His and
much European liberalism is a subjectivized form of supernaturalism where
the ultimate reality casts its shadow upon concrete experience and where
inward and personal experience and the private subjective encounter of the
psyche with transcendent realities is key. This European phenomenology
contrasts with the British empirical and American pragmatic theological
traditions where observation of occurrences in the form of public inquiry
which leads to critical exchange of interpretation and assessment and where
divinity is literal processes observed in natural and historical experience is
decisive.

Horace Bushnell (1802-1876), the "American Schleiermacher" and the
"father of American liberalism," was the most creative theologian from the
New England Puritan tradition during the nineteenth century.[3] Although a
supernaturalist in the sense that he makes a sharp distinction between the natural realm of being governed by law and the supernatural realm not in the train
of cause and effect, these realms are nevertheless consubstantial so that all
living things participate in the supernatural and are in that way divine.

Humanity is the juncture of the natural and supernatural. He held that
humanity is in a state of privation, since knowledge, the moral sense, and
experience are limited. He accounted for the inheritance of sin from previous generations through an organic web of influence. But if sin has its organic effects, so does goodness. Therefore, humanity is an inheritor of a double

---

3. One of the most comprehensive histories of the empirical tradition in theology is
Randolph Crump Miller, *The American Spirit in Theology* (Philadelphia: Pilgrim Press,
1974).

stream. Thus, Christian nurture was also efficacious because human beings can respond to moral influence and objective example. Bushnell was the key influence in the religious education movement within liberal theology.

The impact of the German form of empirical theology represented in Schleiermacher and Ritschl had its influence in America primarily in the figures of William Newton Clarke (1841-1912) and William Adams Brown (1865-1943). Clarke's emphasis on immanence, intuitive knowledge, and his appeal to religious experience bear strong resemblance to the work of Schleiermacher, whereas Brown's resembled more the themes of Ritschl. Methodologically, however, both remained evangelical liberals as opposed to modernists.[4]

JOHN DEWEY

The first key person in the development of a distinctly American empiricist tradition in religious thought is John Dewey (1859-1952). He was part of a movement that was developing a new form of empiricism based on a concept of experience which combined the naturalistic bias of the Greek philosophers and the experimental method practiced by the sciences.

The key concept in Dewey's philosophy is experience. He was concerned with noncognitive and unreflective experience that set the context for all knowing and inquiry, with the plurality of experience, that is, the series of overlapping and interpenetrating experiences, situations, and contexts, and with naturalistic experience, that is, the scientific articulation of the organic character of experience. Experience is the fund of social knowledge and skills and the means by which human beings come into direct contact with a qualitatively rich and variegated nature, which has to be constructed in the light of the experimental method of the sciences. It is through immediate experience that we find our data; it is through operational procedures that we find ways of controlling nature.

Early in his life Dewey began to develop a new theory of inquiry, which he called instrumental or experimental logic, where the actual methods of inquiry practiced by the experimental sciences guided the methods by which we most successfully gain and warrant our knowledge. From felt difficulty to hypothesis to experimental testing to confirm or disconfirm the hypothesis, the original indeterminate situation is transformed into a unified whole. Knowledge, then, is what is warranted by the careful use of the norms and

---

4. The difference between modernism and evangelical liberalism is that while those who represent the latter are concerned to integrate Christian faith with modern thought, they finally stand with the revelation which is guarded by the tradition as over against human experience and reason. Modernists said that even the tradition must be validated with our religious experience and reason. Cauthen, *Impact of American Religious Liberalism*, pp. 26ff.

methods of inquiry. Truth is an instrumental concept directed toward practical ends.

His instrumental or pragmatic mode of inquiry presupposes an evolutionary view of humanity with a strong emphasis on environmental influences and functional adaptation. The data are selected by the senses for whatever hypothesis which has been evoked by previous experience is being tested. The purpose is to control data and their relations so purposive human ends may be met. The procedures of the experimental sciences provide the model, so experience is brought under control by understanding the relationship of data by modifying the data or manipulating the experiment. One inserts change to see what other change results, and the correlation between these changes is the object of knowledge. An idea or concept is identified with the operational method, so that the concept is synonymous with the corresponding set of operations. These operations are part of experience, and they are tested by the consequences, which make them true.

Knowledge directed toward discovery has religious ends. All religious ideas had to be derived on pragmatic or instrumental grounds. Religion has to do with the relation of the possible and the actual, not with beliefs about matters of fact. Religious denotes attitudes that may be taken toward every object and every proposed end or ideal. It means devotion to those ends which serve and promote the actualization of human ideals. "The actual religious quality described is the *effect* produced, the better adjustment in life and its conditions, not the manner and cause of its production."[5]

WILLIAM JAMES

The other main source of the distinctly American brand of empiricism in theology is William James.[6] Like Dewey, he revises the classical view of experience by giving a prominent role to the aesthetic or qualitative dimension of experience. Sense perception is neither the sole nor primary mode of experience but is itself derived from a more elemental and organic togetherness of experiencing subject and experienced environment. Primary to experience is the subject's awareness of itself and others as interacting in an environment of experienced relations, felt transitions, and qualitative feelings. James radicalizes the classical notion of experience through his doctrine of the givenness of relations.

Perception contains knowledge by acquaintance before it issues in knowledge about an object. Perception includes relations, fringes, and patterns of awareness. While classical empiricists considered the clear and distinct aspects of experience the foundation of knowledge, James considers this

---

5. John Dewey, *A Common Faith* (New Haven: Yale, 1934), p. 14.

6. For an excellent discussion of James' philosophy as it relates to empirical theology, see Frankenberry, *Religion and Radical Empiricism*, especially pp. 83-106.

vague fringe of relational experience to be more basic to cognition.

Although James' early and explicit views of religion are sometimes presented as a defense of fideism, the significance of James for empirical inquiry in theology is that his radical empiricism maps out the religious dimension of experience as such. What religion exposes and what "God" means must be found in some kind of concrete experience. The world of religion, then, is not another world but the wider world of "the More," a world of quality and relationship which is operative in the universe outside the subject and can sustain the subject.

DOUGLAS CLYDE MACINTOSH

Douglas Clyde Macintosh (1877-1948), a Canadian by birth, did his graduate work in theology and philosophy at the University of Chicago (1909) and taught at the Yale Divinity School from 1909-1942. He mediated between religious experience in the evangelical and Ritschlian senses of the term and the empirical temper of the Chicago School. His primary interest was not with religion as a social process, as in the early Chicago School, but with religious experience as it appeared in the lives of church people. He was interested in a kind of clinical theology that could guide the work of clergy in the same way clinical medicine could guide the work of medical doctors.

Theology is an empirical science. It is possible to establish a body of experimentally tested theological knowledge based on acquaintance with the divine in religious experience. The data are the special facts revealed in religious perception. God is experienced within a complex of elements in which the divine factor can be isolated. God can be perceived as the real Object which gives rise to the human experience of moral uplift. From these data it is possible to establish an empirically verifiable body of theological laws which derive from the "right religious adjustment" on the part of the individual, the primary element being the devotion to values. From these laws that can be discerned, theology moves from a consideration of what God does to what God is. Theories, then, are constructed primarily on the basis of pragmatic theory. When this procedure is followed, a genuine empirical theology will arise to replace all other theologies which are established on some other basis.[7]

---

7. In many respects Macintosh was similar to Wieman, but they differed in their interpretations of the evidence. Because Macintosh took the evidence to point to a divine mind, will, and personality, he charged Wieman with being a behaviorist. The difference, though, was primarily that the former concentrated on religious experience, while the latter confined the investigation to experience in general. The numinous persisted along with values in his understanding of the data. But they were similar in their idea of God as the value-producing factor in experience.

THE CHICAGO SCHOOL

The primary locus of the development of empirical theology has been the Divinity School of the University of Chicago.[8] So identified has empirical theology been with the Divinity School that it has often been identified as the "Chicago School of Theology."

There have been three phases in the development of empirical theology at Chicago: 1) The early Chicago School (1908-1926), the era of the socio-historical method beginning with the arrival of Shirley Jackson Case; 2) the era of philosophical-theological method (1926-1946), beginning with the arrival of Henry Nelson Wieman; and 3) the era of constructive theology (1946-1966), beginning with the arrival of Bernard Meland.

The first phase is the "early Chicago School," represented primarily by the "socio-historical method" of Case (1872-1947) and Shailer Mathews (1863-1941). These theologians were not interested primarily in philosophical currents of thought but in the socio-historical and functional methods of inquiry.

The empirical effort of the early Chicago School arose out of the study of history influenced by the new sciences of sociology and social psychology. Also influential, primarily through osmosis, was Dewey's pragmatism, which was more a mood than an explicit method. This group, in addition, was shaped by a strong evolutionary view of human beings and groups with its emphasis on environmental influence and functional adaptation.

The empirical study of religion, then, was primarily a study of the functional aspect of religion. A movement or doctrine was known in terms of the function it served. If one can get at the motives behind actions and affirmations and at the purposes for which they are employed, one could unmask the real nature of religious phenomena.

SHIRLEY JACKSON CASE

Case was the primary theoretician of the socio-historical school.[9] His arrival at the Divinity School coincided with the rise of the socio-historical method. He was professor of New Testament interpretation and early church history and sometime dean. His distinctive contribution to the school was to refine the socio-historical method, which began as a type of higher New

---

8. For extensive histories of the Chicago School, see Bernard Meland, "The Empirical Tradition in Theology at Chicago," in *The Future of Empirical Theology*, ed. Bernard Meland (Chicago: University of Chicago Press, 1969), pp. 1-62; Harvey Arnold, *Near the Edge of Battle* (Chicago: The Divinity School Association, 1966); and Creighton Peden, *The Chicago School* (Bristol, Ind.: Wyndham Hall Press, 1987).

9. The best monograph on Case is William Hynes, *Shirley Jackson Case and the Chicago School* (Chico, Calif.: Scholars Press, 1981).

Testament criticism and subsequently inquired into Christian origins and beliefs.

In his New Testament studies he distinguished between historical-literary criticism (literary genre) and historical-social criticism (social experience). In the former, one unravels the literary history of each document; in the latter, the social experience and environmental settings of the tradition. Particular units of tradition are intimately bound up with the life interests of the early Christian society. The test of social experience, their degree of suitableness to the distinctive environment, and functional significance to the life interests must be used to understand any New Testament text.

Case, however, applied this method beyond biblical studies to Christian history. Christianity results from the efforts of individuals and groups to secure and perpetuate their welfare in contact with their environment, particularly those less thoroughly mastered aspects. The ultimate unit in history is not the document but the contemporary social order of which the document is the product. Documents are used as reference points to vital social processes which originally produced them.

All knowledge of history can be derived only from concrete and empirically verifiable data. If past products happen to meet the needs of persons in the present, then they may be utilized in the present. Historical method seeks to go beyond historical products to the beliefs of real people who themselves produced these products in response to stimuli of their environment. The most distinctive feature of the method, though, is its radical functionalism with respect both to the analysis of the past and the didactic use of history in the present.

SHAILER MATHEWS

For Mathews, "*the* representative of the socio-historical method" and the single most dominant figure in the formation of the Chicago School, religion is the adaptation to the environment by social groups who have specific "felt needs." Theology is not a philosophical inquiry into the questions of religious truth in the metaphysical sense. As with most of the practitioners of the functionalist form of empirical theology, he was more concerned with describing, understanding, and enhancing the religious thought and practices of a social movement in relation to its environment than in evaluating them.

This environment was both social and cosmic. Religious practices and beliefs enable social groups to adjust their felt needs to their social resources and cosmic activities. Although religion deals with social experience, undergirding that social experience is a cosmic process that produces and enhances human personality (the "personality producing forces of the universe"). The meaning and value of religious practices and beliefs are discovered by socio-historical analysis of how they function in social experience in meeting the group's felt needs.

Mathews interpreted Christianity as a social movement which gave rise to a series of "social minds" which were produced from analogies and social patterns in an attempt to meet the needs of adaptation to the social and cosmic environment. Theology arises when there is a conscious tension between the religious inheritance of a group and the new conditions in which a group lives, when men and women organize their inheritance in harmony with other elements in their experience. It uses experiences and concepts in general social experience as "patterns" by which to describe and make available the inherited religious convictions of Christians.

Theological doctrine, then, is a form of analogical thinking by which groups can adapt to their environment. Theology meets group needs not by argument but by classifying religious experience and hopes with the social experience and mind of the epoch so that what is accepted in that epoch may serve to unify, clarify, and reinforce the religious inheritance of the movement and make it available in the new conditions. Mathews spent much of his time describing how the organizing social minds, and particularly the "transcendentalized politics" of several creative epochs of Christianity, served as dramatic patterns for such theological ideas as God and atonement.

The normative element in Christianity ("generic Christianity") is the attitudes and convictions of loyalty to Jesus which serve as an inheritance. Doctrines, however, are essential because they are instrumental in maintaining and perpetuating the power of a movement. Doctrine making is group formation or modification of inherited beliefs in accordance with new social analogies.

Mathews was a part of a group of empirical theists.[10] The key to his empirical theism is the idea that humanity has been produced by the natural universe and that through healthful relations with its environing processes humanity may fulfill its life. Mathews referred to his idea of God as "conceptual theism." The term God refers not to a person or principle but is a way of conceiving these cosmic forces by use of analogies and symbols in such a way as to aid in the establishment of healthful relations and adjustment to these forces in the universe. God is an instrumental concept and not an ontological or metaphysical idea that stands for the reality relating humanity and these activities. His concept is a strictly functional one and so is essentially pragmatic.

SOME MILD DISSENTERS

There were some mild dissenters during the first phase of the Chicago School, such as Gerald Birney Smith and Edward Scribner Ames. Ames, a

10. Henry Nelson Wieman and Bernard Meland, *American Philosophies of Religion* (Chicago: Willett, Clark, 1936), pp. 272ff.

colleague of John Dewey in the philosophy department, was the most explicit advocate of the functional method of pragmatism of any of the members
of the early Chicago School. His functionalism led him to an explicit and full-
blown humanism. Unlike Case and Mathews, he was unable to retain a core
of religion which was exempt from a thoroughgoing functional analysis.
The word "God" denotes the reality of the world's life in certain functions
taken in its ideal aspects. Orderliness, love, and intelligence are the characteristic aspects of cosmic life which, idealized, constitute the reality that is
God. Alma Mater, Uncle Sam, and Spirit of the Group, or Commonwealth
serve as analogies to the term God.

Like his colleague George Burman Foster, Smith shared an anguish of
thought that was Nietzschian in quality and was more open to philosophical
and scientific movements than Case and Mathews. Although a proponent of
the empirical method in theology, he was less committed to the strict sociological procedure than they were. He was the bridge between the socio-historical phase of empiricism and the philosophical one inaugurated by Wieman.

Smith was an empiricist of the early Chicago style, yet for two reasons he
was a transition figure in the school. One reason is the collapse of the socio-
historical method, and the other is his own somewhat mystical bent of mind.
By 1929 the socio-historical phase of empirical theology was in deep trouble.[11] Foremost among the changes was the abandonment by sociology of the
modernist project. With the increasing quantification of sociology, the relationship between science and theology changed from support of the modernist
agenda to indifference if not downright hostility. The framework for the
socio-historical method in theology had collapsed.

In addition, Smith was highly critical of his colleagues for wanting to
exempt something in Christianity from thoroughly historical analysis. Finally,
Smith criticized his colleagues for not following the new developments in
biology and physics which were moving science away from strict functionalism. Some new empirical framework was needed, and the coming of Henry
Nelson Wieman to the Divinity School marked the move from the socio-
historical method in empirical theology to a more philosophical empiricism.

There was also a mystical side to Smith's thought that makes him a break
with the early Chicago School. Problems in religious thinking should be
stated in terms of a quality of the cosmic process akin to the quality of our own
spiritual life. Smith did not develop his mystical naturalism into a complete
philosophy of religion. But his belief that religion should address itself to discovering whether the natural universe as described by the sciences was hospitable to the religious response made him more sympathetic to the concerns of Wieman than to the functional method of the Chicago School.

---

11. Delwin Brown, "The Fall of '26: Gerald Birney Smith and the Collapse of the
Socio-Historical Framework of Theology," *American Journal of Theology and Philosophy*
11:3 (September 1990), pp. 183-201.

However, he was convinced that such response would be closer to the arts than the sciences, and so he was cautious about his enthusiasm for Wieman.

HENRY NELSON WIEMAN

When Wieman came to the Divinity School in 1926, a new phase of empirical theology was inaugurated. A new kind of evolutionary and organismic thought, stimulated by Henri Bergson, William James, Jan Smuts, Lloyd Morgan, and Samuel Alexander, and systematized into a creative vision by Alfred North Whitehead, was emerging in the sciences in the 1920s to replace the modernist notion of mechanism.

In 1926 Whitehead's *Religion in the Making* was used by Smith in his seminars on organismic thought. When Wieman translated Whitehead's esoteric terms into language that could be assimilated into the empirical orientation of the Chicago School, he initiated a new understanding of empirical theology which was more philosophical than functional. Although Wieman was eventually to reject much of Whitehead's thought as being over speculative and carrying religious thought away from empirical evidence, Wieman was both a bridge to the philosophical phase of empirical theology which was to issue in a Whiteheadian form of process theology and the initiator of his own form of empirical theology which was primarily philosophical.

Wieman's primary concern was to reformulate religious issues not on a historical or functional basis but on a philosophical basis. The reason is that historic religious symbols were bankrupt. His concern was to go beyond religious experience or historical description of experience to designate in concrete and explicit terms what the religious person meant when employing the term God. His concern was the certainty of religious beliefs and commitment, and so he set out to designate that which in experience was empirically identifiable and describable as the certain object of religious commitment.

Wieman's thought is akin to Dewey, Ames, Mathews, and Smith in that he starts with the experience of value in the environing world of events as a means to deriving criteria for his definition of God. Although Wieman's thought about cosmic behaviors or processes and about creative interchange were consistent with some of the themes of the early Chicago School, especially Mathews' notion of personality producing cosmic forces and of social experience, he nevertheless introduced a different orientation and understanding of empirical method into empirical theology.

Mystical awareness does not yield knowledge of God; knowledge of God can be had only in the same way other knowledge can be had, viz, by empirical observation and formulation. God and the nature of God can be verified on empirical grounds because God is an object of immediate experience. Unlike the conceptual theists, Wieman held God is an object of immediate experience, perceived as well as conceived, apprehended and discerned as any other object in the environment, a process, a movement, a growth, a good not our own which works to shape and reshape human life.

His theory of value provides a vision of an ultimate reality, cosmic in scope, which commands adjustment and loyalty and provides the resources for human growth and fulfillment. God is to be located in value. Value is appreciable activity which can be observed, computed, foreseen, controlled, redirected, elaborated. Activities can be connected in meaningful and supporting ways. What we experience through activity is the nature of objective reality. God is not the universe as a whole or an idealized aspect of the world but an activity empirically discernible.

God is a reality which can be empirically established and amplified. "Whatever else the word God may mean, it is a term used to designate that Something upon which human life is most dependent for its security, welfare, and increasing abundance."[12] God is a creative activity in our midst shaping our lives for good. God is "what operates in human life with such character and power that it will transform man as he cannot transform himself, to save him from the depths of evil and endow him with the greatest good, provided that he give himself over to it with whatsoever completeness of self-giving is possible for him."[13] It is imperative that we come to terms with this working if we are to live full lives.[14]

ALFRED NORTH WHITEHEAD

During the philosophical phase of the Chicago School, Whitehead's metaphysics increasingly was applied to develop a process philosophy of religion and theology.[15] Whitehead's philosophy contains both empirical and rational elements.[16] His thought is primarily empirical in the sense that he

---

12. Henry Nelson Wieman, *Religious Experience and Scientific Method* (New York: Macmillan, 1926), p. 3.

13. Henry Nelson Wieman, *Man's Ultimate Commitment* (Carbondale: Southern Illinois University Press, 1958), p. 11.

14. Wieman's later works were efforts to reformulate with precision that objective reality which he sought. God empirically means "creative interchange" (*Man's Ultimate Commitment*, pp. 22-26), or the "creative event," which includes the four subevents of emerging awareness of qualitative meaning derived from other persons through communication, integrating these new meanings with others previously acquired, expanding the richness of quality in the appreciable world by enlarging its meaning, and deepening the community among those who participate in this total creative event of intercommunication (*Source of Human Good*, Chapter 3, p. 58.). God, then, is a fact, empirically verifiable as existing independently of our perception, superhuman but not supernatural, transcending human but not transcending nature.

15. For a history of process theology, see Gene Reeves and Delwin Brown, "The Development of Process Theology," in *Process Philosophy and Christian Thought* (Indianapolis: Bobbs Merrill, 1971), pp. 21-69.

16. Bernard Lee, "The Two Process Theologies," *Theological Studies* 45 (1984), pp. 307-319.

claims "the elucidation of immediate experience is the sole justification for any thought."[17] But his empiricism includes speculative thought.

Whitehead's controlling purpose was to offer an alternative to the sensationalist doctrine which has been prominent in modern philosophy since Locke and Hume. This he does by developing a theory of nonsensuous perception, perception in the mode of "causal efficacy." The most basic mode of experience is not "presentational immediacy," perception of the world as passively illustrating certain sensa, but an intuitive awareness of our own past mental and bodily states and of the wider world beyond as they compel conformation to themselves in the present. Our intuition that we are related does not arise from inference from sensation but immediately arises from the vast background and foreground of nonsensuous perception. Whitehead, then, relates more to the second than to the first type of modern empiricism.[18]

On the basis of "the reformed subjectivist principle," Whitehead proceeds to develop a coherent view of the world. Accordingly, we can give an adequate account of reality by imaginatively generalizing those elements disclosed in our analysis of the experiences as subjects. The principle requires that we take as the experiential basis of our most fundamental concepts the primal phenomenon of our own existence as experiencing subjects and selves. From the self as we actually experience it we imagine and project a system of general notions, notions of large, adequate generality that will cover all experience and reality as such.

The key person in the development of this direction of Whitehead's thought for theology was Charles Hartshorne, who for more than a quarter of a century was a member of the philosophy faculty at the University of Chicago as well as the Divinity School. Basing his work on Whitehead, Pierce, Hocking, Fechner, and Leibniz, he focused on the ontological argument for God, thereby obscuring the fact that many of the resources for his thought are empirically based.

Combining a realist epistemology and an idealist ontology, he merges the organismic stream of the empirical and process thinkers with a rationalist inquiry that goes beyond the efforts of Whitehead to develop a rationalistic form of empirical thought. His primary function in the history of empirical theology has been to keep the empirical effort attuned to the broader issues of the ontological problems in philosophy and theology. "Grubbing among the facts is neither here nor there. Self-understanding is the issue: someone is confused, either the theist or the nontheist. Which is it? This is the real question."[19]

---

17. Alfred North Whitehead, *Process and Reality* (New York: Free Press, 1978), p. 4.

18. See Schubert Ogden's discussion, "Present Prospects for Empirical Theology," in *Future of Empirical Theology*, pp. 81-82.

19. Charles Hartshorne, *A Natural Theology for Our Time* (Lasalle: Open Court Press, 1967), p. 88.

BERNARD LOOMER

No one represented the philosophical movement within empirical thought
more in his own work or was more instrumental in making it the focus of the
Divinity School in the forties and fifties than Bernard Loomer. He inaugurated
the period of Whiteheadian process philosophy and theology in the Divinity
School with his 1942 dissertation on the significance of the method of empirical analysis in Whitehead's philosophy, one of the basic documents of process philosophy and theology.[20]

In this period of Loomer's thought, while he was Dean of the Divinity
School (1945, at the age of thirty-three, until 1953), he envisioned
Whitehead's metaphysics as the most adequate encompassing vision and
the replacement of all previous metaphysical visions. In some respects he even
advocated a Whiteheadian orthodoxy. Since the theologian never escapes
a philosophical framework, the task of process theology is to master
Whitehead's basic categories and reconceive the historical Christian doctrines within that perspective.

Among the process thinkers during this period of the Chicago School
there was a strong rationalistic bent of mind. Loomer's thought was strongly rationalistic, although not a priori rationalistic. It was, also, empirical
in the sense that he argued that if there is no empirical warrant for an
idea, it is unacceptable, and in the sense that he framed the question about
the general conditions of the ideal of the order of things by asking what
they must be if we are to have any experience at all.[21] Although he did not
appeal to the notion of necessary ideas in the sense that Hartshorne did, he
nevertheless sought an understanding of the most general structure of
experience and a system of general ideas striving toward a continuity of
explanation over an understanding of things in their concreteness, the
emphasis one finds among the more "empiricist" over the more "rationalistic" empirical thinkers. Loomer offered his own version on the
Whiteheadian God as the key to a coherent structure and system of existence.

After Loomer left Chicago in 1965 for the Graduate Theological Union,
his thought began to shift from process metaphysics to "process-relational
thought." He began to question the goal of conceptual clarity and integralness
as too abstract, not related to the ambiguity of life and contexts in concrete
reality through empirical analysis.[22] His naturalism and empiricism began to

---

20. Bernard Loomer, "Whitehead's Method of Empirical Analysis," in *Process
Theology: Basic Writings*, ed. Ewert Cousins (New York: Newman, 1971), pp. 67-82.

21. William Dean, *American Journal of Theology and Philosophy* 8:1-2 (January-May
1987), p. 3.

22. Bernard Loomer, "The Size of God," *American Journal of Theology and
Philosophy* 8:1 & 2 (January-May 1987), pp. 20-52.

overtake his rationalistic bent. The world is a dynamic web of interrelated and interconnected events. The primordially given character of the world is its interrelatedness and interconnectedness. Order is an abstraction from interconnectedness. Good, then, is inextricably bound up with evil. Ambiguity is a characteristic of the nature of all actual events. God is no exception to this "ontology of ambiguity." If God is more than an ideal or principle, then the being of God must be identified is some sense with the being of the world. Hence, for Loomer, in what is essentially a form of pantheism, God as the matrix of interconnected individuals is identified with the totality of the world. The web is the concrete life and being of God. To identify God with the good alone is to make God an abstraction, and empiricism is concerned not with one aspect of God but with the concrete God of experience.

Some process thinkers in their unitary concept of God substitute for a thoroughgoing empiricism a passion for perfection that is not supported by empirical method or the concrete things, people, and actual events of the world. Loomer substituted stature instead of perfection as the desirable quality of God. Stature is not a movement away from the ambiguity of the world or a resolution of ambiguity but is the capacity to absorb more and more dimensions of the world into one's being without losing one's integrity. Stature, or Size, is the capacity not to eliminate evil but to transform the contradictions of life, including depth, breadth, variety, interests, ambiguity, and struggle into compatible contrasts within the individual.

THE LATER CHICAGO SCHOOL

The third phase of the Chicago School was the period following WWII when theological themes dominated the interests of the school. The primary representatives of this phase were Bernard Meland and Daniel Day Williams. Theological reflection was carried on within a perspective shaped by the Whiteheadian vision of reality, but it was also informed by other perspectives and resources as well.

Williams' interests included both the ontological and doctrinal dimensions of Christian faith, and his interpretation of theological themes included a concern for practical matters of ministry. He was the most eclectic of the process group of empiricists at Chicago in his selection of sources, but his philosophical orientation remained consistent with that of process metaphysics, mediating between process theology and other theological perspectives, especially neo-orthodoxy.

Williams was the representative of the second and third phases of the Chicago School who had the most interest in the churches. He remained primarily a theologian, committed to the task of conveying the historic witness of faith within a contemporary perspective and reinterpreting the major themes of Christian faith for the life of the church within a primarily

Whiteheadian perspective, matched in that role only by the work of Norman Pittenger.

As Williams represented the empirical themes outside Chicago through conversation with other theological perspectives with his move to the Union Theological Seminary in New York, so empirical themes were also represented for a number of years at Yale Divinity School through the work of Randolph Crump Miller, who nearly single-handedly carried on the empirical tradition introduced there by Macintosh. Trained as a theologian, his life work consisted primarily of bringing theological resources and criteria to religious education in the churches. He elaborated empirical themes at Yale in his teaching, extensive writing, and editing of *Religious Education.* The basic appeal of empirical thought for him lies in its interpretation of experience, including general, religious, and mystical, in a realistic way. His understanding of empirical theology was shaped primarily by Dewey, James, Wieman, and Meland.

BERNARD EUGENE MELAND

The primary representative of the empirical theme at Chicago following World War II was Bernard Meland. The career of Meland (1899-) in fact embodies the three phases of the Chicago School from the 1920s through the 1960s. He is "a personal summary" of the three phases of the Chicago School.

Meland's thought is primarily empirical. His focus is experiential in that it is oriented toward concrete experience of the relational context. His empirical realism prompted him to focus on the otherness, the richness, complexity of the concrete lived experience and to be critical of the mentalism and rationalistic tendency of much process thought.

Meland was a student at the Divinity School (1925-1929) during a period of transition within the school. Smith was the single most important influence on his theological development, modifying his pragmatic modernism in the direction of a "mystical naturalism" that stressed "elementalism" and the more creatural stance in religious inquiry. The mystical theme was reflected in his mood of "the perilous open" in many of his early essays. He began to find his own voice with a reformulation of his mystical naturalism in a new theory of the religious response as aspirational outreach.

Wieman came to Chicago about the time Meland was ready to graduate. Meland was immediately responsive to the brand of empiricism Wieman brought to the school, namely, devotion to what objectively was the source of human good. This theme as "otherness" or "realism" persisted throughout all of the turns in his thought. However, Wieman was so focused on clarity and certainty about the empirically objective in reality that he bracketed out the more mystical features of the concrete context. There was an eventual break with Wieman, or at least each went his own way over the issue of the manageable and the unmanageable in religious inquiry.

Meland carved out for himself his own characteristic brand of empiricism. During the second phase of the Chicago School, this was done primarily through his distinctive theory of the religious response as the appreciative consciousness and through his concept of the empirical as concrete
lived experience.

Although the socio-historical method persisted in several forms throughout his career, particularly through his focus on history and culture embedded in his concepts of myths, mythos, and the structure of experience and carried forward to the point of rejecting any ahistorical metaphysics even when
he reappropriated Whitehead following his move to the faculty of the Divinity
School, he turned away from modernism and metaphysics to aesthetic sensibilities.

When Meland moved to the Divinity School faculty in 1945 explicit theological themes began to emerge in his effort to reappropriate and reorient
Christian motifs. He conceived his role as theologian as "constructive,"
which meant primarily that theological themes were approached not as systematic theology or historical doctrine but as lived experience.

Upon his return to Chicago, he reentered the discussion about Whitehead
and process philosophy then dominating the Divinity School under Williams
and Loomer. He, however, appropriated Whitehead in his own distinctive way.
His early themes of elementalism, the creatural stance, aesthetic sensibilities,
myth, emergence, and culture qualified and shaped his employment of the
Whiteheadian vision. His summit trilogy on method focused primarily on the
themes of faith, myth, and culture—both religion as a cultural reality in the
history of religions and religion as a part of the structure of experience of
American culture. Redemption more than creation became the dominant
theological theme as the creative act of God as renewal dominated his later
thought about God.

Except for Wieman and Meland, there was little discussion of empirical
theology in the wider theological community during and following World War
II, until the 1960s, when several theologians trained at Chicago under
Wieman, Hartshorne, and Meland began to reestablish the viability of empirical theology with the larger theological discussion.

EMPIRICAL AND PROCESS THEOLOGY

The empirical theme in theology continues today among a second and
third generation of philosophers of religion and theologians who employ
the American empirical and pragmatic tradition. This tradition serves both
as presupposition and beginning point of the movement currently designated
as "process theology" and as a predominant emphasis of one of the groups
within the process movement. Among those whose theological identity is
primarily "process theology," one can distinguish three different method-

ological emphases, viz., empirical, speculative, and rational. All three have a strong empirical component and continue to presuppose the naturalistic and experiential basis of empirical theology.

The claim that process theology is a form of empirical theology is difficult for some to acknowledge, for in contrast to instrumental or radical empiricism, process theologians seem so concerned with delineating or explicating a total structure of thought or vision of reality that they rarely get around to asserting empirical claims or inquiring into them. Most process theology since World War II has concentrated on the speculative side of Whitehead's philosophy and pursued Hartshorne's project to the point that it has seemed as if in both preoccupation and procedure the early Chicago School and the pragmatic and empirical elements of the movement have been eclipsed.

However, process theology is a form of empirical theology in two senses. First, it is the concrete character of the data with which the process thinker is concerned. The concern with categories and vision is not rationalistic in the traditional sense of constructing an abstract framework of thought into which experience can be fitted. Process thinkers begin with and attend to concrete, individual events to discover the persisting and commonly shared characteristics of concrete experience whenever and wherever they occur, lifting them to the level of a vision of experience and subject of further verification and revision as the data from experience become known or a new understanding of the data suggests itself. Experienced events provide the data of reflection in process philosophy and theology. In this sense the method is basically empirical, becoming a generalization of the shared features of concrete experience, lifting the ambiguous flux of experience into a working vision of the whole.

Process theology is also empirical in the sense that it has been influenced by the socio-historical method of the early Chicago School.[23] Indeed, in John Cobb's estimation the two main sources have been Whitehead's philosophy and the socio-historical school at Chicago. Although Whitehead functioned among the process philosophers, especially Hartshorne, to bring the concept of God beyond the relativities of cultural history, process theology has its roots in the socio-historical period as well. Whitehead's own position is as favorable to the socio-historical school as to Wieman or Hartshorne in that his thought was as responsive to socio-historical considerations as to empirical and rational ones.[24] Although he went further than Mathews in tracing the relative independent role of ideas, he laid far more emphasis than either Wieman or Hartshorne upon the role of social factors in shaping thought.

---

23. See Cobb's history of process thought.

24. John Cobb, "The Origins of Process Theology," *Meaning, Truth, and God*, ed. Leroy Rouner (Notre Dame, Ind.: University of Notre Dame Press, 1982), p.107.

SCHUBERT OGDEN

The rational empiricists are occupied with metaphysics as transcendental analysis and the question whether there were logically necessary propositions in the sense that such propositions would be necessary truths if they are true at all. The representatives of this strand of empiricism are the contemporary Hartshornian process metaphysicians and theologians. Schubert Ogden is the primary representative. His thought has been influenced by the empiricism of Wieman and Whitehead, as well as Hartshorne, and enriched by existentialism, especially Heidegger and Bultmann.

Ogden begins with a Whiteheadian empiricism, a brand of empiricism in which the primary awareness is of ourselves, others, and the whole. Because at the base of whatever we say or do there is a primitive awareness of ourselves and the world as both real and important, he locates the reality of God in our experience of value and meaning, specifically, in our fundamental confidence in the meaningfulness of our lives as grounded in the encompassing whole.

Where Ogden goes beyond the empirical foundations for theology and the Whiteheadian speculative vision of reality is to argue that the vision, and specifically the idea of God, which is empirically founded, is not simply a hypothesis but is a necessary idea. His argument appeals to experience, but it is not empirical. The affirmation of God is not an empirical claim that can be falsified, but is a metaphysical claim, viz., that there are concepts of such general adequacy that they are necessary concepts if there is anything at all.

He combines both the empirical and rationalistic strands of the history of empirical theology, arguing that everyone does and must believe in the reality of God because it is presupposed or implied in our actual experience and living, and that the God presupposed or implied there is not a contingent reality; if God exists, God necessarily exists.

The key to Ogden's brand of empiricism and what identifies him as a rationalistic representative of the empirical tradition is his insistence that empirical thought must move to metaphysical thought, even to the point of asking whether there are necessary ideas which a metaphysical scheme must affirm out of an empirical orientation. His rationalism is not the claim that his set of metaphysical principles is the only one genuinely conceivable and so the only set really possible, but the claim that the most basic principles exemplified in our world are in fact metaphysical in character, meaning that they would necessarily be exemplified in any world.

The speculative empiricists are not as much interested in metaphysics per se as in universal commonsense ideas, with cosmology, and with a speculative worldview in which all the relevant facts fit together. They are committed to propositions as speculative hypotheses, so that adequacy is correspondence to all the facts and coherence of vision rather than necessarily true metaphysical principles.

JOHN B. COBB JR.

John Cobb's theology is "empirically oriented" in the sense he maintains a spirit of openness before all the evidence of experience, and his temperament is oriented more toward the empirical than the rationalistic. Although he has never made use of Hartshorne in the way the rationalistic process theologians have, rational criteria are a norm for his judgments in a way not characteristic of the more thoroughgoing empiricists. His theology is empirical in the sense that it includes and is based on broad aspects of experience, such as emotional, volitional, evaluative, and cognitive. The movement toward wholeness in experience, however, moves him from what is given in experience to speculative, confessional, and perspectival elements in theology.

Whitehead is useful for him as a cosmology for interpreting as a whole the evidence of experience. In that sense he does not distinguish radically between the empirical and the rational. The rational is conceived more as cosmology, frankly speculative hypotheses and frameworks of interpretation that might illuminate the experiential evidence. This mixture of empirical temper and speculative vision distinguish Cobb's thought. One might say that he is an empiricist in the sense that we come to beliefs through an open interaction with the evidence and that the most important evidence is experiential, but that his empiricism also becomes an ontological doctrine, so that Whitehead's metaphysics of experience becomes the framework for all of the philosophical and theological doctrines he interprets.

In the earlier part of his career it was the thought of Whitehead that was to the forefront. His first major constructive work was an application of Whitehead's philosophy to the ideas of the human soul, responsible human being, and the doctrine of God. Even in this earlier work, however, there was evident an influence of the early Chicago socio-historical orientation in his insistence of the contextual character and so relativity of theology. He has repudiated the search of the middle period Chicago quest for a literal language in theology and has even juxtaposed the empirical and the historical in a way reminiscent of the early Chicago School. The task of theology is historically given in the sense that the theologian's task is to help the current generation understand its situation and find meaning within it. Among all of the Whiteheadian and Hartshornian expositors of process metaphysics, Cobb has been the one who has emphasized the contextual character and so the relativity of all theological interpretations. Although the Whiteheadian metaphysics continues to be decisive for his thought, he writes more and more in an empirical vein where the appeal to the experience of God as creative transformation and the importance of language and social context as historical construction have come to the fore.

The other major representative of the application of the speculative vision to theology is David Griffin. He has made major contributions of the

Whiteheadian vision to specific theological doctrines, especially theodicy and christology. The role of speculative vision and the importance of an adequate one have been to the forefront recently as he sees the need for a postmodern vision of reality. In his view, a fully adequate theology must seek to be fully empirical (adequate to the facts of experience) and rational (achieving coherence and self-consistency) but also speculative (forming hypotheses about what things are in themselves and how they are related to other things in distinction from how they appear to us).

Thus theology must involve the development of a self-consistent worldview that is adequate to all the facts of experience. He rejects the current claim that the so-called facts of experience are entirely a function of one's theory in favor of presuppositions of practice, which he calls "hard-core commonsense ideas," ideas which cannot be consistently denied, such as freedom, causation, time, truth, possibility, importance, intrinsic value, and ultimate meaning. This entails primarily development of a vision of reality that is intrinsically convincing and inherently understandable and has illuminating power in interpreting the presymbolic perception of experience. The speculative vision, thereafter, is applied to the resolution of conflict between doctrines that seemed initially to conflict with other beliefs and to the interpretation of strictly Christian doctrines in the total theological enterprise. Theology, therefore, is the Christian vision of reality.[25]

This form of process thought has also been highly influential among a group of scientists and theologians whose views of the relation of science and religion have been influenced by empirical and process theology. Especially influential have been the works of Ian Barbour, who has emphasized the value-laden character of all theory and the importance of models and metaphors in science and religion and advocated the process perspective; and Charles Birch, a biologist, whose views of creation, nature, and human life and of God within the natural process have been highly influenced by Whitehead; and Karl Peters whose work on the interrelation of science, religion, and empirical theology, has guided *Zygon* as a major outlet for this application of empirical theology to science.

Although the work of this kind of process theology has been extensive through books and journals, process theology is focused institutionally at the Center for Process Studies at the Claremont School of Theology (California); the primary organ of this version of process thought is the journal *Process Studies*.

---

25. In addition to Cobb and Ogden, this form of process theology continues today in the work of Marjorie Suchocki, who is Cobb's successor at the Claremont School of Theology. As a master of the Whiteheadian vision, she has moved beyond it to reshape and supplement that vision in her own way, informing it with feminist, liberationist, pluralistic, and ecological concerns. Another representative of that speculative side of process thought, who has pursued it in conversation with the empiricists, is Delwin Brown.

Radical Empiricism, History, and Pragmatism

The emphasis of those who stressed the radical empirical foundations of process theology is on the concrete particular and the condition of struggle for meaning. These empiricists want to stay close to the description of concrete lived experience, to an awareness of the nonconscious depths of experience, and are content with a smaller margin of intelligibility. Adequacy is measured by faithfulness to the full range of experience, and general propositions were viewed as hypotheses of interconnections. The view of empiricism shared by the representatives of this type of process theology is shaped primarily by the pragmatic concept of experience.

The two main representatives of the radical empirical theme in empirical theology are Nancy Frankenberry, whose primary contribution is the significance of radical empiricism for the philosophy of religion, and William Dean, whose primary contribution is to constructive theology.

Frankenberry's focus is the critique of classical empiricism, positivism, linguistic empiricism, and neopragmatic empiricism in the light of William James' radical empiricism for the creation of an empirical religious perspective as the basis for the justification for religious beliefs.[26] Although highly influenced by Dewey, Whitehead, Wieman, and Hartshorne, her focus is on the constructive use of James' elemental and organic togetherness of the experiencing subject and the experienced environment of felt qualities. The religious dimension of experience, then, is located as a quality of the "More" within perceptual experience and affectional facts. The justification of religious claims rests in the religious perspective based in radical empiricism. The theistic interpretation of experience as felt qualities in a world of process found in Wieman, Meland, and Loomer are basic, although she also explores the metaphysical implications of radical empiricism in Whitehead and Buddhist thought as the basis for a comprehensive foundation for a larger philosophy of religion.

William Dean's theological agenda consists of an empiricist's conversation with distinctive historicist themes in the American empirical and pragmatic tradition and with European postmodern historicism, particularly deconstructionism.[27] Although he gives some role to the speculative side of Whitehead's cosmology in the construction of experience, he is more interested in an empirical Whiteheadian aesthetic than a rationalistic Whiteheadian metaphysics. The empirical Whitehead is the aesthetic Whitehead.

His own constructive work has been a distinctive blend of the aesthetic/value themes of the radical empirical tradition and human historicity

---

26. See Frankenberry, *Religion and Radical Empiricism.*

27. William Dean, *American Religious Empiricism* (Albany: State University of New York Press, 1986), and *History Making History* (Albany: State University of New York Press, 1988).

which he finds in the social and historical themes of the early Chicago School. He has also been particularly interested in overcoming the bifurcation between nature and history, so that, constructivist as his own thought is, he is insistent that human construction not be done apart from what nature is. Thus he exhibits a strong naturalistic brand of empiricism.

Meland and the late Loomer have been particularly influential in Dean's thought. His thought is a blend of the role of the interpretive response, which is frankly constructivist in the way historicists have argued, and the role of the richness and complexity of concrete experience, which conveys at the pre-conceptual level the vague and dissonant penumbral feelings of value at the fringe of experience. What is distinctive in radical empiricism is the claim that there are other senses than the five senses, such as the sense of beauty, the sense of the "More," the senses of aversion or attraction, the senses of felt quality. Central to Dean's brand of radical empiricism, then, is the experience of aesthetic value.

His effort is to arrive at a theistic hypothesis drawn from the vague, indistinct, unclear, groping sort of empiricist apprehension of the whole or more or creative event that has some hope of pragmatic confirmation, which results in an empiricist/historicist/pragmatic concept of God, "that general complexion or activity within history which makes history meaningful or worth living in."[28]

The kind of radical empirical emphasis represented by Frankenberry and Dean is highly influential among a group of fifty scholars in the Highlands Institute of American Religious Thought. Their emphases are the interface between theology and the American philosophical tradition, the history and development of liberal religious thought, the Chicago School, and naturalism in American philosophy and theology. There is also a group on "Empiricism in American Religious Thought" in the American Academy of Religion. Finally, the research in this group is represented in the journal founded in 1980 by Larry Axel and Creighton Peden, *The American Journal of Theology and Philosophy*.

---

28. Dean, *American Religious Empiricism*, p. 56.

CHAPTER TWO

Major Themes of Empirical Theology

NANCY FRANKENBERRY

INTRODUCTION

My intention in this chapter is to examine some major themes of empirical theology, critically and for their current constructive value. Because my focus is more philosophical than historical, I am less concerned to link the discussion of these themes to particular authors or periods within the complex development of empirical theology than I am to reconstruct from these themes a coherent and challenging structure of thought. I propose to do this, first, by situating empirical theology in the context of the naturalistic principles and worldview common to all of its theological expressions; second, by considering the assumptions of radical empiricism as providing a distinctive epistemological and methodological point of departure for theology; and third, by reflecting on the contemporary place of empirical theology in the overall theological landscape. It will be obvious that my interpretation of empirical theology is a construct which coincides with no particular writer(s) but consolidates what I find to be the best wisdom gleaned from many. To that extent, this chapter is intended as a contribution to, and not simply a description of, empirical theology.

NATURALISTIC PRINCIPLES

The determination of what is to count as "empirical" has always been a highly theoretical matter. This is no less true of the school known as empirical theology. The major themes taken as "empirical" by this theology, as well as the various appeals it makes to "experience," are already effects produced by the particular theory it has adopted to render the "empirical" epistemically accessible to reflection in the first place. The fact that this dependency has not always been explicitly recognized in the complex history of empirical method, even by some representatives of empirical theology, points to the importance of examining the exact account of "experience" presupposed in any particular theory. For without some fairly precise and systematically framed understanding of experience—its sources, limits, ingredients, and possibilities of expression—the empirical appeal to "experience" solves nothing and signifies anything.

In the case of empirical theology, its underlying worldview or cosmological outlook is derived from the presuppositions of evolutionary naturalism and reinforced by the descriptive generalizations of process philosophy. Summarily stated, empirical theology presupposes a naturalistic, neo-materialistic worldview in which the basic constituents of reality are energy-events, happenings, or processes. Nature comprises the realm of the experienceable. Matter turns out to be patterning energy and energy is radiating matter, the only "stuff" of experience. "Substances" are radically deconstructed into their constitutive processes of becoming, and processes themselves are constituted by energy-events. All so-called substances or enduring entities can be understood as processes of becoming which are radically relational. Change the dynamics of relational composition and a novel emergent will occur. In this worldview, no "doer before the deed" is needed to account for ontological identity or agency, for the doer is produced in and through the becoming of the deed, as the effect and not the cause of its own conditions.

This emphasis on process as the fundamental reality out of which things are made, and attention to the organic, profoundly relational, nature of reality, including any religious reality, is a mark of the legacy of Alfred North Whitehead and a variety of organismic thinkers whose work has inspired several generations of empirical theology. In its adherence to a processive-relational conception of reality, empirical theology looks to what is concrete about process, namely, the decisions (in the root sense of "cutting off") and the relations that are constitutive of the very becoming of anything real, including the highest reaches of human spiritual life. As a result, empirical theology is distinguished by its orientation to the analysis of the concrete, where the meaning of "concrete experience" is synonymous with energy-processes in their wholeness or unique qualitative particularity.

No fact-value dichotomy can be presumed at this level of concreteness. Nor is subject-object dualism an inevitable feature of the analysis of concrete experience. Most empirical theologians would affirm William James' definition of what he called a "full fact," consisting in "a conscious field *plus* its object as felt or thought of *plus* an attitude toward the object *plus* the sense of a self to whom the attitude belongs."[1] Concrete reality is variously char-

---

1. William James, *The Varieties of Religious Experience* (Cambridge: Harvard University Press, 1985), p. 393.

acterized in this empirical traditional as duration (Bergson), as creative event
(Wieman), as perceptual flux and *élan vital* presenting a constant "More"
(James), and as the unmanageable depth of the living situation (Meland).
For James and for empirical theology in general, the body is the most immediate and elemental site in human life for experiencing that which is most concrete. Descriptively generalized, the body may even become synecdochal for
all social systems, including that of reality itself.

Theologically, the adoption of a naturalistic worldview marks an important shift from a perspective that regards the resources for salvation as deriv-
able ultimately from a transcendent deity, to a perspective that recognizes
nature's grace as emergent within the depths of concrete experience. More
than simply exchanging the image of "heights" for that of "depths," empirical theology promotes a philosophical articulation of the religious meaning
of nature. It endeavors to spell out the myriad ways in which, in the words of
Bernard Loomer, "all the heights and depths, the originating causes and
final ends, the realities symbolized by the principalities and powers (including the demons and angels) that were formerly thought to inhabit the lower
and upper worlds, are now found within the many mansions of this world."[2]
In the end, it is its preoccupation with the category of "nature" as much as with
"history" that distinguishes empirical theology from existentialist, neo-orthodox, and narrative schools of theology as well as from most varieties of rev-
elationally based or evangelical theology that have surfaced in this century.

By its insistence on the advisability and utility of philosophical categories of analysis in connection with theological method, empirical theology is marked by its own liberal and modernist promptings. Indeed, at the
heart of the debates in which empirical theology has been embroiled throughout its several phases is the issue of whether a post-Darwinian naturalistic
worldview can support or should in any way conspire with Christian theology. Against those who have maintained that Christian theology is necessarily
independent of all worldviews, empirical theology has replied that some or
another contingent relation has always existed between theological interpretation and the historically variable cosmological and speculative aus-
pices under which Christian theology has been constructed. The presumption
of a naturalistic interpretation of the world and the project of articulating a
conception of a deity that is entirely natural has been defended on the grounds
that this auspice not only accords well with current scientific cosmology
but also best accommodates the meaning and truth of the Christian mythos.
It comes as no surprise, then, that throughout the modern period and into
the postmodern era as well empirical theologians who have worked to reconstruct religion naturalistically have routinely played the role of ghostbusters

---

2. Bernard M. Loomer, "Empirical Theology within Process Thought," in *The Future
of Empirical Theology*, ed. Bernard E. Meland (Chicago: University of Chicago Press,
1969), p. 151.

in relation to the supernatural entities that figure in religious mythologies. Indeed, empirical theologians as a rule generally have been less interested in explaining and interpreting traditional doctrines of organized religion than in analyzing observable processes in nature which figure in the various kinds of creative transformation associated with religious living.

But to say that the naturalistic outlook of this theology is skeptical of the postulation of a transcendental realm beyond nature still does not capture the constructive vision of its religious appropriation of naturalism. The major elements of that vision, as I identify them, can be set forth as follows:

1) The conception of nature as co-extensive with "reality" or the "life process" and as constituted by spatio-temporal energy-events entails the corollary that there are no disembodied possibilities, ideals, souls, heavens, or gods. The Word not only "becomes" flesh, but is literally no-thing apart from or prior to its incarnation somewhere. The disembodied Logos which is located nowhere lacks all existence, subsistence, or ordering efficacy. Whitehead's ontological principle illustrates this assumption by postulating that "actual entities are the only *reasons*; so that to search for a *reason* is to search for one or more actual entities," from which it follows that every condition to which the process of becoming conforms in any particular instance has its reason either in the character of some actual entity in the actual world of that event, or in the character of the event itself as it is coming to be.[3] If the one world, with all its incalculable possibilities, is the sole locus of meaning and value, then all principles, descriptions, and explanations must be understood to refer to events and their relations. The ultimate in explanation is finally the most general concrete description of the way in which constitutive relations are coordinated.

2) In an evolving, ever-unfinished universe of ceaseless creative activity the fundamental image of nature in terms of interpenetrating fields of forces and organically integrated wholes has replaced that of self-contained, externally related bits of particles or inert matter. As a result, not only supernaturalisms and transcendentalisms, but all subjective idealisms as well have been superseded by twentieth-century relativity and field theories in physics. For once mechanism is no longer the root metaphor of science, idealism is no longer the only recourse for resolving the tension between science and religion or for introducing "mind" into "matter." Closely related to the assumption that the being of any natural entity is constituted by its relationships and its participation in ever more inclusive fields, the idea that "the whole is more than the sum of its parts" has become central to the development of systems theory, biological ecology, and field analysis. Theologically, this has suggested to some thinkers a vision of the world-totality as a complex, unified individual, itself divine. Empirical theologians have been more cautious in

---

3. Alfred North Whitehead, *Process and Reality*, corrected ed., ed. D. R. Griffin and D. Sherburne (New York: Free Press, 1978), p. 24.

depicting the nature of this totality, preferring to guard against the idealistic tendency which sees the human mind writ large in nature itself. The overarching consciousness of "an all-inclusive divine mind," deemed so essential by the idealist tradition, is usually jettisoned as unempirical.

3) Human nature is a factor within nature and not a mere spectator to it. The processes and events, the qualities and relations which constitute nature are objective in the twofold sense that nature is fully real in its own right and by its own operations and is not dependent on any other order of reality, and, both in its parts and as a whole, it is independent of human thinking. Correspondingly, every item of the experienced world and hence every item of knowledge is an item in nature, a participant in natural processes, and dependent upon the reality of the external world for acquiring knowledge. All objects and all subjects are therefore natural entities. The world of objective actualities enters into the constitution of each subject, which in turn becomes a conditioning cause in the becoming of subsequent subjects.

4) Nature is both pluralistic and continuous, thus ruling out monisms as well as dualisms. While nature may be one, at the same time it is also many and, contrary to Plato, the many, far from being an appearance or an image of the real, are real themselves. William James compared this pluralism to the dried human heads with which the Dyaks of Borneo decked their lodges, the skull forming a solid nucleus, but "innumerable feathers, leaves, strings, beads, and loose appendices of every description float and dangle, terminating, it is true, in a nucleus of common perception, but for the most part out of sight and irrelevant and unimaginable to one another."[4] Likewise, while nature exhibits discontinuities in the form of emergent plateaus, its parts are also bound together by common structures of becoming. Nature, in short, though individualized, is not bifurcated. It does not admit of any dualism, whether of spirit-matter, mind-body, value-fact, possibility-actuality, one-many, religion-science, or God-humans. This principle is illustrated by Peirce's doctrine of synechism.

5) Nature is infinite and inexhaustible. In the presumed absence of any "far-off divine event toward which all creation tends," nature's possibilities are regarded as infinite. Empirical theologians envisage no eschatological "time" in which all possibilities will be completely exhausted or fully actualized. For religious naturalists, the assumption that temporal process is without absolute beginning or absolute end intensifies the sense of wonder, of contingency, and of mystery that attends the living of life.

6) According to this version of naturalism, "quality" and "structure" are aspects of all processes and their analysis is at the heart of empirical method. Quality, or a complex of qualities, is energy as experienced by the human organism. If every event is an instance of energy, insofar as it is accessible

---

4. William James, *Essays in Radical Empiricism* (Cambridge: Harvard University Press), p. 24.

to human experience, it is also an instance of quality. Henry Nelson Wieman goes so far as to say that "quality, then, is the ultimate substance of the world out of which all else is made."[5] Structure, as Wieman also explains, is the term given to the demarcations and interrelations of events whereby we can apprehend them as different events and yet in meaningful relation to one another. Structuring the world so that qualities become more appreciable is the common goal of life, for individuals, societies, and historical epochs. This goal, however, is confounded by the simultaneous interweaving in nature of less than creative processes that are confused, tragic, contradictory, disorderly, and, at best, ambiguous.

7) Nevertheless, "ultimate reality," as construed by virtually all empirical theologians, has a creative character. The very meaning of the term "ultimate reality" here can only refer to the overall character ascribed to the real, not to any supervening reality. In the last analysis, nature is not regarded as dead, blank, and indifferent, as though amounting only to blind, onrushing upsurges of sheer energy without form. Rather, the form that evolution takes is regarded as orderly and characterized by creativity, a creative synthesis which is productive of novel emergents. That is to say, the force of sheer energy is always found ordered, shaped, and possessed of a measure of purposefulness, however meager. Although the process cannot be rendered as linear, some modicum of teleology is asserted or assumed by empirical theology, and it is this claim that distinguishes it from humanistic naturalism and provides the basis for the naturalistic meaning of God.

8) Value is intrinsic to nature. Wherever else in nature value may reside, it is found in the experiences of subjects and is a function of some subject's response. Value is not supernatural or in any way transcendent of nature. It is continuous with "fact" and organic to it, not imposed on nature or projected by the human mind. Creative advance in nature is measured in terms of the emergence of qualitatively richer and more complex individuals and societies. Such increase in value occurs as a contingent outcome of the synthesis of great contrasts, bordering even on incompatibilities, into effective harmonies. Therefore, aesthetic order that yields beauty is regarded as more inclusive, as well as more concrete, than ethical or political or religious order. For some empirical theologians, the overall life process is marked more by a terrible beauty than by the urgencies of Protestant moralism.

9) Transcendence in nature is a function of the nexus of internal relations that comprises the communal ground of all existence. The nexus of relationships, or plenum of interconnected events, that forms our existence is not projected, it is given. We do not create these relationships, we experience them, and to that extent we acknowledge that human life is rooted in a biological reality deeper than consciousness and from which it draws its suste-

---

5. Henry Nelson Wieman, *The Source of Human Good* (Carbondale: Southern Illinois University Press, 1946), p. 302.

nance, nurture, and creative power. Both the creative ground and the redemptive life afforded by the web of internal relations are empirical traces of the transcendence found within nature.

10) Finally, religious naturalism is a recognition and celebration of the common creaturehood of all beings as attested to in many different fields. Ecological studies have shown that human life is intertwined with the movements of the sun and moon, migrations of animals, and the advance and retreat of polar icecaps. Evolutionary theory has found that humankind's roots go back to early primates, backboned fishes, primeval sea worms, and the element-building stars. And biological studies have revealed that life extends to an attenuated prelife hidden in the heart of inanimate matter. Religious naturalism holds that humans have no privileged position above or outside this web of nature and life. We not only live and move and have our becoming within this matrix, but we are, literally, creatures of the earth, born of its evolutionary processes, nurtured and sustained by its intricate interchanges, and recreated within its enveloping environment. This is also the inescapable matrix of perishing of life and loss of value.

The elaboration of these as well as other naturalist principles follows the empirical method of descriptive generalization and is supported by appeals to the several sciences and to widespread human experience. Like all empirical ventures, this method involves a good measure of rational speculation. Some empirical theologians would even stress that speculative philosophy, properly understood, has an important contribution to make to the quest for religious integrity. For in the last analysis, theologians, philosophers, scientists, and poets are all concerned in different ways with the same object of inquiry, awe, and fascination—nature. Some understanding of the whole is necessary for an adequate understanding of any of the parts. But the whole of nature is not accessible as such to empirical inquiry. All that is accessible is mediated through human existence. Unless theologians flatly refuse to place human experience within nature, they need to find in descriptions of human experience factors which also enter into the descriptions of less specialized natural occurrences. If there are no such factors, then the doctrine of human experience as a fact within nature is mere bluff, as Whitehead pointed out, founded upon vague phrases whose sole merit is a comforting familiarity. In that case theologians should admit to a frank dualism, with all the insuperable conceptual problems dualism has entailed in the history of thought.

Empirical theologians, rooted in the worldview of naturalism, are willing to risk descriptive generalization of key notions, such as "becoming" and "relativity," beyond their fields of limited application in order to test their fruitfulness as clues to a tentative and hypothetical understanding of the whole. This rational empiricism differs from transcendental or a priori rationalism which aims to inscribe universal and necessary categories. Empiricists expect to locate only a few recurrent ones.

RADICAL EMPIRICISM AND PRAGMATISM

Just as my account of empirical theology favors the ontology of neo-naturalism and process-relational philosophy, I view its epistemology as distinctively shaped by the assumptions of American radical empiricism and pragmatism. The most important of those assumptions, and arguments in support of them, can be developed in terms of the following theses.

1) The Primacy of Perception. More than any other thesis, this is what distinguishes empirical theology from other varieties of empiricism and also from the epistemology of critical realism. Radical empiricism maintains that the concrete data of perception are the particular actualities that are directly and perspectivally prehended, whereas most other modern schools of empiricism have contended that what is directly given are abstract forms of sense data in terms of which the concrete actualities may be inferred. The claim that perception, or "knowledge by acquaintance," involves a deeper event than analysis and description is a characteristic feature of radical empiricism. According to William James, for instance, "The deeper features of reality are found only in perceptual experience. Here alone do we acquaint ourselves with continuity, or the immersion of one thing in another, here alone with self, with substance, with qualities, with activity in its various modes, with time, with cause, with change, with novelty, with tendency, with freedom. Against all such features of reality the method of conceptual translation, when candidly and critically followed out, can only raise its own *non possumus*, and brand them as unreal or absurd."[6] For Alfred North Whitehead, also, the primacy of perception entailed the judgment that "the deliverances of clear and distinct consciousness require criticism by reference to elements in experience which are neither clear nor distinct. On the contrary, they are dim, massive, and important."[7] It is these data that are intended when empirical theologians employ the general empirical principle that all knowledge arises ultimately from experience or that all theories must be tested in terms of human experience. First and foremost, what radical empiricism contributes to the checkered history of empiricism is a theory about the most concrete data of experience in their full concreteness.

2) The Role of Nonsensuous Perception. In this respect, American radical empiricism stands entirely outside the space of the British empiricist tradition which problematized the status of knowledge derived from sense data. Traditional empiricism depicted a world of experience filled with high abstractions such as "sense data" and other theoretical entities that can not be said to exist concretely. More concrete than sense-data is the non-sensuous

---

6. William James, *Some Problems of Philosophy* (Cambridge: Harvard University Press, 1979), p. 54.

7. Alfred North Whitehead, *Adventures of Ideas* (New York: Free Press, 1967 edition), p. 270.

perception Whitehead called "causal efficacy" whereby we perceive motion, feel actual physical events, and have physical memory. This thesis is an amplification of 1) above, according to which particular actualities, their relations and qualities, are the concrete data of bodily experience, not sense-data. Emphasis is placed on the objective status of affectional and volitional qualities. However, the assertion that experience is of actualities beyond the present moment of experience, actualities that are directly given to an experiencing subject, need not entail a troubling correspondence between verbal expressions and some nonlinguistic reality. Finally, the point of the critique of traditional schools of sense-data empiricism is to suggest that these schools have not been empirical *enough*. Traditional philosophers and theologians alike have failed to provide a precise cartography of the senses in all their natural splendor or to appreciate the full complexity and mystery that attends smell and taste, the sense of touch, of sound, of sight. Rather than furnishing fine-grained, concrete analyses, most empiricists have taken as paradigmatic "this-patch-of-red-here-now," hardly indicative of the acute richness and wonder of sensuous experience in the world. In attending to the importance of nonsensuous experience as well as to the wealth of sensuous experience, empirical theology seeks an elemental basis in experience for designating the kinds of processes religions have repeatedly described.

3) The Reality of Relations. Relations are given in the flux of experience and felt as given. They are as real as the things related. What is radical about radical empiricism is chiefly this thesis. As James put it, "the relations between things, conjunctive as well as disjunctive, are just as much matters of direct particular experience . . . as . . . the things themselves."[8] Other forms of empiricism have recognized only the reality of external relations, but radical empiricism holds that internal relations, the conjunctive experiences, are just as important to the complete analysis of experience as Hume's external relations of "contiguity" or "resemblance." One of several significant themes to follow from this philosophical basis, as it has become explicit in the tradition of empirical theology, concerns *the social nature of the self* as a communal individual who is created out of the internal relations that call that self into being. As articulated by James and Dewey and George Herbert Mead, this theme has produced a much more profound conception of selfhood in American thought than is found in the Continental discussion of Heidegger's analysis of *dasein-mit*. The latter notion is that of an individual who lives in community, while the former conception asserts that the community also lives concretely within the self.

4) The Interactive Model of Experience. Unlike the literature of classical empiricism which problematizes discourse about "the experience of reality" and "experience of the world," empirical theologians have tended to

---

8. William James, *The Meaning of Truth* (Cambridge: Harvard University Press, 1978), pp. 6-7.

talk in terms of "the reality of experience" and "the world of experience."⁹ The difference is subtle but crucial. Replacing the spectator view of knowledge implicated in classical empiricism, radical empiricism relies on an interactionist model in which the ongoing interactive process between organisms and their environment produces the funded character of experience. According to the interactive model, experience is not understood as the raw material knowledge seeks to understand, but rather knowledge is viewed as the active process which produces its own objects of investigations, including empirical "facts." Far from being adequately understood as a passively received tissue of subjectivity, or as an actively imposed layer of ideology, "experience" in the American grain has been theorized as a socially constituted process, semiotically and historically constructed in an interactive process between organisms and their environment. In this discussion, it is clear that experience is not taken to be something immediately present in the form of an unmediated real. "Givenness" for radical empiricism is as much a product of funded experience as it is productive of future experience.

5) The Cognitive Value of Feeling. The model of disembodied reason is repudiated in favor of the view that knowledge is saturated with feeling, mood, affectivity. Following Henry Nelson Wieman, some empirical theologians restrict the term "knowledge" to that which involves interpretation, reflection, and prediction. Others, after the fashion of Bernard Meland, prefer to widen the term "knowledge" so as to include the mode of acquaintance by which what is directly given is grasped feelingly, and feeling is taken to have cognitive import. The issue between these two approaches turns on the type of data to which one chooses to attend. Radical empiricists typically look to the more vague, unmanageable, and only dimly given data of feeling or prehension. They assume such data can be lifted to specifiable structures of expression and articulated faithfully, if not fully. Other empiricists who may be motivated, as Meland thought Wieman was, by the lure of certainty, generally reserve the honorific term "knowledge" for the more manageable data of experience as clearly and distinctly given. In either case, the prehensive feeling quality of experience is thought to have cognitive import, whether directly or indirectly.

6) The Elliptical Quality of Language. In reflecting on the way philosophy has been misled by mathematics to think that its method should be that of deduction from axiomatic certainties, Whitehead issued a warning that has been heeded more often by empirical theologians in this century than by most philosophers until very recently:

---

9. John Dewey's various formulations are particularly illustrative, as in *Logic: The Theory of Inquiry* (New York: Henry Holt, 1938) where he writes: "A universe of experience is the precondition of a universe of discourse. Without its controlling presence, there is no way to determine the relevancy, weight, or coherence of any designated distinction or relation. The universe of experience surrounds and regulates the universe of discourse but never appears as such within the latter" (p. 68).

There are no precisely stated axiomatic certainties from which to start. There is not even the language in which to frame them. The only possible procedure is to start from verbal expressions which, when taken by themselves with the current meaning of their words, are ill-defined and ambiguous. These are not premises to be immediately reasoned from apart from elucidation by further discussion; they are endeavors to state general principles which will be exemplified in the subsequent description of the facts of experience. This subsequent elaboration should elucidate the meanings to be assigned to the words and phrases employed. Such meanings are incapable of accurate apprehension apart from a correspondingly accurate apprehension of the metaphysical background which the universe provides for them. But no language can be anything but elliptical, requiring a leap of the imagination to understand its meaning in its relevance to immediate experience.[10]

The further hermeneutical recognition that all experience is mediated by language, or more broadly, by symbolic systems, carries additional implications for the ongoing development of empirical theology. For if empirical theology has been significant for maintaining a distinctive objectivity of the datum of experience, it is also true that the understanding of that datum rests on conventions generated by systems of signification. Objects, events, relations, and meanings of whatever kind do not simply present themselves to human minds in prepackaged units with labels, ready to be read from the face of experience. Rather, with the intervention of human acts of interpretation, reality becomes organized by languages in terms of certain structures. The thoroughly linguistic, even if elliptical, quality of conscious human thought and knowledge is an important corollary of empirical theology's longstanding subordination of language to primary experience.

7) The Instrumental Role of Conceptual Reasoning. This notion of the relative poverty of conceptual formalizations and linguistic formulations in comparison with the richness of lived experience forms a constant theme in empirical theology. Properly understood, radical empiricism is a complement, not an alternative, to rationalism, and the distinction between the two methods cannot be made in any disabling way. Indeed, empirical theology presumes an underlying rationalism, in the widest sense, that emphasizes continuity rather than discontinuity in explanation. Precisely because it assumes no ontological gaps in modes or dimensions of reality, such as natural versus supernatural, or phenomenal versus noumenal, empirical theology is committed to continuity of explanation. Rationalism within the context of an empirical outlook also entails a resistance to abrupt leaps of faith. And the instrumental value of reason means that ideas emerge from and must be validated neither in logic nor language alone, but in lived experience.

10. Whitehead, *Process and Reality*, p. 13.

8) The Absence of Foundations. Along with American pragmatists, the later Wittgenstein, and contemporary deconstructionists, empirical theology rejects not only the representational theory of knowledge and the Cartesian search for certain foundations but the whole idea of the isolated subject caught in an egocentric predicament of trying to acquire knowledge about a public world on the basis of her or his private experience. This antifoundationalist stance, combined with the continued use of the difficult category of "experience," produces a distinctive voice in the current postmodernist intellectual climate. For the present generation of empirical theologians, not even "experience" can be taken as foundational without privileging the interpreter's partial reading of the meaning of the term. In order not to risk essentialization of that category into an appeal to something fixed and unitary and determinate, empirical theologians, like others today, must constantly be mindful of the countless ways in which any appeal to "experience" is always already transgressed and constituted by axes of difference, involving gender, race, class, ethnicity, and culture.

9) The Mediating Method of Pragmatism. Pragmatism, as it developed out of twentieth century empirical and idealist traditions, had a profound influence on theological method in twentieth-century America and especially on empirical theology's self-understanding of its own practice. Steering between both a naive realism which would assume the theologian simply reads off the face of experience, finding whatever is there to be found, and a personal idealism, which is content to regard its own projections as mirrored and matched by nature, the pragmatic empirical theologian knows that human interpretations do not remold the world, without remainder, into patterns of our own choosing, and they do not simply reflect the world either. Instead, human interpretive schemes create and impose structures of meaning on experience just as much as they also derive meaning from experience. But because the experiential continuum is so diffuse, it affords no single selective principle or set of organizational categories. Even the speculative categories of process philosophy are regarded as one set among many, justified pragmatically by their fruitfulness, not by their correspondence.

10) Neither Realism Nor Antirealism. The extent to which empirical theology is committed to realism, and the exact meaning of "realism" itself, is currently a matter of considerable debate. Given a pragmatic approach to the question, only a minimalist form of realism survives, one that simply asserts that a world exists independently of human life and knowledge and that in some sense that world imposes limits on what humans can sensibly say about it. From the perspective of empirical theology, the assumption that theological concepts originate as social constructions, imaginatively projected, rather than as pure givens, realistically reflected, seems trivially true. However, short of committing some version of the genetic fallacy, this says nothing about the claims to truth these ideas can make or what reference they may have to the world. For theological empiricists, the fact that we inevitably live inside institutionally constituted paradigms, with all the possibilities of distortion and bias and repression this entails, does not prevent our testing and verifying these paradigms against facts that are independent, not of *all* paradigms, but at least of whatever one we are currently interested in testing. In recent writings by empirical theologians, all the relevant tests hinge on pragmatic criteria.

This brief analysis of epistemological themes in empirical theology invites the question of the limits of philosophical analysis itself in relation to theology. As a rule, American theology has evinced less of an antiphilosophical temper than post-Kantian Continental religious thought and has leaned toward immanentism in metaphysics. Nevertheless, the great shadow across the modern period cast by the Kantian restriction on knowledge of a noumenal realm fell also on American empirical theology. Despite the faith of Shailer Mathews in the extent to which experience reveals "personality producing forces" and of D. C. Macintosh in a divine response to human "religious adjustment," both could accept an ultimate barrier between human experience and direct knowledge of the divine. And Henry Nelson Wieman's strict adherence to the method of empirical observation and testing in determining the reference range of "God" could still yield to the final admonition not to mistake human ideas of the divine for the actual reality of the divine. Perhaps it is Bernard Meland's maxim, "we live more deeply than we think," that best sums up American religious empiricism's manner of appropriating the legacy of Kant's first critique.

THEOLOGICAL THEMES

Preeminently, this is *a theology of ambiguity, of freedom, and of creative advance*. All three themes condition each other. Without freedom, in the form of the spontaneity of nature as well as the decisions of humans, there is no creative advance. Yet even in the wake of whatever measure of creative advance does emerge, ambiguity remains. Far from being unified, autonomous individuals exercising freedom, subjects are literally created in their agency through the conditions and constraints conferred on them. If the limitations are, as Whitehead said, the opportunities, it is also the case that the opportunities for creative advance are often severely limited and that anabolic and catabolic processes intermingle in indefinable doses throughout nature. In such a theology, "spirit" is understood materially in the threefold sense that Henry Nelson Wieman developed and described as the continuous creator of ideals, aspiration, and value; as the supreme manifestation of freedom; and as the source and sustainer of human freedom.[11]

This is also a theology that views moral choice as a matter of profound social responsibility but remains deeply skeptical of the Kantian argument that

11. See, for example, Wieman, *Source of Human Good*, p. 300.

since our rational moral demands are legitimate, the fact that they are not ful-filled in this world provides compelling reason to believe that they must be fulfilled elsewhere, in a transcendent realm. Having abandoned the yearning for an absolute of any kind, empirical theology holds, with James, that "all 'homes' are in finite experience; finite experience as such is homeless."[12]

Although it shares in common with existentialist theology such themes as freedom, intersubjectivity, temporality, corporeality, finitude, death, as well as a focus on such particular human experiences as anxiety, hope, despair, guilt, and care, theological empiricism has not been typically preoccupied with existentiality, in the sense of the abstract structures or essence of human existence. Whereas existentialist theology has focused almost entirely on the distinctive structures of the human person, empirical theologians have tended to look for those structures and factors that define our existence as bio-logical organisms. As a result, existentialist theologies may have achieved a depth of analysis with respect to anthropological categories that has not been available among empirical theologians who, for their part, have not tended to be as impressed by the surds, the angst, and the *de trop* character of human existence as have Continental thinkers. The *sense of vital mys-tery*, as an unmanageable depth of existence, figures far more frequently in the writings of American empiricists. Its presence inspires neither nausea nor rebellion, but humility.

The theme of *the baffling ambiguity of good and evil* haunts the efforts of empirical theology to come to terms not only with the theodicy question but also with the human predicament. The multiple ways in which some good may emerge from the disasters of destructive evil and the ways, too, in which the good may be transformed into the demonic defy the usual religious blandishments. Like the intellect in the presence of error, and the emotions in the face of anguish, the will finds in evil a surd that it seeks to overcome, yet without it no quality of the good can be envisioned. Even still, our emo-tional states fail to be a faithful echo of the aims which we have envisioned or accomplished, our actions slip alarmingly past our intentions, and no motivation is ever unmixed. A good action can flood us with sorrow and an evil action, joy. All this makes a mockery of our logic as well as our virtue. Evil, no matter what we do, is part of our every gesture, of our most natural activities, our best institutions. To know evil is also to know the good it makes us betray; and correlatively, every emergence of good, in its turn, carries with it a potential for evil that risks plunging us into deeper ambiguity. Human emotional life unfolds according to a ragged aesthetic form of order, marked by a rhythm of feeling between contrary states, in which the strain to transmute the incompatible data of experience into a unity of effective contrasts can produce, at its extremes, either schizophre-nia or the gift of peace. The keenest and most complex personalities are

12. William James, *Pragmatism* (Cambridge: Harvard University Press, 1975), p. 125.

also those who undergo the deepest and most intense joys and sufferings, pains and triumphs, tensions and attachments. To excise the capacity for suffering is to eliminate that for enjoyment. Any theological effort to disjoin the two terms, good and evil, from each other succeeds only in abolishing both.

The theme that *experience yields knowledge of God*, characteristic of much American religious thought from the Puritans to Jonathan Edwards to the present, needs careful qualification in connection with empirical theology. Varying historically as different conceptions of "experience" have been employed, the appeal to experience in religion usually has raised more problems than it has solved. In general, empirical theology has found that the appeal to experience is methodologically legitimate only to the extent that it is coupled with and refers to an interconnected set of interpretations about what constitutes the nature, scope, and limits of experience. It forfeits legitimacy if it is advanced as a simple appeal to an isolated fact or set of facts. Least credible is any introspective appeal to "religious experience" understood individualistically. On that level, everyone's experience, whether religious or not, is a melange of the attributed, the imposed, and the lived. Interpreting it is always an act of (re)construction, not of dissection.

In the liberal and modernist phase of empirical theology, the theme that experience yields knowledge of God took two major forms. The socio-historical method of Shailer Mathews, Shirley Jackson Case, and Edward Scribner Ames was chiefly interested in analyzing ideas, doctrines, and institutions in terms of functional needs and responses. This phase of the Chicago School had much in common with pragmatism's method of ascertaining the practical consequences in experience of the *idea* of God, whereas the next phase, exemplified in different ways by the systematic-philosophical method of Wieman, Meland, and Loomer, was interested primarily in ascertaining the *reality* of God in human experience, however different that might turn out to be from orthodox religious ideas. In this phase, "experience" was theorized through a unique combination of organismic imagery, phenomenological claims, and process-relational interpretive structures derived from Whitehead, James, Dewey, and Bergson. Now entering a postliberal and postmodern phase, empirical theology emphasizes that the appeal to experience is never an incontestable source of evidence nor an originary point of explanation. The historicizing tendency of this new phase of theological empiricism, as developed by William Dean, highlights the experience of religious meaning in connection with historical events, interpreted within specific communitarian contexts. Here experience, as well as the theological ideas and realities suggested by experience, are seen, not as generic to all creatures, but as historically specific, always partially affected by the social location of the experiencing community. Historicist readings of the texts of previous empirical theologians are productive of new re-visions and recontextualizations of its themes. For example, writing just before the second wave of feminism in America, Bernard Loomer could claim that one way of interpreting the empirical meaning of Jesus Christ for Christians is as the answer to a particular question that emerged in the life of a particular people with a particular history: "How can the strength of our egocentricity be transmuted so that we can live for others?"[13] According to Loomer, the unsurpassable answer for all who ask this question is the cross—a life of self-sacrificial love. But implicit in Loomer's construal was an insufficiently historicized reading, only made visible by feminist critique. Arising out of the event of the women's movement is an entirely different and historically conditioned question that asks: "How can the strength of our relationality be transmuted so that we maintain some autonomy?" A christological figure who would embody an answer to this question for all those who, in fact, ask such a question, would not re-present an ethic of self-sacrifice.

As it arises in empirical theology, the question of God is not a question about another being in the total inventory of What There Is; it is a question concerning the nature of the experienced universe, not only taken as a whole, but taken in its individual parts as well. Empirical theologians have sought to identify an activity operative in the universe and human life that issues in *growth of value*. This growth or progressive integration is regarded as one factor within evolution. It is persistent, but not inevitable, or omnipotent; indeed, it is often reversed or suppressed. Thus, the theme of *a finite God*, defined by a certain type of causality, is distinctive of much empirical theology, although not exclusive to it. Conceived as finite, God is that factor that makes sense of the ways in which harmony and complexity, patterned order and novel emergents, arise and are sustained in nature generally, as well as in the dim regions of organic evolution and amid the conflicts of historical strife. The key to this empirical conception of the nature of God is the idea not simply of "process" but also of "relations," understood as active, dynamic, vectorial transmissions of energy, having both magnitude and direction. The disclosures of twentieth-century quantum physics and field theory persuaded empirical theologians like Bernard Meland that a common core of images such as "a sensitive nature within nature," "rapport," and "matrix of sensitivity" were indigenous in the organic behavior of nature, not simply projections of human nature into the void. On this account, no matter how differently "value" is theorized as to its nature or source, its *increase* can be said to take place in terms of relational activities that yield emergent novelty, more complex integration, and intensified mutuality and sensitive support. Observationally, these "transitive relations," as William James termed them in another context, are the very type of relations that foster the kind of growth and creative transformation that is *organic*. Evil, destruction, and conflict, on the other hand, consist in the blockage or obstruction or decay of just such transitive relations in nature. Because it is organic interconnectedness that leads to the greater good, to the growth of value and qualitative meaning, as

---

13. Loomer, "Empirical Theology within Process Thought," p. 164.

Wieman continually analyzed it, this is what is taken to comprise the empirical meaning of the divine in human life.

This way of depicting the meaning of God, in terms of a complex sustaining matrix of transitive relations in nature which is creative of organic interconnections, displays the close affinity empirical theology has to process theology. However, despite significant overlapping themes, sources, and influences, in at least three crucial respects empirical theology and process theology diverge. In the first place, the confidence among many process theologians in the applicability of personal, agential models of God is not shared by most empirical theologians. Pointing out that we simply do not know, even analogically, the meaning of "love" or "justice" on a cosmic level, empirical theologians have often substituted transpersonal or even impersonal imagery for the personalistic language of devotion. The suggestion that cosmic love might mean something like "sympathetic feeling of feeling," as proposed by some process theologians, still does not offer any empirical warrant for process theology's use of highly anthropomorphic language in connection with the divine attributes.

Second empirical theologians, although not without natural piety, are willing to say with William James that the last word is not sweet, that all is not "yes, yes" in the universe, and that the very meaning of contingency is that ineluctable no's and losses form a part of it, with something permanently drastic and bitter always at the bottom of the cup.[14] Therefore, they find little or no warrant for process theology's claim that the divine totality preserves whatever is good as everlasting and immune to perishing. Value, according to empirical theologians, is a function of its realization, not its conservation. The principle of the primacy of becoming over being leads empiricists to an appreciation of the intrinsic value of radical contingency and temporality, not to an expectation of its everlasting duration, even for God.

Third, empirical theologians are skeptical of the evidential warrants for the idea of a complex all-inclusive totality, especially one that has the concrete unity of an experiencing subject. The difference between the concept of God as one kind of process included within nature (empirical theology) and, on the other hand, the concept of nature as included in God (process theology) is not unlike the difference between a pluralistic, loosely federated commonwealth and a totality leaning toward monism. In the Hartshornian version of panentheism, empirical theologians are inclined to see the same temptations as are inherent in totalitarian systems, namely, a tendency to subordinate the parts to the whole, to make freedom instrumental, to value the present mostly in terms of the formation of a vague future, and to find the lasting meaning of all things in their contribution to the transcendent totality.

The idea that *immediacy and ultimacy traffic together*, best thematized in

---

14. See James, *Pragmatism*, p. 141.

the work of Bernard Meland, calls attention to the primal flux of experience as itself holy ground, generating in its vital immediacy all of the sacred that we are apt to find in the secular. Like the Buddhist teaching that "samsara is nirvana," which depends for its understanding on the further doctrine of codependent origination, this theme of empirical theology rests upon an understanding of organicism and the relational character of process. On the basis of an organismic understanding of the interplay of internal relations in nature, empirical theologians aim to correct the picture that Kantian epistemology paints of the primal flux of experience as a chaos of unformed impressions awaiting form through conceptualization. The countering claim of organicism is that organizing structures arise in the first place in the very process of experience through complex interweavings of internal relations. The vital immediacy of the present moment is structured by distillations of past events as they persist in the present, giving shape as well as openness to possibilities that may emerge from those lines of influence. This is the empirical alternative to the Kantian transcendental ego, a purely artificial doctrine that is the result of an inadequate empirical discernment. Theologically, the significance of this corrective of Kantian epistemology is its provision of an objective referent in experience for such theological terms as love, revelation, or forgiveness, conveyed not simply as linguistic symbols but as dynamic events.

Here, too, in the midst of life's immediacies *now*, the empirical theologian expects to find an empirical referent for the religious symbols of creation, sin, and grace, three of the most powerful insights of Western theological anthropology. The symbol of creation, for instance, rendered empirically, affirms that the realities of existence, though tragic, are not tainted; that the many energies of life are not in malevolent and insoluable conflict with its meanings. Neither nature nor time are closed systems within which the human is starkly determined, but both are open in their continual encounter with the human passion for freedom. This realization makes possible the biblical affirmation, "It is good for us to be here," or, as Robert Frost frames it, "Earth's the right place for love:/I don't know where it's likely to go better." Likewise, the experience of sin, in its way, has asserted against every attempt to submerge human choice under the category of causation or the caprice of change, the reality of human responsibility. The struggle to become human reaches deeper than the realm of finitude or fortune; it can be accomplished finally only in the realm of freedom. A change in chance or circumstance, however welcome, can serve it only when accompanied by a change of heart. The Eden of dreaming innocence is finally uninhabitable by a human life, and if prolonged by sheer force of an isolated will, turns into hell. Yet everyone who endeavors to direct his or her will toward a concern in common, who tries to will the good because it is the good, will encounter very quickly the inner obstacles that the boy Huck Finn ponders in the first pages of Twain's novel:

> I set down, one time, back in the woods, and had a long think about it. I says to myself, if a body can get anything they pray for, why don't Deacon Winn get back the money he lost on pork? Why can't the widow get back her silver snuff box that was stole? Why can't Miss Watson fat up? No, I says to myself, there ain't nothin in it. I went and told the widow about it, and she said the thing a body could get by praying for it was 'spiritual gifts.' This was too many for me, but she told me what she mean—I must help other people, and look out for them all the time, and never think about myself. This was including Miss Watson, as I took it. I went out in the woods and turned it over in my mind a long time, but I couldn't see no advantage about it—except for the other people—so at last I reckoned I wouldn't worry about it any more, but just let it go.

It is so difficult to get any further than Huck on the matter; the obstacles are so relentless and defeat so frequent, that most people retreat from the struggle into the rituals of self-righteousness. The experience of grace, however, calls attention to the human capacity for contrition and change. Poised between the weight of the past and the fear of the future is the possibility of grace in the present. Understood as a goodness within relationships, grace emerges as a concrete social energy. Beyond all sentimentality, the fact is that, against the odds, and in the face of outrageous resistance, the human spirit does from time to time triumph over its own worst temptations, does sometimes discover and other times invent just the resources the moment demands, and does in its religious reflection ascribe this occurrence to grace, as a power not one's own that makes for resourcefulness.

On the difficult question of *the meaning and role of religious language*, empirical theologians have tended toward some agreement around three very general presuppositions. First, the traditional language of religious faith as the Western tradition has known it has become less and less usable in this century. Second, religious language has always been speaking of the dimensions and tensions of human experience, even when it has constructed these into a sacred canopy of supernatural proportions. If the sacred canopy has collapsed, the experience of interconnectedness, of reciprocity, of creatureliness, still needs a language appropriate to the historical moment. Finally, metaphor looks like a reasonably good candidate for this necessary work of languaging. Metaphor locates itself directly in the white heat of the tension between meaning as uncovered and meaning as imposed, between the world of Augustine in the garden at Milan and that of Camus in the plague at Oran. If classical thought erred in exaggerating the discovery of truth by the mind (as if reality were somehow "out there," waiting), perhaps postmodernist thought has erred on the side of imposition (as if, in a faceless facticity, every shred of meaning were the creation of human intentionality). Metaphor is somewhere in between the two: only human beings construct them, but if there were only human beings, there would be no need.

Even among those empirical theologians who have ventured descriptive generalizations of the highest generality, the metaphorical quality of speculative philosophical construction has been emphasized. Whitehead's own tentative and metaphorical understanding of the status of speculative, cosmological categories was evident in his assertion that, in the formulation of first principles, "words and phrases must be stretched toward a generality foreign to their ordinary usage; and however such elements of language be stabilized as technicalities, they remain metaphors mutely appealing for an imaginative leap."[15] Crucially, from an empirical point of view, they *remain* metaphors. It is metaphor which languages the living web of all that is and affirms with Othello that there's magic in its being and unfolding. Metaphor points beyond itself, not to a celestial city, but to a world of concrete particulars, vitally conceived and compellingly rendered, intimating to us our shared community with all living things in which the end result of all "spiritual formation" is, as Whitehead said, a kind of "world loyalty."

Much is omitted from my account in this chapter that will surely be found in subsequent chapters. Empirical theology continues to mean different things to different audiences, and the various authors collected in this volume will each have special emphases to contribute. My own perspective is that the development and elaboration of the above points, too briefly sketched and barely defended here, will be crucial if empirical theology is to remain a constructive project. In addition, there is a final theme which I believe goes beyond the prevailing forms of empirical theology but is implicit in it. This has to do with the way in which the perspective engendered by radical empiricism itself, when exhaustively and thoroughly realized, changes one's worldview in ways that can carry new religious significance. The most far-reaching result of radical empiricism is to convert static nouns into dynamic verbs, thus dissolving what Bergson complained of as "the logic of solids" and Wittgenstein called "the bewitchment of our intelligence by means of grammar." In this way, when their meaning is no longer confined to discrete events "once upon a time," Christian doctrines such as Creation, Incarnation, Redemption, or Resurrection can be understood as ongoing events of a continuously creat-ing universe, a redeem-ing and incarnat-ing nature, an ever resurrecting reality.

Unfortunately, the logic of solids has been the preeminent logic upon which concepts, including theological concepts, have been formed. Empirical theology has suffered from the absence of a language adequate to its meaning, one able to avoid the limitations of "things" and "beings." Indo-European languages have so spatialized our perception of the world that nouns are regarded as self-contained "things" occupying something called space. "Things" are commonly thought of in the way Aristotle did in his *Metaphysics*, as a duality of form and matter. Distinguishing container from

---

15. Whitehead, *Process and Reality*, p. 4.

contained, we ask for "a glass of water" rather than "a water." In the Hopi language, however, we would find it natural to ask for "a water" and unnecessary to fragment the vital immediacy of experience into something called matter, and something else called spirit, which activates matter. As a further source of confusion, the inveterate Indo-European habit of spatializing time entails translating dynamic events into "things" strung out a "long" time ago or a "short" time ago. A spatialized view of time has of course been exploded by the new vision of the world discovered by twentieth-century science, but language lags behind and none quite fits the kind of theology that is being written by radical empiricists. Most theologies, like most Western philosophies, are constructed on the subject-verb sentence pattern, and thus smuggle in an outdated dualistic metaphysic. Theologically, the grammatical logic of solids leads to grave problems with such themes as creation, fall, incarnation, and redemption. In each case the solidified noun form insinuates a metaphysic of agent-action, cause-effect, subject-object, which imposes unempirical distinctions in the guise of theological formulae.

By avoiding nouns and agentive nominalizations, a radically empirical language would emphasize creative advance rather than static completion in a universe of nature that is viewed as more a process than a product, not designed, but designing. As a gerund or a participle, "creating" points to an ongoing process, the working out of a power that is within. If indeed the process is the reality, creation is creating. Employing a language suitable to its own vision of reality, empirical theology would speak not of "creation" and "creator" but of a creat-ing universe, not of "redemption" and "redeemer," but of a natural redeem-ing process, and not of a "revelation" and a "revealer," but of an ongoing reveal-ing of an indwelling spirit in nature that is poured out on all beings.

On the radically empirical principle that there is no doer before the deed, empirical theologians would also see no need to assume the "Father" behind the "Son," the "Word" behind the "flesh," or "divinity" behind "Jesus." As Yeats asked, "How can we know the dancer from the dance?" By understanding the universe of experience radically in terms of the logic of empirical processes rather than of solids, in terms of deeds but no hidden doers, of movement but no prior mover, empiricists will avoid the theological error of reifying observable behaviors into metaphysical abstractions that are thought to underlie, precede, or ground nature. In a radically empirical theology, then, Christian symbols such as Creation or Providence do not refer to the *reason* for nature, but to the fact of its ongoingness.

As far as the human structure of emergence can know, the source is unfathomable, the outcome, uncertain. It begins in mystery, and it ends in mystery.

CHAPTER THREE

Empirical Theology and Science

KARL E. PETERS

Empirical theology has developed in the twentieth century in the context of the social and life sciences. Many empirical theologians have developed their thinking in relation to work in psychology and sociology, and many also are cognizant of the importance of evolutionary theory for philosophy and theology. Therefore it is appropriate to examine some general relationships between empirical theology and the sciences.

Much has been written on the relationship between religion, or theology, and science, mostly within the framework of Western thought. However, almost nothing has been done to explore the relationship of *empirical* theology and science. Major works such as Ian Barbour's pioneering *Issues in Science and Religion* and his most recent Gifford lectures, the first course published as *Religion in an Age of Science*, have little to say about the Chicago School and related thinkers. The same is true of Holmes Rolston III's excellent *Science and Religion: A Critical Survey*, as well as the most recent work by Arthur Peacocke, *Theology for a Scientific Age*.[1] So this essay will work

---

1. Ian G. Barbour, *Issues in Science and Religion* (Englewood Cliffs, N.J.: Prentice-Hall, 1966); Ian G. Barbour, *Religion in an Age of Science*, The Gifford Lectures, Vol. 1 (San Francisco: Harper & Row, 1990); Holmes Rolston III, *Science and Religion: A Critical Survey* (Philadelphia: Temple University Press, 1987); and Arthur Peacocke, *Theology for a Scientific Age* (Oxford: Basil Blackwell, 1990). The lack of attention to American empirical theology is exemplified by the fact that leading empirical theologians such as Henry Nelson Wieman and Bernard Meland are at most mentioned in passing as examples of process theology in discussions of the nature of God or the relation of God and the world. They are not discussed in relation to questions of methodology, although Barbour, in his early book, mentions philosophers Charles Sanders Peirce and William James in this context.

out its own comparisons between empirical theology and science; however, as far as space allows it will do this in the context of more general discussions of the relationship between science and religion. First, I will compare the "spirit" of empirical theology and of scientific inquiry; then I will compare the methods of each. As I do this I also will discuss some specific findings of science insofar as they have a bearing on the spirit and methods of inquiry.[2]

ON THE SPIRIT OF SCIENCE AND EMPIRICAL THEOLOGY

In explaining why the spirit or spirituality of science is just as important as the methods and content of science and faith, human geneticist Lindon Eaves writes that "*spirituality* is nothing less than that orientation of the human spirit toward reality which motivates, directs, and sustains our encounter with the unknown. It embodies our assumptions about the nature of reality, the state of mind normative for the pursuit of truth, the appreciation of the barriers of knowledge, and the sacrifices which must be made on the journey."[3] In discussing the sacrifices science makes, Eaves points out that the primary sacrifice is that of subjectivity in favor of scientific "objectivity." "The sacrifice of subjectivity . . . is itself the spirituality of scholarship."[4] In this section of the essay I will suggest that the sacrifice of subjectivity is related to both a fundamental difference and a fundamental similarity between science and empirical theology. Then I will show how science and empirical theology generally agree in their assumptions about the nature of reality, the state of mind normative for the pursuit of truth, and the appreciation for the barriers of knowledge.

THE OBJECTIVITY OF SCIENCE AND THE TASK OF EMPIRICAL THEOLOGY

Both the basic difference and similarity between science and empirical theology on the issue of "objectivity" can be brought to light by exploring the more general relationship between religion and science in terms of the following working definition of *religion*: A religion is a system of ideas, actions, and experiences that offers a path toward human fulfillment by relating indi-

2. For this structure, which I will develop in my own way, I am indebted to Lindon Eaves, "Spirit, Method, and Content in Science and Religion: The Theological Perspective of a Geneticist," *Zygon: Journal of Religion and Science* 24 (June 1989), pp. 185-215. However, the substance of my essay is based on my twenty-five years of experience with working scientists who have an appreciation for a wide variety of religious thought and practice and with theologians who have attempted to do theology in light of scientific knowledge. In all this I have been strongly influenced by the pragmatism of Charles Sanders Peirce and the empirical theology of Henry Nelson Wieman.

3. Ibid., p. 197.
4. Ibid.

viduals and societies to what is thought to be ultimate.[5]

The basic similarity can be seen by looking at the first part of the definition—"system of ideas, actions, and experiences." In general, science consists of a body of theories that are tested by experiments or controlled observations (the actions of science) against a particular domain of experience. Religions have the same general structure: Poetic stories called myths and rational doctrines constitute the ideas; rituals and codes of conduct specify behavior; and both these lead to as well as respond to a variety of experiences. In science, as in religion, the relation between ideas, actions, and experiences is not one way but interactive: Theories influence the kinds of actions undertaken and the character of the resulting experiences; yet experiences can lead to a modification of theories.

The basic difference between science and religion can be seen in the second part of the definition—"offers a path toward human fulfillment by relating individuals and societies to what is thought to be ultimate." What is meant by *fulfillment*, the nature of the path, and the understanding of what is ultimate vary considerably when one examines what has been called religion.[6] For example, fulfillment may occur in the context of nature—maintaining small-scale societies in harmony with nature, or developing a variety of individual human potentials in a manner integrated with the rest of society and the environment. Or human fulfillment may be independent of nature as we know it—merging individuality into an originating cosmic self, or gathering the righteous at the end of history into a peaceable kingdom in a new heaven and earth. Paths to this completion may be primarily ritualistic, devotional, or meditational and experiential. They may involve only human effort, a complete reliance on a reality greater than human, or both to some degree. The understanding of what is ultimate may be in terms of a state of existence to be attained or an agent that is the source of existence and goodness. And both the state or agent may be simple or complex, personal or nonpersonal. However, the state or agent is usually considered to have the highest value; it is the greatest good.

In all this religious variety there is implied the idea that humans do not exist in a state of greatest good; there is more to life than has been so far realized. Obstacles to fulfillment have to be overcome; potentials have yet to be actualized; various actualized aspects of life have to be integrated into wholes. While *fulfillment* may mean that things need to be brought to completion in some final culmination of nature and history, it also may simply be (as for many empirical theologians) an ongoing succession of states of relative completion here and now. Thus, underlying many of the differences in

5. This definition makes no claim to encompass all religious activity in human history; nonetheless, it is useful in looking at many of the major world's religions.

6. See Frederick J. Streng, Charles L. Lloyd Jr., and Jay T. Allen, *Ways of Being Religious* (Englewood Cliffs, N.J.: Prentice-Hall, 1973).

religion is a common quest for value or what is good, not the value that has been attained but the good to be continued and the further good to be sought.

The quest for increasing value is what basically distinguishes religion from science. In oversimplified terms, we might say that the ideas, actions, and experiences of science are focused more on reality than value, on the way things are rather than on the way they ought to be. Religion seeks greater value and hence in concerned with maintaining and enhancing human well-being. Science seeks to understand human beings and the world in which we live, regardless whether the knowledge attained is beneficial to humans or not; this is one important aspect of the so-called objectivity of science. In more complex terms, if we recognize that even in science there is a commitment to increasing value—the value of knowledge—we can still distinguish religion from science by saying that religion seeks not just knowledge for its own sake, as does science, but knowledge which is "salvational," knowledge that lights the path toward greater good.

Even this distinction, however, needs to be qualified in a number of ways. While it fits much traditional religion and what has been called "pure" science, it does not fit exactly empirical theology and what often happens today when the distinctions between pure and applied science, and between truth and beauty, are blurred.

In discussing how religious ideas (in the form of myths) are salvational, John Bowker insightfully draws out one implication for knowledge that differentiates science from religion. He notes the fact that many religious traditions have a variety of stories of creation, some of which even contradict each other. This means that religions are not interested primarily, like science, in describing the way things are. Speaking of creation stories, Bowker says that "in religions, the *descriptive* account of origins is subordinate to the way in which the conceptualization of cosmos and cosmic origins contributes to the salus (the health and salvation) of the society which it sustains."[7]

However, if one turns to empirical theology, this distinction of Bowker's, based on an analysis of traditional religion, must be qualified. Theology is not religion but it is the rational, critical, constructive exploration of religious ideas, actions, and experiences, in order to understand more clearly what constitutes human fulfillment and how it is attained. In contrast to other theological approaches today, which may stress the authority of past writings, the authority of a church, or individual, nonrational faith as a means of determining the nature of human fulfillment and how it is attained, empirical theology makes the methodological assumption that such questions should

7. J. W. Bowker, "Cosmology, Religion, and Society," *Zygon: Journal of Religion and Science* 25 (March 1990), p.10.

be settled by appealing to experience.[8] In this regard, empirical theology is like science: both are forms of inquiry seeking to gain knowledge and both appeal to experience. In this sense, like science, empirical theology makes Eaves' "sacrifice of subjectivity," favoring results of inquiry that are not biased by human desires, wishes, or hopes. What distinguishes empirical theology from inquiry conducted by the various sciences about the world, human nature, and society is that it seeks to know—really or "in fact"— what it is that brings humans to fulfillment. In comparison with Bowker's assessment of religious thinking and science, empirical theology seeks to be descriptive—and wants to get it right if it can—regarding what brings about human fulfillment.

Some contemporary science also seeks to understand the way things are, in order to assist human well-being and fulfillment. Often scientists seem to be motivated in their inquiry to find out how nature, society, and human personality in fact "work," so that human beings will be better off. Medical research, agricultural science, and psychology and psychiatry are examples of this. At a deeper level, a scientist's search for the way things are may be intrinsically related to one form of human fulfillment: a coming to an appreciation, acceptance, and awe of the universe that creates and sustains us. In discussing the spirituality of science, Eaves appeals to Einstein's "cosmic religious feeling" as an affective element in scientific motivation: "I maintain that cosmic religious feeling is the strongest and noblest incitement to scientific research. Only those who realize the immense efforts and, above all, the devotion which pioneer work in theoretical science demands, can grasp the emotion out of which also such work, remote as it is from the immediate realities of life, can issue. . . . You will hardly find one among the profounder sort of scientific minds without a peculiar religious feeling of his own."[9]

Eaves continues his discussion of the spirituality of science by suggesting that scientists are motivated by three expectations: "First, rightly or wrongly, scientists believe they are engaged in exposing *reality* itself."[10] Second "is expectation of simplicity. . . . The most informative theories are those which

---

8. Of course, empirical theology can include these other approaches insofar as sacred writings, church teachings, and individual beliefs are grounded in the past experience of individuals and communities.

9. Albert Einstein, "Physics and Reality," *Out of My Later Years* (Secaucus, N.J.: Citadel, 1956), p. 28; quoted by Eaves, "Spirit, Method, and Content," p. 198.

10. Much has been written, in light of the sociology of knowledge, about how even science can be culturally biased and therefore how difficult it is for scientists to claim they are "exposing reality itself"; for a survey of some of this literature see Karin D. Knorr-Cetina and Michael Mulkay, *Science Observed: Perspectives on the Social Study of Science* (London: Sage, 1983). Feminist critiques offer a special kind of case regarding cultural bias in the way scientists approach their subject matter, e.g., Evelyn Fox Keller, *Reflections on Gender and Science* (New Haven: Yale University Press, 1984) and Ruth Bleier, *Science and Gender: A Critique of Biology and Its Theories of Women* (New York: Pergamon Press, 1984). Nevertheless, as we will discuss below, science strives for

encompass the greatest range of data with the smallest number of parameters."
Third "is the aesthetic principle. . . . The scientist's sense of what is 'ugly'
keeps alive the quest for a better solution. The sense of what is 'beautiful'
plays a significant part in deciding when a truth is at hand. A sense of what
is 'elegant' determines the degree of enthusiasm for a new scientific strategy. The passion for simplicity and the appreciation of beauty are closely
allied in scientific spirituality."[11]

Motivated by the hope of understanding reality and the aesthetic sense of
beauty, one might say the scientist is seeking a kind of fulfillment, and hence
the scientist is on a "religious quest." In attempting to see things as they
are, the so-called pure scientist, who is not interested in knowledge for the sake
of improvement but knowledge for its own sake, may also be affirming the
intrinsic value of energy, matter, and life in their various forms. In their own
rational-empirical, precise, cognitive manner scientists may be affirming
what Zen Buddhists try to grasp more intuitively, an enlightenment that
involves a direct seeing into the nature of things. Or it might be, in the terms
of psychologist Eric Fromm, a kind of "mature love" that accepts other parts
of the universe, as well as humans, as they are rather than trying to make them
serve one's own interests and therefore controlling and dominating them.[12]

This raises profound questions for religion and empirical theology: To
what extent is the goal of living a coming to terms with the way things are,
regardless of their impact on human well-being; and to what extent is the goal
a reshaping things for human improvement. Or for those empirical theologians
who, like Wieman, seek what in fact transforms: To what extent is the primary
transformation that of human valuing consciousness to appreciate things as
they are without having to change them; and to what extent is the transformation of the human mind a prelude to engineering the transformation of
some other reality. To echo Karl Marx: What is the human quest about, to
understand the world or to change it? Scientists like Eaves seem involved in
the quest for understanding; for others more technologically oriented, the goal
may be to understand in order to change things for some perceived greater
good.

ASSUMPTIONS ABOUT THE NATURE OF REALITY

Like scientific inquiry, empirical theology is conducted within a naturalistic worldview. Naturalism is foremost an appreciation of nature and

objective or intersubjective knowledge that removes both biologically and culturally
grounded biases. In this sense it is critically realistic and tries to fulfill its expectation of
exposing reality itself.

11. Eaves, "Spirit, Method, and Content," pp. 199-200.
12. However, Fromm's discussion of mature and other kinds of love is applied only
to humans, Eric Fromm, *The Art of Loving* (New York: Harper Colophon, 1962), pp.
20-21.

human history as providing the primary if not the sole context both for scientific and scholarly inquiry and for attaining human fulfillment. Human fulfillment and the ultimate source of fulfillment are to be found not beyond the spatial-temporal world but within it. If there are other realms of being other than space-time nature and history (as in supernaturalism), they are beyond our ken and have no relevance to life today. If there is an "eternal more-than-space-time" that is in some way the grounding of nature and history (as in panentheism), still that more can be known only through ordinary rational-empirical inquiry and has relevance for human fulfillment only as it becomes actualized in space-time.[13] The appreciation of nature and history as the arena for God's work and for human fulfillment distinguishes empirical theology from some other kinds of theology; it also expresses a fundamental compatibility between empirical theology and science.

A second feature of the naturalistic worldview, which science and empirical theology hold in common, is that reality is basically organic. By this I mean it is both relational and historical. In discussing the radical empiricism of Wieman, Nancy Frankenberry points out that "the ultimate actualities of the world were conceived of as events, happenings, specific instances of energy. There is no substance or reality underlying this world of happenings. There are only relations, that is, structure, among these units of energy, at various levels of complexity."[14] This statement of an empirical philosopher of religion could just as well have been written by any number of contemporary scientists.

In contrast to the mechanistic, substantive view of reality of Newtonian science, today's science sees everything as dynamic systems of energy, with larger systems being constructed out of smaller energy systems; atoms out of sub-atomic "particles"; molecules out of atoms; complex, self-replicating molecules out of simpler molecules; cells out of complex molecules; organs out of cells; living creatures out of organs. Thus, living creatures are complex systems of energy, organized out of smaller systems of energy. These living systems, built out of (caused by) the simpler systems, in turn exercise control over the simpler systems in what has been called downward causation.[15]

13. Even the "consequent nature" of God, an aspect of the "eternal more" in Whiteheadian theology, depends on the actualization of potentials in space-time.
14. Nancy Frankenberry, *Religion and Radical Empiricism* (Albany: State University of New York Press, 1987), pp. 120-121.
15. Two scientists give helpful explanations of "downward causation" in complex systems: neurophysiologist Roger Sperry, "Changed Concepts of Brain and Consciousness: Some Value Implications," *Zygon: Journal of Religion and Science* 20 (March 1985), pp. 41-57; "Search for Beliefs to Live By Consistent with Science," *Zygon: Journal of Religion and Science* 26 (June 1991), pp. 242-245; and psychologist Donald T. Campbell "Levels of Organization, Downward Causation, and the Selection-Theory Approach to Evolutionary Epistemology," *Scientific Methodology in the Study of Mind: Evolutionary Epistemology*, ed. E. O. Tobach and G. Greenberg (Hillsdale, N.J.: Lawrence Erlbaum, 1990).

Such complex, self-controlling systems also interact with the wider environment to procure more energy (food), in order to maintain, reproduce, and strive in various ways to fulfill their potentials. With this processed energy they interact in other ways with one another and the wider environment, thus forming still more complex systems of relationships.

All of this temporally evolves. Traditional philosophy, theology, and even Newtonian science held that the mark of "true" reality was permanence (no change). However, when nineteenth-century evolutionary thinking was coupled with the slightly older empirical notion that what we observe is real, then change, growth, and development became significant. Time became the cornerstone of a new way of looking at the natural world so that nature became historical.

Thus, when scientists such as astrophysicist Eric Chaisson attempt to portray the "big picture" of the universe, they do so historically; "looking out into space is equivalent to looking back into time."[16] Because it takes illuminating radiation time to travel, even across the room, we are always looking at the past. When astronomers observe stars, galaxies, and systems of galaxies from a few to billions of light years away, they are observing what happened from a few to billions of years ago. In order to speak about nature we must speak about nature historically. And when we speak of human fulfillment, we must speak of it as a continual succession of relative completions or wholenesses, which in turn serve as the stage for further events that make actual the potentials of existence in still wider and deeper integrated relationships.

Even though change is fundamental in the current scientific worldview, so is continuity. If everything is patterns of energy, with more complex patterns evolving out of and made up of simpler patterns, then there is no sharp distinction between energy and matter ($E = Mc^2$), between viruses and life, between higher primates and *homo sapiens*. And human history, whose various culturally evolving institutions are built on energy-matter-life foundations (brains, books, and computer chips), is simply the latest phase in the evolutionary history of the universe.

In light of this continuity it would be somewhat artificial for empirical theologians to limit their interaction with science primarily to the social sciences. While religion and other human activity is primarily cultural, still the humans engaged in such activity are also biological, chemical, and physical creatures. Further, as knowing subjects conducting scientific and theological inquiry in a rational-empirical manner, humans still are conditioned in their various inquiries by the biological, chemical, and physical systems of energy out of which we are composed.

16. Eric Chaisson, *Cosmic Dawn: The Origins of Matter and Life* (Boston: Norton, 1981), p. 8.

THE HUMAN MIND AND BARRIERS TO KNOWLEDGE

In addition to the "sacrifice" of subjective bias for "objectivity" and to assumptions about the nature of reality, the scientific spirit includes assumptions about the human mind and an appreciation of the limits on human knowledge.

First, there is a general limit on what all normal humans can experience with the senses. Taking into account a general evolutionary perspective that includes the evolution of the human brain and human culture, the latter including religion and science, one can make the statement that the human knowing apparatus and the methods of knowing have evolved in an earth environment through natural selection, and later through cultural selection pressures. While the capacities of the human brain and the methods of inquiry may go beyond what seems necessary for biological survival and reproduction, still, according to well-established contemporary scientific theory, humans and their brains evolved from other higher primates in local environments. Thus, for example, the range of what humans see and hear is sufficient for what cooperating humans have needed to be successful so far in the biological, evolutionary "game." However, we now also know that what humans perceive in the visible and auditory ranges of energy wavelengths and frequencies is only a small percentage of the total wavelength-frequency spectrum of radiation. We know this because of scientific-technological advances within the twentieth century that have allowed us to process information from other wavelengths and frequencies, not immediately perceivable by the human body. These other frequencies and wavelengths of energy are marked by such names as cosmic rays, x-rays, radio waves, and microwave radiation.

The import of this for empirical theology may be considerable. Insofar as empirical theology considers experience to be only direct sense experience or direct felt experience, we are limited by the evolved structures of our own bodies and brains. Of course, for matters of human fulfillment, these evolved structures may be primary. However, the fact that we now know there is much more to nature than we can directly perceive and feel is an important example of the kind of barriers that confront empirical knowledge.

A second limit on human knowing is related to individual variability. Genetic defects limit the rational-empirical capabilities of some humans. And even within the normal range of knowing capabilities there is considerable variation. Some people are more adept at mathematics, while others are more adept at art, and still others are more adept in processing information important in social relations. According to one reliable test for personality traits, the Myers-Briggs test, humans vary considerably on a number of factors that affect the way we perceive and process information about the world and other humans. Various combinations of these factors form "personality types" that have an effect on how we work and play.[17] This might also include how we work as thinkers—as scientists and empirical theologians— and how we practice religion. In *God's Gifted People*, Gary Harbaugh interprets the Myers-Briggs types as "gifts of the spirit."[18] From an evolutionary perspective the types result from genetic variations as well as from experience in the human life cycle.[19] Although factors in personality types limit the cognitive activity of each individual, all together they enrich total capacity of the human species for gaining knowledge.

These findings from some of the biological and social sciences fit well with an important assumption of inquiry in science and empirical theology: The methods of each must be self-critical and self-correcting. Thus it is recognized that all knowledge is tentative and not absolute. Neither science nor empirical theology finally appeals to methods of authority, "blind faith" that is no more than an assertion of belief in the face of or beyond experience, or rational agreement in a particular community. As Charles Sanders Peirce pointed out, such appeals cannot resolve differences between competing authorities, competing faiths, or competing communities, because each party appeals to what is already established by each respective method as true, making the truth of each absolute. The only way out is to recognize the tentativeness of all human knowing, the limits of our capability as knowers, and then to use a method that appeals to future experience as a way to resolve conflicts between present ideas.[20] The appeal to future experience that is repeatably accessible to all who are trained and in a position to have the experience is a hallmark of both contemporary science and empirical theology.

ON THE METHODS OF SCIENCE AND EMPIRICAL THEOLOGY

When one begins to consider the methods of science and empirical theology one is faced with a complex set of relationships between experience and concepts. On the one hand, experiences present to the human mind phenomena to be explained and interpreted with concepts. On the other, concepts we inherit from our culture and from specialized communities, such as a particular scientific or religious tradition, influence how we experience the

17. Judy Provost, *Work, Play, and Type* (Palo Alto, Calif.: Consulting Psychologists Press, 1990).

18. Gary L. Harbaugh, *God's Gifted People* (Minneapolis: Augsburg Fortress, 1990).

19. For a survey of recent evidence for the genetic basis of personality, though not focused on Myers-Briggs indicators, see L. J. Eaves, H. J. Eysenck, and N. G. Martin, *Genes, Culture, and Personality: An Empirical Approach* (New York: Academic Press, 1989).

20. Charles Sanders Peirce, "The Fixation of Belief," *Collected Papers*, ed. Charles Hartshorne and Paul Weiss (Cambridge: Belknap Press of Harvard University Press, 1965), vol. 5, pp. 223-247.

world and what experiences we select as worthwhile for consideration. Furthermore, the development of concepts, both in religions and the sciences is a complex process of mental construction. Beginning with a wealth of inherited ideas, our human imagination constructs metaphors, analogies, and models to extend existing ideas to cover new experiences. Then these ideas are tested by their coherence with other ideas, their ability to account for experiences, and, perhaps most important, their ability to lead to new experiences. Those concepts which meet the tests become part of the historical reposit of ideas for others to use. In what follows I shall simplify these complex relationships by loosely employing Eaves' shape of scientific exploration as a movement in the growth of a particular science from taxonomy or "identifying those contours of reality which demand our special attention, setting the subject-matter of the discipline," to the hypothetical-deductive constructing and testing of possible theories, and finally to the development of ongoing research programs in the "paradigmatic or technological phase" of mature science.[21]

TOWARD A TAXONOMY OF SCIENTIFIC AND RELIGIOUS EXPERIENCE

One function of taxonomy is to map out a domain of experience to be considered as subject matter for inquiry. We will begin by claiming, in line with the radical empiricism affirmed by many empirical theologians, that all our experiencing is of unified wholes. It includes at the same time a feeling of being acted upon; a sense of particular features including such phenomena as shape, size, and color; and a feeling of value or affective tone.[22] In initial states of awareness, these aspects of the experience are not clearly distinguished.

Experience as value- and theory-laden. However, specific aspects of experience can become the center of our attention, depending on our particular interests. Our interests may be ones most humans hold in common, such as meeting basic physical needs or achieving emotional satisfaction in interpersonal relationships. Or they may be more specialized interests such as we spoke of above in comparing the basic objectives of science and religion. Or they may be the interests expressed in a particular scientific theory such as the genetic theory of DNA that focuses inquiry on the search for particular kinds of observable data. Or the interests may be expressed in a religious belief system, for example, in a claim one must be "reborn" to enter the

---

21. Eaves, pp. 201-202. Also underlying the following discussion is Ian Barbour's helpful analysis of the interrelationships between experience and concepts in science and religion in general, *Religion in an Age of Science* (San Francisco: Harper & Row, 1990), pp. 31-39.

22. Alfred North Whitehead's notions of causal efficacy and presentational immediacy underlie this statement regarding the aspects of a complete experience, e.g., Whitehead, *Symbolism* (New York: Macmillan, 1927).

"kingdom of heaven," so that followers of this belief system seek experiences of rebirth or interpret experiences already had this way. In both science and religion, concepts help shape our interests and actions and thereby the experiences we seek. In this sense, in both science and religion experience is "theory-laden."

Furthermore, and perhaps even more interesting, is the possibility that experience is also "value-laden." Consider again our initial characterizing of experience as the experience of wholes that includes valuational or affective aspects as well as perceptual aspects and the feeling of being acted upon. Results of scientific research on the human brain support the notion that as we process sense data, the stimuli we are processing pass through a particular region of the brain called the limbic system (located behind the nose above the palate of the mouth) and thereby acquire emotional tones. According to neuroscientist John Eccles, "by their projections to the prefrontal lobes [located above the eyes in the forehead], the hypothalamus and the limbic system modify and color with emotion the conscious perceptions derived from sensory inputs and superimpose on them motivational drives."[23] Our experience is value-laden because we are genetically informed and biologically constructed to experience this way.

It also is value-laden because cultures program human brains to respond in different ways to different kinds of experience. This is done through learning as a child grows up and encounters different facets of the culture—parents, peers, schools, mass media, computers, churches. Likewise, more specialized communities educate us to focus our experience in terms of what that community values.

Experience and Values in Science. The scientific community values a certain kind of knowledge, "objective" or intersubjective knowledge that is free from personal and cultural bias due to genetically programed feelings and other cultural values. One way science seeks to be free of bias—to sacrifice subjectivity in favor of its own bias for "objectivity"—is by precision in its use of language, eliminating connotations as it tries to refer to experiences only with the denotations of the words it uses. This is coupled with the kind of analysis that breaks down the whole of experience into precisely identifiable parts. And the relationships experienced in the whole of experience are made more precise by the application of mathematics, by quantification.

Thus, in these ways science seeks to dampen some values and orient other values in experience in the service of the value of knowledge. This dampening of biological feelings and cultural values is necessary for intersubjective testability—the empirical methods of theory confirmation and their resulting observations that are "public," that is, repeatable by those

23. Karl R. Popper and John C. Eccles, *The Self and Its Brain* (Berlin: Springer International, 1977), p. 273.

who are qualified in the particular scientific discipline. And the values of appreciation, care, and even love for the subject matter being studied, say a one-cell organism, while they may help a scientist "listen" to the material and attend to all that is there, are nonetheless put into the service of the goal of understanding this part of reality for what it really is.[24]

Furthermore, even as it seeks intersubjective knowledge, science affirms value in another way—in appreciating the beauty of precisely defined and quantitatively related structures, the beauty of abstract order such as one finds in mathematics. Physicist John Albright compares the beauty of mathematics with that of the order in music: "If a Bach fugue can bring one closer to God, then what is to prevent Maxwell's equations of electromagnetism (just to name one particularly beautiful scientific theory) from producing a similar effect? To those who appreciate such things, the beauties provided by science and mathematics ought to be recognized as enablers of faith in almost the same ways as those beauties provided by the arts that are more conventionally associated with religious experience."[25]

Values and Experience in Empirical Theology. If the scientist dampens biological feelings and cultural values, and orients other values toward the search for the value of inter-subjective knowledge and the beauty of abstract relationships, empirical theologians open up the value dimension of experience to encompass a still wider range of values, such as the beauty of felt qualities and not only the beauty of formal structure. Empirical theology also seeks to orient all values, including genetically and culturally programed biases, toward human fulfillment. However, in doing this the empirical theologian may also be somewhat selective; not everything people value will be highlighted, for some things people think worthwhile may not contribute to long-term human fulfillment. The standard ethical distinction between what people desire (or value) and what is desirable (valuable) still applies.

In terms of a naturalistic view of the world and history, empirical theologians speak of human fulfillment in terms of a successive series of completions that expand the valuing consciousness of persons. Expansion of the valuing consciousness can be understood as coming to see and appreciate an ever richer set of relations of mutual support and the qualities so related. These richer relations may be cognitive, aesthetic, interpersonal; they may involve other individual humans, other communities, other species, or the wider natural world. Hence the valuing consciousness may be expanded not,

---

24. That some scientists take this "personal" approach to their subject has been stated in meetings of the Institute on Religion in an Age of Science by Eaves and by microbiologist Ursula Goodenough. It also is a point made sometimes by scientists who are familiar with a feminist perspective. See Evelyn Fox Keller's discussion of Barbara McClintock's work in *A Feeling for the Organism* (San Francisco: Freeman, 1983).

25. John R. Albright, "Science and Faith," *Insights: The Magazine of the Chicago Center for Religion and Science* 3 (June 1991), p. 17.

only in knowledge and formal beauty (as in science), but also in love and justice in regard to other persons, other types of people, other animals, and the rest of the natural world.

Also the valuing consciousness may on occasion be expanded to include "classical" religious experiences, such as conversion in which a guilt-ridden divided-self is transformed into an integrated, self-affirming person in loving relationships with others, or the mystical experience of being unified with the creative ground of existence with feelings of joy, harmony, serenity, and peace. Empirical theologians do not interpret these kinds of experience in terms of supernaturalism but in terms of a more extensive form of naturalism than that affirmed by more traditional empiricists, positivists, and many scientists. Following William James' idea of "radical empiricism," which sees our normal experience as the experience of wholes that includes the experience of both perceptions and values in what may be called "full facts," many empirical theologians affirm that "not *another* world but a *wider* world is the locus of religious interests."[26] This wider world allows for more extensive events of becoming complete or fulfilled.

Thus, in comparing the experience involved in scientific inquiry with that of the empirical theologian, one might say that scientific analysis, the precise use of language to speak of experience as experimental variables, and the quantification of relations, all act like the zoom lens of a camera to focus more deeply on more narrow ranges of experience. In contrast, the empirical theologian seems to be using a wide-angle lens in an attempt to encompass as much of experience as possible, even the totality of experience, insofar as it is related to human fulfillment.[27]

On the other hand, the empirical theologian may also be interested in

---

26. Frankenberry, writing on James, *Religion and Radical Empiricism*, p. 104. The term "full facts" is in Frankenberry's discussion on p. 105.

27. In one way the experience of the scientist seems to be wider than that of the empirical theologian. This is because empirical theology has tended to limit experience to what can be directly sensed and felt by the human mind alone. However, science goes beyond this to use a variety of technologies to make "indirect observations" of a wide range of phenomena not directly accessible to the human sensing apparatus: e.g., subatomic particles, activities inside a cell, human brain-waves, weather systems, the high-energy centers of galaxies, and astronomical phenomena billions of years old. Data from such indirect observations may be relevant to the empirical theologian because the technologies involved are, in the final analysis, instruments of human observation. And humans, in using them, finally observe what the technology makes possible with the same combination of sense and affective experience that is present in direct experience, without the aid of technology. For example, those who see the photographs from computer enhanced telescope images of the center of the Milky Way Galaxy may be just as emotionally affected by the beauty of the images as they would be by directly observing a sunset. Such experiences can become part not just of a rational structure but of an aesthetic matrix (cf. Frankenberry, ibid., p. 111). They can expand the human appreciative consciousness, enrich our values, and therefore be relevant to human fulfillment.

"zooming in" on specific instances of fulfillment or increases in the valuing consciousness, in order more precisely to define in an operational manner what can be expected to occur if one is properly related to whatever it is that brings human fulfillment. Even though the empirical theologian takes into account a wider range of experience than the sense data and quantified relationships of scientific inquiry, this does not necessarily mean that in speaking of increases in experience of value, considered as relations of mutual support, the empirical theologian has to sacrifice precision in specifying concrete and in some cases even measurable growth of the valuing consciousness. Later, we will develop this part of the taxonomy of experience in showing how concepts about the source of value can be justified empirically in scientific-life research programs. But first we must turn to the formation of concepts in science and empirical theology.

CONCEPT FORMATION IN SCIENCE AND EMPIRICAL THEOLOGY

Experience, though essential, is not sufficient for understanding; instead, experience often presents problem situations that "ask" to be understood. Humans seek to understand by forming concepts that in one way or another make "sense" of experience, of why and how certain experienced events happen. Forming concepts is a constructive task of human imagination. In the construction of ideas, science and empirical theology employ some of the same mechanisms and share compatible goals.

Two aids in concept formation: affirming the opposite and analogy. In his pioneer writings on pragmatism and the methods of inquiry Peirce argued that the construction of theories was not a matter of induction (generalizing from observations) or of deduction from already established principles. Instead it involved an imaginative leap he called "abduction."[28] If one examines historical examples of the imaginative thought construction, one discovers two kinds of thought processes that assist in forming new concepts. One can be called "affirming the opposite," the other analogy.

Affirming the opposite has been exemplified in traditional theology in the *via negativa*: forming concepts about God as infinite, eternal, and unchanging in contrast to the human experience of finitude, temporality, and impermanence. It is also seen in Hegelian dialectical thinking: positing an idea, which then gives rise to its negation, which in turn brings forth the negation of the negation that unites both the original thesis and its antithesis in a higher level concept. Affirming the opposite was employed by Einstein in developing his special theory of relativity: He denied the then-accepted theorem of the addition of velocities, that the velocity of light emitted from a moving object was calculated by adding the velocity of light to that of the object from which it was emitted. Instead he held the velocity of light con-

---

28. Peirce, "Three Types of Reasoning," *Collected Papers*, vol. 5, pp. 94-111.

stant regardless of the motion of the frame of reference from which it was emitted, thus leading to the conclusion that measurements of space and time were relative to an observer's frame of reference. Affirming the opposite was also an aid for nineteenth-century mathematicians whose denial of the Euclidean postulate of parallel lines never intersecting provided the basis for non-Euclidian geometries. Empirical theologians may, in effect, be affirming the opposite when they argue that becoming rather than being, or events rather than substances are fundamental features of reality.

A second aid to creating new concepts is the use of analogy. Throughout history in a variety of cultures, religious people have used their own inner experience of themselves as persons who have intentions, plans, and purposes, and who then act to carry them out, to develop via analogy the idea that the observed forces of nature acted the way they did because they possessed an inner, personal spirit. Such personal analogies have also been used to develop concepts about a single invisible divine reality. Sometimes the analogies express the relationship between humans and divinity, as when God is conceived as king, father, mother, or friend. However, personal analogies have also been used as aids for thinking about the nature of the divine in and of itself; based on human introspection, God has been thought of as thinking, intending, or suffering. On the other hand religious thought is not limited to personal analogies. Often the divine is simply understood as "the way," for example, the Tao as the way of heaven and earth. Or physical realities such as wind are used as analogies to speak of God as Spirit, which like the wind is invisible but has observable effects.

Science, too, develops new ways of conceiving things by using analogies. In physics, radiation (for example, light) has been thought of as a fluid, like water manifesting itself in waves; radiation has also been thought of as consisting of discrete particles, packets of energy that are either in one place or another. These two analogies for radiation lie at the foundation of the problems of wave-particle dualism in quantum physics. In the nineteenth century, biologist Charles Darwin took economist Thomas Malthus' essay on expanding population in a world of finite resources (leading to shortages and a struggle for survival) as an analogy to explain the origin of species by natural selection. Finally, empirical theologians, who think of God not as being but as a process (affirming the opposite?) may fruitfully use analogies from a developing new science, systems theory, to speak of the divine event as a dynamic system.

When the implications of analogies are systematically developed, the analogies become models. For example, as Sallie McFague points out, the analogy that God is like a king has been systematically developed in Western religious thought into an extensive monarchical model that speaks of the behavior of God, of how humans should respond to God, and in the Middle Ages in Europe how all of society should be ordered hierarchically into a feudal system.[29] Darwin's basic analogy of competition for available resources with the fittest more effectively reproducing was further developed in the late nineteenth century in combination with American individualism and free-market economic theory as social Darwinism.

Both these extensions have been challenged and are considered by many to be factually incorrect and even, in terms of values, morally flawed. This raises an important point regarding the methods of science and of empirical theology. The way an idea is formed does not determine its validity. In the past many have used some notion of affirming the opposite as a logic of existence to establish the validity of ideas, for example, the idealistic dialectical thinking of Hegel and its materialistic Marxist counterpart. Similarly, others have attempted to arrive at valid knowledge simply by making analogies. However, even though useful in forming new concepts, for an empiricist neither affirming the opposite nor making analogies can be used to justify them. The process of justification, as we will see later, depends on how well ideas so formed account for experience and lead to new experiences.

Two goals of concept formation: explanation and interpretation. In terms of forming concepts, we have seen that both scientists and theologians can use the same procedures as aids in constructing new ideas. However, if one asks more specifically what the goals of such construction are, or how science and religious thought each try to understand experienced events, one can discover a difference in emphasis between the two. Oversimplified, science seeks to understand *how* events happen; theology seeks to understand *why* they happen. Or, as Rolston puts it in his discussion of "scientific and religious logic": "Science and religion share the conviction that the world is intelligible, susceptible to being logically understood, but they delineate this under different paradigms. In the cleanest cases we can say that science operates with the presumption that there are causes to things, religion with the presumption that there are meanings to things. Meanings and causes have in common the concept of order, but the type of order differs."[30]

A few years ago I found myself in a situation that provides an example of the difference Rolston identifies. A friend, a man in his seventies, was diagnosed as having terminal cancer and given six to eighteen months to live. He was a physician and his scientific leanings led him to attempt to understand and then inform his friends about the complex set of conditions that were the efficient cause of his cancer. After he died, in my grief I also attempted to understand this event. However, I was not content with knowledge of efficient causes; I wanted instead to know the meaning of the event—not the how but the why. In seeking the meaning, I thought about my friend's death in the context of other, similar events. In particular I thought about the general

---

29. Sallie McFague, *Models of God: Theology for an Ecological, Nuclear Age* (Philadelphia: Fortress, 1987), pp. 63-69.

30. Rolston, *Science and Religion*, p. 22.

pattern of death and life in the universe: the "death" of stars bringing about the creation of new kinds of atoms from which our own solar system and planet are made; the death of political systems, such as the Greek system when conquered by the Romans, leading to the rebirth of Greek culture within the much larger Roman empire; the death of Jesus of Nazareth and his rebirth in the minds of his followers as the spirit guiding the development of Christianity.

In thinking this way I was not arriving at a set of causal explanations for my friend's death, but I was interpreting its meaning for me and those still alive. Rolston puts it this way: "In science cause is restricted to outward, empirically observable constant conjunctions, attended by an elusive notion of necessary production of consequent results by the preceding spatiotemporal events. Where causes are known, prediction is possible. . . . 'Meaning' is the perceived inner significance of something, again a murky but crucial notion. Occasional apprehension of meanings does not constitute a religion, any more than occasional recognition of causes constitutes a science. But where meanings are methodically detected out of a covering model, which is thought to represent an ultimate structure of reality, one has some sort of religion or one of its metaphysical cousins in philosophy."[31] The ultimate structure I thought I discerned in my friend's death was the creative relationship between death and new life. By linking my friend's death to other deaths and new creations in nature and history, I discerned the possibility of new lives for those who were close to him—new opportunities for living for his wife and friends. And this understanding provided guidance in the form of the maxim, "look for the new opportunities for living."

In light of this difference between explanation by prior conditions and interpretation according to repeating patterns that give meaning, one might partly understand another difference between science and theology. Science tends to use nonpersonal analogies or metaphors and then develops these into nonpersonal models and quantified relationships. In so doing, it tends to rule out any interior dimension of things (including intentions, plans, and inner purposes). Of course, psychology might talk about human purposes and plans, and hence use models that are personal in speaking of humans as causes of events. However, when one moves into events beyond the human, into the nonhuman realm of energy, matter, and life, scientists construct theories based on nonpersonal analogies and mathematical models. The almost exclusive use of nonpersonal metaphors and models is perhaps the best way to understand what is meant by science being materialistic.

On the other hand, if meaning is to be sought for human living, many find it helpful to be able to think of the activities taking place in the universe and on our planet as being a part of a larger plan or purpose. It also is helpful, in a conciliatory way, to be able to interpret the plan or purpose as

---

31. Ibid., pp. 22-23.

coming from a reality that acts for human well-being and fulfillment. Hence metaphors are developed that the ultimate source or cause of all events is a benevolent ruler, or a loving parent who at times might discipline what it has created for its own good, or a companion who is a source of strength in a time of crisis. At first glance, these personal metaphors and their more extended models appear to offer a kind of causal explanation for events. However, because of the difficulty of discerning the exact inner intentions of such a reality as a variable in a causal sequence, many regard such concepts as offering an interpretative rather than an explanatory kind of understanding. Yet, for interpretation's sake, a nonintentional relationship such as "death and rebirth" might be just as helpful.

The goal of concept formation in empirical theology. So far what has been discussed applies to science and religious thought in general. When we turn to empirical theology and compare its construction of concepts with that of science, one can conclude that empirical theology has both the objectives of explanation and interpretation, with perhaps some degree of variation among particular empirical theologians depending on which objective is more the center of focus. Wieman, for example, offers a view of ultimate reality as the "creative event." With this general notion one can move toward seeking causal explanations of how humans find fulfillment through commitment to the creative event by asking what are the conditions under which the creative event is most effective. Or one can move toward interpretation and meaning by arguing that the creative event is a general, repeating pattern in the universe involving a breaking down of old structures, activities, and thought in order to give rise to new actualities (a death-and-rebirth pattern). As such, the creative event is an activity or process throughout nature and history; in light of it one can examine one's own life and discover meaning, or lack of it, by determining to what extent one allows oneself to participate in this kind of process. Further, in those times when one's life begins to "fall apart," one can live in the expectation that this is a phase of the creative event, which in the end will give rise to an experience of new value and thereby to a richer and fuller life.

CONCEPT JUSTIFICATION IN SCIENCE

The human imagination in using analogies and models exhibits the capability of going far beyond experienced events even as it tries to understand conceptually the causes and meanings of such events. Therefore, a crucial part of any method is to have a way of justifying concepts, of sorting out between competing concepts those that are most true or valuable.

From the scientific perspective there are a number of aspects to the justification of proposed theories. They should be rationally consistent with previously justified theories. They also should fit with the body of observations that are regarded as significant in a particular scientific discipline.

They are further evaluated for their simplicity: Theories with fewer assumptions are better than theories with a greater number of assumptions to account for the same set of experiences. Also theories that are more comprehensive in their scope or ability to explain a wide variety of phenomena are better than theories that are more limited in what they explain. Finally, theories are evaluated for their fertility or ability to provide a framework for an ongoing research program. This means not only their ability to predict logically any previously made observations but also their ability conceptually to predict what has not yet been observed.

Often, theories are not evaluated in isolation but in comparison with competing theories. In some cases two or more competing theories might be judged to be equivalent in their ability to account for experienced events, their coherence with other theories, their simplicity, and their comprehensiveness. In such cases a critical question becomes what kind of ongoing research program each of the competing theories establishes.

The notion of research program has been developed by philosopher of science Imre Lakatos as a way of solving problems left by competing notions of scientific discovery and justification advanced by Karl Popper and Thomas Kuhn. Popper's objectivist idea of justification with his important notion of falsification of theories does not sufficiently take into account the persistence of theories that had been disconfirmed in particular experimental situations. Evidence from the history of science suggests that scientific theories are simply not subject to a "quick kill" by refutation. On the other hand, Kuhn's notion of paradigm theories and the shift from one paradigm theory to another is problematic because it makes science at crucial points of development too relativistic and irrational.[32] Without going into details because of space, suffice it to say that the problems Lakatos points out with both Popper's and Kuhn's views of advances in scientific knowledge are significant, because both thinkers are frequently cited in talking about possible advances in religious knowledge as well.[33] Insofar as they have been surpassed by Lakatos' idea of research programs, the notion of research programs is very important for any theology that seeks to be empirical.

According to Lakatos, a research program contains two basic features, a hard-core or basic theory and a set of auxiliary hypotheses. The auxiliary hypotheses serve as a protective belt around the hard-core theory. They may be modified or replaced due to observations that falsify them, but because this happens they prevent the hard-core theory from being falsified in any direct manner. As long as the auxiliary hypotheses of the research program can

32. Imre Lakatos, *The Methodology of Scientific Research Programmes*, ed. John Worrall and Gregory Currie (Cambridge: Cambridge University Press, 1978), p. 6.

33. Lakatos discusses the problems with Popper's and Kuhn's views, as well as other positions regarding scientific methodology in a section on "Fallibilism versus Falsificationism" in his essay "Falsification and the Methodology of Scientific Research Programmes," ibid., pp. 10-47.

be modified in a manner that allows for the emergence of new observed events or facts, the hypotheses being modified become part of a progressive research program. Progress is due to the uncovering of new, unforeseen facts, even as the system of hypotheses in a research program continues to explain old facts. On the other hand, if the auxiliary hypotheses are simply ad hoc explanations made to protect the basic theory and there are no predictions of new facts, the research program is degenerative. If this continues for a period of time, the core hypothesis, even though not directly falsified, may be abandoned.[34]

Eaves gives some examples of hard-core hypotheses of both degenerative and progressive research programs.[35] Theories such as the earth is flat and the world was created in six days may indeed appear to explain observed phenomena; however they are degenerative because they do not lead fruitfully to new facts. Eaves writes, "Indeed, the earth may be flat, but the theory does not produce many good experiments and has not produced much insight. Indeed, the world may have been created in six days, but there are few papers in scientific journals which describe experiments based on that theory. As Claude Bernard observed, 'Theories in science are not true or false. They are fertile or sterile'"[36] One theory that has become the core of a progressive research program is the double helix model of the gene, DNA. Eaves calls this kind of theory an "icon"—a part of reality that serves as a window to a much more extensive picture of reality. "The place of the double helix in biology provides a model system for the interaction between model and matter, the icon, in science. Molecular genetics is unlikely to revise the DNA icon because it has played such a crucial part in making biology a 'hard' science. . . . Once James Watson and Francis Crick had 'got it right,' DNA became the unifying feature which gave coherence to the facts of reproduction, evolution, chromosome behavior, Mendelian inheritance, protein synthesis, mutational change, and other processes. Furthermore, the icon became the key to new horizons—the details of gene regulation and biotechnology."[37] In other words, the Watson-Crick model of DNA has become a hard-core (or paradigm) theory of a progressive research program in biology.

TOWARD A PARADIGMATIC EMPIRICAL THEOLOGY

According to Eaves, the mark of a mature science, that is, a science that has moved beyond the taxonomic and the hypothetico-deductive stages into

34. See Lakatos, *Methodology of Scientific Research Programmes*, pp. 48-52 for his more detailed characterization of scientific research programs.

35. The core hypotheses are basically the same as Kuhn's "paradigms."

36. Eaves, "Spirit, Method, and Content," p. 195. The quotation by Bernard is from Hans J. Eysenck, *Fact and Fiction in Psychology* (Harmondsworth, United Kingdom: Penguin Books, 1965).

37. Eaves, ibid., pp. 195-96, referring to James D. Watson and Francis H. C. Crick, "A Structure for Deoxyribose Nucleic Acid," *Nature* 171 (1953), p. 737.

the paradigmatic and technological stage, is the establishment of a major progressive research program. As we have seen, in many respects empirical theology is quite similar to science in the degree to which it has resolved issues of taxonomy and the formation of concepts in keeping with its own goals of seeking to understand human fulfillment. As we will see, empirical theology also has some clarity on the question of how theological ideas should be justified. However, if empirical theology is to become a mature discipline, comparable to a mature science, it will need to establish a progressive research program that unites the efforts of many theologians and philosophers of religion in justifying the concepts of empirical theology in relation to the rich understanding of experience in this field.

In my judgment empirical theology is already part way toward its mature phase because, as we saw earlier, empirical theologians share the same spirit as science, one feature of which is consistent with the idea of a progressive research program bringing to light newly observed facts and continually improving models. This is that we live in a world that is much richer in its reality than what is to date conceptually known. For the empirical theologian this richer reality is embodied in a notion of experience that is broader than distinct sense data and includes a "deeper and qualitatively richer form of apprehension." Bernard Meland, one of many empirical theologians who identifies this kind of experience, cites Whitehead's idea of consciousness: "Consciousness is the weapon which strengthens the artificiality of an occasion of experience. It raises the importance of the final Appearance relatively to that of the initial Reality. Thus it is Appearance which in consciousness is clear and distinct, and it is Reality which lies dimly in the background with its details hardly to be distinguished in consciousness."[38] Meland cites this passage when he raises a major problem in the thought of Wieman, namely, how to incorporate the "More" of the rich fullness of experience that is a source of Wieman's naturalistic mysticism with his more critical rational-empirical method that is more selective of what is given in experience. One possible solution to this problem is to suggest that the uncovering of new facts in progressive research programs is a way of accessing the richer, qualitative dimension of experience, even though this does not exhaust that dimension. This we will discuss a little later.

However, Meland's point also calls our attention to a broader notion of empirical justification than one finds in science, the justification of religious ideas in living, both by individuals and by whole communities. Because theology tries to understand ways to human fulfillment, because empirical theology attempts to understand what in fact brings about a continuous succession of completed states of living with a growth in what individuals and

---

38. Bernard Eugene Meland, "The Root and Form of Wieman's Thought," in *The Empirical Theology of Henry Nelson Wieman*, ed. Robert W. Bretall (Carbondale: Southern Illinois University Press, 1963), p. 62.

communities can know and appreciate, and because fulfillment so conceived is only accomplished in the course of human living here and now, in the final analysis religious research programs are carried out in the fullness of daily life and not only in carefully constructed situations in which experiments or controlled observations can be made. In other words, the justification of a theological concept is a general, pragmatic one of the concept's effectiveness in shaping behaviors that help one to an ever greater richness of experienced value.

This pragmatic form of justification need not conflict with the following, more limited but also helpful, method of justification that has much in common with that of scientific research programs. Yet, even in this more restricted sense of justification, there is a difference between what the empirical theologian does and what most scientists do. While progressive scientific research programs are expected to yield new facts, theological research programs are also expected to yield a growth in value. Both fertility of facts and fertility of values are criteria for the justification of the claims of empirical theology.

Nancey Murphy, in her seminal essay "Acceptability Criteria for Work in Theology and Science," argues that "Lakatos' methodology provides criteria for distinguishing science from non-science and for distinguishing acceptable scientific theories and modifications of theories from those that are unacceptable." She goes on to say, however, "it would be useful at this point to have a widely accepted theory of acceptability criteria in theology, but I believe it fair to say that there is little agreement on this point among theologians."[39] What I am suggesting here is that, on the one hand, empirical theologians not only justify their concepts according to acceptability criteria in science; following Lakatos, concepts are acceptable "insofar as they contribute to *research programs* that are *empirically progressive*—that lead to the discovery of novel facts."[40] On the other hand, empirical theologians have the added burden of justifying their concepts according to how well they can lead to behavior that increases the experienced richness of value and thereby human fulfillment. As this is done, the increases in value are operationally defined as expected facts that can be observed and even measured. To understand this let us outline a possible research program in empirical theology.

There are many possible research programs in which empirical theologians could engage. However, their hard-core hypotheses would all reflect certain basic assumptions about the nature of reality that we discussed earlier in comparing the spirit of empirical theology with the spirit of science: nature is the sole context for human inquiry and for attaining human fulfillment; reality is organic, that is, relational and historical; and, against dualism, there is a continuous development of ever more complex systems of energy, matter, life, and mind. In this context the empirical theologian can develop research programs to better understand what increases human fulfillment or the ever continuing enrichment of the experience of value.

In seeking to understand what increases human fulfillment, one is seeking to understand empirically "the source of increasing value," one way many empirical theologians formally define *God*. One core hypothesis about the source of increasing value could be that it is a creative system. This core hypothesis is not directly falsifiable because it is protected with a belt of auxiliary hypotheses generated in terms of the core, because empirical testing is directed at the auxiliary hypotheses instead of the core. Examples of possible auxiliary hypotheses are 1) the creative system of value is a two-stage temporal system, one stage being the disruption of the status quo by the experience of new events, the second being a new integration of what formerly existed with the new events, that is "death and rebirth"; 2) a mechanism of disruption is seeking out values that are different from one's own, that is, "loving the enemy"; 3) a mechanism of integration is the deferring critical judgment as one tries out new possible integrating patterns of thought and behavior, that is, "faith in things yet unseen."

Such hypotheses can then be operationally defined as ways of behaving in controlled situations, say a social-psychological experiment in interpersonal relationships and decision making regarding abortion, in order to see the degree to which the valuing consciousness of each person in the experiment is increased or the sense of community between participants deepened.[41] The situation can be controlled by having experimental and control groups that are equivalent in all significant respects except the auxiliary hypothesis to be tested. All groups might be asked so to try to resolve the abortion problem; however half the groups might be instructed to incorporate their "opponents'" values into their own way of thinking, an operational definition of "love your enemies"; the other half, as the control groups, would not be so instructed.

The point of this would not be to actually resolve the abortion problem but to see if there was a difference before and after the experiment in the degree of "depth of community" between experimental and control groups. A measurement of "depth of community" could be constructed by operationally defining (partly) this idea as the degree of caring that people have for those of opposing views, using a standard type attitude scale constructed by social

---

41. An operational definition is here the same as Peirce's pragmatic understanding of defining the meaning of abstract terms in terms of "practical consequences either in the shape of conduct to be recommended, or in that of experiences to be expected, if the conception be true." This phrasing is by James in "A Definition of Pragmatic and Pragmatism," Peirce, *Collected Papers*, vol. 5, p. 1.

psychologists.[42] When this is done, one has defined values as facts to be observed and measured.

That this kind of experiment can be designed suggests that empirical theology, using justification in this more limited sense, can make use of studies done about creativity in the social and natural sciences. Like Eaves' DNA icon, hypotheses about the structure and conditions of the creative event can possibly unite work done in a number of fields, including social-psychology, biology, and ecology.[43] Using this work as a source of possible ideas, to some extent already confirmed scientifically, if the "creative event" research program leads to new auxiliary hypotheses and new ways of observing increases in value, thereby increasing one's knowledge of God as the creative system of value, the program is progressive. If auxiliary hypotheses about the creative event do not bring to light how an increase in value occurs but some other core hypothesis and its auxiliaries do, then the hypotheses that define God as a creative system, while not directly falsified, will probably be abandoned in favor of the more fruitful program.

In this manner concepts about God in empirical theology can be justified in a way that is comparable to that of justification in science. Any hypotheses so justified can then be put into practice in daily living to see if they meet the pragmatic test of leading to greater value in "real life." Together, the two methods of justification can help move empirical theology toward something comparable to Eaves' third stage of science, the paradigmatic-technological stage.

In conclusion, empirical theology has much in common with both the spirit of science and its methods. The differences between the two are related to what are often regarded as differences between "facts and values." This is a reflection of a basic difference between the goals of science and religion, one attempting to understand reality and the other seeking ways of human fulfillment. However, when empirical theology and science are compared, this difference is more a difference in degree than in kind. And when values and their source are operationally defined in possible research pro-

---

42. The auxiliary hypotheses and the means of testing them are a development of Wieman's fourfold creative event, Henry Nelson Wieman, *The Source of Human Good* (Carbondale: Southern Illinois University Press, 1946), pp. 58-69. However, I have separated Wieman's first two phases (stated in the first auxiliary hypothesis) from the last two (stated as the expected results). For further information of how one can develop and test empirically under controlled conditions, and hence scientifically, hypotheses about Wieman's concept of God as the creative process, see Karl E. Peters, *The Concept of God and the Method of Science: An Exploration of the Possibility of Scientific Theology*, Ph.D. dissertation, Columbia University, 1971.

43. For work in social psychology, see *The Journal of Creative Behavior*; for relating biology to creativity and values in a way helpful to empirical theology see Charles Birch and John B. Cobb Jr., *The Liberation of Life* (Cambridge: Cambridge University Press, 1981); for relating ecology to creativity and values see Holmes Rolston III, *Environmental Ethics* (Philadelphia: Temple University Press, 1986).

grams, the fact-value distinction is overcome and empirical theology becomes equivalent to a mature science. Even if this is done, however, empirical theologians should keep in mind the basic religious quest, the quest for real-life human fulfillment. Because this quest involves integrating value-laden experiences that are much richer than what can be considered in more focused experimental situations, the final justification of religious thought and practice is in the ongoing lives of human beings in an ever-changing world.

CHAPTER FOUR

Empirical and Classical Theology

MARJORIE HEWITT SUCHOCKI

To discuss major differences between empirical and classical theology requires adopting some rather broad working definitions of both kinds of theology. While recognizing that broad definitions overlook nuances and thus tend toward oversimplification, I nonetheless will work with the understanding that empirical theology refers to that tradition which takes experience itself (variously interpreted) as the fundamental source of religious insight, whereas classical theologians place a primacy on revelation and reason (often speculative) as complementing sources of insight. Revelation is posited as coming into history from a transhistorical source in God, in which case the locus of truth has no essential relation to history; whereas for empiricism, the locus of truth *is* history.

The other major distinction is the philosophical heritage within which each form works, which of course relates to the different cultural matrix of each. Classical theologians drew their suppositions about the nature of reality primarily from the ancient philosophers and philosophical schools, such as Plato, Aristotle, the Stoics, and Plotinus. Augustine, for example, is best understood in conjunction with *The Enneads*. Through the early Middle Ages Plato's *Timaeus* exercised great influence, and by the high Middle Ages, Aristotle provided the frame of metaphysical reference. The great controversies over whether or not universals were real in themselves (realism) or whether they were but names given to individual things (nominalism) shaped the later Middle Ages and the period of the Reformation.

Empiricism certainly had forerunners in the high and late Middle Ages in some aspects of the thought of Duns Scotus, Roger Bacon, William of Occam, and Gabriel Biel, but its primary philosophical heritage must be traced to the Enlightenment era. Cartesian rationalism made the thinking subject the primary locus for philosophical reflection. However, since Descartes understood the world to be divided into two substances, mind and matter, and since substance was by definition that which requires nothing other than itself in order to exist, there was a problem in relating the thinking self causally to the staff of matter. The English response was to make the locus of knowledge sensory perception, which linked the mental knower with the material world. However, this device did not resolve the problem of dualism, given the predilection even in the empiricist camp for defining mind and matter as two different substances. The American philosopher William James offered a resolution to the issue through what he called "radical empiricism," which entailed that the mind is continuous with matter, emerging from its environment through relation. James critiqued the English empiricists as concentrating on separate things and senses, and failing to note that relationships are just as solidly sensed as are things. Conjunctive and disjunctive relations are among the most important elements in our experience. What we call mind is a series of experiences, linked by conjunctive relations. A similar position was later developed by Alfred North Whitehead in his organic philosophy of reality as a relational process of many instances of becoming. Contemporary radical empiricists continue in this tradition, but often with an increasing importance given to history.

REVELATION IN CLASSICAL THEOLOGY

To develop the distinctions between classical and empirical theologies further, I will proceed first by probing the role of revelation in classical theology, particularly in relation to reason, and then by focusing on the contrasting views of God. Given the scope of classical theology, this exploration will be necessarily brief and therefore incomplete, but it should be sufficient to indicate not only the broad differences between the two modes but also the remarkable similarities that demonstrate that they both are, after all, variations within a common Christian tradition.

Earliest Christian thinkers from apostolic times and from their successors in the antignostic period regarded the Hebrew scriptures, the sayings of Christ, and the writings of the apostles as final authorities in matters of faith and practice. The worldviews of the time facilitated this position, since mystery religions and philosophies alike tended to assume that the mundane world was but a small portion of reality. Beyond the habitats of time and space there was a deeper reality, rational in nature, that provided the pattern for the human world. Revelation was like the irruption of that which was Real into the realm of a world struggling toward its own approximation of the Real. Thus revelation was a source of knowledge and a sure guide to conduct as one aimed to live in consonance with the Real.

The Christian variation on this sensitivity understood God to be the creator of a complex world of many layers, including spheres of principalities and powers that could hold humanity hostage in delusion and evil. God's truth broke through the webs of confusion first in the Hebrew scriptures, and ultimately in Jesus Christ as God's own presence in history. This central breakthrough resulted in a period of many pneumatic utterances, where God as Spirit continued to speak through those who were participants in the revelatory event of Jesus Christ. Thus by the end of the second century the early church venerated not only the writings of what are today the Hebrew and the Christian canons but other writings as well, such as those of Hermas, Barnabas, and the Didache.

The gradual narrowing of revelation to what became the canon came about through controversies generated by the many variations of Christianity that were evolving. In the perceived urgency of establishing "right belief," the church limited the source of faith to those writings it considered apostolic. As for the continuing controversy over the varying interpretations of even these writings, the church turned to the interpretive authority of the church itself, lodged in its bishops. Thus "revelation" and "scripture" became virtually identical.

The allegorical use of scripture dominated the first centuries of Christianity. Origen, writing in the third century, developed this mode most fully, suggesting that scripture holds a threefold sense: the literal, the moral, and the spiritual. The spiritual sense is allegorical, hiding and yielding wisdom at the same time. Under the guise of its literal statements lurks the deeper meaning, accessible to the mature in Christ. But of course once this principle of interpreting scripture enters into theological use, the "closed canon" is in fact an open canon into which many ideas might be read, and therefore be established as authoritative. This amounts to a merging of revelation and reason, with the authoritative status of revelation conferred upon reason insofar as speculative thought was given allegorical presence in a text. Thus revelation in fact became a continuing event, even while ostensibly confined within the specific texts of the canon.

Augustine continued the allegorical use of scripture, using it in support of his own monumental construction of doctrine. The intertwining of revelation and reason is nowhere more apparent than in his *City of God* exposition of the fall of Adam. The actual scriptural text gives the barest outlines of the story within several pages; Augustine's exposition takes several chapters of *City of God*. The elements of the text are expanded through allegory to embrace Augustine's own creative interpretation of the human plight. He ostensibly based his thought on a biblical story and then so elaborated that story that it could bear the cultural, mythological, and philosophical elements that he needed to develop his own perception of creation, evil, and redemption. Thus he demonstrated how revelation and reason merged into a single authority in the patristic period of the Christian tradition.

As for reason, Augustine connected it strongly to the will. What one knows is directed by what one desires, which is to say, by the will. Thus knowledge is attained through the complex operation of one's will, which is itself directed by one's loves. Augustine divided love into two diametrically opposed categories: the love of God, which embraced within it the love of the world in and through God, or a love of self, which entailed a love for the world insofar as the world served the ends of the self. All humankind could be divided according to these two loves. Love shapes the soul and, therefore, defines the parameters of what one may know.

When the will toward love of self is turned by God toward God, then true knowledge can take place. This occurs insofar as the soul, united with God, participates in the reality of God. Knowledge of God is then direct, mediated through the union with God, and forming the soul in conformity with that love. Insofar as revelation is concerned, this aspect of Augustine's thought provides the basis for mystical knowledge of God and for the doctrine of illumination that became prominent in medieval and renaissance Christianity.

THE ROLE OF REASON

While scripture continued as a normative authority in the Middle Ages, the role of reason came far more strongly to the fore. This is particularly obvious in Peter Abélard, who introduced dialectics into Christian theology. He collected passages from the Bible and patristic literature that were mutually contradictory and then in the sentences of *Sic et Non* attempted their reconciliation. With regard to the patristics, his rigorous inquiries led to judgments that the patristic writers had, in fact, erred, but he stopped short of applying such judgment to scripture. When scripture contradictions defied reconciliation, he assumed that the transmission of the text had corrupted the text. This position then put reason and scripture on the same plane: that is, the scriptures must be reasonable, tested by sure reason, and sure reason can at least potentially find its corroboration in the scriptures.

Thomas Aquinas gave the definitive medieval position on revelation and reason. He argued that the object of all theology—indeed, of life itself—is God, but that God by definition exceeds the powers of the finite intellect. Therefore, revelation is necessary if humanity is to achieve its destined goal, which is the knowledge of God. Revelation is thus given by God through inspiration, resulting in the scriptures. These are attested by the faith that they generate, as well as by miracles and signs. Thus the scriptures, since they originate from God and supplement human knowledge, are a sure and binding authority for faith. Reason is not made irrelevant by the scriptures. Faith and reason then work together to bring about the increasing knowledge of God.

There is a certain parallel between revelation and reason in Aquinas. Revelation gives knowledge of God, or that which is above the human intellect and therefore in principle indiscernible by the intellect working through

its own powers. But natural reason also works with that which is in principle beyond itself, the universals. According to Aquinas, the universals inhere
in matter, giving it form. The active intellect is able to abstract these universals
from the matter in which they are embedded and thus arrive at knowledge.
These universals, while available through sense perception, have their ultimate locus in the mind of God. Thus both knowledge through revelation
and knowledge through nature deal with that which is eternal, be it God or
the universals within the mind of God. Both likewise deal with degrees of revelation. God reveals the matters of faith through scripture and through the
incarnation; God reveals the stuff of finite knowledge through creation by
shaping the potentiality of matter into form through universals. Knowledge
occurs through nature as matter displays its form and thus the universals to
the natural mind, and knowledge occurs through grace as God reveals truths
such as the triune nature and the things of salvation. In the first instance,
the mind is active; in the second instance, the mind is passive. There is no
inconsistency here, for the mind abstracts universals from matter through
sense perception. God, however, is not given to sense perception, so the
mind is not equipped naturally for the knowledge of God. Only as God is
revealed is it possible for reason to grasp its divine object. In a much later age,
theologians will claim that God is not an "object," but in the epistemology
of Aquinas, the mind's engraced ability to grasp God is no diminution of
God but rather God's own gracious mode of bringing creation to its divinely appointed end of the eternal contemplation of God.

The work of reason in building from revelation for the development of
sound doctrine was controversial, as is witnessed by the many interpretations
that were proclaimed heretical by the church. Consequently, the theologians
of the scholastic period confirmed the authority of the church itself to judge
correct interpretation of scripture and thus the correct development of doctrine. This authority resided in councils, which were convened by the pope.
While in actuality there was much tension between the authority of the councils and the authority of the pope, theologically the ultimate authority was
lodged in the pope. This coincided with the political situation, in which
Innocent III ruled kings and empires under the edict that, as Vicar of Christ,
his spiritual authority superseded all secular authority. Given the papal
authority over the political world, it would have seemed strange had he not
exercised the same authority within the sphere of the church, councils not
withstanding.

THE RECOVERY OF THE GREEKS

All this was to change in the fourteenth and fifteenth centuries, as the cultural and political forces set loose through the Renaissance recovery of
ancient Greek texts radically changed the climate of thought. The recovery
of the Greeks not only began the movement toward humanism, with its new

emphasis upon the individual and the powers inherent within humanity, it also facilitated the deeper veneration of ancient authority over contemporary ways and wisdom. This heightened the authority of the ancient biblical texts and provided a norm against which to judge scholastic theology, and also the authority of the papacy. While revelation had always been venerated, the location of the correct interpretation of scripture within the church hierarchy effectively made the hierarchy itself the actual norm. In the fourteenth and fifteenth centuries, the ancient was vaunted over against the modern. The Renaissance humanists had already begun the critical investigation of texts, and whatever was not found in scripture—such as the temporal power of the papacy—became suspect. Certainly most of the themes sounded by Martin Luther in the sixteenth-century Reformation were already beginning to appear in the thought of persons such as William of Occam and Gabriel Biel.

Sense perception began to play an increasingly prominent role in the theory of knowledge, and so to lay the seeds for an incipient empiricism. The way had been prepared for this when the authority of Aristotle gained ascendancy over Plato. What remained of the Platonic forms had become the universals in the mind of God. However, these universals were considered accessible to human reason insofar as they shaped matter into form and therefore could be abstracted from matter by the intellect. Occam's famous "razor" simply did away with the universals as existing outside the mind. It was vain to utilize more explanations when fewer could settle the issue: If the human mind could effectively abstract universals from things, then there was no need to locate the universals elsewhere than in the mind that forms them. The mind as such tends toward generalization through the various impressions of objects that it receives. The theory of knowledge thus developed was a correspondence theory of truth: The mind forms a true copy of the object that it sees, and the categories of generalization developed by the mind correspond to the reality of the external world.

Revelation in Occam's view occupied an ambiguous but politic place. On the one hand, he used his keen reason to raise radical questions concerning doctrines, going further than his predecessor Abélard in his willingness to raise questions concerning scripture. But on the other hand, he proposed a rule of faith whereby that which the church believed and taught was to be believed by all within the church. This faith was infused into the soul of the believer, primarily through the grace of God given through the sacraments. The position borders upon a fideism that tears asunder the scholastic marriage of revelation and reason, making them into two separate spheres. The "things of faith" no longer necessarily conformed to the laws of reason.

The eve of the Reformation, then, saw the fully developed classical view of reason and revelation and an incipient empiricism emerging in the fourteenth and fifteenth centuries. The contrast had to do with the sufficiency of the human mind and senses to account for knowledge. The classical view held to the insufficiency of human reason—because of the fallen will for Augustine and those who followed him, and because of reason's finitude for Aquinas and his followers. The Reformation thinkers tended to follow Augustine's distrust of reason, in a strange reversal of Occam. They, too, separated matters of faith from matters of reason, but whereas in Occam the priority is clearly on the side of reason, the Reformers put the priority on faith. Reason was sufficient to deal with the mundane world, but what was that to salvation? The things of faith, inaccessible to reason, made for the triumph of the soul.

The various options within the classical position on revelation and reason were fairly well developed in Christianity by the end of the medieval era. The empiricism was nascent, and as is evident from the Reformers, easily absorbed into the classical position so that it was not applied in matters of faith. Another essay in this volume develops the intellectual history of empiricism; fundamentally, empiricists eventually applied Occam's razor to religious knowledge as well as to secular knowledge, eliminating the notion of revelation altogether and substituting philosophy of religion for theology.

ALFRED NORTH WHITEHEAD

Yet within the empirical tradition represented by Alfred North Whitehead, the divorce from the classical position is not quite so sharp. His own theory of knowledge is indeed empirical, but in such a way as to incorporate speculative reason. His famous image of this incorporation is in the image of the "aeroplane" that must be grounded in order to take off into its flights of free thinking and must touch ground again in order to be sustained. That is, empiricism is not against speculation, it is the ground of speculation. One observes the experienced world, whether through one's unaided senses or through those refined extensions of our senses represented by the experimental tools of the sciences. The fundamental issue is to be able to describe the way "reality" is, which includes asking the question, "What must be the case in order for reality to be like this?" Through our reason we take note of the data of our experience, and still through our reason we postulate the cosmological situation that allows the particular data of our experience. The cosmology is tentative, not certain, befitting its speculative nature—but it is a cosmology nonetheless.

Whitehead's observations of experience yielded an inexorably relational world, where everything that is, is through its relation to other actualities. His similarity to the classical position on reason and revelation comes from his speculative thought concerning the necessary conditions for such relationality. He, too, had recourse to a theory of "universals," which he called "eternal objects." At first these "eternal objects" functioned much like the universal forms of things that could be abstracted by one entity in relation to another—no longer necessarily as an action of mind, since it is a process describing all reality whatsoever, but simply as the nonconscious prehension of that which had preceded one. The "one," in this case, may indeed be the human mind, but it could also be an element within a puff of smoke, or a piece of rock. Relationality *is* the feeling of the other, together with the abstraction of its "form" that takes place as any becoming entity feels the force of its predecessors. This is the very process that produces a new actuality.

By the time of writing *Process and Reality*, Whitehead needed a locus for the sheer togetherness of the hierarchy of forms, each of which was what it was in infinite combinations of possible relations. The small essay, *Mathematics and the Good*,[1] gives the most brilliant description of Whitehead's vision of the togetherness of the eternal objects. In *Process and Reality*, he locates the realm of the eternal objects in the primordial nature of God in a way that certainly bears parallels with Aquinas' location of the universals within the mind of God. For Aquinas, the forms inhere in the matter they shape by God's creativity; for Whitehead, the eternal objects "ingress," or are embodied in actual entities, through the creativity of the occasions themselves.

Reality operates in and through relationality: Every entity comes into existence through its feeling (prehension) of the past, including the forms (eternal objects) resident in the actualities of the past, and through its own creative unification of those forms which involves their contrasting in a dynamic process of integration whereby the entity moves toward its own unique embodiment of form. In this process, the actual forms of the past are supplemented with the potential-become-actual form of the present; each new entity is uniquely itself—like many others, indeed, but in its own individual mode of likeness, which is in fact the creative actualization in time of a new form of existence.

Because of Whitehead's ontological principle that everything that comes into existence must have its reason in itself or in some other existent realty, Whitehead needed a source actuality for the new form that each new entity becomes. That which the entity becomes preexists the entity, since at its initial stages the form it will become is only possible, not yet actual. In fact, it is just as much the new possibility as it is the past that evokes the becoming of each new occasion. The past can only call for some form of recapitulation of its own achievement; the future, calling forth instantiation of a new possibility, combines with the past to explain the present. But if every reason must be within an actuality, and if the actuality of the past cannot account for the new possibility, what actuality does? And so Whitehead developed a notion of God in order to account for the presence of the new. God functions to provide novelty to each becoming occasion and in the process, to provide the principle of limitation, or order, as well.

---

1. Alfred North Whitehead, "Mathematics and the Good," in *The Philosophy of Alfred North Whitehead*, ed. Paul Arthur Schilpp (LaSalle, Ill.: Open Court, 1941).

The entire process is like this: In a relational world, every reality receives from its entire past and has an internal, relational effect on the future realities that will succeed it. God, as part of this world, receives the effects of every reality whatsoever. God integrates these effects into the divine nature, and from the fullness of God's consequent knowledge of the past God knows what possibility at any particular standpoint is optimum for the next moment of becoming. But not only God receives the effects of the past—the world succeeds itself; the energy of the past demands a successor present. The present, having been affected by its own past, now demands its effect and calls forth its future. Relative to the evoked future—or the becoming entity—God as well as the world is in its past; hence it receives the influence of the past toward its own repetition, and the influence of God toward a novel way of dealing with the past for its own becoming. The new entity thus feels the past according to the new perspective provided initially from God. To use the language of Aquinas, the entity abstracts the forms from the past *and* also abstracts the form of its own becoming from God. It would be akin to the "active intellect" in both cases. Or, the past and God propose to the entity what it might become; the entity itself actively disposes of those proposals as it itself comes into concrete existence. What is the "ingression of the eternal objects" from the point of view of God is the "prehension of eternal objects" from the point of view of the becoming entity.

I should note that each form the becoming entity abstracts from the past was in its own time of becoming a form or variation thereof offered to the occasion by God. Thus the parallel with Aquinas; whereas for Aquinas natural knowledge is made possible because of God's act of creation, forming passive matter according to an inhering form, for Whitehead natural knowledge is made possible because of matter's active disposition of a form it received from God. In both cases, universals inhere in the finite world, and in both cases God is creatively involved in that inherence. For Whitehead, unlike Aquinas, the world's disposition of God's proposed form is the freedom of the world to become what it will within the limitations it has received. For Aquinas, matter must receive the form God gives; resistances to form are not due to the freedom of matter but due to the natural limitations of matter. For Aquinas, religious knowledge is made possible through the direct act of divine revelation; for Whitehead, religious knowledge is formed no differently from any other kind of knowledge, and the direct relation of every finite reality to God is natural, not supernatural. But what the finite entity prehends in prehending God is not necessarily the nature and attributes of God; it is far more restricted than that—the entity prehends its *own* possibilities through its prehension of God. In short, Aquinas posits two types of knowledge, natural and supernatural, with the universals in the mind of God related only to natural knowledge. Whitehead has but one form of knowledge, all natural; but natural knowledge now necessarily includes prehension of God as the source of universals, or eternal objects.

The other item of contrast is that for Whitehead, unlike Aquinas, prehension is not primarily sense perception. Rather, it is the direct flow of relation; what was there, is felt here, and contributes to the creation of the "here." For Aquinas, knowledge of universals in matter is mediated by sensory perception. The ground of the difference is that Whitehead is analyzing all reality at a microcosmic level; prehension is a universal activity accounting for the relational character of reality. Prehension is thus the presupposition of what will be called knowledge at the level of social complexity that is involved in self-conscious beings. Sensory perception is made possible by a complex nervous system composed of billions of actual entities, most of which do not involve consciousness. Prehension is a primary mode of nonsensory perception which, through a particular organization of entities, becomes the basis for sensory perception and knowledge. A conscious being, then, does indeed perceive and know through the five senses, but underlying this knowledge is the prehensive activity itself which is more than sense perception, even while it grounds sense perception. Human knowledge cannot be restricted to what one knows via the five senses. The "sixth sense," and fundamental mode of transmission of information, is via the primal activity of prehension. This is experienced in its most direct form through one's experience of oneself in memory; there is no sense perception involved in the experience of reliving an experience through memory. Rather, one prehends one's own past. Sense perception is the simplified organization of data, aiding in one's disposal of the direct prehensive information as it is selectively mediated to consciousness.

The more complex theory of knowledge that emerges when prehension is taken into account allows the experience of relation itself into the data of knowledge. That is, it is not simply the things that one knows but the relations of things with respect to others and oneself. The sense of relation is so pervasive an aspect of existence that it can be overlooked; one is so used to it that one hardly notices it. A Whiteheadian perspective suggests that the experience of relation was indeed overlooked in the classical theories of knowledge and that this oversight resulted in an oversimplification of reality as a conglomerate of discrete things. Sensory perception, taken on its own, leads to a dualism that separates the experiencing, thinking subject from separated, inert objects.

Thus while there are notable similarities between Whitehead and Aquinas as one probes their theories of knowledge relative to universals, the inclusion of prehension as the pervasive experience of relation divides them. Whitehead becomes a "radical empiricist" in James' sense of grounding all knowledge in experience. This deeper interpretation of experience is vastly different from that intended by the scholastics in Christian history and by the early empiricists, whose theory of knowledge was based only on sense perception.

Is revelation possible within Whitehead's radical empiricism? Given the fact that God is the universally related one, relating to every creature and receiving the effects of every creature, there is no reason in principle to deny the possibility of revelation. Presumably God could so influence a people that they would corporately be attuned to God's own hopes for human history. The point is that in Whitehead's system God *does* influence everything—but God cannot control what is done with that influence. Revelation would require a responsiveness to the divine influence. Again, there is no reason in principle to deny that a people could or would be responsive to the divine will in such a way that God's character could be revealed through them. Since such a possibility is entirely consistent with the metaphysics, the issue of revelation would have to be decided on grounds of history and faith, not cosmology. The point of it in a Whiteheadian system is that revelation would be natural, not supernatural, and that it would require the cooperation of the creature. Given the fact that revelation would require the cooperation of the creature, and further, that the creature/s could only receive a revelation that was consonant with its or their past, then what finally would be revealed would reveal God *and* history, or God *in* history. It would necessarily be perspectival, revealing the world as well as God, and insofar as it revealed God it would reveal the relation of the world to God at that particular standpoint. Revelation would necessarily be relative. Thus anything that was called revelation could not be beyond criticism, nor could the critic escape her or his own standpoint in such a way as to make that particular standpoint irrelevant for the critique or interpretation of revelation. There is no skyhook, hanging objective and pure outside the universe, from which one can view God. Revelation must necessarily be relative, participating in all the ambiguities of human history.

I have used Whitehead to contrast classical and empirical theologies of reason and revelation because Whitehead provides the greatest point of such contrast among empiricists. This is because of his inclusion of a relational God within his understanding of experience. There have been a number of empiricists who radically question this inclusion of God, much as Occam objected to Aquinas' location of the universals in the mind of God. Whitehead thought that since possibilities were a-temporal, they required a locus, and, as indicated above, that locus had to be an entity that included an a-temporal nature. But Whitehead's point was quite controversial, and a number of empiricists claim that the entity itself is sufficient to account for the rise of novelty in a relational universe. "Eternal objects" are not needed; novel possibilities are simply emergents along with actuality in the process. The "Whitehead with God" debate has raged for several decades. How one decides may depend less on how one develops the metaphysics of Whitehead's cosmology, and more in one's own religious experience.

THE NOTION OF GOD

The other major point of contrast to be made between classical and empirical theology is in the notion of God itself. The two major fountainheads for classical theology are Augustine and Aquinas; I will indicate the broad outlines of their understanding, this time contrasting them with Bernard Loomer, whose understanding of God may be the most radical among the radical empiricists.

The most obvious entry point to the classical notion of God is through the doctrine of the trinity, since this was often considered the prime example of revealed as opposed to natural theology. As Augustine noted, there are many examples within nature of three elements combined in a unity, but these are not sufficient in themselves to lead one to a notion of the trinitarian nature of God. Rather, God as triune is a revealed understanding that then leads one to note examples of threeness in unity within nature.

If the trinity is a revealed doctrine, the question to ask is under what circumstances and how was it revealed? The answer rests with patristic soteriology. The suppositions about the world in early Christianity were deeply influenced by a gnostic mistrust of the material world as opposed to the pure reality of spirit. Insofar as the Hebrew worldview continued to influence Christianity through its incorporation of the Hebrew scriptures, the dualism of the gnostics was mitigated, but only by being rendered ambiguous, not by elimination. The mitigation was that God did indeed create the material world through the divine Logos, and the ambiguity was that the world does not exist as it was created but as it is fallen from its created condition. Sin is the creature's participation in its own fallenness, so that hapless individuals help to create the very trap that catches them. For the problem in existence was that only as we participate in immortality is there human happiness—but to participate in immortality is to participate in the immortal God, and we are separated from this God, not only by our very creatureliness, but also because of our sin. The plight is that by definition our salvation from sin does not lie within our own abilities; we have not the means to participate in God's immortality in our separated state. Therefore, only God can save us.

Many religious belief systems of the early Christian era followed such a mythic construction of the human plight. Christianity, however, claimed that we have been saved from our miserable condition by God's own act: God participated in our existence in order that we might participate in God. Through incarnation, God assumed human flesh in Jesus of Nazareth and lived the sinless life of conformity to the will of God. Being sinless, there was no natural reason for Jesus to die, but die he did through the particular and common torture of crucifixion. It was customary to assume that a criminal's undergoing such a terrible death constituted an expiation of the crimes that led to the cross, but in the case of the sinless Jesus the expiatory power of the cross was given for sinful humanity. Therefore, God in Christ atoned for the sins of the world, removing the barrier that separates the creature from participating in God.

These are the broad outlines of the soteriology in early Christianity; there were many variations on the theme, particularly as the notion of a devil began to play a prominent part in the subjugation of human beings to sin. Thus the scenario varied greatly in its details, but the broad strokes were those outlined above. God, incarnate in Christ, resolves the problem of human sin such that the creature might be joined to God. The connection of this soteriology with the trinity was simply the question of how an incarnation could be possible. The metaphysical suppositions were material, even with regard to the ephemeral realm of spirit, which was often considered simply a rarified matter. How could God be present in history and at the same time retain the suprahistorical position of the creator God who governed the universe? The answer would be the triune nature of God.

The mythic substructure of the doctrine of the trinity should not dissuade us from noting the complexity and sophistication of the doctrine as it was finally developed through the tumultuous fourth century. Again in broad summary, God was considered the unoriginate creator of the universe, who created the universe through the Logos. The Logos doctrine itself entered Christianity through Stoicism, where Logos functioned as the principle of rationality that was threaded throughout the universe. In Christian hands, the Logos became a center within the Godhead that related to the Creator as thought to mind. God was such that the activity of thinking generated a second center within the divine reality, so that God's thought is present to God's self. This abstract terminology became personal by applying the terminology of Jesus as the Son of God to the Logos as God the Son. The creator God, then, was eternally Father to the Son. It was through the Son (Logos) that the Father created, and through the Son (Jesus) that God became incarnate. The two are yet one, since it is the nature of God to generate the Son. The unity of God in and of its own nature pushes toward and is—not a dyad—but a trinity.

While the focus at Nicea was intensely upon the relation between Father and Son, the final formula concluded with reference to the Holy Spirit as third person of the trinity. The very deity of God was such that three principles, or centers, or hypostases, were necessarily entailed. Following Nicea, more attention was given to the relation of the Spirit within the trinitarian structure of God. The Spirit was considered active in soteriology, since the Spirit united human beings to the Son by infusing them with faith. With regard to the Spirit's intratrinitarian role, this was defined differently from the Son. The Son was generated by the Father, but the Spirit proceeded from the Father (whether through the Son or with the Son became a contention that caused a great schism between Roman and Greek forms of Christianity). Practically speaking, God as Father was accorded a kind of primacy, but ontologically, the unit of God generated a threeness that admitted of no subordination within itself: Father, Son, and Spirit were one nature, one will, one immortality—in short, one essence.

The formulations surrounding the Nicene confession are fundamental to classical theology; Augustine and Aquinas each expanded and expounded upon the doctrine in different ways. Augustine emphasized God as will, and Aquinas emphasized God as intellect. But both men assumed Nicea and carried the discussion further.

AUGUSTINE

Augustine's contribution follows from his great stress on the unity of God and by his further delineation of relation itself as that which constituted God as triune. Since it was the relations that accounted for the differences within God, and since relation is not a substance, the trinitarian structure of God did not violate or compromise the unity of the divine substance. The relations are fundamentally of origin and reciprocity: only the Father generates the Son; only the Son is generated; only the Spirit proceeds from Father and Son together. But the Father is not a Father apart from the Son, nor would Father and Son be Father and Son together unless they spirated the Spirit—each relation is constitutive of the whole; no relation is isolated.

The original impulse toward trinitarian theology came from soteriology, or God's actions in history for salvation; this was named the "economic trinity," or the trinitarian work of God. Most of the discussion, however, focused on the "immanent trinity," or ways to resolve the conundrum of how God could be one and yet three without tritheism or internal contradiction. By focusing on the unity of the immanent trinity, Augustine also contributed to the explication of the economic trinity. Given the difference in relations, a specific work could be appropriated to one of the relata within the divine life, but given the unity, the whole of the trinity was involved in every work of God. Thus with regard to the incarnation, the Son indeed became incarnate in history, but this required the entire trinitarian work in that the Son, as Word of the Father, participated in the sending, as did the Spirit which is the expression of the union between them. In creation, which is the work peculiarly appropriated to the Father, the Father creates through a Word that is effected by the Spirit. And the Spirit's extra-trinitarian unifying work is that of unifying persons with the Son for reconciliation with the Father. There is no work of the triune God that does not involve the wholeness of God; this follows from the essential unity of God.

Augustine, like those before and those who followed him in continuing to develop the classical notion of God, saw no problem in combining the trinitarian God yielded by the soteriological approach with the philosophical God that was at hand in the classical culture. The Greeks had laid out the requisites for deity in a substance dominated world: God could require nothing other than God's own self in order to exist; otherwise, God would be dependent upon that other, compromising the sufficiency of divine power. God, to be God, must be the unoriginate cause of all that is; but if God is cause of all that is, then clearly God must precede all that is and therefore be independent of all that is. God, to be God, must be perfection itself; but if God is perfect, then God can admit of no change, for to change would be to be different from time to time, in which case God would be more or less perfect and no longer perfection itself. Thus God, to be God, must be immutable. God, to be God, must be omnipotent, having all power; for if God were not omnipotent, how could God be sufficient to sustain the infinite divine life. By definition the infinite divine life requires infinite power for its preservation. God, to be God, must be infinitely knowing; for if God were not infinitely knowing, then there would be that in the created world that was outside the divine knowledge. If it were outside the divine knowledge, it would be to that degree self-sufficient. However, there is only one substance that can require nothing other than itself in order to exist, and that is by definition God. Accordingly, there can be nothing in the universe that is outside of the divine knowledge, and God is omniscient. It similarly follows that God is omnipresent, for God's knowledge of something is at the same time God's presence to that which is known. Thus the philosophical attributes of self-sufficiency, immutability, omnipotence, omniscience, and omnipresence were added to the soteriological attributes of the trinitarian God. The fundamental difference that this wedding created was that it made the classical God personal and triune.

One final mention to be made concerning Augustine's contribution to the understanding of God is his tendency to emphasize will and love as the character of God. Will plays such a prominent role in Augustine's anthropology and theory of knowledge that it would be strange to find the emphasis missing in his doctrine of God as well. But the emphasis on will primarily follows from the personal nature of God involved in the soteriology. It is inconceivable, given the omnipotence of God, that anything should occur apart from the will of God. Yet over against the mighty will of God stands the paradox of a human will defiantly turned away from God. Given this paradox, Augustine extends the will of God into a predestining will that permits evil for the plenitude of creation, for the aesthetic beauty of contrast, and for the manifestation of divine mercy. Thus all of human history, inclusive of the freedom to turn from God, is the unfolding of the divine will. The classical God is a purposive God, toward the end of God's own love.

AQUINAS

This contrasts with Aquinas, who saw intellect as the primary character of God. He asked the question, how is it that there is a difference between generation and spiration with regard to the trinitarian structure of God? Why are there not two sons? His answer was the distinction between knowledge and will. God's knowledge generates God's own image, since God most surely knows God's own self. Thus there is a reflected, filial quality to God's own self-knowledge. But will, on the other hand, is directed toward otherness. The relation of the Spirit is therefore not generation, but spiration, and since

God and God's self-knowledge are one, the spiration must proceed from both Father and Son. Father, Son, and Holy Spirit are then names for the God who is fundamentally intellect, thinking and willing.

We noted above that the object of human life for Aquinas is the knowledge of God—and indeed, the final goal toward which all the universe must drive is God. This is of a piece with the understanding of God as thinking and willing, for thinking and willing are purposive activities, and, indeed, for Aquinas God is pure act. But God's thinking and acting, united in love, must necessarily be toward the highest, which is to say, toward God's own self. Therefore, for God to create the world is for God to love the world, and to love the world is to will that it might achieve its highest good—which is the everlasting contemplation of God as a full participant in the love of God. The existence of the world, then, is the outward expression of God's inward act of eternal self-contemplatory bliss.

Should one question whether the outward parallel to the inward work borders on pantheism, the answer would follow from the trinitarian analogy. That is, within God's own trinitarian being there is an otherness that is nonetheless a deepest unity, being an otherness within a common substance. The outward work of God models the inward act of otherness by producing that which is fully other to God, and yet capable of unification with God. The full otherness of the created universe is not simply its materiality as opposed to the pure spirituality that is God, but also its true freedom.

This freedom finds its most sober witness to the otherness of creation in the act of sin, or the defection of the creature from its original righteousness. Original righteousness included, as would be expected in Thomas' system, an illumination of the intellect that gave a knowledge of God, self, and the world proportional to finite power, along with a concomitant harmony of body, soul, and spirit, and the experience of loving God wholly. This original righteousness was maintained by the grace of God, but not so as to annihilate human freedom. When the creature used freedom concupiscently to cease from the whole reliance on God's grace, original righteousness was lost, and with it, the harmony of body and soul. Thus the fallen state is a defect of original righteousness that becomes like a sickness in the body and the unregulated disposition of the soul. Clearly, the ability of the creation so to move from its created order into its own poor imitation of creation in disorder is sufficient to establish the otherness of creation.

The story of creation is not only the story of fall but of redemption by grace toward the attainment of creation's end—which is also God's end—in the contemplation of God. Hence God's work of creation includes redemption, or the turning of the creature back toward its final goal. Since only God can do this given the insufficiency of the creature first through its misuse of freedom and second through its finitude, God supplements fallen nature by infusing grace into the creature. This grace then operates by making the creature acceptable and by prompting the will toward God in faith so that the creature might then live a life of love and good works. Such a life is on the one hand possible only insofar as God acts graciously in the creature, but on the other hand, given the freedom of the creature, by the cooperation of the creature. It thus conforms to the grace of God and is made fit for its final reward, the beatific vision of God in all eternity. The end of all things is God.

Thus the heart of the classical notion of God is a trinity defined by salvation history, whether the doctrine be taken with a primacy of will as in Augustine, or on intellect as with Aquinas. The traditional attributes of omniscience, immutability, and omnipotence are assumed unquestionably as belonging to the notion of God, but even these tended to be defined in terms of soteriology insofar as they involved the perfection and power necessary to accomplish salvation. Throughout, the method utilized in developing the notion of God is the concept of reason and revelation discussed in the first section of this essay.

EMPIRICISM AND GOD

When we turn to an empirical doctrine of God, the contrast is extreme partly because the questions as well as the method are so different. That is, the classical notion of God depends heavily upon certain assumptions concerning the human plight. Certainly these assumptions were grounded in a particular interpretation of experience—but experience is never raw; it is always interpreted. In the classical period, the shaping assumptions concerning the human condition were that we were fallen from an initial purity of being and that in our fallen state we are incapable of attaining the immortal end for which we were created. Only God could save us—and salvation was experienced through Jesus Christ. Two thousand years of Christianity have perpetuated much of that original story, but changing cultures and continents provided the context for a shift in the basic assumptions. Notions of evolution succeeded notions of an instant creation with original righteousness, and increasing individualism challenged the corporate sense of guilt. As we saw in the scholastics, already in the medieval era a greater confidence was emerging in the fundamental dignity of the human person as a rational being. This confidence was brought to full term in the Enlightenment period and only modestly shaken by Immanuel Kant's critique.

The questions of empiricists do not frame the issue in terms of how fallen humanity can be saved. Rather, in a world challenged with pluralism, industrialism, an interlocking world economy, and environmental disasters, empiricists tend to ask how we might live as a socially responsible community of the world's peoples. The question gains an added poignancy in recognition that human history, at least in our own time, is marked by massive genocides—the Indian in the conquest of the American west, the Armenians, the Jews in the Nazi holocaust, the Cambodians in the Khmer Rouge atrocities. Animal species have likewise met with genocide through sheer human rapaciousness, and willful human shortsightedness and greed wreak havoc to the environment. The question of living as socially responsible communities is not asked in any illusions of optimism regarding the human condition; rather, it is asked in view of the tragic dimensions of the human power for evil. The word salvation is not used, nor is there much talk of any immortal end—rather, the concern is with history and its consequences for the world's well-being.[2] How, then, do empiricists talk of God, and how does it relate to our needs? Is it still the case, for all the changes, that the doctrine of God gains its cogency and power from its relation to the experience of human need and human hope?

There is no one empiricist doctrine of God, any more than there is any one classical doctrine of God—but there are common themes. Given the empirical basis, God would have to participate in the relational basis of reality. The old classical requirements for God, rationally developed from Greek philosophy, give way to a more ambiguous God whose power relative to history is not absolute, but limited necessarily by the freedom of the world, and whose knowledge could therefore not be a predestining foreknowledge. Rather, God's knowledge would have to be of the actual as actual, the possible as possible, and the probable as probable. The future is open, even to God.

The most prominent developments of the notion of God are from the more rationalistically inclined empiricists such as Alfred North Whitehead, Charles Hartshorne, and those who base their thinking on the structures they provide. But the more interesting developments may come from those who follow more persistently the radical side of empiricism, such as Henry Nelson Wieman, Bernard Meland, and perhaps the most radical of all, Bernard Loomer. Despite the fact that Loomer's considerations on God are on the face of it radically discontinuous with the classical notions cited above, I will summarize his understanding of God as given in the essay, "The Size of God,"[3] and then conclude by noting the implications of the contrast.

BERNARD LOOMER

Loomer departed from his mentors, Whitehead and Hartshorne, not by eschewing speculation, but by increasingly demanding that speculation stay closer to the data of experience. For Loomer, as for William James and

---

2. See, for example, William Dean's *American Religious Empiricism* (Albany: State University of New York Press, 1986). Dean's fundamental thesis is that "history constructs reality, that history is simply a chain of interpretations, and that whatever might lie outside history lies outside religion, empirically considered" (p. x).

3. *The Size of God: The Theology of Bernard Loomer in Context*, ed. William Dean and Larry E. Axel (Macon, Ga.: Mercer University Press, 1987). Loomer's initial essay is followed by a number of critical responses from theologians such as Nancy Frankenberry and John B. Cobb Jr.

Whitehead, experience denoted the vast flux of physical feelings inundating every momentary process of becoming. Because of our complex embodiment, humans are capable of channeling this vast amount of data first through sensory perception, and then through consciousness and the modes of thought consciousness entails. The earliest, prehensive levels are distilled toward the foci of consciousness. Paradoxically, as consciousness is focused, the pervasive relationality that marks the basic level of existence becomes more diffuse, with its immediacy melded into the more distinctive data produced through consciousness. The "blooming, buzzing confusion" of the world becomes ordered into discrete bits of knowledge.

Value is achieved in this matrix by what Loomer called "stature," or the amount of contrasting experiences of intensity and variety that one could integrate within the self and still maintain one's "integrity and individuality." This calls upon the conscious self to draw more of its primal relational sensitivities into the realm of consciousness itself, expanding one's concerns correlatively with the relations that give rise to one's becoming.

With regard to the evil in the world, this, too, is to be admitted into one's self-integration. The ambiguity of inclusiveness rather than the sharpness of exclusion is the goal. This provides a certain aesthetic resolution to issues of evil: The tragic and the good together have the potentiality to increase the depth and richness of one's ongoing experience. Holding the contrasts together in the fullness of oneself is the achievement of stature.

But stature is not simply contrasting experience, such as the tragic and the good; stature is also the contrast of variety. To open oneself to a variety of cultural experiences—not as a tourist, but as a participant—is again to increase one's stature through increasing breadth. Depth is also involved, insofar as one is open to commitments that involve one fully in the ongoing well-being of another. In each case—contrast, breadth, or depth—the deciding factor is that these elements can be integrated into a unit of harmony, where the many become one. This unity achieved through the integration of the many is of ultimate value in human experience; it is "stature."

Immediately, of course, one must note that stature is necessarily ambiguous. It derives from the stuff of this world, from histories that include genocides as well as great loves, of scenes of rot and decay as well as scenes of beauty surpassed yet again by beauty. The openness to experience that is necessary for the achievement of stature is an openness to the ambiguity of existence—its sanities and insanities, joys and sorrows. Such attenuation to experience is admission of the full complexity of experience into who we are, and the purchase of this price is stature.

If this is the value yielded by experience, what then can we say of that to which we have traditionally ascribed the greatest value, God? *The Size of God* concludes with, "The conception of the stature of God that is presupposed in this essay may be indicated by the speculative suggestion that the world is an interconnected web endeavoring to become a vast socialized unit of experi-

ence with its own processive subjectivity."[4] The implication in this statement is that just as we know and categorize many forms of organized experience that are less complex than the human level, even so there are organized
forms more complex than the individual. Many we know as the complexity
of the very institutions we create, though these exist through intersubjectivity rather than subjectivity. Loomer suggests that the world itself struggles
toward the highest possible unity, which would be the integration of all its
components into a contrasting synthesis of unified experience. "God" is
both the process and the hoped for outcome in the greatest stature possible.

The ambiguity of the process is retained, and the God thus produced is not
a transcendental being possessing all power—rather, the God would be the
unified power of the whole. Evil as well as good inheres in the process, but
it would seem that the bent would be toward the good, given the value of unification. That is, the process would be constructive, retaining values, rather
than destructive. The ancient category of omnipresence would certainly
apply, for nothing actual is beyond the divine milieu, whether that actuality
be relatively good or relatively evil. Omniscience would not apply in the
classical sense—but if such a God is struggling toward its own subjectivity,
then one might posit that its very stature would be an awareness of all its component parts. Yet in Loomer's thought, that subjectivity is only an ambiguous reality at present—in which case "omniscience" in the sense of full
awareness may be a future category. Transcendence in the sense of a God over
and above (or even against) the world would be vastly transformed into a transcendence yet to be—for a God who is the future of the world is a God
whose fullness transcends the current world. Transcendence becomes a temporal and an emergent category, rather than a spatial and static category.

This radical notion of God drawn by Loomer from his radical empiricism puts a new meaning on salvation relative to the issues of human evil.
Oddly enough, they may seem more akin to classical notions of salvation by
grace that enables one to do works of love than is immediately apparent.
Loomer, like Meland and James before him, considers the matrix of experience to be more than we can think (Meland's phrase)—indeed, stature is the
result of pulling more of the matrix into integrated, subjective awareness. A
God who is in the process of becoming "a vast socialized unit of experience with its own processive subjectivity" is necessarily part of the "more"
of our experience; this is the empirical base of Loomer's thinking. But if
this is so, then it is so with regard to every element in the world; the becoming God would be part of the "more" affecting the becoming of each part.
Would not the emerging subjectivity of this God be dependent upon the sub-
jectivities of the parts? And if so, would not the nudge toward greater stature
for each individual be an aspect of God's own stature? In Loomer's development, stature includes "the strength of . . . spirit to encourage others to

---

4. Ibid., p. 51.

become freer in the development of their diversity and uniqueness . . . the power to sustain more complex and enriching tensions . . . the magnanimity of concern to provide conditions that enable others to increase in stature,"[5] all of which seems remarkably like the works of love promoted by classical theology. The classics held that such works were enabled by the grace of God; if the emerging God encourages such stature in the individuals that make up the world, is not this encouragement something like an enabling grace?

Salvation in a Loomerian world would require—necessarily—the cooperation of the world. For salvation could itself be construed as "size." If so, the one who is grasped by this notion of God would view all of the world as more or less of a piece, with the well-being of the world essential to the well-being of each part. The Buddhist saying, "Not one soul enters Nirvana until all enter Nirvana" would apply; each, knowing oneself to be essential to the whole, must cast one's welfare in with the whole. There would be a wholesale need, "for God's sake" and for one's own, to take tragedy or evil anywhere in the world, insofar as possible, into one's own being—not as a voyeur, but as one with a vital interest in the creative outcome, so that one works to overcome the tragedy, redress the evil. In so doing, one is indeed "doing the works of God." And since God is through the whole, would not one then rely on God's enabling force? For such works would be the strengthening of the emergent God, which in turn would reinforce the strength of that God for one's own continuing participation in works of stature. And if God is throughout the relational whole, why could it not be plausible that what one does in one corner of this teeming world might be utilizable by the becoming God in some other corner?

The most prominent aspect of the classical notion is its trinitarianism, and clearly there is no place for such a nonempiricist doctrine within Loomer's work. But the trinity certainly suggested that God is in some sense communal and that the very nature of God requires an irreducible diversity that is nonetheless deepest unity. The Loomerian God is hardly trinitarian—but isn't this notion of God communal in a sense even more radical than the trinitarian mode? And if the trinity includes an irreducible diversity within unity, is it not the case that Loomer's notion of God embodies this notion in extreme ways? Thus while Loomer's empiricist God is not trinitarian, the essentials of that trinitarian God might be seen as clinging to the edges even of its Loomerian replacement. The classical notions die hard—if, indeed, they die within those who are shaped by its history.

These remarks are hardly definitive and are certainly extrapolations of Loomer's amazing suggestion. But they are given in the interests of illustrating

5. Bernard M. Loomer, "S-I-Z-E," *Criterion* 13 (1974), pp. 5-8. Reprinted in *Religious Experience and Process Theology*, ed. Harry James Cargas and Bernard Lee (New York: Paulist, 1976), pp. 69-76.

that what at first might appear to be the most radically opposed construal of God within the radical empiricist school might in fact find odd meeting places in the contrast with classical theology.

This essay, covering so vast a subject as classical theology and the complexities of empirical theology, can hardly hope to do more than indicate some of the features of each and to note the points of contrast and similitude. I am painfully aware of the shortcomings entailed in condensing rich periods of history into a few paragraphs and the many tomes of a writer's thought into several pages. Yet I am bemused by the conviction that the spirits of classical theologians and of empirical theologians are not so far apart after all. They each struggle from their own perspectives in time, culture, and individual temperament to ask the questions concerning our human experience: How is it that we find ourselves in the anguish and ambiguity of an existence which is at once beautiful and ugly, wondrous and terrifying? How might we maximize the good? How is it that we experience the aid of God in maximizing the good—and how shall we understand this God? In the hard work of forging the questions and their possible answers, Christian theology continues to be created.

PART TWO

"Being sure in religion does not entail being certain in theology."

Ian T. Ramsey

CHAPTER FIVE

Empiricism and God

WILLIAM DEAN

INTRODUCTION

The makers of empirical theology have sought to represent what Emerson had called "an original relation to the universe." They were not willing to concede that, because "foregoing generations beheld God and nature face to face," their lot was to be "retrospective," to twist their new world necks to see God through the eyes of others.[1]

The empirical theologians' concept of God can be understood as, in large part, the function of one, distinctly American perspective. This American perspective departs from its European ancestors in that its historicism is more thorough and deep-running. That is, the Americans who adopt this perspective typically argue that to a great extent their world is based on historical experience—in that it is known, tested, and finally made from and by historical interpretations which are free or accidental. Their historicism, nevertheless, is distinctive in being partial. That is, some of what these Americans know, test, and make is accomplished in and through history, but some is accomplished as though it were impervious to history; some is naturalistic-humanistic (referring to natural as well as cultural activities) and some is philosophically idealistic and rationalistic (involving ideals or reasons in some sense independent of natural and cultural activities). This partial or half-way historicism characterizes not only a distinctly American perspective, but also the God specific to this perspective, the God of American

---

1. Ralph Waldo Emerson, "Nature" (the 1836 version), *The Complete Essays and Other Writings of Ralph Waldo Emerson*, ed. Brooks Atkinson (New York: Modern Library, 1940, 1950), p. 3.

empirical theology. In this descriptive essay, written in the early 1990s when ideas of a more complete historicism are entertained, that partiality is prominent. It seems to me to have explanatory importance and to give the empirical theologians consistency with tradition but also to make them vulnerable to challenge.

More than anything else empirical theology is a claim about a people, a claim about that people's religious history, and a claim about that people's God in that people's history. Thus, empirical theology is more about a world than about a method, whether empiricist, realist, naturalist, American, or even historicist. While it is based on experience, uses pragmatic tests, is distinctly American, and is more historicist, perhaps, than any antecedent theology, empirical theology, nevertheless, is first of all, even if unselfconsciously, a claim about what a particular religious history means—just as ancient Hebrew theology was a claim about what a particular religious history means.

Accordingly, for the empirical theologian God is, or should be, largely a reflection of a local, American history. All this said, an adequate account of the distinctiveness of empirical theology's God requires a certain consciousness of method, particularly of the historicism of the empirical theologians.

THE AMERICANNESS OF EMPIRICISM'S GOD

The writings of empirical theologians or philosophers of religion fall primarily in the twentieth century, beginning with Douglas Clyde Macintosh's 1919 *Theology as an Empirical Science*, extending through works by Henry Nelson Wieman, Bernard Meland, and Bernard Loomer, until today. These writings are traceable not only to the philosophies of William James, Alfred North Whitehead, and John Dewey, but to Ralph Waldo Emerson, even to the theology of Jonathan Edwards. These writings are related to the more empirical work of process philosophers of religion and process theologians of the second half of the twentieth century (principally, Charles Hartshorne, John Cobb, Schubert Ogden, and David Griffin), and the socio-historical approach of the "Chicago School" theology of the first half of the twentieth century (George Burman Foster, Shailer Mathews, Gerald Birney Smith, and Shirley Jackson Case).[2] I focus here, however, on the major empirical theologies proper—those of Macintosh, Wieman, Meland, and Loomer—and see their writings in the light of an American lineage.

Consciously or unconsciously, empirical theologians spoke for peoples who

---

2. My own brief attempts to describe the roots of empirical theology and the sources I use in those attempts can be found in *American Religious Empiricism* (Albany: State University of New York Press, 1986), Chapter 1; and *History Making History: The New Historicism in American Religious Thought* (Albany: State University of New York Press, 1988), Chapters 2 and 5.

had faced perilous tests of historical survival. Most seventeenth- and eighteenth-century Americans stood in natural and social history almost naked— unable to clothe themselves sufficiently in the European traditions from which they had physically removed themselves. Immigrants of the nineteenth and twentieth centuries, along with Africans throughout American history, stood equally naked in history, but with less confidence that they were running the show. They were united in asking whether, within this new and brutish American history, they could find God . . . or a version of God that made particular sense to them.

Empirical theologians answered by locating their God in their history, in the midst of their historical struggle. Like the ancient Hebrews, they wandered in strange lands and through strange events; and like the Hebrews, they had little choice but to find God in those lands or not at all. But while their God stood within history, it was not totally dependent on history. Not only did they typically understand their God to be in some respect independent of historical influences, but in some respect to be irrelative to the local particularities of history, or absolute.

For the empirical theologians, history was, first of all, natural. Like Emerson,[3] the empirical theologians found themselves in the thick of natural process (*natura naturans*) rather than contemplating from a distance the natural scene (*natura naturata*). Contrary to European convention, nature and science were integral to American theology. The God of the Americans lived at the center rather than on the edges of nature. The culture of the Americans sprang largely from rather than stood beside nature and science.

Yet, the empirical theologians retained for their God a moral character impervious to pressures of natural or human social history. This divine imperviousness parallels a self-ascribed American imperviousness to history. The Americans understood themselves to be innocent of many of the historical corruptions of other peoples and thus to be in God's eyes an historically exceptional people, God's New Israel. This combination of divine and national independence from history parallels a Hebrew sense of divine and national independence from history: both communities credited their God with exceptional justice and themselves, as God's chosen people, with exceptional status among the world's peoples. Thus for both communities, while God is so deep within historical forces that God can be found only within history, God's moral character is independent of history's prevailing corruptions.

Thus, empirical theology's concept of God is distinct and parallels a certain distinctivenesses in the American self-understanding. In both cases, the distinctiveness is formed by an extreme ambivalence about history: first, history encloses all that is real; second, history is to be escaped. On one

---

3. Ralph Waldo Emerson, "Nature" (from the second series of essays published in 1844), in *Ralph Waldo Emerson*, p. 410.

hand, nothing escapes historical process, so that even God is its creature. The Americans jettisoned in a land that is strange and largely uncoupled from the institutions of Europe, had little choice but to find themselves and their God in just their own vague and solitary historical wanderings or not at all. Accordingly, for them God is a God of and within the natural and cultural history of America. On the other hand, historical processes do not touch the exceptionalist stature of God's people or the character of God. Americans are in one sense free from history, distinguished (by means of their divine election) from all other peoples, who are sullied by the ambiguities of historical time and place. Appropriately, their God, like nothing else in history, is purely just.

In these respects empirical theology and its God are distinctive, even as empirical theology moves from Jonathan Edwards, whose learning was so European that his Americanness was unconscious, to Bernard Loomer, who was so American (he spent one hour outside the United States) that his Europeanness was unconscious. Empirical theology is heavily affected by the fact that the Americans were physically separated from and, to a large extent, psychically weaned from European ecclesiastical and cultural institutions, from the traditions of these institutions, and from the God of which they spoke. It was as though the Europeans, steeped in an ancient culture, could rest in the bosom of the ancient God who lived beyond history and thereby could afford to be optimistic about their God and pessimistic about this world. Their God's power was unchecked by the powers of history and, thus, capable of intervening in history to rescue them from history's stain and annihilation. Equally, not looking to natural or human history as the final court of appeal, they could afford to be fashionably insouciant, even pessimistic about history. For the Europeans life in the long run was secure if the right spiritual moves were made, even if life in its immediate historical context was theologically vacuous. It was different for a distinctively American group of Americans. Their God, even if its character was insulated from historical corruption, nevertheless lived quite within history. That is, although God was perfectly good and had universal influence on the world that centered on America, God's power was imperfect, blocked, and subverted by what history would allow. While this meant that history day by day was filled with theological and religious urgency, it also meant that nothing was finally secure, for God could be overpowered by history and history, in all its terror and ambiguity, was the final arena of human salvation. Even if others misread them (just as they misread Emerson) as naive and optimistic, the Americans of the empirical theologian felt almost-naked in the often destructive swirl of history and knew that neither was their God altogether clothed.

But for the empirical theologian the American lot was not quite tragic.[4]

---

4. Sidney Hook not withstanding; see Sidney Hook, "Pragmatism and the Tragic Sense of Life," *Contemporary American Philosophy*, Second Series, ed. John E. Smith (New York: Humanities Press, 1970), pp. 170-193.

What the Americans lost in security they gained in intimacy. When their God fell into natural and social history, this gave to nature and to politics a religious significance unknown to Europeans (but not unknown to the ancient Hebrews). While this natural and political significance was not guaranteed by a God whose power was unlimited because protected from the limits of history, it was rooted in a divine character that was unambiguously good. The God of the empirical theologians was not totally present in history, for God's character was perfect in an ahistorical way. Accordingly, where history failed, it simply deviated from God's will so that there, at that point, God was absent from history and history was evil. Not only was the American's God not totally naked in history; neither were the Americans. In their religiousness they could appeal to ideal possibilities, call them God's will, and proceed confidently with a moral program for history, a program superior to what history ever would deliver. In this respect the empirical theologians stood with Reinhold Niebuhr, who could include as a part of his political "realism" the notion that Christians must issue mandates for history that are "impossible possibilities." That is, because there is a divine morality superior yet relevant to history's morality, it is appropriate to ask history to accomplish what history would inevitably fail to accomplish.[5] Thus, the God of the empirical theologians did not entirely float in history but instead offered a moral stillpoint in the chaos of historical processes and pluralities.

Empirical theology moved closer to history than typical European theologies, but stopped short of total immersion. Empirical theologians moved God from beyond history to a particular position within history—just that position at which God's power is limited by history's power while God's character is protected from history's moral and spiritual ambiguities. The empirical theologians would not concede that God is so naked to history that even God's character is as local as any historical contingency is local; and, with the exception of Loomer, they would not concede that God is as ambiguous as any historical event is ambiguous. And in this, too, the empirical theologians reflected their American culture, which saw itself as never quite naked to the ambiguities of natural and cultural history. Empirical theology, then, was and is a claim about history. It is the claim that both Americans and their God are almost historical, almost naked within the processes of natural and social history.

This was a vision that grew out of a modern people's struggle with natural and human social forces. Lost in America, pressed for survival, unbalanced by the steadying pressure of old institutions and old traditions, the Americans

---

5. Reinhold Niebuhr argues that *agape* "has its primary justification in an 'essential reality' which transcends the realities of history, namely, the character of God." *The Nature and Destiny of Man: A Christian Interpretation*, vol. 2 (New York: Scribner's, 1949), p. 96.

were an uncommonly agonistic, a struggling, even a violent people. It made
no sense to see history as controlled from beyond by an absolute God; no
benign powers were simply given; there was no alternative but to wrest
from the maw of history whatever contributes to survival. But this picture was
not merely grim. Something of the European sensibility survived, something about God's old faithfulness was preserved: through historical reality
there shone a quality, even a perfection, that could be (or better, had to be)
trusted. Thus, for the empirical theologians the Americans were not only a
violent, but a morally idealistic people—a condition that alone would seem
to explain America's baffling wars in Vietnam and Iraq, and its righteous
yearning to own guns and to box.[6] The God of the empirical theologians
reflected that strange combination of violence and moral idealism.

THE MODERNITY OF EMPIRICISM'S GOD

Empirical theologians seek this distinctively American God not on the basis
of authority but through experience of history. The moral idealism of the
empirical theologians is evident in what is always their basic empirical contention: that the value realized in history cannot be exhaustively explained by
reference to ordinary historical forces alone. History is marked, or vectored;
it bears the stamp of something; it is valuable in ways that cannot be explained
except through postulating the influence of something perfect on the course
of history. The grimness of the empirical theologians is evident in their
acknowledgement that the ambiguities of history are inescapable. Their
moral idealism leads them to affirm that history, nevertheless and ironically, suggests something beyond ambiguity. Thus, even if history does not
move to a destiny beyond history, that does not mean it moves in no direction at all. Even if history is not controlled by a perfection outside of history, it may be influenced by a perfection within history—a perfection with
which people might cooperate to make history better than what otherwise it
might be.

The empirical theologians amplify this claim about history by using language about God. God is a power within this world that encourages history,
as much as any finite power might encourage history, to become better than
it would otherwise be. God is the inexplicable vector in history, coaxing it to
greater value.

When they spoke of history's movement toward greater value, the empirical theologians on occasion may have been just the optimists and progres-
sivists their neo-orthodox critics charged them with being. However, the
empirical theologians knew that history is irredeemably spoiled—because
God, while morally perfect, has not the power single-handedly to right what

---

6. See Joyce Carol Oates, *On Boxing* (Garden City, N.Y.: Dolphin/Doubleday, 1987)
for an account of the combination of brutality and idealism in this sport.

is wrong. Further, because there is no recourse to a suprahistorical world, history's ambiguous accomplishments remain the only accomplishments there are. (Some optimism.)

Whether optimistic or pessimistic, in associating God with history's moral advance, the empirical theologians remain fundamentally consistent with Jewish and Christian scriptures. Typically, the Hebrew scriptures see God as the central but not overriding determinant in the history of Israel's spiritual, political, and military life and see the nation as religious to the extent that it reacts to history as if history were guided by God. Equally, the Christian scriptures see God as the central but not overriding determinant in the history played out in the life of Jesus and in the history preceding, surrounding, and succeeding Jesus; and one is religious in a Christian way to the extent that one sees God acting in the life and history flowing to, through, and from Jesus.

While the empirical theologians concur with biblical traditions about God's action in history, they (except for Macintosh) reject those Western theological traditions that understand God to be omnipotent in that action. This omnipotence derives from a God-world duality which they all (even Macintosh) reject and in which God's extra-historical status enables God to do anything in and to history. These latter theological traditions, the empirical theologians tended to claim, entered Western religious thought out of a largely mistaken loyalty to ancient Greek dualism and to modern European philosophies that revived that dualism. For the empirical theologians, then, God is a creature known and operative within history, even if God does not, because God cannot, control history. Rather, God's power is not absolute but relative to what historical circumstances will permit.

Empirical theologians suggest,[7] and I elaborate, one way of arguing that the relativity of God's powers is simply a corollary of the absoluteness of God's goodness. First, if God's power were absolute, there is no way to understand how God could be absolutely good, for, given history's evil, a God with absolute power would cause history's evil as well as its goodness. Second, if God's power were absolute, God's love would be one-sided, immutual, even tyrannical—and, thus, hardly love. With absolute power, God could act on history but could not react to history. An absolute God could not permit independent actions by other historical players (even if, incomprehensibly, they had any power at all, after God had absolute power), because this would locate God's power in a field of interacting powers, thus making God's power relative to other powers. But if creatures have no real powers, God cannot respond to historical creatures simply because they could never initiate action to which God might truly respond. Thus, if God's

---

7. This reasoning is fully explicated only in the writings of process theologians; see, especially, David R. Griffin, *God, Power, and Evil: A Process Theodicy* (Philadelphia: Westminster, 1976) and "Creation out of Chaos and the Problem of Evil," *Encountering Evil: Live Options in Theodicy*, ed. Stephen T. Davis (Atlanta: John Knox, 1981), pp. 101-118.

power were absolute, God would be incapable of entering into anything analogous to the highest form of human love—which is reactive as well as active. Accordingly, if God is to love, God's power must not be absolute, even if this spoils what otherwise would have been the perfect effects God would have had on the course of history. Finally, that this good God's power is limited, the empirical theologians said, is empirically obvious: look at the moral ambiguities of history.

However, the empirical theologians, with the exception of Loomer, remained consistent even with classical Christian theology in claiming that God is perfect in character, even if not in power. God is absolutely good— that is, God's moral guidance is absolutely good (relative to nothing evil) and, thus, should always be honored and served. Further, this perfect character is everywhere available (which assumes that, just as God's goodness is uniform, so must history be uniform in some crucial ways).

Accordingly, empirical theologians conform to the modern spirit, which seeks formal and uniform structures in history. They aim to discover the real and uniform structure of history and to work out human meaning by reference to that structure as it stands and as it is discovered. Specifically, they aim to discover (not create) God's absolute, perfect, and uniform character as it operates throughout all history.

This discovery, in turn, enables humans to augment God's finite power with their own finite actions. There may be a tendency to moral growth in history but, because that tendency's power is limited, it will fail if it is ignored or rejected by historical creatures. Accepting the challenge implicit in this, the empirical theologians propose that religion's pragmatic justification is the moral action it promotes. The empirical theologians' modernist task, thus, is to discover the divine process as it has operated universally and eternally in natural and cultural history, and then to collaborate with it.

Today this characterization of God and the religious task can assume greater definiteness when it is compared to the new alternatives of constructivism, pluralism, and an as yet unarticulated relationalism. First, the empirical theologians clearly do not accept the postmodernist task of constructing (as well as discovering) the divine process.[8] While humans through their interpretations might construct their natural and social contexts, they do not construct their divine context; they do not even seek to alter the moral character implicit in history's course. Thus, empirical theologians seek only obediently to serve history's universal and uniform vector toward moral growth. Second, the empirical theologians do not accept the postmodern idea that histories are local and plural. While national histories, for example, may be radically different and informed by different social and intellectual qualities, the nature of God's action in history is always

8. Most obviously, see Mark C. Taylor, *Erring: A Postmodern Theology* (Chicago: University of Chicago Press, 1984).

and everywhere the same, so that religious history in this sense is uniform and singular. Third, when they choose obedience, the empirical theologians give primacy to God itself, rather than to relations with God. The empirical theologians may believe that people should live for the relations (of, say, love) they mutually construct; and they may be repelled by the suggestion that anyone should give primacy, instead, to the other and its constructs, seeking only to imitate the other. Nevertheless, the empirical theologians refuse to give primacy to the relations between people and God and believe that the religious task is to serve God's purposes rather than for people to develop a constructive interaction between those purposes and their own. Where relationality is paramount, the emphasis is on the evolving relations between those in relation and on the constructive contribution of all parties to the relationality; where imitation is paramount, the emphasis is on the object of imitation and its construction, so what is sought is the conformity of the imitator to the imitated. The empirical theologians were unwilling to make the changing parties to relations, human as well as divine, the shapers of the deepest realities. That is, the empirical theologians see God, at least God's character, as an object for human imitation, rather than as a party to causal interaction. To risk an analogy, by the empirical theologians God is understood on the analogy of a timeless friend whom one venerates rather than on the analogy of an attentive friend with whom one historically evolves.

Here the empirical theologians follow classical Christian theologians. For both groups, humans have no local or general affect on God's own character. Humans may choose whether or not to sustain relations with God; but if these relations are sustained, they must be treated as coming from God and passively accepted. This is simply a corollary of the absoluteness of God's character; because God's character (the value-generating energies implicit in the world) is absolute, formally it will remain as it was regardless of how humans change. That is, where the character of God is concerned, empirical theologians affirm the classical aseity of God. The character of God is relative to nothing.

Thus the empirical theologians accepted rather completely what the postmodernists would call the modern "myth of the given."[9] While people are free to interpret God's character, in this they guess what is. They do not augment their guesses by their own constructive interpretations, assuming that their interpretations will have some effect on what will be. Creatures are free to support or to work against God's moral "intentions" but not to change them; they are there for discovery but not for creative interpretation, if creative interpretation means that the interpretation alters the identity of the

9. See Wilfrid Sellars on "The Myth of the Given" in "Empiricism and the Philosophy of Mind," in Herbert Feigl and Michael Scriven, eds. *Minnesota Studies in the Philosophy of Science*, vol. 1 (Minneapolis: University of Minnesota Press, 1956), pp. 253-329.

interpreted. When it comes to relations with the deepest character to history, the empirical theologians adopt a venerative stance, opposing the fullest implication of what one day would become the postmodernist's conceit that the observer in the very act of observing always creates to some extent the observed. The empiricism of the empirical theologians is always appreciative or descriptive rather than critical and constructive.

FOUR EMPIRICAL THEOLOGIANS AND THEIR GODS

My account is far too manifold to permit more than a very sketchy and selective historical corroboration of its definition of empirical theology's God. The many elements I have set forth can only be alluded to and then only as the occasion warrants in my commentaries on Macintosh, Wieman, Meland, and Loomer.

MACINTOSH

In the first paragraph of his 1919 *Theology as an Empirical Science*, the first book in explicitly empirical theology, Macintosh calls for an academic "counter-attack, having as its object the recovery of a scientific status for theology." He renounces not the ambitions of the medieval "science of God" but the timidity of modern theologians who retreat before criticism emanating largely from the new sciences.[10] To make science "the best friend in disguise that religion has ever had,"[11] Macintosh would adopt a scientific approach; he would open with weak, formal, provisional, but experientially prompted hypotheses and then test and refine those hypotheses empirically. He would proceed "'from the vague whole to the definite whole.'"[12] Wary of a pragmatism that ignores verification and accepts whatever has desirable results, Macintosh wants a scientific pragmatism that would require "full verification"—meaning that definition finally must be shown to correlate in some way to experience.[13] He is equally wary of rationalistic, mystical, psychological, and historical approaches to experience (particularly those of Ernst Troeltsch and Albrecht Ritschl), calling them all subjectivistic. What Macintosh valued in what he called the scientific approach was its realism, its insistence on verification to confirm that there is "a numerical oneness, an existential identity between the object as perceived and the object as inde-

---

10. Douglas Clyde Macintosh, *Theology as an Empirical Science* (New York: Arno Press, 1980), p. 1. See Preston Warren, *Out of the Wilderness: Douglas Clyde Macintosh's Journeys Through the Grounds and Claims of Modern Thought* (New York: Peter Lang, 1989) for a complete overview.

11. Ibid., p. 5.

12. Ibid., p. 27.

13. Ibid., p. 23.

pendently real."[14] Accordingly, Macintosh models theology on science's empiricism. The resultant "empirical theology" would first establish "theological laws" ("statements of what in human experience God can be depended upon for, under certain conditions"), then generate "theological theories" (what the religious "object must *be* . . . in order to account for what the object *does*").[15] He first would establish how God acts and then infer what God is; he would move from the promises and deeds of God to the nature of God.

Macintosh asks: Can we not learn from religious behaviors what difference God makes and, thus, who God is, just as the sciences have learned from natural behaviors how nature works and, thus, what general principles describe nature? If this is accomplished, the scientific theologian can hope to restore "the predictive element to its central place in prophecy; on the basis of the laws of empirical theology he ought to be able to guide individuals to the religious adjustment that conditions the most desirable religious experience, and to predict, within limits, the results of the right adjustment."[16] Theology cannot warrant serious attention until it learns empirically and pragmatically how to describe what God does and who God is.

When theology becomes a *bona fide* empirical science, it will become "the one and only 'New Theology,' destined to displace all rivals for the honor of that title." Further, this will make theology philosophically important. Is not philosophy's impotence attributable to the fact "that she has been waiting, without realizing it, for theology to become an empirical science? When once this has been accomplished, the way will have been opened, for the first time in the history of thought, for the making of a philosophy at the same time adequately spiritual in its appreciations and adequately scientific in its method."[17]

However enthusiastic this call for method, Macintosh's ostensible objective was theological content: the practical work of discovering specifically how God works and thus who God is, thereby to propose how people should adjust themselves to God. To begin this inquiry Macintosh introduces premises he considers obvious: 1) that God is dependable; and 2) that through Jesus we learn that God promotes changes of behavior that are primarily moral. These are premises, mere working hypotheses, suggested by what seems basic to experience. First, according to Macintosh, we know God is dependable because "we simply assume (in the scientifically tentative or empirical way) that God *has* character and will therefore be found depend-

---

14. Douglas Clyde Macintosh, *The Problem of Religious Knowledge* (New York: Harper & Brothers, 1940), p. 5. Macintosh goes on to call his position a "critical monistic realism," wherein "there is a core of existential or numerical identity, a practical identity or overlapping of the immediately experienced and the independently real" (p. 6.).

15. Macintosh, *Theology as an Empirical Science*, pp. 41,43.

16. Ibid., p. 41.

17. Ibid., pp. 45, 46.

able."[18] Second, we assume that Jesus's life is exemplary and that Jesus sought above all "the promotion of moral efficiency in the interests of true human welfare."[19] God, we will assume for the time being, is not only dependable but, above all, moral.

Macintosh's empirical argument is that these assumptions can be confirmed and given specific content through empirical-pragmatic analysis. This confirmation is worked out through the analysis of religion. In 1919 Macintosh argues that "the history of practical religion may fairly be regarded as a prolonged empirical investigation."[20] In 1931 he amplifies this by contending that religions are extended experiments, seeking by trial and error to understand and to adopt divine values.[21] Not only are religions differentiated from each other, but they are characterized by progress, or the achievement of better understandings and adjustments to divine values. Now through the analysis of the history of religious experimentation, we verify a posteriori not only that God is, after all, dependable and seeks moral results, but what God's moral objectives are. Thus, in his 1940 *The Problem of Religious Knowledge* Macintosh pithily states, "We discover God as divinely functioning reality when we find what we can always get by praying for it, in the sense of entering into the right religious adjustment with reference to it, the rightness of adjustment being itself indicated by the dependableness of the result."[22] Thus we can move from assumptions about God to verified truths about God.

In short, Macintosh argues that when we look at our moral experience we are led to an inescapable conclusion: There is a process occurring at the deepest level of nature and history; it promotes certain kinds of moral activities with utter reliability. Macintosh concludes, "God is a constant Source of unfailing spiritual power."[23] Our obligation is to adjust our behavior to this Source—thereby, through collaboration, to make possible what otherwise would not be possible. "On condition of the right religious adjustment . . . God the Holy Spirit produces the specific moral results desired."[24] Macintosh is laconic when it comes to naming just what moral results God would promote; but they appear to center on "unselfish love toward God and man," which, in turn, leads to beneficial physiological effects and to secular and ecclesiastical community.[25] Finally, Macintosh argues briefly that God is a personal Being but one who, unlike all other per-

18. Ibid., p. 141.
19. Ibid., p. 143.
20. Ibid., p. 5.
21. "Experimental Realism in Religion," in *Religious Realism*, ed. Douglas Clyde Macintosh (New York: Macmillan, 1931), pp. 318-323.
22. Macintosh, *Problem of Religious Knowledge*, p. 196.
23. Macintosh, *Theology as an Empirical Science*, p. 141.
24. Ibid., p. 148.
25. Ibid., pp. 152-156.

sons, both experiences and influences the entire world.[26]

Ironically, after setting forth this new scientific theology, Macintosh then proceeds to defend essentially prescientific theological ideas: God's absoluteness ("the absolute sufficiency for man's religious needs,"[27] which would seem to require something like omnipotence) and God's moral perfection. Macintosh saw no immediate problem with the orthodoxy of these concepts, arguing that consistency with traditional concepts of God might be taken "as ground for satisfaction rather than complaint."[28]

Further, Macintosh argues repeatedly, there is no problem in the fact that each of his concepts of God begins as an assumption. Not only are those assumptions sparked by experiences,[29] but as assumptions they function just as assumptions do in science. "The religious expert has the same *logical* right to presuppose it [the existence of God] as the physicist has to presuppose the existence of electricity. *That* it is, is sufficiently sure on the basis of prescientific experience; scientific method is to be employed to find out more exactly just *what* it is."[30] Furthermore, these "unverified elements in scientific theory may turn out to be exceedingly fruitful in directing further experimental research."[31]

To acknowledge that speculation plays a necessary role in all research programs is merely fashionable in the late twentieth century.[32] What Macintosh fails to note is that this speculation affects in particular ways the outcome of the analysis it launches. When he assumes God is dependable (both universally effective and undeviating from an original purpose) and moral, he establishes a research agenda capable of exploring and adjusting to just those characteristics and only those characteristics. This agenda omits entirely, for example, the opposite notions and the outcomes to which their adoption might lead: 1) the absence of dependability in God (that God is local and that the purpose of God can be changed) and 2) the moral ambiguity of

26. Ibid., pp. 189-190.

27. Ibid., p. 162.

28. Macintosh, *Problem of Religious Knowledge*, p. 200.

29. Macintosh, *Theology as an Empirical Science*, pp. 160-161.

30. Macintosh, *Problem of Religious Knowledge*, p. 192.

31. Ibid., p. 201.

32. I refer to the literature spawned either by Thomas Kuhn's *The Nature of Scientific Revolutions* (Chicago: University of Chicago Press, 1972) or, more importantly, by quantum physics. For the latter, almost randomly, one could name Dietrick E. Thomsen, "Going Bohr's Way in Physics," *Science News* 129 (January 11, 1986), pp. 26-27; John Archibald Wheeler, "Beyond the Black Hole," in *Some Strangeness in the Proportion: A Centennial Symposium to Celebrate the Achievements of Albert Einstein*, ed. Harry Woolf (Reading, Mass.: Addison-Wesley, 1980), pp. 341-375; Gunther S. Stent, "Hermeneutics and the Analysis of Complex Biological Systems," in *Evolution at a Crossroads: The New Biology and the New Philosophy of Science*, ed. David J. Depew and Bruce H. Weber (Cambridge: MIT Press, 1985), pp. 209-225.

God.[33] If these opposite concepts were adopted, they might well illuminate different worlds and/or alter local worlds in unpredictable ways, thus becoming empirically verifiable. When Macintosh not only unselfconsciously assumes that God must be dependable and morally perfect, he may find verification; but this may be only partial verification at best—rather than strict correspondence of his description to what must be universally and eternally the objective case. In fact, not only does Macintosh fail to confirm a correspondence theory of truth realism, but he may have confirmed the very relativity he opposed. Further, he set a particular course for the empirical theologians that were to succeed him.

I point to both the strength and, perhaps, the weakness of Macintosh's partial historicism. As I have noted, his concept of God does conform in important ways to the historic tradition. Nevertheless, the coherence of Macintosh's proposal might be more intelligible today if he had either abandoned empiricism and accepted the dependability and moral perfection of God or embraced his empiricism, but acknowledged that it could indicate nothing more than the dependability and moral perfection of God for D.C. Macintosh or for his Christian community. On his own admission, Macintosh begins by assuming the truth of several highly specific, Western, Christian notions of God—e.g., based not only on Jesus as the world's moral exemplar but on the specifically Christian tradition of the absoluteness of God, the aseity (the complete self-dependence) of God,[34] and the perfection of God ("we must have a perfect God, or we can have no God at all"[35]). Does the very specificity of Macintosh's Christianness deconstruct his own critical realism? Has not his very Christianness introduced an ineradicable arbitrariness, contingency, and relativity into his view of the world? How then does he claim for these same views a universal "reality"—that they describe the entire world as it is, apart from the religious observer's influence on the world? Equally, what happens to Macintosh's aim to discover "real" comprehensive and static theological laws and to perform theological prediction in an ostensibly uniform world? Or if Macintosh's realism is ahistorical, unaffected by local dynamics of history, is that ahistorical realism compatible with his historicist empiricism?

WIEMAN

Henry Nelson Wieman was Macintosh's most immediate and prominent successor, although Wieman makes little mention of Macintosh. Wieman also wanted a theology based on science's empirical and pragmatic methods.

33. See, e.g., C. G. Jung, *Answer to Job*, trans. R.F.C. Hull (New York: Meridian, 1960).
34. Macintosh, *Theology as an Empirical Science*, p. 181.
35. Ibid., p. 164.

At the beginning of his theological career, in his 1926 *Religious Experience and Scientific Method*, Wieman states that "all knowledge must depend ultimately upon science, for science is nothing else than the refined process of knowing."[36] Like Macintosh, Wieman did not allow this to drive him, except perhaps briefly in mid-career, to anything like a positivistic epistemology. Just as Macintosh allowed pre-scientific experiences to play a role in the formulation of hypotheses, Wieman recognized that most important religious hypotheses depended for their formulation on vague and noncognitive experiences beyond the reach of rigorous, scientific scrutiny.[37] Nevertheless, Wieman, like Macintosh, adopted scientific methods to develop and test that sort of religious truth that could be developed and tested with any precision at all. He too wanted to avoid dependence on subjective experience, not because it is unimportant, but because its relativity and arbitrariness threaten scientific realism.

If Macintosh's primary interest was religious epistemology (how to know God), Wieman's primary interest was soteriology (how to be transformed through relation to God). Accordingly, if Macintosh's concept of God must be inferred from his epistemological commentary, Wieman's concept of God must be inferred form his soteriological commentary.

The highest human need is to evolve creatively, to seek new growth and to surpass old growth. God is simply that in the world that fosters this growth. Religion is the name for activities that promote this new growth. Religion, like science, is based on experience; but while science describes the regularities of life, religion promotes the evolution beyond these stated regularities. Science and religion are interdependent, for all regularity needs novel improvement, and all novelty needs the discipline of what is regular. "Religion needs the constraint, guidance, and tests of scientific method just as much as scientific method needs the freedom, spontaneity, and creative impulsiveness of religious experience."[38] And, again, God is what fosters religious experience.

Reasoning from effect to cause, there is no doubt that God exists. People do creatively depart from previous regularities; for this they must depend on something; and God is that Something on which they depend. People do base their creative action on experience; and all experience is experience of something; God is simply the name for that object of experience that fosters this creativity.[39] Wieman assumes that growth is an effect and, thus, that

---

36. Henry Nelson Wieman, *Religious Experience and Scientific Method* (Carbondale and Edwardsville: Southern Illinois University Press, 1971), p. 23.

37. See, e.g., Wieman's rebuttals to Randolph Crump Miller, Daniel Day Williams, and, especially, to Bernard Eugene Meland in *The Empirical Theology of Henry Nelson Wieman*, ed. Robert W. Bretall (Carbondale and Edwardsville: Southern Illinois University Press, 1963).

38. Wieman, *Religious Experience and Scientific Method*, p. 132.

39. Ibid., pp. 9, 10, 29.

it has a cause beyond itself, and he calls this cause "God." Calvinistic theo-centrist that he is, Wieman is assured that human growth (the highest human good) cannot be self-caused, independent good. Thus, a person must rec-ognize that the source of this dependent good is "the grace of God alone and not his own reason or sense of value or other human power."[40] Of course, in some situations human collaboration is a necessary cause of human growth ("in many cases [the growth of value] could not occur at all if men did not assist"[41]); but this does not detract from the fact that God also is always a nec-essary cause of human growth. God is that something acting on the histori-cal process that cannot be found entirely within that process but that is a necessary cause for all the good that occurs within the historical process. And, apparently, God is not local or relative to any particular history but is the necessary cause for human good whenever or wherever it occurs. That is, as necessary cause for human good, God is absolute and universal.

Of course, to be assured of God's existence is not to be assured of how God fosters creativity. Thus, Wieman's task is not so much to ask whether God exists, as it is to ask what we need to know about God if we are to best exercise our religious freedom. Wieman answers the latter question most directly in his 1946 *The Source of Human Good*, where God is called the "creative good" that fosters history's actual "created event." The creat-ed event, the movement beyond past regularities, can be analyzed: 1) It is receptivity to meanings different from or deeper than one's own meanings; 2) it is integration of these new meanings with old meanings; 3) it is devel-opment of wider conceptualities, capable of including new with old mean-ings; 4) it is the use of these wider meanings to form wider and more pro-found communities. God as the source of the created event is the "creative process working in our midst which transforms the human mind and the world relative to the human mind."[42] Thus, the task of people is to be recep-tive to the creative event in order better to avail themselves of God's cre-ativity.

Finally, in all this God is unambiguously good. The "creative good" is pure-ly good, and its effects on "created goods" are purely good. As Wieman insists in *Normative Psychology of Religion*, God is the supreme value; the supreme value is good; and what is good is unambiguously good: that is, "good is good and evil is evil regardless of their relative quantities and their relative power."[43]

Some of the questions asked about Macintosh's God might be addressed to Wieman's, because his historicism also is a partial historicism. First, the moral perfection and universal influence of Wieman's God brings that God

---

40. Wieman, *Source of Human Good*, p. 49.

41. Henry Nelson Wieman and Regina Westcott-Wieman, *Normative Psychology of Religion* (Westport, Conn.: Greenwood Press, 1971), p. 52.

42. Wieman, *Source of Human Good*, p. 17.

43. Wieman and Westcott-Wieman, *Normative Psychology of Religion*, p. 50.

clearly into the Christian tradition. Second, there are the tensions introduced when Wieman's historically particular empiricism is brought face-to-face with God's transcendence of historical particularity. Jesus, the prime empirical object, initiated a chain of social and historical events in which the creative event was lifted "from the subterranean depths to the level of domination." This chain of events was specific and canalized; it began in the life of the first Christians, was "perpetuated in history. Otherwise, it could not reach you and me."[44] Further, the very empirical method that equips people to appreciate this historical locus of inheritance was derived from a specifically Jewish-Christian insight, wherein "the sovereign good works creatively in history," rather than, as with the Greeks, through static forms that emanate from beyond history.[45] Further, it is Wieman's highly particular Calvinist theocentrism (or equivalent assumptions) that was to convince people of the necessity of God. But, as with Macintosh, readers might ask, How can all this historical particularity generate universal claims about God? Why are the four parts of the creative event (the sub-events) not confined to the Christian history to which Wieman refers? How is God uncontaminated by history's evils, thus to remain unambiguously good in all historical situations?

MELAND

Bernard Meland and Bernard Loomer can be read as successors to Wieman. Meland is primarily what might be called an appreciative thinker, rather than an epistemological or soteriological thinker. His 1976 *Fallible Forms and Symbols* argues from beginning to end that theology's great enemy is the demand for clarity. By contrast, Meland believes that theology's highest obligation is to become as open as possible to whatever is ultimate, even if that leads to murky language and untied ends of thought. Accordingly, he looked with deep suspicion on Wieman's rigorous functionalism—as well as on Charles Hartshorne's rationalism and on the process theologians' commitment to Alfred North Whitehead's metaphysics. Meland found it demented, absurd in a quite uncomic way, to insist that experience of what is deeper-than-human bow before the human demand for clarity. If there was anything Meland thought wrong-headed, it was the desire to make knowledge of God empirical in some reputedly scientific way. Yet he remained an empiricist, only now looking to the errant margins of experience rather than to some core, "scientific" order in experience. Meland chose an appreciative openness to whatever appears to be the realities of faith, even as they violate theological schemes. He looked to William James's radical empiricism as a way to be open (whatever the costs) to the full range of

44. Wieman, *Source of Human Good*, p. 42.
45. Ibid., p. 7.

experience, not just to experience with functional or experimental application.[46]

Thus, in his last major book, Meland will say, "I have recoiled from trying to envisage or to define God in any complete, metaphysical or ontological sense, preferring instead to confine attention to such empirical notions
as *the creative act of God* and *the redemptive work of God in history*." In short,
Meland will define God by reference to the historical events that he interprets
to be the effects of God. Meland allows that "much of the meaning we appear
to find in life we bring to it"; nevertheless, Meland will balance this apparent Kantianism with a Jamesian and Bergsonian realism: "the nexus of relationships that forms our existence is not projected, it is given." Meland proceeds, then, to describe the divine effectiveness as "this goodness in existence
which we do not create, but which creates and saves us."[47] God, so conceived, is a creativity operating within the broad "Creative Passage" of existence. As people receive this creativity, largely through myth and symbol, they
are enabled to be good in ways that exceed their own ways of being good.

However nuanced Meland's last major statement on God, it remains fundamentally consistent with his comments on God from the 1930s through the
1970s. God is a term to refer to a creativity operative in history that enables
people to be sensitive and good in ways they could not be by themselves.
Despite his skepticism, Meland has a distinct concept of God. According
to Tyron Inbody, "Meland's pluralism stands between Wieman's monism
and Loomer's pantheism."[48] Unlike Wieman or Macintosh, Meland will say:
"The very assumption, in fact, that there is a single organic tendency at work
in the universe which may be designated God, seems an over-simplifica-
tion of the facts. . . . The richest reality may not be the One, but the Many."
Or he will say that the sustaining activities in life, while they may be conceptually synthesized, "cannot be abstracted as a single behavior" . . . but are
more accurately seen as "a community of activities, rather than a single
behavior."[49] Nevertheless, unlike Loomer, Meland is unwilling to identify God
with all creative processes whatsoever, evil as well as good. The consequence, Inbody suggests, is that Meland's "naturalistic God stands between
Wieman's singular and undifferentiated goodness as an object of devotion and

---

46. See Bernard Eugene Meland, *Higher Education and the Human Spirit* (Chicago:
University of Chicago Press, 1953), Chapter 5.

47. This and preceding three quotations in Bernard E. Meland, *Fallible Forms and
Symbols: Discourses on Method in a Theology of Culture* (Philadelphia: Fortress 1976),
p. 151, emphasis in original.

48. Tyron Inbody, "Meland's Naturalistic God," in *New Essays in Religious
Naturalism*, ed. Creighton Peden and Larry Axel (Macon, Ga.: Mercer University Press,
forthcoming).

49. Bernard Meland, "Toward a Valid View of God," *Harvard Theological Review*
24 (July 1931), p. 203; Bernard Meland, *Modern Man's Worship* (New York: Harper &
Brothers, 1934), p. 185.

Loomer's undifferentiated power of nature."[50] For Meland God can be identified with the sources of creativity *only to the extent that they promote goodness*. God, quite simply for Meland, "is a structure of infinite goodness."[51]

But again, the same conundrum arises for Meland: Given the fact that God can be known only at the margins of historical sensibility and only through historical forms and symbols of local cults and cultures, how on empirical grounds does Meland know that God is not only infinitely good (free of contaminating interactions with history) but that this same infinitely good God operates wherever humans live?

LOOMER

Bernard Loomer, by contrast, argues that the unambiguous goodness of God, as that is described by Wieman, Hartshorne, and Whitehead, is not empirically sustainable. This argument is only the most important conclusion in Loomer's most important theological writing, "The Size of God"—a manifold essay that will be remembered for its effort to carry the empiricist mandate to its full extension.

Loomer took with full seriousness Wieman's claim that growth occurs in receiving, integrating, and personally and socially incorporating just those things that contrast with already created goods. Loomer coined the terms "stature"—or, synonymously, "size"—and made it the single most important religious measurement. It measures "the volume of life you can take into your being and still maintain your integrity."[52] The more stature the better, so that the person who incorporates greater diversity without losing integrity (personal coherence) is the person with greater achievement. Thus, for Loomer empirical theology finds value in growth, where growth is described by the movement toward greater stature.

Equally, theology is empirical to the extent that it, as an inquiry, has stature. Theology is empirical just in refusing to replace the breadth of concrete accounts of experience with the narrowness always endemic to abstractions about experience. Translated, this meant that theology must give sustained attention to the ambiguities of experience, where "ambiguities" refer to the irrational diversities implicit in concrete experience. Accordingly, Loomer offers a virtual ontology of ambiguity. He concludes that the very structure of experience involves the fullest ambiguity—even the ambiguity of good and evil, where the attainment of good seems to require a corresponding attainment of evil. Because the experienced world is always and

---

50. Inbody, "Meland's Naturalistic God."

51. Bernard Eugene Meland, *Faith and Culture* (New York: Oxford University Press, 1953), p. 212.

52. Bernard M. Loomer, "S-I-Z-E," *Criterion* 13 (Spring 1974), p. 6.

everywhere riddled with ambiguities, it is incomprehensible through abstractions (which focus on unambiguous uniformities). The empirical adequacy of a theology is its capacity to incorporate the breadth of these ambiguities in its very formulation, thus attaining, itself, a kind of stature. This is what empiricism really means; it is not ambiguity and stature themselves that are prized but authenticity to the breadth of experience—which, properly read, involves ambiguities and stature.

From this follows Loomer's concept of God. If "God" refers to that which has the highest value, then God must most completely incorporate and promote growth. But most completely to be involved in growth, God must be resident in the full breadth of diversities and have the fullest conceivable stature. Clearly, this God could not be God if it were resident in a part rather than the entirety of the world, for any part could not involve the fullest stature; thus, Loomer supports a pantheism. But because ambiguity, including the inseparable intertwining of good and evil, is implicit in the very structure of experience, God must participate in the world's ambiguities fully and without a loss of integrity. As such, God participates in the fullest ambiguities of good and evil.[53] Finally, this God, "the organic restlessness of the whole body of creation," affects the world. "God" is the term that "signifies a richness of resources for the living of life at its depths"—thus promoting the human drive for stature.[54] Ostensibly, Loomer reached these conclusions, not deductively as my account would suggest, but empirically. This is to say that when Loomer looked at life in its religious depths, he saw nothing beneath ambiguity. Ambiguity seemed to go all the way down.

Directly and simply, this means that Wieman's defense of the goodness of God is not sufficiently empirical. When it makes God unambiguously good, it becomes a defense of a desired abstraction, rather than an account of the depth of experience that, in all its ambiguity, we experience and call God.[55] Equally, Loomer worried that Meland's account of God as the "tender working" within nature (one way in which Meland refers to the infinite goodness of God) omits the "roughness" of the world as we feel it in its precognitive physical impact. Meland, also, equates God "with the abstract aspects of the world."[56]

In making this step, Loomer not only decisively abandoned the unambiguous goodness of God but brought to full expression the aestheticism

53. See Marvin Shaw's objections to this move: "The Romantic Love of Evil: Loomer's Proposal of a Reorientation in Religious Naturalism," *American Journal of Theology and Philosophy* 10 (January 1989), pp. 33-42.

54. Bernard M. Loomer, "The Size of God," in *The Size of God: The Theology of Bernard Loomer in Context*, ed. William Dean and Larry Axel (Macon, Ga.: Mercer University Press, 1987), pp. 41, 42.

55. Loomer, "The Size of God," p. 49.

56. Bernard M. Loomer, "Meland on God," *The American Journal of Theology and Philosophy* 5 (May and September 1984), p. 140.

implicit in the thought of both Wieman and Meland. Wieman devoted the sixth chapter of *The Source of Human Good* to beauty, and Meland's characterization of faith as "appreciative awareness" more than suggests that what is religiously most profound is to be understood by analogy with aesthetic experience, rather than cognitive, moral, or conventional mystical experience. Loomer finally said, "The basic order of the world is aesthetic in character, dynamically aesthetic. The metaphysical conception of aesthetic order is, among other things, a generalization of the value principle involved in the notion of evolutionary advance."[57] In other words, the historicism implicit in evolutionary theory leaves no static category standing, whether cognitive, moral, or conventionally mystical. For, if flux dominates, then the only category is the category that will describe the experienced value in the flux, as aesthetics can. Accordingly, Loomer was to say, "My thesis at this point is that stature may be understood and achieved most fully in terms of beauty. Beauty is the concrete quality, and aesthetic order is the structure of relationships present within the concrete actualization of beauty."[58] One implication that Loomer (conveniently) did not state: God, while not unambiguously good, does have perfect stature and is unambiguously beautiful.

All this notwithstanding, Loomer shared with Macintosh, Wieman, and Meland certain strengths and problems. In his later writings Loomer gives witness to a traditional reverence for the awesome depths of history that mysteriously generate the world's evolutionary and valuational energies. Nevertheless, his empiricism stands in the tension with his universal claims. It is true that in the last fifteen years of his life Loomer took with increasing seriousness local narratives. Stories about his father, who was a sea captain, often were used to argue that "nature is the measure, and not man," and that nature is marked by wildness or at least by "a kind of roughness."[59] Nevertheless, it is also true that "The Size of God" opens with a metaphysical exposition more than merely reminiscent of Whitehead's metaphysics and gives to God a perfect beauty, unsullied by the inhibitions to stature so prevalent in history. Also, whatever Loomer's ostensible empiricism, his arguments about God seem based not on immediate experience as much as on quite abstract and ahistorical deduction: Because stature is the deepest value and because "God" refers to the deepest value, then God must be characterized by stature.

CONCLUSION

The distinctiveness and the genius of the empirical theologians lie in their step toward the historicization of the concept of God. They extend in new

57. Bernard M. Loomer, "Theology and the Arts," (An unpublished lecture manuscript dated March, 1974; place and exact time of delivery unknown), p. 5.

58. Bernard M. Loomer, "Notes on Beauty as a Design for Life," (An unpublished lecture manuscript dated March, 1978: place and exact time of delivery unknown), p. 16.

59. Loomer, "Meland on God," pp. 142-143.

ways the historicist approach already implicit in American religious thought. Particularly, they insist that God is known through historical experience and is found in the locus of history—natural as well as cultural history. As a consequence, their God, in order to be truly historical, could possess only finite, or imperfect, power.

However, the empirical theologians set a limit to the historicizing process. They contend that God has a character that is everywhere the same; and they argue that God is valuationally perfect in the way that only something protected from the full impact of history can be perfect. That is, there is something about the character of God that is quite independent of historical influence, so that it is neither localized nor compromised. The empirical theologians contend that God, to be God, had to have such a universal and perfect character, and this tied them to Western religious tradition. But it also stood in tension with their historicist empiricism.

Bernard Loomer, an unwitting postmodernist,[60] challenged the moral perfection of God in the name of an empiricism that is historicist. Empirical theologians who continue to participate in this living theological movement have yet to determine whether God must be more completely historicized or not. The question remains quite open.[61]

---

60. See William Dean, "Bernard Loomer and the Irony of Empiricism," *Process Studies* (Fall 1988).

61. The question could be stated as a dilemma: Either sustain a partial historicism that allows empirical theology to stay within the Western theological tradition at the price of at least temporary inconsistency with late twentieth century questions about coherence or choose a more complete historicism at the price of losing consistency with much of the Western theological tradition.

CHAPTER SIX

God as Spirit

BERNARD J. LEE

INTRODUCTION

God as Spirit. God's Spirit. The Spirit of God. The Holy Spirit. The Spirit of Holiness. Spirit from God.

In the Judeo-Christian tradition, this kind of language hints that one is very, very close to the vortex of religious experience. Only primal symbol has the verve to catch Spirit in act: great furnace fires, the kinder flame of the heart's passion, friendly fires against the chill; wind in a rage; breeze that departs as unbidden as it entered; flood waters and spring waters and womb waters.

The issue here is not the Greek emphasis upon God's immateriality as spirit, to meet the philosophical requirements of simplicity. It is upon the Hebrew metaphor *Ruach*: divine breath that blows into history right from the Who of God.

Empirically, what justifies speaking religiously or theologically about God is the claim to have experienced God, or at least the claim to have experienced a God-experiencer. Abraham Heschel observes that there are no proofs for the existence of God, there are only witnesses.[1] In the pages that follows, most of the witnesses are from the Earlier Scriptures [Old Testament], especially during the prophetic period.

In the time of the great prophets there are two major metaphors that mediate and articulate the living presence of YHWH in human history: *Ruach*, often translated as spirit, and *Dabhar*, often translated as word. These are not the only metaphors, but they dominate the record. And even though our

---

1. Abraham J. Heschel, *The Prophets*, vol. 1 (New York: Harper, 1962), p. 22.

attention here is upon *Ruach*, some attention belongs also to *Dabhar*, for the two work together in the mediation of Jewish religious experience of the period.

All of the reflections in this book are efforts to theologize in the empirical mode. While there are some central meanings to empirical in this context, namely, fidelity to experience, the applications are myriad. I intend to name some of the meanings of empirical for me along the way.

HISTORY AS LOCUS THEOLOGICUS

We are in a world and can only experience what is given us relationally in this world. If God is available to us, it would have to be on the basis of God's being somehow and somewhere in the world with us. To note the somehow and somewhere of God, Bernard Meland often uses expressions like "where ultimacy traffics with immediacy."[2] In that vein, William Dean insists that all theological statements are always also historical statements.[3]

Some witnesses to the experience of God find God trafficking in the more obvious events and others in the more secret innards of historical movement. As I shall indicate, *Dabhar* is a metaphor that tends to note the more palpable events and *Ruach* the more elusive. In both cases, it is a metaphor that names the experience of God. It can name the experience because it was actively there already in the making of the experience.

What I shall be doing below is looking at the *Ruach* texts to see what kinds of events are occurring, who is involved, and what YHWH is interpreted as being up to. I will attempt generalized theological insight from the accumulating particulars.

Empirical theological reflection, in this rendition, is an effort to read what historical witnesses indicate about their experience of YHWH as present and active in their world, especially when the metaphor *Ruach* interprets YHWH's traffic with immediate lived experience.

METAPHOR

Ruach and *Dabhar* are both metaphors. Every metaphor is based upon an analogy. One thing *is like* another thing. If they were exactly like each other, they would be identical. In every metaphor, then, it is also the case that the one thing *is not like* the other. The *is not like* feature is usually a guarded secret, because the focus is upon the *is like*.

Popularly, people tend to think of metaphor as being pressed into service

---

2. Bernard E. Meland, *Fallible Forms and Symbols* (Philadelphia: Fortress, 1976), p. 148.

3. William Dean, *American Religious Empiricism* (Albany: SUNY, 1986), especially Chapter 2.

to express a powerful experience descriptively, and for the most part that means after the fact, i.e., some quite new experience of remembering/interpreting an old experience. While that is a valid meaning of metaphor, it is not the one I intend in my reflections here.

In the final chapter of *The Symbolism of Evil*, Paul Ricoeur makes a case for thought arising from symbol, not vice versa.[4] I agree with that and presume it hereafter in the text. And in his introduction to *Metaphoric Process*, by Mary Gerhart and Allan Russell, Ricoeur makes the same case for metaphor.

> Metaphor, far from being limited to a linguistic artifact, is characterized by its epistemological function of discovering new meanings. . . . A metaphor is a thought process before it is a language process.[5]

We are symbol makers and metaphor makers, and our knowledge of the world comes into being through our symbol/metaphor making. In these functions, symbolic activity belongs to the process of knowledge coming into being, "not with the explanation of an idea but with the invention of an idea."[6] Metaphor has an epistemological function; it mediates the coming into being of our understanding of something. It doesn't happen after the experience, it is a causative factor of the experience itself. That, then, is the metaphoric function of *Ruach* to which I shall attend, for it is a *maker* of the experience of God—not the sole maker but a real maker.

The most basic literal meaning of *Ruach* is probably "moved air." Thus it can mean wind and it can also mean breath. Hebrew anthropology is physiological in character. Spiritual or psychological functions are interpreted with very physical referents. Because living and breathing are so obviously and intimately connected, *Ruach* names not just breath, but life itself, or what another system might call the soul, or personality, or personhood. But soul and personality are very abstract concepts and play no conceptual role in ancient Hebrew experience. So *Ruach* is the metaphor for the "who" of a person, and also for the impact of that "who" upon the larger world.

The clearest way to approach the meaning of God as Spirit is to visit the instances in which spirit mediates/interprets religious experience. Then we need to estimate what is claimed for Spirit in the events in which the Hebrews see *Ruach* at work. Finally, we shall generalize from those many experiences of *Ruach* and see how this generalization finds its place in the larger schema of Judeo-Christian religious understanding.

---

4. Paul Ricoeur, *The Symbolism of Evil* (Boston: Beacon, 1967), "Conclusion: The Symbol Gives Rise to Thought."

5. Mary Gerhart, and Allan Russell, *Metaphorics Process* (Fort Worth: Texas Christian University Press, 1984), p. xii.

6. Ibid., p. 108.

The Ruach Trail

I will follow H. Wheeler Robinson's accounting of *Ruach*.[7] There is in his or anyone's listing some arbitrariness that cannot be overcome, because we cannot always be certain whether *Ruach* is more primarily speaking of just wind, or just breath, or indicates that the Who of YHWH is directing the movement of history.

Ruach occurs 378 times. Wind is the referent 131 times (sometimes literally and sometimes figuratively). In 39 instances *Ruach* refers to the life principle, without specific reference to God. *Ruach* names psychic functions 74 times. But *Ruach* refers to the influence of God in the world 134 times, and in these we are especially interested.

To begin with, *Ruach* interprets historical events as being directed by YHWH. God's *Ruach* is always a gift for the sake of the community, never for an individual for personal good. Whatever happens to individuals happens to them as parts of the corporate personality of Israel.

The key personages who guide the destiny of Israel are the prophets, priests, and kings. Kings means any kind of "civil" leadership, e.g., judges and generals as well. Prophets tend to assert the claim of the Age to Come upon the a community's life. Kings and judges, like good administrators, tend to safeguard the claims of the present. They make things work now, and work well. Priests are especially concerned with the claims that the past makes upon the present. They protect sacred history. Typologically—therefore not always true all the time for every prophet, priest, or king—prophets assert the claims of a future age; kings/leaders the claims of the present; and priests the claims of the past. As I have surveyed *Ruach* passages one by one, I find none that mentions the Spirit of God with direct reference to priests. There are numerous passages in which the Spirit works with kings/leaders. But above all, we find *Ruach* cavorting with prophets.

Ruach and Leaders

We begin with witnesses to God as Spirit when leadership issues are the historical events that testify to God's effective presence as *Ruach*.

Pharaoh is so impressed by Joseph that he places him in a key leadership position in Egypt. What impresses Pharaoh is Joseph's ability to interpret dreams. "Then Pharaoh asks his ministers, 'Can we find anyone else endowed with the Spirit of God like him?' So Pharaoh said to Joseph, 'Since God has given you knowledge of all this, there can be no one else as intelligent and wise as you. . . . I hereby make you governor of the whole of Egypt'" (Gn 41:37-39,41).

---

7. H. Wheeler Robinson, *The Religious Ideas of the Old Testament* (London: Duckworth, 1964), pp. 17-18.

Two things are to be noted here. The more obvious is that Spirit and leadership are connected. But it is also noteworthy that Spirit enables Joseph to interpret dreams, i.e., there is some coalition between the Spirit and the unconscious or the nonrational. The ability to read those deeper stirrings is important to the function of leader.

When Moses finds his leadership task overwhelming, he asks YHWH for additional help. YHWH gives Moses seventy elders to help, and "took some of the *Ruach* that was on Moses and put it on the seventy elders" (Nm 11:25). Then when Moses realizes that he will not lead the people into the promised land, he prays, "May YHWH, God of the spirits that give life to all living creatures, appoint a leader for this community." YHWH instructs Moses to "take Joshua . . . a man in whom the Spirit dwells, and lay your hands of him" (Nb 27:18).

The testimony continues with the leadership of the judges. "The Spirit of YHWH was upon Othniel and he became judge in Israel" (Jgs 3:10). God's Spirit was also on Jephthah (Jgs 11:29). The Spirit of YHWH began to stir Samson in the camp of Dan (Jgs 13:24-25).

Saul is the first king. By most standards, he wouldn't be a remarkable candidate. He needs a lot of help! Samuel anoints Saul and then says the YHWH'S *Ruach* will put him into a prophetic frenzy and make him into a new human being. And YHWH changes Saul's heart (1 Sam 10:5-9). Two notable points: *Ruach* turns a life around; it is done in a prophetic ecstasy, and heart is where the work gets done. When Saul is a disaster, David is anointed king while Saul still lives. "With a horn of oil, Samuel anointed David surrounded by his brothers, and the *Ruach* of YHWH seized David from that day forward" (1 Sam 16:11-13).

When David is dying he refers to himself as the singer of Israel's songs and says that "the Spirit of YHWH speaks through me" (2 Sm 23:1-2). And it is interesting that when Saul is overcome by a bad spirit, it is only the music of David that can return a good spirit to him.

The texts themselves witness the Hebrew experience of the Spirit of God as present to Israel's leaders, remaking them, guiding them, changing their hearts, rendering acute their instincts about the deeper and nonrational recesses of the human soul.

RUACH AND PROPHETS

We will now consider the prophets, and how God as Spirit is interpreted to impact upon historical events in and through the prophets.

Prophecy names two kinds of experiencing. Sometimes we find prophets in very excited and frenzied states of ecstasy. More often we think of prophets as those who proclaim how people must live now because of what YHWH is about to do for them. The two are not mutually exclusive. Sometimes one's spirit must be convulsed, turned upside down and inside out, to be ready for what YHWH wants to do. Getting ready for YHWH often calls for abandoning one's own cherished commitments, and that is wrenching. It is the deconstruction that must occur before the reconstruction is able to take place. I will be focusing upon the more traditional meaning of prophet.

Balaam is the first prophet with whom YHWH's *Ruach* is associated. Balaam, a Moabite, is dispatched by Balak, the Moabite king, to curse Israel. But the *Ruach* of YHWH comes upon him, and he blesses Israel instead, with great affection even: "How fair! How fair!" (Nm 24:5).

Just as Spirit is transferred from the one leader Moses to seventy other leaders, the *Ruach* of the prophet Elijah is transferred to the prophet Elisha, and the brotherhood of prophets can see even from a distance that the distance that "the *Ruach* of Elijah has come to rest on Elisha" (2 K 2:15).

Among the preexilic prophets, Amos is without reference to YHWH's *Ruach*. Although Hosea is intolerant of prophet and priest alike. Hosea nonetheless acknowledges that the prophet is a man of the Spirit (Ho 4:5). The prophet Micah is quite clear about the Spirit and his own vocation as prophet:

> I am full of strength,
> full of YHWH's *Ruach*,
> of justice and of courage,
> to accuse Jacob of his crime,
> and Israel of his sin.
> (Mi 3:8)

For Micah, having YHWH's *Ruach* is clearly related to justice and to the courage to pass judgment when justice is violated.

Justice is a far richer Hebrew notion than our English word normally carries. It names the essential rightness of things when they are the way God would have them. Rightness and righteousness are how history is meant to be ordered, precisely because God is that way ("be holy as God is holy"). Justice/righteousness is the deep story of God. It is rooted in the Who of God. God's *Ruach* in the world calls the world to justice and the prophet with YHWH's *Ruach* judges the world according to justice.

Even though first Isaiah never directly invokes *Ruach* to validate his own prophetic call, he does certainly see *Ruach's* agency in the restoration of Israel. The key operative words are justice and judgment:

> When the Lord has washed away the filth off the daughter of Zion and has cleansed Jerusalem of the blood shed in her, then with the *ruach*/spirit of *mishpat*/judgment and with the *ruach* of fire, YHWH will come and rest upon the whole stretch of Mount Zion. (Is 4:4-5)

The people of a restored Israel must be a justice-people because YHWH's *Ruach* is a justice-*Ruach*. The value structure upon which judgment is passed is a *Ruach*-justice structure. It is a judgment that sears!

Scorching fire is a partial report on Isaiah's *Ruach* experience. There is a tensive but gentler experience concerning the Age to Come. *Ruach* is also like water that turns desert into garden, where justice prevails (cf. Is 32:15-16).

Isaiah also implicates *Ruach* in the messianic leadership for the great New Age. The *Ruach* of YHWH which will rest upon this leader is also a *Ruach* that gives wisdom, insight, counsel, power, and knowledge of God (Is 11:1-2). Here a contrast might be initiated between *Ruach* and *Dabhar*. *Ruach* will not tell the messianic leader concretely and precisely what is to be done, for that is more the *Dabhar* task. *Ruach* is responsible for the interior qualities that attune one's instincts and intuitions to the kind of world that needs to be made: a justice-world, because of Who YHWH is. In nonbiblical language, but as a growing generalized insight into God as *Ruach*/Spirit, the moral character of the reign of God which *Ruach* presses is at base a valuational structure grounded in the deepest Who of YHWH's own self.

Jeremiah's witness to God is primarily in terms of *Dabhar*. He is so irritated with would-be prophets that he is, in fact, rather negative about these "spirit" motivated people.

But it is Ezekiel with whom, as George Montague says, "an entirely new 'wind' is blowing."[8] A vision initiates Ezekiel's vocation as prophet. While a voice speaks to him, YHWH's *Ruach* comes into him and sets him upright on his feet (Ez 2:1-2).

In his prophecy, Ezekiel announces the renewed covenant which YHWH shall make. The following text is particularly instructive:

> I shall pour clean water over you and you shall be cleansed. . . . I shall give you a new heart and put a new *Ruach* in you; I shall remove the heart of stone from your bodies and give you a heart of flesh instead. . . . I shall put my *Ruach* in you, and make you keep my laws, and respect and practice my judgments (Ez 36:25-27).

Much is happening in these verses. *Ruach* names the spirit of both God and Israel. Israel has a new spirit because YHWH's spirit has been put into it. The place of the new spirit is Israel's heart. In Hebrew anthropology, the heart is the metaphor for personhood. Heart names the deepest place in a person. It is the seat of personality. The transformation worked by *Ruach* is in the heart. Who Israel is—that is what is transformed, nothing less.

In metaphor, water names the experienced effects of *Ruach's* agency: being cleansed and purified. Getting a new heart amounts to a new valuational structure, as a result of which Israel is attuned to YHWH's own judgment making.

---

8. George T. Montague, *The Holy Spirit: Growth of a Biblical Tradition* (New York: Paulist, 1976), pp. 23-24.

In Ezekiel there is quite a comprehensive metaphorical theology of *Ruach*. And it is consistent with the wider witness to YHWH's experienced presence as Spirit. It is the Who of God who enters into and transforms the Who of the prophet, or king, or Israel itself. What counts and what doesn't is grounded in the justice of YHWH, and when YHWH's *Ruach* shapes another's *ruach* to be like it, that person or nation knows how to judge with YHWH's own judgment.

Having followed the *Ruach* trail for a while, it is necessary briefly to amble through the territory of *Dabhar*. If during the same time as the *Ruach* testimonies the same people also speak repeatedly of YHWH's *Dabhar*, we must presume that there are two different metaphors because there are two sufficiently different experiences.

THE DABHAR TRAIL

The Hebrew *Dabhar* is regularly translated as "Word." There is no closer word than Word in English, even though the translation is profoundly inadequate. The entire Indo-European language system does not have an interpretation of reality corresponding to the Hebrew concept for *Dabhar*.

To the contemporary Western ear, "word" means a sound that stands for a concept of things, events, qualities, ideas, etc. Word has to do with our linguisticality. Being human and being linguistic are causally interconnected. While the linguisticality of Jewish experience is just as interchangeable as being human, the word *Dabhar* names something further.

In a well-known biblical narrative, Jacob tricks Isaac into giving him the blessing and inheritance that should have gone to Esau. Pronouncing the blessing effects the blessing. Isaac speaks the words and effects the deed by the speaking. Word is a dynamic force that makes something come into existence. Esau's pain, and Isaac's too is palpable:

> When Esau heard his father's words, he cried out loud and wept bitterly to his father, "Father, bless me too!" Isaac replied, "Your brother came by fraud and took your blessing." Esau said to his father, "Was that your only blessing, father? Give me a blessing too." Isaac remained silent. Esau burst into tears (Gn 27:34-38, passim).

In no Western court would Isaac's fraudulently given will and testament be upheld. For an ancient Hebrew, however, the speaking did the deed and that was that. The saying made a deed, formed a thing, caused an objective fact.

This, then, is the daily meaning of *Dabhar* in Hebrew culture. Just as *Ruach*, with a daily meaning, mediates one kind of experience of God, so too does *Dabhar* with its daily meaning get metaphorically pressed into service in the experiencing of God. *Dabhar* and *Ruach* are both metaphors that witness to God's self-communication into human history.

In the Earlier Scriptures there is not a crystal-clear distinction between *Dabhar* and *Ruach*. Occasionally they overlap. However, if two metaphors are used very frequently in the same period, there must be different experiences of God that people are naming. It is my assessment that if two separate meanings are not clearly demarcated and always operative, there are nonetheless two families of meanings that constellate around the two metaphors. The way to assess *Dabhar* is to examine the many times it occurs and generalize as best one can the experience of God being named therein. I will offer here a brief summary on *Dabhar*. A fuller treatment will appear elsewhere.[9]

DABHAR AND PROPHECY, DABHAR AND LAW

The expression *Dabhar* YHWH, the Word of Yahweh, occurs about 240 times in the Earlier Scriptures, and about 20 more times in the plural.[10] There are related texts that have to do with YHWH speaking. About half of the Word of God texts address how the prophets know what they know about God when they proclaim: "The *Dabhar* YHWH came to me . . ." This kind of prophet validation text occurs especially in the later prophets. *Dabhar* is also used to refer to the Law, both the *Torah* generally and to the specific contents of the Law (about sixty usages of *Dabhar* refer to the Ten Commandments). Preponderantly, the *Dabhar* texts have to do with the prophets (as do the *Ruach* texts).

THE DABHAR CONSTELLATED MEANING

The *Dabhar*/Word of YHWH tends to be far more specific in its historical directives than *Ruach*. *Dabhar* often gives considerable detail concerning the shape that YHWH would have history take, e.g., the Ten Commandments. *Dabhar* is transformative like *Ruach* but is occasion-specific. *Dabhar* is not God uttering vocables, or prophets turning what they know God wants into vocables. *Dabhar* is the active, dynamic, effective presence of Yahweh experienced as a pressure upon historical experience. It's YHWH accosting human history makers into collaboration with the divine history maker.

THE COLLABORATIVE COMPLEMENTARINESS OF RUACH AND DABHAR

I want to develop *Ruach's* meaning using a model from philosophical anthropology.[11] Every culture lives out of a narrative that is deeper and wider

---

9. Bernard J. Lee, *Jesus and the Metaphors of God* (New York: Paulist, forthcoming).
10. Robinson, *Religious Ideas*.
11. I am indebted in this discussion to the work of Stephen Crites. Cf. Stephen Crites, "The Narrative Quality of Experience," *Journal of the American Academy of Religion* 39:3 (September 1971), pp. 291-311.

than anyone can ever fully express, although every poem, song, artifact, all the meanings people live from—all of these instance the deep story, and these particular stories are the only clues there are to the deep story. The deep story is something like the spirit of a culture, and people who have been socialized well in the deep story have a keen sense whether some particular story is faithful to it or not. The deep story doesn't demand any one particular instance of it, only that all instances honor its basic story line, its cherished values. A culture's deep story can be transformed, but only slowly and organically at levels beyond conscious control. No one can just dream up a new deep story.

Societies all have exclusion procedures when a radical violation of the deep story is attempted by someone's particular story. Sometimes exclusion occurs even when the violating story does break some specific regulation. In their instincts, committed people sense that a way of putting life together "is just not right."

I think *Ruach* and *Dabhar* can be generalized with this distinction in mind. God's *Ruach* is like the deep story in God, and when God's *Ruach* transforms any person's or community's *Ruach*, they can read the world with God's own sense of the world. This is clearly Paul's reading:

> These are the very things that God has revealed to us through the Spirit, for the Spirit reaches the depths of everything, even the depths of God. After all, the depths of a person can only be known by that person's own spirit and not by any other person. Now, instead of the spirit of the world, we have received the Spirit that comes from God, to teach us to understand the gifts he has given us. . . . Someone who has God's Spirit [a spiritual person] is able to judge the value of everything, and his [or her] own value is not to be judged by others (1 Cor 2:10-12,15).

In Jewish anthropology, when the deepest part of a person was named, the ownmost "who" of a person, *Ruach* was the metaphor. When YHWH's effective presence is felt like the Who of God coming upon the who of the prophet, or upon the who of Israel, *Ruach* YHWH interprets the experience. And if there is any best clue to the deep story of the Who of God, it is justice through and through.

But a deep story is only as good as its particular, concrete historical embodiments. The *Dabhar*/Word is a perception of God that understands God to have an effective presence in helping the deep story fall into place in all of Israel's particular stories.

GOD AS SPIRIT

Here, then, are some generalizations drawn from the 134 or so witnesses to God as Spirit in the Earlier Scriptures, a few of which have been noted here.

There is not a perfect logic that flows through them, but enough clustering of meaning to claim something like a constellation based interpretation.

1. To speak of God as *Ruach*/Spirit is to claim that *Who* God is makes huge claims on *who* we are.

2. Because God's Spirit is more active in prophecy than anywhere else, it would seem that God is above all up to creating new futures. There are eschatological and apocalyptic auras to God as Spirit. God as Spirit asks the world to live forward.

3. The efficacy of Spirit is especially in the heart, which in Hebrew anthropology is the seat of personhood. Experiencing the *Ruach*/YHWH is an affective experience felt especially in regard to values and structures of value.

4. If one had to choose a single best word to note the character of the deep story of God's ordering, it would be justice.

5. Being attuned to the Spirit of God calls for a way of living that is profoundly sensitive to the movements of history, especially to the inner movement inviting our collaboration.

These reflections have been my attempt to ground the meaning of God as Spirit empirically in the deliverances of ancient Hebrew experience, especially—though not exclusively—from the prophetic period. I have no interest here in what the classical tradition with its Hellenistic roots meant by spirit (nonmaterial and simple). That is interesting and important but not my subject.

The people of the Earlier Scriptures did not argue God's existence. They did not discuss the characteristics of God. References to God often included the events in which the experience of God occurred: The God of Abraham, the God who led us out of Egypt, God who made the world, God whose Spirit comes into our hearts, God whose Word shows us a path. They experienced all this and became God's witnesses.

AN AFTERWORD: PROCESS THEOLOGY

My exposure to Whitehead's philosophy and to process theology (John Cobb and Norman Pittenger were the first two I read) alerted me to the presuppositions that undergirded classical theism, in which my faith had all its early roots. Before long, process theology facilitated my recovery of the Earlier Scriptures, the Old Testament, to which the process/relational interpretation of deity has genuine affinities. Ownership of the Hebrew scriptures helped me recover the Jewishness of my own Christian origins, and I continue to be amazed at the Jesus that I have met in his thoroughgoing Jewishness.

These final reflections are meant to be conversation with those who have read through Alfred North Whitehead, and through the history and literature of process theology.

In what I take to be a very important clue, Whitehead said that God is effective in the world in respect to both his primordial and consequent natures.[12] In nearly all of *Process and Reality*, Whitehead explores the power of God in the world as primordial. The human experience in which God's primordial agency is interpreted to be effective is an urge toward the future based upon desires activated in the present.[13] In *Adventures of Ideas*, Whitehead calls this primordial agency the supreme Eros,[14] and says that the soul has a tendency to remain attuned to this Eros.[15] It is my reading of the Hebrew witnesses to God that *Ruach* has many similarities to God's primordial agency.

In Whitehead's natural theology, all order for the world is from God as primordial. This order is effective in nature because it is constituted by the subjective forms of God's entertaining all possibilities. While that order has a character, it doesn't require any particular scheme of things, only that whatever the scheme of things actually is, that it be faithful to the Eros of God and transformative of historical experience. Prayers to the Spirit in the Christian tradition have this sense: "Come Holy Spirit, fill the *hearts* of the faithful. *Enkindle* in the them *the fire* of your love. Send forth your Spirit to your people and they shall be recreated and [with them] you shall renew the face of the earth."

Only in the final pages of *Process and Reality* does Whitehead return to God as consequent. Nowhere in his natural theology does he spell out how the consequent agency of God functions or how people might identify it in their experience. There is one hint, however, I would like to pursue briefly. Whitehead refers to God's particular providence for particular occasions.[16] Effective attention to particular occasions would require that God who first experienced events would then address them intentionally in their particularity. That implies that God as consequent, God the experiencer of the world, speaks to the world out of that experience. In technical terms, this would seem to involve God in the propositional phase of a concrescence, perhaps in relationship to the subjective form for nonconformal propositions. I am suggesting, therefore, that the consequent agency of God in the world is very similar to the Hebrew experience of YHWH called *Dabhar*.

Martin Buber ponders what God's speaking in history is like. He says that most of the time we do not hear the word because we expect something to happen alongside of or above daily events. Rather,

---

12. Alfred North Whitehead, *Process and Reality*, corrected edition (New York: Macmillan/Free Press, 1978), p. 32.

13. Ibid.

14. Alfred North Whitehead, *Adventures of Ideas* (New York: Macmillan/Free Press, 1967), p. 198.

15. Ibid., p. 251.

16. Whitehead, *Process and Reality*, p. 351.

God's speech . . . penetrates what happens in the life of each one of us, and all that happens in the world around us, biographical and historical, and makes it for you and me into instruction. Happening upon happening, situation upon situation, are enabled and empowered by the personal speech of God to demand of the human person to take [one's] stand and make [one's] decision.[17]

If, as I recommend, Bernard Meland's appreciative consciousness is a condition of human receptivity to Spirit, then skills in social analysis speak to sensibilities to Word. For situation upon situation, happening upon happening, to be empowered as God's personal *Dabhar* events must be understood on their own ground. Once they are read accurately, they must still be adjudicated with God's judgment, which God's Spirit in us makes possible. This is the political side of process theology that has long gone undeveloped. It is a political side in both analysis and acted out strategy.

When Edward Schillebeeckx was asked about prayer in an interview, he replied that prayer without social commitment is romanticism and sentimentality and that social commitment without prayer often becomes crass and dangerous. That may be the sort of thing that *Ruach* and *Dabhar* signal in a very ancient tradition. I think there are fine resources for a pneumatology in Meland's writings. It is conceivable to me that as compelling as so much of process theology is to the mind, there has not been a *Dabhar* development to complement the formidable *Ruach* dimensions.

There has been a tendency in process theology to make connections between Spirit and the consequent nature, and Word and the primordial nature. The earlier metaphors for God are *Ruach* and *Dabhar*. But it is a *Logos* christology that has dominated the Western Christian tradition. Because *Logos* is the principle of order in Stoic thought (which has influenced *Logos* christology), there is justification for making correlations (John Cobb and David Griffin) between the *Logos*/Word and the primordial nature.

In the very first issues of *Process Studies*, Thomas Altizer opined that Whitehead was "twice born."[18] I understand this to suggest that Whitehead's philosophical system bears the marks of some of his own religious experience. It is not my position that Spirit and Word simply correspond to the primordial and consequent natures of God—only that there are some resemblances and some similar instincts about deity and deity's efficacious presence in the world.

---

17. Martin Buber, *I and Thou*, (New York: Scribner's, 1958), pp. 136-137.
18. Thomas J. J. Altizer, "Dialectical v. Di-Polar Theology," *Process Studies* 1:1 (Spring 1971), p. 37.

CHAPTER SEVEN

Jesus and History

GERARD S. SLOYAN

The central figure of Christian faith under God was a man in history.[1]
Within a hundred years of his death and resurrection certain believers in
him were reverencing him as the heavenly Christ, a person of spirit to whom
birth and death and the sheer materiality that lies in between were foreign.
These possessors of a secret "gnosis" are with us still—claiming the name
Christian but embarrassed by the basic conviction of the worldwide company
of Christians that the salvation of humanity—from its own worst self and from
all that threatens it—is a work of God accomplished through one of its own.

Christianity has never lacked those who have had a poor view of the
human creature and its possibilities. In awe at the magnitude of unchangeable
deity with its boundless purity as spirit, these votaries take their chief comfort from the divine spark that is in them. At the same time they deplore the
mortal frame in which it is housed. For them it is inconceivable that this
frame should be fated for greatness. A fruit of this outlook is the fact that the
largest threat to faith in Jesus Christ has always been, not a weak faith in his
divinity, but a hesitancy to accept the fact that he is human—in every sense
one of us.

Human beings have a history. Things happen to them in time. From womb
to tomb, whether this be a mausoleum or a shallow grave, their days are
numbered by recurring events. Some grind cereal grain and bake it, others

---

1. Writings on this subject are voluminous. One might profitably consult Marcus
Borg, *Jesus, A New Vision* (San Francisco: Harper & Row, 1988); Howard Clark Kee,
Jesus in History. An Approach to the Study of the Gospels, 2d ed. (New York: Harcourt
Brace Jovanovich, 1977); E. P. Sanders, *Jesus and Judaism* (Philadelphia: Fortress,
1985); Norman Perrin, *Rediscovering the Teaching of Jesus* (New York: Harper & Row,
1967).

hunt and fish or traverse continents and oceans. Many produce crafts or works of art, a few build empires or towers to the skies. Life for every one of them is a matter of before and after. When their lives are done, these lives can be delimited by the events that preceded and followed them. Chronicling the lives of peoples and individuals came to be called by the Greeks "history," people's story. But it was history as lives lived long before it was history as lives recorded. That is because history is what people do in any place and time.

Jesus of Nazareth, a Galilean Jew born in the Augustan era and put to death in the reign of Tiberius, lived in history like the rest of us. His life and times were recorded by four separate biographers—or so they were thought to be—fifty and more years afterward. One and two centuries later, spurious writings proliferated that purported to fill in the gaps left by the four writers. Most of this pious fiction was produced by people who had an axe to grind in the realm of ideology or doctrine. They used the familiar gospel form in an attempt to gain acceptance for their views.

In 1945 a library of papyrus manuscripts assembled by late second-century Christian monks was discovered in Upper Egypt (i.e., the south). It contained, among other writings, all in Coptic, a collection of 114 sayings of Jesus—but no copy of any of the four gospels. Some of these sayings occur in the first three gospels in identical form, others in different and usually briefer form. A few had surfaced in other papyri around the turn of this century. Numerous other sayings, perhaps the most interesting, were divided between those consistent with Jesus' gospel utterances and those edited with the bias of spirit over matter—even a contempt for matter—that characterizes gnostic Christianity.

There are no other dependable sources on the words and deeds of Jesus than the four canonical gospels (meaning trustworthy as guides to Christian faith and life). To these, with a caution, can be added certain sayings of the Gospel of Thomas, a name given to the Coptic collection from its opening claim of authorship.

Numerous sayings and figurative expressions used by Jesus occur in different form in the Jewish scriptures, especially the folk wisdom found in Proverbs, Ben Sira, and Wisdom. The latter two are books of the Greek Bible of postexilic Jews, the Septuagint. A lively question is, how many of the canonical sayings and parables were attributed to Jesus by the early Christian prophets whose oral and written work preceded the gospels? A similar question is, which of the many parables and sayings that resemble those of Jesus, among the many in the two Talmuds and other rabbinic writings (roughly 400-1400 of the Common Era), might have had currency before him? Both questions are impossible to answer.

One that can be answered is that Jesus must have so characteristically taught in parables that he was identified in memory with this form of teaching. This meant, among other things, that some of his cryptic short stories to illustrate the rule of God may not be his but may simply have accrued to him. The same is true of Luke's parables of the divine mercy. A few of these may owe as much to Luke's artistry as to Jesus' more abrupt style—if such was his only manner of teaching. But that Jesus was a master of verbal imagery and parabolic inventiveness can scarcely be doubted.

This poses squarely the question of how much reported of Jesus in the form of a narrative of events, with stories and aphorisms interspersed, was actually his. It is a modern question, no more than three hundred years old. Up until then no distinction was made between the gospel accounts of his career and the facts that underlay them. This in turn is part of a larger problem. We do not have a faithful account told in modern fashion of any of the ancients, not Julius or Augustus Caesar, Hillel or Shammai, Herod the Great, or Josephus. Plutarch and Suetonius, it is true, wrote "lives" of the Caesars and Josephus reported much on Herod. But these were mere summaries of their exploits mixed with the character traits that lingered in the popular mind. Caesar's *Gallic Wars* were almost certainly the work of another hand, while Josephus in *The Jewish War* and even his *Life* presents only the self-image that he wants remembered. It has been hazarded that not until Marcus Aurelius do we have an insight into any "real" person of history. His *Meditations* reveal much of his inner self that can be joined to the chronicle of his deeds.

JESUS IN THE GOSPELS

The Jesus who comes to us in the gospels is one reported on by believers in him. This is not a necessarily suspicious detail. The same is the case with Moses and Gautama (in whom some "believed" as the Buddha), Muhammad and St. Francis. In those instances, and Jesus constitutes no exception, a person of history made such an impact that the man and the myth became inseparable. Only great ones—and this would include great tyrants—have myths woven of them after their deaths. These are not legends, which by definition may be assumed to be in good part untrue, but elaborations and developments faithful to the reality of the momentous lives. No myth is possible that departs sharply from the actuality of the person recalled. Saints do not become sinners or vice versa (although the latter *is* infrequently the case, as with great national leaders like St. Knut and St. Vlodymyr). In myth, however, as contrasted with legend, miracles are not ascribed to a life unmarked by wonders. Wisdom can be attributed to the craftily intelligent but not to fools. The evil do not become good by some alchemy worked by biographies. In Jesus' case, to use a modern image, he was remembered as "eight feet tall" because he stood at six feet and one half.

But to speak of him in this way is to make the error of assuming that his life story was a matter of basic concern to his early followers. It was not. More accurately, only the story of how he ended was important to the first generation. The earliest thing recorded of him was that his new life as risen had become the life of those who believed in him. That this was being said of him is a matter of demonstrable history. It is also obviously a statement of religious faith and in that sense not subject to historical inquiry. It had, however, an important presupposition: "He *died* for us," or, "He *died* for our sins." These statements are as theological as the first but with this difference. They speak of death, and death terminates a particular human history. The affirmations about Jesus' new life after death and the death itself are called "pre-Pauline" because they occur so frequently and in so many forms in St. Paul's correspondence. His extant letters begin in the year 50 or so. The faith convictions expressed in them go back some fifteen years to when he first experienced the risen Lord and believed in him as the Christ of God. The termination of Jesus' brief career and what came directly after it mattered most to Paul. The same is true of the writings spurred by Paul's letters, which would include Colossians and Ephesians, the epistles to Timothy and Titus, 1 Peter, and independently Hebrews and Revelation.

In all of these there is no record of Jesus' life and teaching beyond a few fragments: his birth of a Jewish mother in Galatia, his death on a cross and resurrection throughout Paul's letters, several mentions of his innocent sufferings in 1 Peter, one reference to Pilate in 1 Timothy and one to the transfiguration in 2 Timothy. That is the sum of the mention of events in Jesus' life outside the gospels.

The only conclusion to be drawn from this is that Jesus was proposed widely in the Hellenized world as an object of faith without reference to his healings and exorcisms, his nature miracles, or his teachings. An exception to St. Paul's silence would be the handful of mentions of a "word of the Lord" in his correspondence. That Jesus died in a certain way and for a certain purpose was the matter of great importance to these early believers. Of greater importance still was his having been raised from the dead after his earthly history was over. His was now a life of heavenly existence that could benefit those whose life story was still in progress. At no point do the New Testament books present Jesus as less than human, always more. He is described there as an earthbound creature who experienced the limitations of humans generally. There are two exceptions to this. In the first three gospels he is at times superhumanly perceptive about his impending fate and the thoughts and motivations of others. In John he simply is not bound by the limits that hem in the general run of humanity.

Careful inspection of these narratives yields two things about what their authors are up to. None of the four holds fast to the intention we may wish was theirs of presenting Jesus as he was before he died and rose. The faith the first three have in his present state in glory keeps creeping into their accounts of the earthbound mortal man. John, for his part, abandons any attempt to confine his narrative to the words and deeds of the pre-resurrection Christ. He opts instead for presenting in Jesus the figure of the optimum believer in him: a person who speaks in his own words the faith the John community has in him.

Once one sees how the evangelists have gone about their tasks it is easier to take each gospel on its own terms. They are documents written from a vantage point of faith and addressed to faith. They are, at the same time, writings about a historical character and not a legendary one. Hence they can be read with a view to exploring how much history in the modern sense is reported in them. But they cannot profitably be read in only that way.

THE SEARCH FOR JESUS

The search for Jesus in the modern post-Enlightenment sense has been going on since the late-eighteenth century, the period of Samuel Hermann Reimarus. Up to that point the gospels were heard and read largely in the spirit in which they were written. That spirit was one of conveying the significance of Jesus, his importance to a faith community as manifested by what God had accomplished in him. Former centuries did not realize that the evangelists described his words and deeds by way of the pictorial reconstructions of the biblical narrators; but they at least saw that their intent was to encompass their hearers in the scenes depicted. The gospel writers challenged his contemporaries.

Progress in studying the historiography of the classical world was responsible for bringing about the change. If Attic, Ionic, and Roman histories could be plumbed to see "what really happened," why not Hebraic, Israelite, and early Christian history? The Hebrew Scriptures were the first bastion to be taken, on the false assumption that they were basically a work of history. The post-Enlightenment outlook was such that the Bible was not viewed seriously as the literature of a people in narrative, poetic, or otherwise imaginative form. If it was to be "true" it could only be true as history. No other vehicle of truth was admitted. As a consequence, archaeology flourished and with it comparisons with the history of Egypt and the other ancient empires. No stone went unturned, literally, to yield a historical record that would complement that of the Bible. When inconsistencies or contradictions arose apologists tried to explain them away while rationalists rejoiced in them. Since history of this recently developed kind was taken as the standard, the debates proved inconclusive. An ancient library of writings was having norms applied to it quite different from those that underlay its composition.

The Jesus story was at first spared this type of inquiry but not for long. Reimarus' work, published ten years after his death by G. E. Lessing as *The Wolfenbüttel Fragments* (from the city of their discovery), was a calculated attack on the dependability of the gospels as history. Since the gospels often report different events in different fashion, it was concluded, they must have been clever fictions by men who failed to synchronize their stories. Their whole performance was an attempt to create a universal system of thought that promised salvation, based on the wrecked nationalist hopes of a failed messiah. Such was Reimarus' starting-point rather than his conclusion.

David Friedrich Strauss's *Life of Jesus* was perceptive in identifying the mythic quality of certain gospel accounts, such as the baptism and transfiguration of Jesus and the stilling of the storm. He correctly saw that these narratives were constructed on biblical paradigms, but concluded wrongly that they could not be true since no verifiable historical basis could be provided for them. A period of rationalist-based criticism followed in which all the gospel miracles were interpreted as having a natural explanation. This culminated in a not quite dead Jesus who was revivified by fragrant spices in a cool tomb. Such interpretations of Jesus' wonders and his resurrection are too familiar to bear repetition here. They reached their zenith early in this century in sober denials that he had ever existed. Writers like the German Arthur Drews held that the evangelists simply conflated all of Israel's hopes as recorded in the Bible and fixed them on a fictitious ideal Jew of the Second Temple period.

Certain scholars of Germany and France of this time, who continued to be men of faith, were no less empirically oriented. They set about employing history's new methods rigorously, checking gospel data against near-contemporary sources where they existed, exploring the Jewish writings in Greek of the immediately pre-gospel period for religious commonplaces, and seeing what the rabbinic writings of a later period might yield (in translation, since few knew Aramaic) in the way of similarities to the gospels. Because these scholars knew Greek well they were able to sift all the pagan witnesses to the emerging Christian community and the inaccurately denoted "apostolic fathers," those second-century writers of moral and liturgical handbooks and apologetic treatises.

When Ferdinand Christian Baur died in 1860 this giant of the Protestant faculty at Tübingen had produced a small library of writings that identified the "Petrine" and the "Pauline" spirit latent in the New Testament's twenty-seven books. From the tension between them he established a Hegelian synthesis that was the Catholic reality of the second-century church. All of this was done with as little bias and as much historical evidence as he could muster. The master discipline underlying Baur's attempt and others like it was history. Because the nineteenth century had an overweening historical concern it was assumed that that of the New Testament authors was no less. They may have written in cryptic and figurative ways but they were primarily reporting in their fashion on what "really happened."

Martin Kähler in conferences delivered to Protestant clergy in 1892 issued a caution to the effect that the century-long search for the so-called *historical* Jesus had been fruitless because the gospels were not concerned with that person. Their concern, rather, was with the *historic*, biblical Christ. The two adjectives in the title of his slim book were meant to distinguish between

the happenings in Jesus' life and the impact of his person upon his followers. Kähler's warning was not offered in a spirit of skepticism of history's possibilities but was based on the conviction that a faith portrait of the risen
Christ, whose words and deeds were colored by belief in his risenness, was
the church's legacy. Søren Aabe Kierkegaard had repeatedly sounded a similar note in mid-century with his insistence on the impossibility of basing religious faith on historical conclusions. Some of what was believed may have
happened in history but Christians do not believe in history. Their faith is in
the revealing word of the living God.

Kierkegaard's plea for faith on the part of the believing subject was filtered
down as, "Faith is subjectivity." Kähler's distinction led to a conclusion
quite opposite to the one he intended, namely, that faith in the historic Christ
placed in doubt any and all certitudes about the historical Jesus. The one
became known as the apostle of fideism, the other of historical skepticism.
Neither, however, could slow down the rush to a favorable judgment on history as the key to all knowledge of Jesus and Christian origins. The search for
empirical, i.e., demonstrable, conclusions continued on which alone faith
could reasonably be based. The researches of Weiss and Schweitzer late in
the last century and the form critics Bultmann, Dibelius, and Schmidt during
and after World War I centered on how the gospels may have been composed and why.

DISTRUST OF THE CHURCH

A basic distrust of the church as a faithful witness was at the heart of
these inquiries. However early the interpretations of believing communities may have been applied to the acts and utterances of Jesus—even the
fragments that long preceded the written gospels—they were suspect as
"church sayings" or theologized teaching. If they had not departed from
Jesus' original intention they at least could not be certified as having
retained it. Any aphorism or story claimed to be his that resembled too
closely materials that might have survived into the Talmudic period were
likewise discounted—not because he had not spoken them but because
their unique appearance as credited to him was the one assurance that he had
said them at all. There was no desire in all this to reduce Jesus to the status of a man of few words, only to place beyond all doubt the words that
could be identified as his. The net effect of this was to set aside the trust-
worthiness of the evangelists as having reported the teachings of Jesus
accurately. In the search the question of their having conveyed his spirit and
influence faithfully did not arise. What he had actually said, what he had
in fact done was all that mattered. How else than this could the real Jesus
be known?

Most of our contemporaries with a theological education will remember
clearly the empirical study of the historical Jesus they were exposed to.

They have come through it in various conditions. A few are reduced to near silence in the pulpit and classroom about what Jesus said and did. Some return to the literalist view they had of the gospels before their seminary studies. The great bulk remain committed to the tradition-minus-redaction Jesus in whom they can believe. But this is a much more bloodless figure than the Jesus of the gospels. A major problem that hovers over the churches is whether their expositors of the gospels can speak of the Jesus who was and the Jesus Christ who is in perfectly good conscience. Only the thoughtful among the ordained and the nonordained have the problem. They are by no means the most influential among the churches' teachers. Only a few are influential on others through their writing and speaking. But all, and especially ministers to congregations, have been affected by the question of whether those who appear to be writing a history of Jesus in the Christian Scriptures are to be trusted.

WHAT IS HISTORY?

The basic question at issue here is, "What is history?" Where is history's true repository: in voices once living but now long stilled; in written records, archaeological finds; in chronicles only but not in any form that breathes faith, imagination, elaboration? A pole that has as one axis Jesus and the other history can only tell something about Jesus if a proper valence is assigned to history.

All history is interpretation. That must be said at the start. Even a book of documents is a book of interpretations. There is no human writing that can convey what actually happened aside from certain basic facts. Such would be that Jesus was crucified in a Friday afternoon by Roman troops acting under orders. Who was responsible for it, and why, is a matter of interpretation. Not even court depositions by all the parties concerned would have put the matter beyond all doubt. People rationalize, people lie. They surely do both when they suspect that history will judge their shameful conduct. Above all, people do not supply motives for their deeds. The evangelists had no living, first-hand witnesses for much that they reported on. They had fragments of narrative, of teaching, of reminiscence that had been spoken publicly again and again, some of it committed to writing. With consummate skill they had set down what it all meant, a matter they were much more interested in than in the events themselves. Why was it fitting that the popular desert solitary John should have testified to Jesus? Why was it that in some gospels Jesus was said to be active in pagan and Samaritan territory and in others not? Why did his three resuscitations from the dead so closely resemble those of Elijah and Elisha, his multiplication of the loaves the story of the manna and Elisha's feeding of a hundred men with bread? In short, what do the gospels mean to convey about Jesus in their carefully crafted compositions? The initial mistake

on the reader's part would be to take these writings as histories of Jesus
when in fact they are proclamations of this significance to help believers
live their lives in him.

The books of the New Testament are surely historical, but they tell the history of a movement, not a man. They chronicle the faith of the Jewish sect that
was coming to realize its likenesses to and differences from its parent, the religion of Israel, and its notable divergence from its sibling Judaism, the religion of the rabbis. The focus of Paul's letters seems to be on the death and resurrection of Jesus. These events recede in time with each journey he takes and
letter he writes. In fact, it is the community life of the believers in
Thessalonika and Corinth, Philippi and the indeterminate Galatian towns
that the apostle chiefly records and the history of Jesus only insofar as it is
part of theirs.

Jesus in Capernaum and on the lakeshore, on the temple porches or in its
outer courts appears to be the evangelists' concern. But that Jesus is not
the center of their concern. Jesus in the minds and hearts of believers in
Sepphoris and the Syrian cities and wherever else he was being prayed
through to the one he called Father, is. This writing is an existentialist literature, all of it, which in some measure looks backward but has an eye
chiefly to the present that then was and uncannily to the future. The gospels
tell no "life of Jesus," only of the lives of people trying to live with his
life. Each of the four is not the picture in motion out of the past it seems to
be but a still frame of the now at the time of the writing. Every parable and
discourse, every encounter with demons, disease, and death is a summary
in the little of many lives lived and many proclamations uttered. From
Jesus' departure in glory down to the moment Mark and the others began
their labored task, each gospel speaks history. It is church history and the
church is the teller of its own story. No process of acceptance later known
as canonization was required to make it such. It was history when it was first
lived, first spoken, first recorded. The question that matters is, can believers trust the community that transmitted the tradition, that told the tale then
and tells it now?

It may seem that the direction in which the present line of inquiry is leading is one that ends not in faith in Jesus but faith in the church. But, as the perceptive will immediately grasp, there can be no ultimate trust reposed in
the believers of the first, second, and subsequent centuries. Faith is placed in
God alone. Even the creedal formula, "I believe in the holy Catholic Church,
etc." does not mean the same thing as "I believe in God . . . in Jesus Christ
. . . in the Holy Ghost." The latter says *credo in Deum*, etc. a complete
reliance on the one God whom we conceive as tri-personal. With the "goods
of salvation," as they are called, or the "works of the Spirit," it is "*credo
sanctam catholicam ecclesiam*, etc.," "I believe the church [to be a work of
God but not something worthy of divine honors]." Regarding the trustwor-
thiness of the gospels, the main issue is what is believed about the church as

the corporate believer in the Jesus Christ the gospels tell about. Christians possess the faith of the church. Through this faith they believe in God and the revelation God has made. The faith by which this community believed in the resurrection appearances is the same as that of the spread of belief outside Jewish circumstances, of the evangelization accomplished by Peter and Paul in Rome, Ephrem in Syria, Athanasius in Egypt, Boniface in Germany, and Augustine in England.

A CHANGING FAITH

But did not the faith change once its object was altered? At first it was faith in the risen Christ who was identical with Jesus, a person whose words and deeds were well remembered. The Spirit's action among the disciples was both the cause and the object of that faith. Soon there came to be believers, Palestinian Jews, who had none of those experiences but knew those who had. The circle widened. Jews and gentiles with no direct link to the earthly Jesus or the risen Christ evangelized others and they in turn others. How could the account be trusted, especially when in the near diaspora nothing seems to have been transmitted beyond the fact that Jesus died and rose?

The answer lies in the fundamental fact that belief was never a matter of accepting human testimony. Men and women who instructed in the new way may have been believed by others in the sense of having had human credence placed in them. They were never believed *in*. Only God and Christ were that, with the Spirit of God making it possible. The agent or instrument in this act of faith was always the church, the community that is the "body of Christ" in whom the Spirit dwells. The language is Paul's, but we have no earlier, Palestinian expression of the same conviction. Those earliest believers did express it somehow.

As the materials that lay behind the gospels were being formed, they surely contained departures from the ways Jesus was initially remembered. There were tellings of his deeds and words that were influenced not little, but much, by resurrection faith in him. Local communities engaged in departures from previous tellings—it was initially a Palestinian phenomenon, remember—because their purpose was to convey the reality of Jesus in ways that seemed best to them. Later, for example, when Mark made the multiplication of loaves and fishes to be two rather than one for his pedagogic purpose, there was probably no outcry. Again, the Matthew people may have been using Mark as their lectionary for years before their scribe or scribes expanded it to give us Matthew's gospel. There probably *was* an outcry then of diehards unhappy with the change—not an unhappiness that the new product had so many added words of Jesus and a midrashic birth narrative, but because it was different. The prophets and evangelists of the communities were expected, after all, to add color and make changes, telling the Jesus story in a new way. That was their gift and task.

CREATIVE FIDELITY STOPPED

At a certain point this work of creative fidelity stopped. The likely reason was that God had raised up no more than the four evangelists of genius whose work we know. The "many" Luke's gospel speaks of in its prologue would include besides Mark and Q,[2] the collectors of miracles, parables, and sayings and perhaps certain literary craftsmen whose works are well forgotten. After the acceptance of the four gospels by consensus of the churches—achieved roughly by 175—an adverse judgment was passed on all the later attempts. The church's faith held that these inventive accounts did not convey the Christ believed in. This nonacceptance established the limits of development of narratives about Jesus as vehicles of the church's faith.

Was accuracy of detail in reporting the standard employed to determine what was of faith regarding the words and deeds of the earthly Jesus? It was not, as we know from the critical scholarship of the last 150 years. Was a careful transmission of the faith tradition concerning his person the standard? We know from the same researches that it was. A difficulty is that a historical search yields only historical results, in this case of a highly tentative nature. Admission of the fact that we are faced with an ecclesiological question here—the nature of the faith of the apostolic church—and not a historical one would help greatly.

The reports of Jesus' activities and faith in him are inextricably intertwined in the gospels. To change the figure, they are in good part miscible liquids that become one, like water and wine. Faith and history in the gospels are simply not immiscible, like oil and water. But such is the presupposition of those who seek to discover Jesus' history as totally separable from the early church's theology about him. The venture of complete separation is fated to failure, even though a few brute facts like Capernaum as Jesus' Galilean headquarters can stand on their own. Some few things like this have not been subjected to a faith interpretation.

AN ECCLESIAL JESUS

This sounds perilously close to the claim that in the gospels we have an ecclesial tradition about Jesus. Quite simply, that is what we have. We know him, not in his person alone or in writings about him alone but as the history of belief in him reveals him to us. We call this "traditions," in Christian usage *the* tradition. This means that the history of believers in him from

2. The hypothetical sayings source of between 50 and 70 utterances of Jesus, depending on how they are divided, which occur in identical or near-identical wording in Matthew and Luke. See Ivan Havener, *Q: The Sayings of Jesus* (Collegeville, Minn.: Michael Glazier, Liturgical Press, 1987); John Kloppenborg, *The Formation of Q: Trajectories in Ancient Wisdom Collections* (Minneapolis: Augsburg Fortress, 1987).

Pentecost down to the completion of 2 Peter (if that was written last) is taken as seriously as the history of Jesus himself. Nor did the chain of believers stop there. It was only the end of a particular era. Faith went on.

There is no record of the lineaments of faith in the earliest age, the years 30 to 50. Then we begin to learn of the faith of Paul's churches in Christ Jesus as he proclaimed and nourished it. The undatable Q—it may go back to as early as 40—tells us that some church or churches viewed him as God's wisdom in the flesh. Seemingly, faith in his death and resurrection was not essential to the Q community. Only with Mark does there begin to be an interest, that we know of, in the man of history. But by this time it is no longer his history alone. It is history as seen through the prism of the histories of those who believe in him. The Jesus of the gospels is the Christ of early Christian tradition.

That should not distress persons of faith. They may pursue Jesus' earthly history as rigorously as the limits of critical method allow. Their comfort is that their starting-point and finishing-point is the same: the faith in him, reflected in the gospels, held by the church that believers constitute.

EMPIRICAL AWARENESS OF JESUS

This brings us to the basic question with which the essays in this collection are concerned. Can there be any such thing as an empirical study of, or relation to, Jesus of Nazareth?

Since the word "empirical" has two senses quite different in their connotations, the answer must be twofold.

The more modern of these—going back two centuries or so—sees the empirical as that which relies or is based solely on experiment and observation rather than theory. Such are the many theories and the fewer indisputable facts of the physical sciences. They rely on sense data: the palpable, the measurable, in many cases that which is deducible from the above two. When "empirical" is used in this sense, it describes methods of observation or research quite different from those used by history. Both use the word "evidence," but two distinct things are meant. Sometimes the term "scientific history" is used but it is a misnomer. All that is intended is the application of careful research methods to testimonies of various sorts to the past: written records; concordant or discordant witness to events or persons of the past; human artifacts, human remains, and the like. In every case critical history tries to determine whether the various testimonies constitute a dependable record. It is in no sense an empirical study as chemistry, physics, and astronomy are.

A second and older meaning of empirical is that which relies or is based on practical experience without reference to scientific principles. Thus, various seventeenth and eighteenth expressions of Christian faith were described as empirical or experimental (where nowadays we would say experiential).

In this sense, knowledge of Jesus by believers in him has always been empirical. They know him, not as a figure out of the past only—someone read
about in the New Testament and other confirmatory evidence—but as the
Jesus Christ, head and members, of their everyday experience. They know
him as the church, whose head he is and whose body they are. This knowledge is not to be confused with the special gifts accorded to mystics or the
claims of enthusiasts (the word is not here used pejoratively) who say that they
have experienced Christ's presence in the Spirit. All of these experiences
of Jesus may be granted for the sake of argument but something else is being
spoken of.

An empirical awareness of the reality of Jesus Christ in the sense above
is a correct description of knowing him directly, whether in private prayer,
in Christian worship in community, in deeds of justice and love, in his sisters
and brothers the baptized, or indeed in the whole human family. He is known
because he is experienced in all these ways.

CHAPTER EIGHT

Humankind and the Religious Dimension

WILLIAM C. TREMMEL

ALONG THE WAY

I found, circled with
    chaos, in stillness centered,
the hurricane's eye. (WCT)[1]

Modern scientists tell a fantastic story about how sometime between 15 and 20 billion years ago it all got started in a pinhead-size explosion of sufficient energy to eventuate into all that now is and whatever is yet to come. They tell an incredible story; not quite detailed enough in the beginning Bang, but detailed enough to support Pierre Teilhard's speculations on geosphere, biosphere, noosphere (mindsphere).[2] It was and is a creative process, an evolving ongoing operation.

We may never know what really happened in the first billions of years, but we are fairly sure that about 4.6 billion years ago that geosphere, one day to be called earth, was swirling and whirling into orbit and compactness; and cooling down gradually, gradually, gradually. When it cooled sufficiently, hydrogen and oxygen combined (water happened) and oceans began to form. And then suddenly in those oceans life began to happen.

But that part should not have happened—not the life part; not the biosphere part. The oceans should have all frozen solid. And that would have

---

1. For haiku introductions see William Calloley Tremmel, *Running on the Bias* (Tampa: Tumbleweed Press, 1989).

2. See Teilhard de Chardin, *The Phenomenon of Man* (New York: Harper & Row, 1959).

been that. No life, no biosphere, then or now, because if the oceans had ever frozen solid they would be solid still. They should have frozen, but they did not. Instead a "miracle" happened, or something like a miracle. From some source or other a fantastic saving maneuver occurred. At least that is how Owen Gingrich,[3] who is a scholar of sufficient stature for our attention, sees it. Not long ago Gingrich delivered a lecture at the University of Pennsylvania. The lecture was entitled, *Let There Be Light*.[4] In his lecture/article Gingrich sketches the creation of the universe: the cosmos, from Big Bang to current times. He then argues that the whole evolution of the universe since that ground-zero explosion is simply too grand a design to have been accidental. And he gives an interesting example; an example that Aquinas in his fifth argument would be tempted to endorse.

When the earth was forming as one of the planets around the sun, the sun was not as hot as it is today. It was probably 25 percent less luminous. Now, if the sun were 25 percent less luminous today, with the kind of ozone layer we have, all the oceans would be frozen solid. And if the oceans had ever been frozen solid, they would still be frozen solid because the sun has never been, and is not now radiant enough to unfreeze once-upon-a-time frozen oceans.

So what happened? As the earth began to form, the swirling clumps of stone began to compress into our geosphere. The compression got tighter and tighter, and the interior got hotter and hotter, and volcanic gases began to break through the crust. Just as the land mass was forming, and then the oceans, so was a new outgassing-volcanic atmosphere of carbon dioxide and water vapor [CO_2 and H_2O] forming around the earth. This was a very thick atmosphere at least 25 percent thicker than our current ozone. And it produced a strong greenhouse effect that raised the earth's surface temperature above the critical freezing point, thus saving the oceans' liquidity.

But that hothouse/greenhouse was also a threat because as the sun got hotter, so did the surface of the earth. The earth's oceans were threatened with boiling away. The planet that we would one day need was threatened by a runaway greenhouse effect. Then just in the nick of time a single-celled, algae-like organism exploded into life in the oceans of the newly formed geosphere. This life-form, extracting hydrogen from the water and releasing oxygen into the air, gradually replaced [parallel to the sun's increasing radiation] the original opaque atmosphere with the blue, gaseous atmosphere that encircles our earth protectingly even to this day, and especially that precious ozone layer that we are warned to concern ourselves about.

As Gingrich puts it: "The perfect timing of this complex configuration of

---

3. Owen Gingrich is professor of astronomy and history of science at Harvard University.

4. The Owen Gingrich lecture is printed in *Is God a Creationist?* ed. Roland M. Frey (New York, Scribner's, 1983), pp. 119-137.

HUMANKIND AND THE RELIGIOUS DIMENSION

circumstances is enough to amaze and bewilder many of my friends who look at all this in purely mechanistic terms—the survival of life on earth seems such a close shave as to border on the miraculous. Can we not see the designer's hand at work?"[5]

At least we know that there is a world going on, and it exemplifies direction and progress and meaning. It moved from Big Bang to geosphere, to biosphere, to mindsphere. And in all this motion we can see at least two basic dimensions of world process: 1) There is direction to it all, and 2) each level of development exemplifies increasing, organized complexity; organized complexities seen, for example, in earth itself, in life, mind, self-consciousness, thinking, love, empathy—with exquisite and overwhelming beauty in it all.

But, and this is the question of this chapter, why are we humanoid types the only ones who make such speculations. What is it about us that makes us the myth-making, storytelling, philosophical, scientific, theological animals. And the simple answer is: Because we are an integral part of that whole meaningful process that began at least as early as the Big Bang. We are part of the process. Emergents in the process. Self-creating and world-creating in our own particular ways. But how did we get this way?

THE HUMAN ANIMAL

> On day six, late, God,
> somewhat disappointed, made
> his first sunflowers. (WCT)[6]

Twenty-five thousand years ago, Cro-Magnons (early *Homo sapien sapiens*) made tools.[7] They also made religion. We have some of their artifacts to prove these claims. Why Cro-Magnons made tools and religion is not hard to answer. They needed them; needed technology and metatechnology[8] to deal with life and death problems. We will examine this at some length, but later. First we must ask a prior question: Not why did they do these things, but how could they do these things: make tools and religion? What made them different from all those other animals that did not make tools and religion? How did Cro-Magnons get that way?

---

5. Ibid., p. 133.

6. As one might poetically interpret Genesis 1:26; 6:6.

7. Anthropologists now recognize the period 35000 to 10000 years ago (the late ice age also called Upper Paleolithic period) to have been one of the most creative times in the history of humankind—creative in language, in art, in music, in class distinctions, in the origins of commerce and trade. The time of the first fully modern species of human kind; now called man twice wise—*homo sapiens sapiens*.

8. Metatechnology is any attempt to go beyond technology and introduce extranatural and/or supernatural techniques into natural processes; e.g., praying for rain.

Like everything else, the Cro-Magnons were part and parcel of the creative process that some fifteen-twenty billion years after the first bang still bangs away. But they were special parts: those parts that quietly in their lifespheres evolved themselves into mindspheres. And that made all the difference. To this we must give some attention.

A basic metaphor in empirical/process thought is the term "event"—translated here as "a happening." We shall for our special purpose target a special kind of event: the human event, which is basically a social event; that is, an organic happening. In every happening, in every passing present, there is harmonious, creative process. Also in every happening, in every passing present there is unpredictable newness. This can be observed, for example, in a concert featuring the Tchaikovsky Fifth, performed by a competent orchestra. Here is a sociality of sound, made possible by the fusion of notes being played by musicians who, under the baton of a good conductor, create a grand sociality of sound. But also at times in the performance, from the grand fusion of sound, an individual melody-line will stand out as the mass of sound gives way to a solo passage. At one point, within the very structure of harmonious accompaniment,[9] a French horn asserts itself with enchanting, commanding freedom. And this line of solo-sound, in its very being, makes a fusion of the whole, and the whole is changed into a new whole. The mutuality, the interconnectedness of part and whole, constitutes the reality of this special social event. And this special individual-social fusion is never quite the same twice, even if it is the same orchestra, the same director, and the same soloist. There is always a newness in the performance.

Even though it might appear that the sociality and emergence of sound in the performance of the Tchaikovsky Fifth is mostly in the hearer's ear, this is not so. Sociality (emergence and fusion) is not merely a matter of psychology. It is a real and dynamic relatedness of parts to wholes and wholes to parts. And this relatedness, this fusion, is as extensive as the events of the entire cosmos. Which is to say that the term "social event" is a usable metaphor for interpreting the nature of nature itself. It is also *the* event for understanding the nature of the human animal.

In addressing questions about the nature of the human animal, George Herbert Mead[10] concentrated attention on 1) the emergence of new entities from basic social structures—entities which he saw as true novelties, and 2) the dynamic of those new entities in restructuring the social structures from

---

9. For evidence try the beautiful French horn emergent independence in the first few minutes of the *andante cantabile* section of Tchaikovsky's Fifth.

10. George Herbert Mead, born in South Hadley, Massachusetts, in 1863. Educated at Oberlin College, continued studies at Harvard, later went abroad for three years of advanced study in philosophy and psychology. He taught at Ann Arbor from 1890 to 1893; then joined the faculty at the University of Chicago, where he taught until his death thirty-eight years later, in 1931.

which they emerge; in reforming their environments into new social structures.

As social philosopher and/or behavioral psychologist, Mead, in illustrating his position on sociality, was right at home with our symphony concert. He, too, held that although overall social structure is basic, it is not to be regarded as being either absolute or self-contained. The part, the individual, is not merely a cipher, or a quantitative statistic, but a creative quality that gives to the social structure from which it emerges quite as much as it takes from that structure. The soloist recreates a whole new symphony sound quite as much as the orchestra makes possible the individuality of the soloist's accomplishments. The whole is creative of the part, and the part is creative of the whole.

The social relation is basic, but not final. The whole thing is an interrelated process. This is true of all living things, but especially true of humans. Mead held that human mind and human selfhood depend upon social intercourse. Human animals do not spontaneously emerge full-blown from social structures. Rather they invent themselves within various social structures. And the main device for this self-creation is language communication.[11] All animals communicate. They make gestures (even noise-gestures) to which other animals, especially animals of the same species, respond. But human animals do their gesturing (language communicating) much more dramatically, meaningfully, effectively. Humans are the talking animals, and it is in their talking that they get the basis for their human maturation. Significant human communication is made possible, first, because of the sophisticated nervous system in humans and, second, because of the also sophisticated larynx system with which they are also endowed. The human brain is the instrument that makes it possible for humans to remember the past, experience the present, and (and this is of crucial importance) imagine the future. The vocal system is the instrument that makes it possible for humans to communicate (past, present, future) rememberings and imaginings to each other and to themselves. The brain and the vocal mechanism, arising in a matrix of social action, make possible the process of communication and place human intelligence at human disposal. We can think imaginatively. This special thinking ability comes about, apparently, not simply because of a wonderful brain and vocal structures inherent in humans, but because of certain deficiencies in the human inheritance. Erich Fromm put it succinctly when he wrote:

---

11. George Mead also identifies the playing of games as important in a person's development of self-consciousness and maturity. When a child is active in a game, that child "must have the attitude of everyone else involved in that game." That child must be able to envision the others and their parts in the game, and himself/herself and his/her part of the game. See *Mind, Self, & Society* (Chicago: University of Chicago Press, 1934), pp. 151-163.

The first element which differentiates human from animal existence is a negative one: the relative absence in man of instructive regulation in the process of adaptations to the surrounding world. . . . The emergence of man can be defined as occurring at the point in the process of evolution where instinctive adaptation has reached its minimum.[12]

Which, more simply stated, is to say that we are short on instinctive "know-how." It is not being born of human parents (being endowed with human brain and vocal cords) that makes us truly human. It is the transformation that occurs as we invent ourselves (recreate ourselves) in the process of human communication. We transform ourselves into the sophisticated maturity that makes us truly human animals—*Homo sapiens sapiens*. We are the animals who, as Sartre puts it, have our existence before our essence.[13] An acorn, in hospitable environment, just naturally grows up to be an oak tree. A duck just naturally is always a duck, and just that kind of a duck. It is born that way. All of the necessary instructions—how to swim, how to fly, and, apparently, even the migratory flight route—are all in its genetic structure at the beginning of his time.

But humans are dramatically different. Humans begin to exist before they are really human—existence before essence. In a special sense, we humans are the nonprogramed animals. We are here before we are really human. Initially we are just candidates for humanity. It is true that at birth, even at conception, there is an instructed part laid down. Our physical attributes are pretty much all there. The body begins, and the instructions for its physical maturity are all there; but not the humanity, not the mind, not the language; not our attitudes, our loves, our antipathies, our sadnesses, our religions. All of this—and all else that makes us persons, personalities, human beings— is yet to be learned; yet to be created.

Illustration: A bunch of years ago, a friend and I took our then-young sons on a canoeing vacation in the Boundary Waters Canoe Area Wilderness (BWCA)—a million acres of wonderful wilderness that divides one section of Canada and the USA from each other. We rented two canoes, lashed them together in pontoon fashion, and with a small boat motor, putted our way off into the wilderness. The second day out, I was at the helm, Jim Worrell (my vacationing physician friend) was sitting up ahead, the boys were in the other canoe. As we moved through the magnificence of the natural world around us, unexpectedly Jim twisted around, looked at me and said, "Tremmel, do you know the most wonderful thing in the world?" Just off hand I couldn't think of it. He held up his thumb and said, "The length of my

---

12. Erich Fromm, *Man for Himself* (New York: Rinehart, 1947), p. 38.

13. See Jean Paul Sartre's *Existentialism Is a Humanism*, Mairet's 1946 translation of *L'existentialisme est un humanisme*, in Walter Kaufmann's *Existentialism from Dostorvsky to Sartre* (Cleveland and New York: World, 1956), p. 290.

thumb." Then he continued. "Think about it. . . . At the moment of my conception the length of my thumb was laid down, was genetically set: just that long, and no longer. And my whole hand. The same thing. My five fingers. My wrist. My whole arm. . . ." and on, and on, and on—everything. And I must admit that it was fascinating—all that he told me about the wonders of genetic programing. But that was not the really fascinating thing happening. The really fascinating thing was *his fascination* with the length of his thumb. And that was not laid down at the moment of his conception—not his fascination, not his medical degree, not his delightful personality, not his love for people, not his dedication to his profession, not any of the things that really made him Jim Worrell. What made him what he really was, what made him truly fascinating and truly human, was a deficiency in instinctive "know-how," and how he made up for that deficiency.

In a crucial sense, humans are the nonprogramed animals. Being nonprogramed, having existence before essence, makes it possible for the emergence of an animal that can be both keenly rational and passionately emotional—both for good and evil. And this came about because of the self-conscious and imaginative nature of the human animal. First, in their emergence through the language communication aspect of human development, humans became not just conscious animals, but keenly self-conscious animals. In the use of significant symbols (language) we humans not only talk to other people but we talk to ourselves. We hear ourselves talking, we become self-consciously aware of ourselves talking. When we talk to others (and/or to ourselves quietly inside), we talk of the past, the present, and the future—or as Tennessee Williams puts it: the past, the present, and the perhaps. In the combination of self-consciousness and imagination the creative dynamics of human behavior occur: the rational dynamics, and the feeling dynamics.

It was Aristotle who early on called humankind the rational animals, and he was right up to a point. We do have cool, rational minds. We build fabulous computers and space technology with our cool, rational minds. We explore inner space and outer space and four dimensional space-time with our cool, rational minds. We use our sophisticated rational minds for all kinds of marvelous inventions and productions (even theology and philosophy), but that is only part of it. Much more characteristic of humans is not cool rationality, but impassioned actions and rationalizations. And it is in this dimension that humankind becomes, among other things, a religious animal.

THE RELIGIOUS ANIMAL

> Some night when early
> winter's in the air I'll
> hear an owl call my name. (WCT)

As far as anybody seems to be able to determine, humans are the only animals that do religion. Dogs don't do it. Cats don't do it. Chimpanzees, elephants, porpoises. None of them. These facts seem to make it proper to call humans the special animals—the religious animals. But, of course, humans are the only animals who do quite a number of things: philosophy, theology, science, retail merchandising, plumbing, war. But because religion is our interest here, we shall target religion.

We are back to that earlier question: Why do we do religion? Why are humans the religious animals? A beginning insight into this question is humorously revealed in a squib that appeared in the *Wall Street Journal*, July 13, 1984. It was titled "From the Mouths of Babes." A Sunday school teacher asked a little boy if he said his prayers before he went to bed at night. The little boy said, "Yes." The teacher then asked if he said his prayers when he got up in the morning. The little boy said, "No." The teacher asked why not, and the little boy answered, "Because I'm not scared in the morning."[14]

More academically we might approach this question about the religious animal by observing that as humans we have the kinds of minds [emerging as Mead tells us from a special central nervous system and a special larynx system and within a special system of sociality] that present us with a vivid awareness of ourselves. We do have at times, as Aristotle proposed, cool, rational minds. But we also have minds that inform us, in a most uncool fashion, that we are living in a self-defeating world. The self (any person) is disturbed because once old enough to have much sense, he/she gets the sense of the true situation into which he/she has been born. All humans are involved in, even trapped in a human environmental condition (a world) that sooner or later defeats and annihilates all selfhood. Which is to say, nobody ever gets out of life alive, and nobody ever gets out of life half of what he or she might reasonably want. And (and this is the crux of it) humans are the animals *who really know this* because, as we said above [as Mead informs us] humans are the animals of educated maturity, not instinctive maturity. Which means, among other things, that humans are the animals of extravagant self-consciousness and imagination.

To say that humans are self-conscious is to say that they see *themselves* in the present, remember *themselves* in the past, and *imagine* themselves in the future. Largely through the mechanisms of speech and games, as Mead informs us, made possible by a distinctive physiological and neurological inheritance, Mr. Jones knows himself to be Mr. Jones. Jones sees himself as both a subject (inside himself) and as an object (a self looking at others and at himself). Jones knows himself, experiences himself, in his own immediate awareness and in his remembering himself in the past. And he sees himself in imagination as he may be later on.

It is not intended here to deny that other animals have some degree of

---

14. Created by T. H. Fallon.

self-consciousness and imagination. But if they do to some degree see themselves and imagine themselves in other places doing other things, they do not do so very effectively, because generation after generation they go on living in the same old way. If things are imagined differently, changing modes of operation and ways of life ought to occur. But nonhuman animals rarely change their modes and ways. And when they do change, it is usually an evolutionary change, not a deliberate, thought-out change. Apparently other animals live in the immediate world, with some memory of the past, but little thought about, or imagination of, themselves living *or dying* in the future.

Because of the size of self-consciousness and imagination in human animals, they endlessly want what is not and are afraid of what is not. They live positively and negatively: live not only in the actual world around them but in a *wished-for-world* and in an *afraid-of-world*. Positively they imagine what is not and desire it, sometimes passionately. Negatively they imagine what is not and fear it, sometimes devastatingly. This puts humans, as Paul Tillich has suggested, in the condition of *angst*—the condition of anxiety and estrangement. The world does not measure up to human wants and ambitions and down the road it threatens with annihilation.

Because things are never quite as humans want them and because humans can always imagine things differently, and want them so, they rebuild the world endlessly, closer to their heart's desire. 1) They reform the world with technology and science. 2) They try to make it reasonable, to make sense of it, with mythology, theology, philosophy. And 3) they try to relate to it adequately or transcend it successfully with religious beliefs, devotions, and commitments. Religion, so regarded, is definable as the way that a person believes and behaves in his/her efforts to overcome and transcend the existential estrangement in which humans so often find themselves—the vivid awareness of finitude.

This last item (#3) identifies religion as an adjustive behavior and targets what might be called the function of religion. Indeed, that is exactly what William Bernhardt calls his method of establishing a meaningful definition of religion;[15] a method and definition that he researched and established

---

15. William Henry Bernhardt was born in Chicago in 1893. He grew up in Beatrice, Nebraska. His family was of German Lutheran affiliation. Apparently no thought was given to his attending college until a Methodist minister recognized the young man's keen intellect and encouraged him to do so. He graduated from Nebraska Wesleyan in 1921 at age 28. After Nebraska Wesleyan, he took advanced degrees at Garrett Biblical Institute (B.D., 1924), Northwestern University (M.A., 1925), University of Chicago (Ph.D., 1928). While in school Bernhardt served several years as a Methodist minister in River Forest, Illinois, and as a YMCA Secretary in Chicago, and two years as Professor of Philosophy at Central College, Fayette, Missouri. In 1929 he accepted a position in theology and philosophy at the Iliff School of Theology in Denver, Colorado. He served on the Iliff faculty for thirty-five years, part of the time as academic dean. He retired from Iliff in 1964. From 1964-1970, he was Professor of Philosophy, and had various other

in order to speak intelligently to classes on religion in his new position at the Iliff School of Theology, where he taught from 1929 to 1964. His problem was not that there were no definitions available for him to appropriate, or that there were no good definitions. The problem was that there were too many "good" definitions. As he stated his problem,

> Students of religion . . . find it practically impossible to agree upon what it is they are to study. This state of affairs becomes evident as soon as one examines books purportedly written on religious subjects. [They] may find [themselves] reading ethics tinged with emotion; or [sociology] written with more than customary fervor; [or abnormal psychology] written by one who finds the field wholly absorbing and therefore concludes that it is religious; or [they] may find [themselves] reading the impassioned writings of some philosophical physicist whose chief emotional satisfaction is found in his struggle with fundamental concepts, and who is thus convinced that his physics is religion.[16]

In his research of definitions, Bernhardt concluded that probably most of the many definitions of religion can be classified in four groups: First, there are supernaturalistic definitions; for example, James Frazier's definition defining religion as "the propitiation or conciliation of powers superior to man which are believed to direct and control the course of nature and human life."[17] Second, there are definitions that stress the ethical-social interest of humankind; for example Alfred Eustice Haydon's "religion is the shared quest of the good life."[18] Third, there are definitions (which Bernhardt himself was inclined to endorse) that can be called adjustive definitions, or as Bernhardt called them, functional definitions. For example, Bernhardt referred to that first-century slave-philosopher, Epictetus. As a slave Epictetus knew all about unsatisfactory/inescapable aspects in human existence. As philosopher he made an adjustive/functional, serenity prayer type, pronouncement: "We must," he said, "make the best of what is under our control, and take the rest as its nature is. How, then, is its nature? As God wills."[19] Finally, fourth, Bernhardt identified those definitions that are based in deep emotional experience—based in feeling, in thrill, which may at times become intense enough to be an ecstasy.

---

administrative assignments at California Western University in San Diego, California. He died on September 5, 1979. See William H. Bernhardt, *A Functional Philosophy of Religion* (Denver: Criterion Press, 1958).

16. Ibid., p. 1.

17. James Frazier, *The Golden Bow* (New York: Macmillan, 1922), one volume edition, p. 50.

18. A. E. Haydon, *The Quest of the Ages* (New York: Macmillan, 1929), p. ix.

19. *Arrian's Discourses of Epictetus*, trans. W. A. Oldfather (London: William Heinemann, 1926), Book I, i.17.

Bernhardt concluded that the glut of "good" definitions was the result of the method used in making most definitions of religion. The method was John Stuart Mill's method of agreement, also called empirical generalization. First we come up with an hypothesis that seems to make religious sense; e.g., Alfred Eustice Haydon's religion is "shared quest of the good life." Then we verify our definition by a simple enumeration—by counting noses. After the counting, "shared quest of the good life" certainly seems to add up to a definition. That is what a great many people seem to be doing, or trying to do. Definition accomplished. Or again, upon careful empirical investigation we conclude (as did Rudolf Otto) that religion is essentially an experience of sacredness. This investigation bears out and we conclude on our empirical evidence that religion is the experience of the "Holy Other." Religion is the numinous experience.[20]

To get around the glut of definitions and become more definitive, Bernhardt shifted the definition method. He accepted the method that Louis Pasteur used in solving the mystery of "spontaneous combustion" in the origins of bacteria.[21] This method is the method of concomitant variations or functional analysis. It is based in the premise that concurring variations may be indications of causal relations; i.e., concomitant variations may be indications of functional connections. If two phenomena are observed to change with regularity, it is likely (not guaranteed, but likely) that they are somehow causally related.

In examining the functioning of religion in primitive, ancient, and modern cultures, Bernhardt found a concomitant relationship between the use of technology and metatechnology [see note 8]. Where people have sufficient technological know-how to solve critical problems, they solve those problems on their own. Where they do not have adequate technology to solve critical problems, they often seek supernatural/extranatural help. Bernhardt did not equate religion and metatechnology, although metatechnology is employed in most religions. Rather, Bernhardt used technology and meta-technology to identify the relationship between human need and the religious enterprise. He defined religion as a primary adjustment system in which and through which people endeavor (often using metatechnology) to live their lives in sustaining morale, no matter what. As Bernhardt put it,

Religious behavior is a complex form of individual and group behavior whereby persons are prepared intellectually and emotionally to meet the nonmanipulable aspects of existence positively by means of a reinterpretation of the total situation and with the use of various techniques.[22]

20. See Rudolf Otto, *The Idea of the Holy* (Oxford: Oxford University Press, 1924).

21. For a more detailed account of the Pasteur experiment and of Bernhardt's use of that experiment see the Tremmel chapter in *God, Values, and Empiricism*, ed. Creighton Peden and Larry E. Axel (Macon, Ga.: Mercer University Press, 1989), p. 234.

22. Bernhardt, *Functional Philosophy of Religion*, p. 157.

By "nonmanipulable aspects" Bernhardt was referring to those aspects in human living that are beyond immediate human control and are of critical importance to human life and well-being: circumstances that are horrendous and uncontrollable. Nonmanipulables threaten humans with nonbeing—nonbeing meaning, in this consideration, the loss of values that are essential to genuine human life—such as 1) life itself, 2) a sense of personal worth, 3) an awareness of moral integrity. Here we can see Paul Tillich's: fate and death, emptiness and meaninglessness, guilt and condemnation.[23]

Death is, of course, a major example of a nonmanipulable that demands religious attention. It is not only an uncontrollable problem, but a horrendous problem. The death of a loved one, one's own death, anyone's death, is horrendous both in fact and contemplation and evokes religious responses. But by no means is death the only steely nonmanipulable that confronts ordinary everyday living. For those who live past the tender years, the basic tragedy of life may not be death but disillusionment: in discovering that so often life must be lived in little, picayune ways far beneath the expectations of our youthful dreams and ambitions. The real frustration is not that life must end, but that it must so often be lived in hopeless, frustrating, meaningless, distressing ways.

The world is, of course, full of problems that are nonmanipulable but are not problems demanding religious attention; e.g., the rising and falling of the tides, the progression of our galaxy toward Andromeda, the coming and going of the seasons. I cannot manipulate the ocean, but the ocean may be of little religious significance to me until, in a storm, that ocean threatens to swamp my boat.

As seen from Bernhardt's perspective, religion is a complex attempt to deal intellectually and emotionally with those aspects of human existence that are of critical significance in human life and are unavoidable in human life. All of the other definitions stated above simply define aspects of this basic functional need. We may want Haydon's shared quest of the good life. We may experience Otto's numinous Holy Other, or James' something more. We can feel Kant's demanding conscience, and Whitehead's solitariness. All this, and more. But all of this happens for a more basic reason. It happens because we are those self-conscious, imaginative animals who must deal intellectually and emotionally with what it is to be humans trying to make our way in a world that is obviously not made for humans only.[24]

---

23. See Paul Tillich, *The Courage To Be* (New Haven: Yale University Press, 1952, 1965), Chapter 2.

24. Coming from a different direction, William James seems to have arrived at a similar conclusion. In the chapter called "Conclusions" in his *Varieties of Religious Experience*, referring to the wide range of religious beliefs, he asked, "Is there under all the discrepancies of the creeds, a common nucleus to which they bear their testimony unanimously?" He then answered his question: "There is a certain uniform deliverance in which religions all appear to meet. It consists of two parts:—1. An uneasiness; and 2. Its

First, then, there is the function of religion. Second, there is the "how" of religion. How do people do religion?

THE GOD-WORD

> First thaw running clear
> and cold. Up there somewhere a
> glacier in the sun. (WCT)

As observed above, Bernhardt identified the first dimension of religion as being a complex human activity wherein persons attempt intellectually and emotionally to develop and retain sustaining morale in the face of potentially overwhelming vicissitudes. Bernhardt calls the second dimension of his definition the "Reinterpretational Level. This is the level normally spoken of as theological or metaphysical. . . . The primary problem at this level is the problem of God."[25]

One thing people do when they do religion is think about it and talk about it. They do *theos logos*. They make words about God. Traditionally, historically, in all true religions, people have striven to deal with Bernhardt's "nonmanipulables" in a conviction that "at the center of human experience, and even of all reality, there is a being, or beings, or process (a divine reality) in which and through which a person (or community of persons) can transcend the life-negating traumas of human existence, can overcome the sense of finitude."[26]

To avoid the "parable arguments" of recent language philosophy [especially the delightful God-word parables of John Wisdom and John Hicks], we might utilize, as people ordinarily do for determining what words mean, Lewis Carroll's insightful Humpty Dumpty. Alice and Humpty were having a conversation and the subject of unbirthdays came up. Humpty told Alice that the King and Queen gave him a fine cravat as an unbirthday present. Alice was puzzled. She had never thought of unbirthdays or unbirthday presents

---

solution. The uneasiness, reduced to its simplest terms, is a sense that there is *something wrong about us* as we naturally stand. The solution is a sense that w*e are saved from wrongness* as we naturally stand. . . . The individual, so far as he suffers from his wrongness and criticizes it, is to that extent consciously beyond it, and in at least possible touch with something higher, if anything higher exists . . . *He becomes conscious that this higher part is conterminous and continuous with a MORE of the same quality, which is operative in the universe outside of him, and with which he can keep in working touch with, and in a fashion get on board of and save himself when all his lower being has gone to pieces in the wreck." Varieties of Religious Experience* (New York: Modern Library/Longmans, Green, 1902), pp. 497-498.

25. William H. Bernhardt, *The Cognitive Quest for God and Operational Theism* (Denver, Criterion Press, 1971), p. 22.

26. William Calloley Tremmel, *Religion: What Is It?* (New York: Holt, Rinehart and Winston, 1976, 1984), p. 6.

before. Upon her inquiry, Humpty told her the obvious. There are 365 days in a year. Each person has 1 birthday each year. So, obviously, there are 364 unbirthdays in a year. And, continued Humpty, "There's a glory for you." Again confused, Alice complained that she didn't know what Humpty meant by "there's a glory." Humpty Dumpty sneered contemptuously.

> "Of course you don't—till I tell you." I mean "there's a nice knock-down argument for you."
> "But 'glory' doesn't mean 'nice knock-down argument,'" Alice objected.
> "When I use a word," Humpty Dumpty said, in a rather scornful tone, "it means just what I chose it to mean—neither more nor less."[27]

This is the stance usually taken by people concerned to talk about things—including religion and God. It is the ordinary human approach. They/we may not go as far as Humpty, but in general people employ the same basic notion. Words mean what people say they mean. Words mean what communities of persons agree upon. Language is a product of human/community invention (as, with George Mead, we saw earlier). Physicists in usage define what they mean by their scientific jargon in the discipline of physics. Computer experts agree on what they mean by computer jargon in the discipline of computer talk. Football fans invent football jargon. Theologians (in their different theological postures) invent theological jargons. And people everywhere apparently use the God-word to stand for what it is they believe originally and basically causes things to be, and/or to be the way they are; and/or makes it possible for things to happen, and go on happening. The God-word is humankind's common answer to Martin Heidegger's penetrating question, "Why are there things instead of nothing?" In one translation or another people answer, "God."

As people think about themselves in their world, as they rationalize their lives in this world, the concept of determining power emerges in their thinking. In terms of this (discovered and/or invented) determining power, or powers, people explain and arrange their religious beliefs and actions in order to deal intellectually and emotionally with religious needs. God is the answer given by religious people to the problems of the human condition—to the threat of nonbeing; to the awareness of human finitude.

Concerning the functioning of the God-word in religion, William James referred to one of Leuba's publications on the psychology of religion. "'The truth can be put,' says Leuba, 'in this way: *God is not known, he is not understood; he is used*—sometimes as meat-purveyor, sometimes as moral support, sometimes as friend, sometimes as object of love. If he proves himself useful, the religious consciousness ask for no more than that. Does God

---

27. Lewis Carroll, *Alice's Adventures in Wonderland and Through the Looking Glass* (New York: Magnam Books, 1968), pp. 221-222.

really exist? How does he exist? What is he?' are so many irrelevant questions. Not God, but life, more life, a larger richer, more satisfying life, is, in the last analysis, the end of religion.'"[28]

Traditionally in the Western world people [guided by their theologians] have identified God as different from the world that God created, or is creating. God caused the natural order, or is causing the natural order, but God is not part of that natural order.[29] If God is different from the natural order, then knowledge of God is only partially available through a rational examination of the natural order (as Aquinas philosophized), if available at all. In traditional Western theism, God knowledge is fully available only when God reveals God's supernatural dimensions through special religious means and/or persons; e.g. Moses on Mt. Sinai, God's son Jesus Christ in Galilee and Judea, Muhammad in Arabia.

Prior to the coming of the modern world—back before Copernicus, Kepler, Galileo, Boyle, Newton; back before the eighteenth-century enlightenment; back before the twentieth-century explosion of science and technology—confidence in supernatural revelation as a central theological method was the sensible way to operate on the religious "Reinterpretational Level." But today people of the modern world [especially in the Western world] live increasingly in a zeitgeist of empirically based, natural world information. This means, among other things, that basic knowledge concerning "the real world" [the everyday-lived-in-world] is based on a process of empirical investigation, hypothesizing, and verification/falsification.

In such a zeitgeist it is not surprising that not only scientists but also some theologians are turning away from revelational epistemologies and utilizing modern-world methods of empirical investigation. God knowledge is to be sought within the natural order using the best epistemological methods possible; namely, empirical investigation and rationally ordered data in what Bernhardt calls the method of increasing cognitional efficiency.[30] And quite possibly what empirical theology discovers will become increasingly the way that modern world humans will conceive of God and do their religion.

Empirical theology targets God's immanence. Apropos of this, Bernhardt writes that "God, no matter how conceived, is believed to be within the cosmic totality. . . . The term God . . . symbolizes some phase, character, struc-

28. James, *Varieties of Religious Experience*, p. 497. Taken from Leuba's "Studies in Psychology of Religious Experience," *The American Journal of Psychology* 7 (1896), p. 309.

29. This is not necessarily the case in Eastern world religions. In Indian Hinduism, for example, the ultimate cause of the world is a spiritual energy system of which all apparent realities are but appearances. Again, in Chinese Taoism, God is not outside the natural world but is the dynamic energy (Yang-Yin) and the directional dynamic (Tao/Way) of the natural world.

30. Bernhardt, *Cognitive Quest for God*, p. 7.

ture or behavior pattern of the Environmental Medium."[31] From his studies, Bernhardt affirms that in searching for God in either supernaturalistic or naturalistic categories, people see God not only in the dimension of creativity, but also in the dimensions of value and saving grace. These two dimensions constitute basic categories for God as God is depicted throughout religious literature. First, the agathonic dimension—"that which is of use to or enjoyed by human beings or the source of that which is of use and enjoyment."[32] Of contemporary naturalistic theologians, Henry Nelson Wieman has been most productive in this dimension. According to Wieman, as interpreted by Bernhardt, "God may use mechanisms for the creation or the furtherance of values, but he is not responsible for mechanisms as such."[33]

A second category for deity, Bernhardt calls the dynamic. Here one identifies as God not simply value but the entire creative process itself, or some basic dimensions of that process. Concerning the agathonic and dynamic dimensions of the God concept, Bernhardt writes:

> The categories which one adopts governs the choice of data considered admissible in determining the nature of God. From the agathonic approach, the world-as-value or the world-experienced-as-value constitutes the primary source of data. . . .
>
> From the dynamic approach, it is the world-as-experienced or the world-as-known which constitutes the source of data. The thinker who accepts this approach may not impose any value criterion as test of data-admissibility. . . .
>
> The traditional attributes of God may be divided into two general classes: the moral-personal and the absolute or existential. The first class includes those which belong to the realm of value, goodness, and character. The second class consists of those which belong to the realm of power, structure, being or existence . . . The attributes of God which will eventually emerge from the agathonic approach belong to the moral-personal group. . . . The attributes of God which emerge from the approach of the dynamic category are more absolute or existential in character. God as dominant phase or determinant behavior pattern of the existential medium may not possess the list of value or character attributes which are found in the agathonic approach. Analysis of the total environing medium may prove that God possesses some or all of the moral-personal attributes which many consider essential to the nature of God. . . . If, on the other hand, the facts which emerge from observation lead one to conclude that human values, as generally understood, are relatively unim-

31. William H. Bernhardt, "The Meaning of God in Religious Thinking," *The Iliff Review* (Winter 1946), p. 28.

32. Bernhardt, *Cognitive Quest for God*, p. 7.

33. Ibid.

portant in the local scheme of things, this conclusion may also have to be accepted. It will be necessary for the contemporary thinker to adjust himself to a rigorous theology. . . . It may be necessary for him to face the fact of God in much the same fashion that he contemplates the atomic bomb, with awe rather than sentimentality.[34]

In both agathonic and dynamic dimensions of naturalistic theology, creativity is a central concept. The creative activity everywhere apparent in the world appears to be the active "desire" to drive creative advance endlessly onward. Unlike older interpretation, we now say that God does not create by fiat and omnipotence but with passion to have becoming happen. In God's creative dimension, God is the source of creative dynamic, the principle of process, a divine impulse, a passion to change. God, however defined, operates with creative passion.

JOY

> Didn't plan it when
> I came out, but there . . . up there!
> See! - a shooting star. (WCT)

With all we have said thus far about the function of religion, and theologizing in religion, "religion turns out to be for people not simply a method of dealing with religious problems but is itself an experience of great satisfaction and immense personal worth. Religion is not only something people "do" and "use"; it is also something that happens to them. It is an experience—a highly treasured experience, and even, at times, an experience of sheer ecstasy."[35] As Ioan Lewis puts it in the opening lines of the Preface to his *Ecstatic Religion*, "Belief, ritual, and spiritual experience . . . are the corner stones of religion, and the greatest is the last."[36]

Religious experience happens on at least two levels of human experiencing: the exoteric and the esoteric. I can sing a song with you, say a prayer with you (exoteric), but I cannot share a mystical experience with you (esoteric). On the exoteric level, religion has historically exploited sensuous experience, sexual experience, love experience (both C. S. Lewis' eros variety and his agape variety).[37] On the esoteric level, religion involves at least the experiences of worshipful presence and mystical identity (mysticism).

Exoterically religious experience has been stimulated through some of the greatest of mankind's artistic, aesthetic accomplishments—all the way

34. Ibid., pp. 9-10.

35. Tremmel, *Religion: What Is It?*, p. 7.

36. See I. M. Lewis, *Ecstatic Religion* (Middlesex, England: Penguin Books, 1971), p. 11.

37. See C. S. Lewis, *The Four Loves* (New York: Harcourt, Brace, 1960), pp. 131-192.

from Notre Dame Cathedral in Paris to the modern rock music opera *Jesus Christ Superstar*.[38] Artforms play a dramatic role in religious experience. God words, theology, like science and technology, are severe abstractions. And people are, to be sure, abstracters. But first of all, people are feelers responding directly to colors, shapes, sounds. They are art born. Of course, art is also abstract, but whereas philosophy, theology, science seek the true proportions of reality, art seeks vivid awareness of reality. It can give a person not only an intellectual awareness of his/her God but a feeling of that God. And art in its religious forms also targets a social awareness of reality. Religious art forms speak not only to individuals but to individuals in their sociality. Religious art forms can effect both individual stimulation and social stimulation. As well as personal spiritual experience, art can create spiritual togetherness, and has done so, and is doing so, for people everywhere.[39]

Sexuality, as one would expect, has also played a role in religious experience—all the way from Herodotus's startling discovery of temple prostitution in Babylon to the Song of Songs in the Jewish Bible, to the Qur'an's promise of heavenly delights, at least for men, wherein they shall be "in gardens of delight, enjoying what their Lord has given them. . . . Reclining on couches . . . [and] wed to [dark-eyed] maids."[40] Christianity has been more circumspect about exploiting sexuality in religion, but it is there, underground, subconscious. Try "brides of Christ" for example.

In the dimension of eros, religions everywhere promote love for the members of the sacred community, and even for those outside the sacred community—so much love for outsiders that believers often go to great lengths to missionize them into "the real love": God's love—agape.

In all this we can share. It is exoteric. But the most precious religious experiences of all are unsharable. They are esoteric. First, the experience of divine presence, a feeling of the nearness of God—worship. Worship might be defined as an enraptured concentration in which the worshiper feels himself/herself to be in intimate personal relation with divine reality. In this condition a person feels caught up in a heightened awareness of religious values. He/she senses the reality of something mysterious and awesome, which is, at the same time, congenial, sustaining, and concerned. Try Otto's

---

38. Lyrics by Tim Rice; music by Andrew Lloyd Webber.

39. Early in his writing career, Henry Nelson Wieman declared that aesthetic experience can be a doorway to mystical experience: "A profound aesthetic experience may approach the mystical. But we do not call it mystical until the wealth of stimulation and multiplicity of reaction have become so great that distinctiveness and clarity of perception and thought fade into deep emotion. Aesthetic experience enhances vivid clarity of perception. Mystical experience submerges clarity under a wealth of richness of feeling so great that the order required for clarity can no longer be maintained." *Normative Psychology of Religion* (New York: Crowell, 1935), p. 180.

40. Koran, sura 56.10-39.

numinous consciousness, or James' something more, or Taylor's go-between God.[41]

In worship experience there remains a distance between the I and the Thou. I am here and God is there. Mysticism is something more than that. In it one slides in the direction of unity. The I-Thou distance tends to collapse. It is an experience 1) in which the consciousness is flooded with an awareness of the interrelatedness and unity of all things: a spiritual ecology which gives all things, including the mystic and God, a common identity and 2) an experience of bliss and contentment which passes all human expectation and explanation.

According to Walter Stace there are two general types of mysticism.[42] He calls one introvertive mysticism. The other he calls extrovertive mysticism. Without elaborating, we might say that introvertive mysticism turns the world off (as one would want to do in a Hindu theological system) and accomplishes a transcendent consciousness far removed from the natural world of every day. Extrovertive mysticism, in an opposite concern, turns the world on. In extrovertive mysticism the mystical event is an intense feeling that the world is somehow an overwhelming unity—a spiritual ecology, affording a sense of intense belonging.

A truly sensitive description of exoteric mysticism appears in Eugene O'Neill's play *Long Day's Journey Into Night*.[43] A father and a son, in a love-hate relationship, in lives full of tension and distress, are sitting at a dining-room table late at night. They begin to open up to each other in deep honesty. Edmond the son speaks: "You've just told me some high spots in your memories. Want to hear mine? They're all connected with the sea. Here's one. When I was on the Squarehead square rigger, bound for Buenos Aries. Full moon in the Trades. The old hooker driving fourteen knots. I lay on the bowsprit, facing astern, with the water foaming into spume under me, the masts with every sail white in the moonlight, towering high above me. I became drunk with the beauty and singing rhythm, became moonlight and the ship and the high dim-starred sky! I belonged, without past or future, within peace and unity and a wild joy, within something greater than my own life, or the life of Man, to Life itself! To God, if you want to put it that way. . . . Then another time, on the American Line, when I was lookout on the crow's nest in the dawn watch. A calm sea, that time. . . . Dreaming, not keeping lookout, feeling alone, and above, and apart, watching the dawn creep like a painted dream over the sky and sea which slept together. Then the moment of ecstatic freedom came. The peace, the end of the quest, the last

41. See John V. Taylor, *The Go-Between God* (Oxford: Oxford University Press, 1972).

42. See Walter T. Stace, *The Teachings of the Mystics* (New York: Mentor Books, The New American Library, 1960), pp. 15-23.

43. Eugene O'Neill, *Long Day's Journey Into Night* (New Haven: Yale University Press, 1956). By permission of Yale University Press.

harbor, the joy of belonging to a fulfillment beyond men's lousy, pitiful, greedy fears and hopes and dreams. And . . . other times in my life, when I was swimming far out, or lying alone on a beach, I have had the same experience. . . . Like a saint's vision of beatitude. Like the veil of things as they seem drawn back by an unseen hand. For a second you see—and seeing the secret, are the secret. For a second there is meaning! Then the hand lets the veil fall and you are alone, lost in the fog again, and you stumble on toward nowhere for no good reason!" *He grins wryly.* "It was a great mistake, my being born a man. I would have been more successful as a sea gull or a fish. As it is, I will always be a stranger who never feels at home, who does not really want and is not really wanted, who can never belong, who must always be a little in love with death."[44]

Always a little lost and alone, except in moments of tremendous joy. Religion is not only something that people do but something that happens to them, and sometimes the happening is an ecstasy. *Pax tecum.*

---

44. Ibid., pp. 153-154.

CHAPTER NINE

The Nature of the Church

BERNARD J. LEE

THE NATURE OF "NATURE"

The Spanish existentialist philosopher, Jose Ortega y Gassett, once remarked that we human beings do not so much have a "nature" as we have a history. We know what we are through the events in which we are implicated and what they tell us about ourselves. "Nature" is the best generalization we can make based upon the experience we have.

The church is a social response to the Christ-event. That social response over the centuries has its origins in the social response to Jesus in his lifetime, of which there were two forms: resident followers in the towns where he spent time and itinerant men and women who traveled with him in both the north and the south of what was the Jewish nation at that time. Jesus gave his disciples no specific structure, only some images for how power should function among them (shepherd, servant, steward).

Phenomenologically, then, church is a social response to the Christ-event, whose "nature" will always be partly founded in the Christ-event and partly in the historically and culturally conditioned appropriations of that event. That sentence is loaded with complexity! Who is interpreting the Christ-event and its requirements? Is it a Matthean interpretation with a stress upon community? Is it a Johannine interpretation with an emphasis upon one's personal relationship with Jesus? Is it a Pauline church that dwells upon the salvific character of faith or a Jamesian interpretation insisting upon the good works without which faith appears graceless?

Further, to what culture and in what time of history are we attending to assess the nature of the church? The French church of the Middle Ages, influenced by the great monastery of Cluny and by the theological prowess of the University of Paris? Or Christianity in Paris in the decades after the French revolution? Suppose it is Italy instead, or Greece, or India? In other words, what slice of history offers itself to generalization about church?

Also, how are the historical and cultural dimensions being interpreted. What sociological presuppositions shape judgments about community? Shall one try to interpret culture with Margaret Mead in mind, or Clifford Geertz, or Mary Douglas?

Because church has histories, it also has natures. The steadiest currents come closest to "nature" in the singular. But these theological judgments are also and always historical assessments.

I will explain in more detail below my selection of very early church experience and the effects of retrieving *that* church's nature into constitutive roles in the church today in U.S. culture.

EMPIRICAL AND BIASED THEOLOGICAL REFLECTION

That the deliverances of experience are the data for empirical theology is what makes it empirical. That the experiencers claim to have experienced the presence of God is what makes it theology.

When the topic is church the issue is especially complicated. Upon which of the many deliverances of the experience called church are we reflecting? Reformation churches? Roman Catholic churches? Anglican Catholic churches? First century churches? Fourth century churches? Eastern Syrian or Armenian churches before the schism? Or contemporary Egyptian Coptic churches or Russian Orthodox churches long after the schism? Simply: what cultural and historical prejudices are operative? There is never a question of whether they are, only what they are.

To add to the complexity, we need to know who is doing the reflecting, and with what ideological biases? I do not mean "ideology" in a pejorative sense. I just mean the presuppositions that one brings from one's own experience, one's language and culture, one's own rearing, one's own vested interests. There is an experience base, both personal and collective, that undergirds every interpreter's reflection. Presbyterians and Baptists, Lutherans and Catholics do not interpret redemption the same way, and that is a bias which alters the meaning of church. Within the same tradition, the liberals and conservatives, the fundamentalists and the historicized critics do not understand in the same way how God calls community into existence through Jesus Christ.

I want to name some of the context for my own reflections regarding the historical slices of church I am examining and some of the personal biases of which I am aware, i.e., my experience base.

While I cannot count in detail the effects of my conditioning, a few of the many factors are worth naming, for they surely operate in the selected early and late church experiences that I have chosen to address.

I am a First World Christian. That came home to me more vividly than I can convey recently at an International Consultation on Basic Christian Communities. I do not ever think in terms of my faith possibly costing me my life. But people in Brazil and El Salvador do. I am a U.S. Christian, and I do not know the daily and deadly tensions between the south and north of Ireland. I have seen the impassioned paintings on the walls and fences all over Belfast. I was stopped on a country road in northern Ireland by six men with automatic weapons, whom I soon learned were British soldiers. The five minutes before learning their identity were not very funny!

Further, I am male, and I recall quite clearly my surprised embarrassment when I first read Elisabeth Schüssler-Fiorenza's *In Memory of Her* and realized the New Testament presence of women that I many times passed over. I am Roman Catholic, deeply conscious of pre-and post-Conciliar Catholicism. I am a priest in the Marianist religious community. That shapes my perspective on the church, heightens my interest in community, and accounts for my strong interest in the figure of Mary as an insider in Catholic religious imagination (although that is not part of my focus here).

Empirical may name a commitment to the deliverances of experience, but the conditioning factors that impinge upon the selection and interpretation of experience need to be affirmed.

TWO SOCIOLOGICAL PERSPECTIVES

In the earliest years of Christianity the "churches" are gatherings that meet in people's homes: households of faith, or house churches. There are at this time no superstructures above and beyond them. Contact with the founding apostles help maintain connectedness beyond the immediate setting.

In the time lapse between Paul's letters to the Corinthians and Thessalonians and the pseudo-Pauline letters to Timothy and Titus, structures emerge that name roles and qualifications. Before long, already in the second century, the episcopus (Greek for overseer) is recognized as the key leader in each local church, and the key Roman *episcopus* speaks with authority to members of other local churches. House churches are still normative units of church, but there are now larger structures in which they exist.

The smaller units are what Victor Turner calls *communitas*. The larger structure is *societas*. We use church to talk about both of these. For many Christians, "church" tends to name the larger institutional structure, the *societas*. It pleases institutions when that happens. But *communitas* is where people gather and where their lives rub against each other. Only *communitas* involves whole persons in their relationship with other whole persons, where the scale of gathering is small enough to allow it.[1] Martin Buber says that *communitas* is where people are not just side by side (many Sunday parishes) but where they are truly with one another.[2] They meet face to face. They experience [or should] genuine mutuality. Here is also where life rubs against culture and history in all the daily, hands-on ways. *Societas* is more insulated from those cultural currents in the making. It needs *communitas* to present them.

Societas is concerned with ordering the whole. While both need structure of one sort or another, *societas* is far more preoccupied with the existence and maintenance of structure. A *communitas* that does not have the support of a *societas* is less likely to endure. *Societas* that does not have liveliness of constituent *communitates* bulks and atrophies. They need each other. They must neither absorb nor discount each other's specificity. The dialectic can be stirring, discomforting, even chaotic. But it needs to be there.

I want to name another sociological paradigm which I have found helpful to understanding the nature of church, for which I am indebted to Evelyn Eaton and James Whitehead.[3]

The word "community" is used so widely that it hardly names anything specific unless one defines it: the community of nations; the neighborhood community; the Hispanic community; Women's Community; the school community; etc. Whenever I speak of a social unit that I consider to be truly church, I presume the following interpretation.

A primary group is one whose fundamental reasons for being together are the relationships that bind: friends, family, and the like. The expectations that people in a primary group have of each other are encompassing and loosely defined. You can call a friend anytime. Parents do not tell a crying child at 3:00 AM that getting up now is not part of their job description.

A secondary group is one whose main reason for being together is because they share some task in the world: members of an athletic team; faculty members in the same school; people who work in the same office; etc. It helps of course if they also have good relationships, but that is not basically why they have come together. One's role in a secondary group is not all-encompassing and is likely to be fairly well defined: what a quarterback does on a team, what a vice president does in a corporation, what a bagger does in a supermarket.

A community that merits being called church is a hybrid group. It will have some characteristics of a primary group, for members of the Body of Christ are responsible for and to each other. It will also have some characteristics

---

1. Victor Turner, *The Ritual Process: Structure and Anti-structures* (Ithaca: Cornell University Press, 1969), p. 127.

2. Cited by Turner, ibid., p. 122.

3. Evelyn Eaton and James D. Whitehead, *Community of Faith: Models and Strategies for Developing Christian Communities* (New York: Seabury, 1982), Chapter 3, "Basic Questions of Group Life," pp. 34-46.

THE NATURE OF THE CHURCH

of a secondary group, for a Christian community that is church cannot not be in mission. If God has intentions for the world, and if Christians believe that those intentions are disclosed for them in the Christ-event, then their community has to reach out to the shape of history.

There are Christian groups that are mostly primary groups, others that are basically secondary groups. These are good and the church needs them, but I do not consider them to be units of church. Rather they are organizations within the church.

It can be said slightly differently. Every true church community has both a private life (among its members) and a public life (with the larger world around it).

These two paradigms, the meanings of church involved in *communitas* and *societas*, and in church community as a hybrid of primary and secondary characteristics, will appear in the discussion that unfolds.

THE EARLY PERIOD OF CHURCH: SOME DANGEROUS MEMORIES

Memory . . . mobilizes tradition as a dangerous tradition and thereby as a liberating force in respect of the one-dimensional character and certainty of the one "whose hour is always there" (Jn 7:6). It gives rise again to the suspicion that the plausible structures of a society may be relationships aimed to delude. Christian faith can and must be seen as a subversive memory. *The church is to some extent the form of [this memory's] public form.* The criterion of its authentic Christianity is the liberating and redeeming danger with which it introduces the remembered freedom of Jesus into modern society and the forms of consciousness and praxis in that society.

Johann Baptist Metz[4]

To pursue the question of the nature of church, I will return to the very early history, to those times when the followers of Jesus were engaged in the social construction of a new religious reality.

Creation stories, i.e., our "beginnings," are privileged memories because they are presumably closer to the original voice and to the wilder charisms that even the legitimate pursuit of order frets to domesticate. Johann Metz calls them dangerous memories. They are "dangerous" to the present church's received culture because they remember a freer, less encumbered time when even the first formative period had yet to arrive at secure conclusions. Any social group's recognition that there were other times, rich and flourishing times, that were very different from present times is an emancipatory mem-

---

4. Johann Baptist Metz, *Faith in History and Society: Towards a Practical Fundamental Theology*, p. 90. English translation © 1980 Search Press Ltd. Reprinted by permission of Crossroad Publishing Company.

ory. Dangerous memories disclose the finitude of the status quo and recall the suppleness of the original charism to lead many lives.

Emancipatory memories set boundaries too, of course, but often far broader ones than we would now be tempted to entertain without them. In the case of the church, they disclose how open to alternative incarnations is the authentic Christ-event.

It would be a naive biblicism that simply passed from 100 CE to the present, as though the rich experience of nineteen intervening centuries carried no wisdom. What I am pointing out in this short chapter, therefore, is very limited and incomplete, yet I believe of towering import, i.e., that early memories put the late church under requirement. In the latter part of this chapter, I will focus upon the worldwide movement of small or basic Christian communities, not just for that movement itself, but for what they disclose to all churches about the experience of being church for the Third Millenium.

I intend to focus upon the first sixty or seventy years of Christian existence (and it isn't called "Christian" until midway through that period). The earliest written record of church experience is the collection of authentic Pauline letters. However, in the gospels and in Acts there are some earlier oral traditions that remember times before Paul, even though recorded in writing only after Paul.

The major topics will be these: the word "church" and its ancestral voices in the world of Jewish meanings; Jesus as an interpreter in the Pharisaic tradition and the church as interpreter; the discipleship of equals as the inexorable logic of Jesus' experience of God; Jesus and the preferential option for the poor; and finally, the nature and role of house churches in formative Christianity and their contemporary reappearance.

For Christians to hear their beginnings accurately we must let words and structures have the meanings they had for Jesus and the earliest followers when a gathering formed about him. We must in part listen with Jewish ears, with first century ears, with mid-Eastern ears. We cannot do this perfectly, but we can get closer to that voice through the deliberate effort to let another culture speak on its own.

THE WORD CHURCH AND ITS ANCESTRAL VOICES

The Greek word *ekklesia*, the New Testament word most often translated into English as church, occurs about 115 times in the Christian scriptures. Only three of these are in the gospels, and all three of those in Matthew (Mt 16:18 and twice in 18:17). The word occurs over 50 times in authentic Pauline letters, written before any of the gospels. The word does not occur in Q which also antedates the Gospels, and may be not only very early material but from Galilee itself or southern Syria.[5] I think it likely, therefore, that "church"

---

5. Ivan Havener, *Q: The Saying of Jesus* (Wilmington, N.J.: Glazier, 1984), pp. 42-45.

(in its Aramaic form) did not color Jesus' sense of the disciples who followed him. The word was so familiar to the early communities that if the oral
traditions that preceded the written traditions had remembered Jesus as using
the Aramaic analogue, it seems there would be stronger traces of it in the
gospels. What these words indicate in Matthew's gospel, as Andrew
Overmann demonstrates, is the social construction of Christian reality in
the Matthean community.[6]

When the Greek word *ekklesia* occurs in the Septuagint, it is quite regularly a Greek rendition of the Hebrew word *qahal*. Both words name a gathering of people, an assembly. When the Hebrew scriptures are translated
into English, *qahal* normally appears as assembly. Gatherings of people,
especially the disciples, are part of the Jesus movement in Jesus' own life. So
the fact of *qahal* is not foreign, even if the word is not current.

Two features of the "church" word and the *qahal* meanings that are the
ancestral voices for a Jew using the word are important to our empirical
exploration of church.

First, even though the word church is used very early it did not in either
Paul or Matthew indicate an institution that displaced or transcended the
Jewish Covenant. There were (re)New(ed) Covenants all along the way in the
Jewish relationship with YHWH.[7] In a statement whose radical implications
remain to be laid out, the Second Vatican Council affirmed a Catholic conviction that God has not abrogated his covenant with his chosen people.[8]
Both a continuing covenant with YHWH and chosenness by YHWH are
affirmed. While I refer to a specifically Roman Catholic utterance, I believe
that it is not optional for any Christian churches to have a permanent, caring
relationship with the synagogue.[9] The truth of our originating experience
requires it. That is an empirical grounding. And it is a radical reorientation
after nineteen hundred disastrous years of almost unrelieved tragedy in the
orientation of Christians to Jews.

Against this background I find it increasingly fruitful to explore the notion
of Judaism and Christianity as siblings, as some Jewish writers also suggest.[10]

---

6. Andrew Overmann, *Matthew's Gospel: The Social World of the Matthean
Community* (Minneapolis: Fortress, 1990), esp. Chapter 3, "The Social Development of
the Matthean Community," pp. 72-149.

7. Delbert Hillers, *Covenant: The History of a Biblical Idea* (Baltimore: John Hopkins
University Press, 1969). Hillers shows how successive interpretations of religious covenant
are shaped by changes in secular treaty forms in the Mid- and Near-East.

8. *Nostra Aetate*, section 4.

9. Clark Williamson, *Has God Rejected His People: Anti-Judaism in the Christian
Church* (Nashville: Abingdon, 1982).

10. Hayim Goren Perlemuter, *Siblings*, (New York: Paulist, 1989); and A. Segal,
Rebecca's Children: Judaism and Christianity in the Roman World (Cambridge: Harvard
University Press, 1986), p. 179.

An honored, familiar form of mainstream Jewish life came to an end with the destruction of the Temple in 70 CE, the pillaging of the Essene communities, the dismantling of the Jewish body politic, the incredible disruption of Jewish life. In this version, rabbinic Judaism and Christianity engaged in the construction of a new religious social order side by side. The bitterness everywhere present on the Christian side is not matched on the Jewish side.[11]

In Jesus' time, Jewish religious life itself is quite sectarian. While there is indeed tension between Jesus and the center of Jewish religious life,[12] Christians did not take up a separate existence until the waning decades of the first century. Before that, following Jesus is perceived by the disciples to be a way of being Jewish. Christians break bread in their homes but also go regularly to the temple. There is noticeable tension but no rupture.

While what we call church today is clearly founded in the Christ-event, there is little New Testament evidence indicating Jesus' conscious intention actively to initiate a new religious foundation outside of normal Jewish life, along side of or superseding temple and synagogue. The new Jerusalem Bible translates Jesus' words in Mt 16:18 as "You are rock and upon the rock I will build *my community*" not "my church." One should not see a second century (and later) institutional meaning of church in the texts of the Christian scriptures. That new Jerusalem Bible translation better reflects the truth of a gathered group *and* the truth of its Jewish location (at that time).

The second important feature of *ekklesia/qahal* I will indicate initially by contrast. I, and very many Christians socialized in the Western Christian tradition, were reared with huge concern about individual salvation, which translates often into daily concern about my individual relationship with God. While that is in significant ways a forthright concern of the Johannine community, it is not thematic of the synoptics or of Paul.

H. Robinson Wheeler has detailed the corporate personality of Israel as a systematic framework of Hebrew anthropology.[13] Joshua and his army lost the battle at Ai because Achan, one of the soldiers, had violated YHWH's specific instructions. Before the community knew that Achan was the guilty one, they were only told "that Israel sinned." The nation lives its way through the life of every Jew, and vice versa. When Achan is stoned, his family and servants and animals are stoned with him. And we are told that all Israel stoned him, meaning that at that moment the few people there who act are all Israel acting.

---

11. The bitterness has been much deeper on the Christian side. For a presentation on the treatment of Jesus in the Talmud, cf. Jacob Lauterbach, "Jesus in the Talmud," in Weiss-Rosmarin, Trude, *Jewish Expressions of Jesus: An Anthology* (New York: KTAV, 1977), pp. 1-98.

12. E.P. Sanders, *Jesus and Judaism* (Philadelphia: Fortress, 1985). As an example of conflicted interpretation, cf. chapter 6, "Jesus and Sinners," pp. 174-211.

13. H. Wheeler Robinson, *Corporate Personality in Ancient Israel* (Philadelphia: Fortress, 1964).

It would be easy to write this off as a primitive tribal identity that must be overcome. That, I believe, is partly true. But there is a great experience that we ought not to have lost, that of a primal connectiveness that knits our human destiny into a single historical fabric.

Salvation comes through the covenant that YHWH makes with a people. They are assembled by covenant, and both the full assembly and all of the smaller groupings within it are *qahal* when assembled. One is redeemed through the covenanted people because one's life is lodged there. And it is personal because it courses its way through each and every member, but it is never individual, i.e., never something that happens via some direct connection between YHWH and an individual person that is outside of covenant or irrespective of it.

In Luke's gospel, Jesus' opening public statement is a self-interpretation taken from Isaiah: "Unrolling the scroll he found the place where it is written, 'The Spirit of the Lord is upon me. He has anointed me to preach the good news to the poor. He has sent me to heal the brokenhearted, to preach deliverance to the captives, and new sight to the blind; to deliver the downtrodden and to preach an acceptable year of the Lord'" (Lk 4:17-19). Gerhard Lohfink argues that when Jesus heals it is not primarily a gift to an individual because of Jesus' compassion, though that is surely there. Rather, Jesus proclaims and initiates the reign of God, and that is what happens to people because God's reign is breaking in. The healed ones belong to a world being healed by the reign of God.

> We do not really grasp Jesus' cures . . . if we understand them solely as miracles performed for individuals out of sympathy for their illness. Since the eschatological horizon of Jesus' activity has reentered consciousness, it has been clear that Jesus' miracles of healing must be seen in connection with his preaching of the kingdom of God. . . . We must express this very pointedly: the *sole* meaning of Jesus is the gathering of God's eschatological people.[14]

Jesus evokes and occasions the faith that heals through participation in a people within whom God's reign breaks through. The church then is not an agent of private salvation but a Body in whom God's power is regnant. The Body experiences redemption.

We sometimes speak about Paul's image or metaphor of the Body of Christ. That's only fair if metaphor is allowed, as I think it must, to carry ontological weight. Body is not *merely* an image. We are members of one another and what happens to the Body happens to its members. We expect God to care for Christ's Body. I believe Martin Buber's remark is as "indigenous" to the early Jewish Christian world as it is to the Jewish experience of which

---

14. Gerhard Lohfink, *Jesus and Community* (Philadelphia: Fortress, 1984), pp. 12,26.

he speaks: *We expect a theophany of which we know nothing except the place, and the place is called community.*[15]

As far back as Alexis de Tocqueville, through David Riesman, Philip Slater, and most recently Robert Bellah et al., both the achievements and the excesses of individualism are tallied.[16] Bellah suggests biblical religion as a redemptive resource in our tradition that might possibly socialize (or relationalize) American individualism.[17] I agree, but only insofar as church recovers its original instincts about people as already and always interconnected, interrelated, and interdependent. The recovery would have to be operational, not merely a cognitive grasp. I doubt that it can be recovered without the worldwide movement of small or basic Christian communities. Church as *societas* is always in need of church as *communitas*. There is value-added importance in U.S. culture, because unsocialized individualism cannot open itself very well at all to God's intentions for history as these are put forth in the Christ-event when it speaks with its original voice.

JESUS THE INTERPRETER

My desk *Webster's New Collegiate Dictionary* reflects the tragic effects of two millenia of Christian misinterpretation in defining "pharisaical" as "marked by hypocritical censorious self-righteousness." The next entry on "pharisaism" defines this spirit as "hypocrisy." Christian scholarship increasingly acknowledges that the Pharisees were the finest flowering of Judaism in Jesus' time.

In their hard-to-assess origins, the Pharisees react against a narrow commitment to the written Torah, insisting that no period or events can disclose YHWH's intentions with finality, for God is disclosed ongoingly and forever in God's traffic with human history. Therefore, they affirm a living tradition, an oral Torah, which carries equal authority with written Torah.

The Pharisees appear quite suddenly in the mid-second century BCE during the Hasmonean period. There is no documentation about their origins. When they make their first recorded historical appearance they are already a well-defined group with substantial religious and political power. Because they appear in the Hasmonean period we can situate them in one of those crucial periods where Jews are fighting for their soul against the impingement

---

15. Martin Buber, *Martin Buber: The Way of Response*, ed. Nahum Glatzer (New York: Schocken, 1966), p. 117.

16. David Riesman, *The Lonely Crowd: A Study of the Changing American Character* (Princeton: Princeton University Press, 1960); Philip Slater, *The Pursuit of Loneliness: American Culture at the Breaking Point* (Boston: Beacon, 1970); Robert N. Bellah, Richard Madsen, William M. Sullivan, Ann Swidler, and Steven M. Tipton, *Habits of the Heart: Individualism and Commitment in American Life* (Berkeley: University of California Press, 1985).

17. Bellah et al., *Habits of the Heart*, pp. 219-249.

of other cultures upon their religious inheritance. In this case, Hellenism is the antagonist. So as not to oversimplify, some of the antagonists are Hellenizing Jews in Jerusalem whose own vested interests are served by their coalition with Hellenized power centers.

The Pharisees show up as realistic compromisers and at the same time faithful Jews. They are realistic enough to know that, like it or not, they must come to terms with Greeks and later with Romans. They are willing to make compromises in the civil political order, as long as they retain responsibility for the Jewish religious soul. They come to terms with giving to Caesar what is Caesar's so long as it does not prevent anyone from giving to God what is God's.

One of their transformations of Jewish daily life that is often misrepresented by Christian interpretation is the transferral of many Temple rituals (e.g., purification rites) to the Jewish home so that Jews would find their daily life sacred. These rituals and sabbath observances are at the core of conflicts between Jesus and the Pharisees in the gospels.

The conflict between Jesus and the Pharisees is most virulent in Matthew's gospel. While I want to name some elements of tension that I believe are historical in Jesus' relationship with the Pharisees, quite an amount of the polemic in Matthew's gospel is between the Matthean Community and Formative Judaism following the destruction of the Temple and the devastating war between the Jews and the Romans, as Andrew Overmann's recent book demonstrates.[18] Two competing religious social constructions of reality are at war.

Side by side with the Matthewan polemic, Jesus affirms the validity of the Torah: "Not one piece of what has been written (written Torah) shall be laid aside." And he declares the valid authority of the Pharisees: "You must listen to them (oral tradition), for they do indeed sit in Moses' chair." I think the total break with Judaism has not occurred, or the community would not be "remembering" Jesus' positive appreciation of both written and oral Torah.

In the earlier phases of historical biblical criticism, Rudolf Bultmann judged that the presence of Jesus at table fellowship with the Pharisees appears genuinely biographical. This is an important clue to Jesus' relationship with the Pharisees, for it seems likely that the fairly exclusive table fellowship practice (*haveroth*) of the Pharisees begins with Hillel and is operative in Jesus' time. The Pharisees must be basically comfortable with Jesus' teaching.

The influence of the Pharisees over the synagogue is also rather clear. That Jesus would have often been invited to comment upon scripture in the synagogue again testifies to their basic approval of what Jesus teaches. In Acts

---

18. J. Andrew Overmann, *Matthew's Gospel and Formative Judaism: The Social World of the Matthean Community* (Minneapolis: Fortress, 1990), esp. pp. 72-89.

we also learn that some Pharisees were among the early community of followers of Jesus.

Of all the major sects of Judaism of which we have some knowledge, there is clearly more affinity between Jesus and the Pharisees than with the Sadducees, Essenes, or Zealots. I think it fair to understand some genetic connection (which is not to make a simple identification) between Jesus and the Pharisees, a position which I have laid out in more detail elsewhere.[19] Further, I would understand that one of the results of the genetic connection is Jesus' willingness to add new interpretation to the historically accumulated interpretation. In the "sermon on the mount" Jesus repeats, "You have heard it said [the oral Torah] . . . but I say to you." (Mt 5). Jesus does not reverse the behaviors of the oral Torah but asks for their deeper intentionality and seeks to radicalize them. It is easy enough to see how some irritation arises, but it does not seem to have been at the high pitch that severs relationships.

Another point of irritation is that, while Jesus joins the Pharisees at table, he also has table fellowship with those whom that religious culture found unholy, i.e., those excluded from the Pharisees' *haveroth*. If God gives sunshine and rain equally to the good and the bad, then we must be holy with God's holiness—as Luke has it, to be compassionate as God is compassionate.

The Johannine community, in fact, understands Jesus to say that people who have faith in ages to come will not only do what Jesus does, but greater things (*meizona*) than Jesus does. Unmistakable here is the sense of ongoing events that continue to disclose the works of God in the unfolding of the Christ-event.

The religious sensibilities of Jews in the early scriptures (OT) are radically historical. Ortega y Gassett's remark that human beings don't have a nature, they have only a history, is exemplified by YHWH's relationship to the Jews of old. There are no ponderings over the nature of God. Who God is for them is precisely the history that God has with them: YHWH who led us out of Egypt; YHWH who took us across the Red Sea; YHWH who promised us our land: the Father of Abraham, Isaac, and Jacob. Because YHWH is constantly and newly there in history, the need to reinterpret YHWH is equally constant and new, a need incumbent upon a community.

What is the dangerous memory here? It is a reminder to churches that solidify self-articulations that their origins lie in a constant openness to new self-interpretation. There are several important aspects to getting regrounded in an original openness to reinterpretation, to calling upon early experience to be a constitutive agent in new experience.

Alfred North Whitehead, writing as historical consciousness was making

---

19. Bernard J. Lee, *The Galilean Jewishness of Jesus: Retrieving the Jewish Origins of Christianity* (New York: Paulist, 1988), pp. 96-118.

its way into the Western mind, said that "you cannot claim absolute finality for a dogma without claiming a commensurate finality for the sphere of thought within which it arose."[20] To do that would freeze experience in an icy moment of stopped time. One cannot, in fact, do that. But the inclination is easily there, and the attempt is perilous.

There is a particular benefit for people in U.S. culture who look for religious mooring. William Dean is right, of course, in citing the pragmatic, historical disposition of Americans. In our system of jurisprudence, for example, we create new situations as normative by reinterpreting previous situations (judgments).

> Hebrews [sought] to found themselves on historical actions rather than on transhistorical ideals. Americans, like Hebrews, are a nation of wandering emigrants who continue to reinterpret their covenant with God as they restlessly cross space and time, and who, in that series of reinterpretations, create their religious identity. . . . [They] create their religious truth from actions—present actions reinterpreting earlier actions, thereby becoming new actions, over and over again.[21]

Let me suggest a particular instance where the dangerous memory of Jesus, located in the nurturing matrix of the grand interpreters, seems especially relevant.

In the Christian tradition, the "Father" name for God has been at the heart of the religious perception and experience of God. The meaning of God has, of course, flowed through the meaning of church. The pervasive presence of father figures in leadership and ministry is one of the most visible testimonies.

New Testament scholars tend to agree that the retention of the Aramaic word "Abba" in the mouth of Jesus is authentic. James Dunn says that when people have had genuine religious experience they ransack their culture for the best ideas and metaphors they can find to articulate the experience.[22] In a culture that is undeniably patriarchal, the Father metaphor would fast present itself. Paul Ricoeur suggests that the ransacking doesn't just go after the experience but metaphors are there as the experience emerges, helping to create the experience in the first place.[23] This is the epistemological (rather than the elaborative or decorative) function of metaphor.

Fatherhood is human experience that mediates and interprets God, and

---

20. Alfred North Whitehead, *Religion in the Making* (Cleveland: World), p. 126.

21. William Dean, "Hebrew Law and Postmodern Historicism" (1987), p. 1, ms.

22. James D.G. Dunn, *Christology in the Making: A New Testament Inquiry into the Origins of the Doctrine of the Incarnation* (Philadelphia: Westminster, 1980), p. 196.

23. Paul Ricoeur, Preface to Mary Gerhardt, and Allan Russell, *Metaphoric Process: The Creation of Scientific and Religious Understanding* (Fort Worth: Texas Christian University Press, 1984), p. xii.

undoubtedly discloses the God people have experienced. The metaphor works (tells the truth) because the God who is experienced is in some ways truly like the most perfect of human fathers. But the likeness in metaphor is never total. If one thing were totally like another, they would be identical. In every metaphor there is also something that is not like the other. In some ways God is not like a human father. The daughters and sons of God are not children of a sexual reproductive act.

The feminist critique of patriarchy makes us aware of how much that pervasive social system has affected operational religious metaphors. Perhaps even more fundamentally, the feminist hermeneutic makes us aware that the fatherhood of God is a metaphor and not a gender determination of deity.

I venture the speculation that the church, in the tradition of Jesus and the grand interpreters, should be eager to enlarge our understanding of God with additional metaphors and would further be open to the transformations of ecclesial identity that relates to deity as mother no less than a father.

In summary, if we dangerously remember our origins in a tradition of grand (re-)interpretation, which I believe is essential to understanding the life of Jesus, then we uncover some church nature that surprises the tradition a bit. The church in fidelity to its origins is a social "place" where God's intentions for history are ongoingly disclosed through a mutually critical dialogue between faith and culture. We need be honest enough to recognize that not only does religion disclose God's intentions for history, but so-called secular history sometimes carries God's impulse more authentically than religious history, and may, therefore, also put religion under requirement.

THE CHURCH AS A DISCIPLESHIP OF EQUALS

As a Roman Catholic, I know that the church of this tradition is in a period of great change after the Second Vatican Council. But we are not alone in this because all of the churches are responding to similar features of our shared world. Slithering out and away from secularization theology, sustaining the impact of historical consciousness, using historical critical methods of biblical interpretation, listening to the feminist critique, experiencing deconstructionist impulses whether one has heard of Jacques Derrida or not, learning that pluralism is a normative condition, etc.—these leave no Christian tradition in the West untouched.

To be in between an old, settled order and a new place whose configuration is still indeterminate feels, according to theologian/psychologist Jim Zullo, like "having your feet firmly planted in mid-air." It is also what Victor Turner refers to as a community's liminal period. Liminal communities are reactive to previous structures (they are rich in antistructure tendencies). They are often in quest for more egalitarian structures. If that is where many churches are today, and I believe it is, then our present condition is a bias that perhaps helps us recover elements of egalitarian community in our tradition. Power words in an egalitarian community are less evocative of domination, less typologically male, and more attuned to collegiality and collaboration.

In reaction to stringent hierarchies, egalitarian communities sometimes try to eliminate or at least minimize structure. Paul felt the strong need to call for people's acknowledgement of diverse gifts and the different functions they have. These need not pull the Body apart! Chapter 18 in Matthew's gospel is basically a manual for handling conflict. It ends with a parable about a person in authority who does not use power to dominate. But the one dealt with in this way in turn uses power to dominate, a behavior condemned by Jesus. Victor Turner refers to the counter-cultural communes of the sixties in this context also. Very few of them endured. Mary Douglas points out, in the foreword to Robert Adkins' new study of *Egalitarian Community* in Paul, that these communities are fragile. "They tend to break apart, often in anger."[24]

With all of those forewarnings, it does seem that the call to a discipleship of equals is authentic in the teaching of Jesus and is a redemptive dangerous memory for today's church.

While Jesus is not the first to dwell upon the fatherhood of God, he leans hard on the inexorable logic of that parenthood. If all women and men have the same parent, then all are siblings and all are equal in the power structure. It is painful to watch a ten year old act out "parent" to a five-year-old sibling, and the acting out is invariably destructive of harmony in their own relationship. Sound parental behavior in a real parent with a real child is one thing—but between adult sibling equals quite another.

In Mark's gospel (Mk 10:35-45) James and John approach Jesus while Jesus and the twelve are on the road and request power privileges: one of us on your right, the other on your left. The other ten hear about it and are indignant. Jesus tells them that they have missed the point entirely. Leaders must not behave like pagans who lord it over each other but like servants to each other. The story is basically the same in Matthew except that Matthew rescues James and John from their childishness and has their mother do the asking (Mt 20:20-28). It is telling that Luke relocates the story. The discussion, in abbreviated form, does not take place on the road, but at table at the last supper. The Lukan community is keenly aware that it is dealing with the function of power in its own community life and community ritual.

The rationale is most clearly present in Matthew 23:8-12. Jesus indicates that titles must be foregone since all of them are siblings. Don't be called rabbi or teacher or father. It is the parenthood of God that has "siblingized" them into equality that the functions of power must not violate. Elisabeth Schüssler Fiorenza summarizes it well:

---

24. Mary Douglas, Foreword to Robert A. Atkins, *Egalitarian Community: Ethnography and Exegesis* (Tuscaloosa: University of Alabama, 1991), p. x.

The short Matthean injunction, "Call no one father, for you have one father," thus maintains the same relationships as the saying in Mark 20:29-30 did. The new kinship of the discipleship of equals does not admit of "fathers," thereby rejecting the patriarchal power and esteem invested in them. . . . The saying of Jesus uses the "father" name of God not as a legitimation for existing patriarchal power structures in society or church but as a critical subversion of all structures of domination. . . . Neither the "brothers" nor the "sisters" in the Christian community can claim the "authority of the father" for that would involve claiming power and authority reserved for God alone.[25]

In Paul's letter to the Galatians, this profound intuition is again articulated. For those baptized in Christ, privilege may neither be given or withheld on the basis of race, social position, or gender.

The most basic way of talking about a discipleship of equals is to recognize that the character and function of power are the issues at stake. Clericalism, for example, is a deep violation of the discipleship of equals in Christian community. The way that power is to function, i.e., at the disposal of the legitimate agenda of the community rather than a community at the disposal of the leader's agenda, is redemptive not merely in religious settings but in human settings. The church should be a primary place where this relentless experiment in the functions of power in a discipleship of equals should be instanced for the sake of *all* social systems. All of us in the world are siblings, not only the explicit followers of Jesus.

One of the reasons that egalitarian communities often fail is through a misguided perception that all power-related roles are violations of equality. As Bernard Loomer has pointed out, power is always an issue whenever two or more people are engaged in social interaction. Community, like its larger analogue society, needs roles and structures. The issue is not between power and no power but between what Bernard Loomer has called linear power (effects go one way only) and relational power where the flow of affecting and being affected is one of mutuality.[26] I have found the power discussions of Elizabeth Janeway[27] and Marilyn French[28] especially germane to a contemporary appropriation of a biblical model.

In summary, if we dangerously remember the originating voices in which church begins, we must affirm the discipleship of equals as the nature/history

25. Elisabeth Schüssler Fiorenza, *In Memory of Her: A Feminist Theological Resconstruction of Christian Origins*, Copyright © 1983 by Elisabeth Schüssler Fiorenza. Reprinted by permission of the Crossroad Publishing Company, pp. 150,151.

26. Bernard M. Loomer, "Two Kinds of Power," *Criterion* 15:1 (1976), pp. 11-28.

27. Elizabeth Janeway, *Powers of the Weak* (New York: Morrow Quill, 1980).

28. Marilyn French, *Beyond Power: On Women, Men, and Morals* (New York: Ballantine, 1985), Chapter 7, "The Long View Forward," pp. 489-546, esp. sect. 4 on Power, pp. 504-512.

of the church. I have indicated my judgment that the character and function of power is at stake in a discipleship of equals. If there are many church histories vis-à-vis power issues—and there are—which is to be invoked? To word it more empirically: If there are varied, multiple experiences of power dynamics, which of them—if, indeed, any of them—is to be the experiential basis for an empirical theology of the church, i.e., for an empirical ecclesiology? I am holding out for that early charism rooted, I believe, in Jesus' experience of the father/parenthood of God and its implications for equality for all God's children in all of their/our social systems.[29]

THE PREFERENTIAL OPTION

Based on a Q saying, Matthew has Jesus teach us to "be perfect" like God. Luke's Jesus says to "be compassionate" like God. Under both of those is the recurring Hebrew directive to "be holy" like God. One looks at God's holiness and attempts to live according to it, which is of a piece with being in God's image.

In the Jewish religious matrix in which the religious consciousness of Jesus was educated, there are two words above all that define the operational nature of God's holiness: *sedeq* and *hesed*. *Sedeq* is usually translated as justice or righteousness, *hesed* as mercy, or love, or tenderness. *Hesed* is what God lives out of that keep God's rage creative even when *sedeq* is violated. I think *hesed* is a prudent inclination to leniency based upon love. I will focus attention upon *sedeq*.

Two references to the Jewish scriptures set the context for *sedeq*. In Exodus 16 YHWH provides desert food to God's grumbling children. There is manna each morning. Someone from each tent gathers it for the tent's household. If someone gathers a huge amount, it's just the right amount for everybody when it is distributed. If someone gathers only a very small amount, it too gives the same measure to each when it is distributed. In time of need and limited resources, the goods of life must be equitably distributed. The earth is everyone's one home, and everyone's table in the earth home must provide for life. The issue is not mere distributive justice but the right order that must be in place for human happiness. It is the order that looks after goodness. When *sedeq* is there, so is *shalom*, i.e., so is harmony and contentment.

On the other hand, God's holiness is expressed in God's lavishness. When God's intentions for human history are in place, it will be like a banquet that YHWH has set for the world (Is 25:6). Isaiah says that the food will not be merely good, but food rich and juicy. There will not be ordinary wines, but fine strained wines. *Surplus and bounty are not wrong, evident-*

---

29. Charles Hartshorne, *The Divine Relativity: A Social Conception of God* (New Haven: Yale University Press, 1969), p. 50.

ly, but they are not allowed until all the basic needs for everyone's decent life are met, and until they are met those needs must be the preferred place where we opt to direct our transforming energy and effort. That is a preferential option for the poor.

A preferential option for the poor does not, I think, mean that the poor are loved more. I think of parents who love all of their children, but a child in need or in trouble gets privileged attention. The others are not loved less in the meantime. Jesus drew the nonunderstanding if not the scorn of the Pharisees because he not only sat at table with "the clean," but with all of his sisters and brothers. In different contexts he explains that, like a doctor, he first notices those who are sick, or like a good shepherd he leaves the ninety-nine who thrive and seeks out the stray.

The Matthean community hears Jesus instruct it to live beyond conventional wisdom. We owe our care not only to our friends—even pagans do that—but to everyone and that even includes enemies. God gives sunshine and rain to everyone, Jesus argues, not distinguishing between the good and the bad. When we behave that way, we are behaving like God's children, i.e., in the only way that honors the fact of siblinghood effected by God's parenthood (Mt 5:43:48).

The early communities, in Luke's idealized portrait of the early communities, share all things in common. The first attempt to create community roles is a response to the need for a more equitable distribution of the community's resources to meet needs, whether Greek or Jewish (Acts 6:1-6). The Greeks complained that their widows are getting less than the Jewish widows. Seven people were chosen to be in charge of food distribution.

I am suggesting, therefore, that a preferential option for the poor is built into the nature of the church because it is built into the history out of which the church came and continues to come. This is the history—the experience—that should nature the church.

Christians today sometimes cite a Chinese proverb that says if you give a person a fish, the person can eat today, but if you teach that person how to fish, that same person can eat everyday without your daily help. In scenario one, we provide goods. In scenario two, we empower people to provide their own resources. But the fish story needs a third variation: Sometimes we might have to change the ownership of the stream!

Neither Isaiah nor Jesus could have used the language of systems, for that belongs to our century. But the point of *sedeq* is that sometimes injustice is so embedded in how systems function that until the system is changed goods and empowerment cannot terminate injustice. In fact, if the roots of injustice are not addressed, then patching up the malfunction with food and empowerment can in fact enable the unjust system to flourish, because someone is picking up the pieces and subverting the uprising.

Jeremiah has a sense of systems, even if not the word, when he reminds the people even in exile to be concerned, not just about their individual needs, but about whether there is *shalom* in the city, since their own *shalom* is tied up with the welfare of the city. In Greek, the city is the *polis* and to be concerned about the welfare of the city was to be *poli*-tical. Politics is about how people are together in a social system.

Given the preferential option for the poor, a telling phrase that comes to us from liberation theology, and given systemic roots of much injustice, the church cannot *not* have a political dimension, a public face. Metz sums it up well:

> Following Christ always has a twofold structure. It has a mystical ele-
> ment and one that is situational, one that is practical and political. And in
> their radical nature the two do not work against each other but propor-
> tionately in step with each other. The radical nature of following Christ is
> mystical and political at one and the same time. . . . When the double
> mystical and political composition of following Christ is ignored . . .
> what happens is either the reduction of following Christ to a purely social
> and political dimension of behavior or its reduction to private religious spir-
> ituality. What is lost is the following of Christ in which Jesus' kind of
> standing up for the glory of God in the midst of individual and social
> contradictions of our life is continued.[30]

If justice is one very central way of naming God's intentions for the world, then commitment to God and commitment to the transformation of his-torical structures cannot be put asunder. Further, if Jesus is a further unveil-ing of those intentions, and if the church is a social embodiment of a com-munity's response to the Christ-event, then it is in the nature of church to have profound political concern. Public life belongs to church as much as pri-vate life. Mystical and political are not opposed. In my Roman Catholic tra-dition there has been critical reserve about the presence of church in the political arena. I do not understand this as an absence from public discourse and public action but as a refusal either to be a political party or to give alle-giance to any party or candidate across the board.

In the empirical tradition, I believe that Henry Nelson Wieman under-stood this about as well as anyone. In his intellectual autobiography, he holds that only that which operates in our midst can transform us. "Therefore, in human life, in the actual processes of human existence, must be found the saving and transforming power which religious inquiry seeks and which faith must apprehend."[31] Lest anyone think that Wieman has fallen prey to a one-sided religiosity fixated on social involvement, his friend and colleague

---

30. Johann Baptist Metz, *Followers of Christ* (New York: Paulist, 1978), pp. 42,44.
31. Henry Nelson Wieman, "Intellectual Autobiography," in *The Empirical Theology of Henry Nelson Wieman*, ed. Robert W. Bretall (Carbondale: Southern Illinois University, 1963), p. 4.

Eugene Meland thinks it accurate "to classify Wieman the theologian as a mystic concerned with the immediacy and certainty of the presence of the living God."[32]

I believe that the development of praxis or practical theology especially in the last two decades is a retrieval of one of the dangerous memories associated with Christian beginnings. "Practical" is not an easy English word to rehabilitate. Too often it conjures up a sense of instrumental efficiency, i.e., what really works. But in the tradition of Aristotelian political philosophy, that instrumental activity is rather a matter of *techne*. "Praxis" or "practical" has more to do with concern about the kind of world we are committed to help usher in. Practical theology is a response to our belief that God expects and requires our collaboration in world-making. Dermot Lane says that a Christian subject can never be immunized from the real hazards of history, because "the God of Jesus Christ is a God who stirs up and encroaches upon the practical interest of the person who is trying to think about him. The reality of God is one that disarms yet enlivens, haunts yet heals, disturbs yet enables."[33]

In a word, the church has a political nature which ecclesiology has traditionally passed over in thundering silence. The church has this nature because its historical origins are in Jesus Christ. Lane emphasizes the performative character of Jesus' mission,[34] since the kingdom of God which he proclaims has begun changes the plight of the poor, the captive, the blind, the disadvantaged. We know that the healing of dysfunctional systems is essential to the healing of those who are wounded by them.

BASIC CHRISTIAN COMMUNITIES AND THE NATURE OF CHURCH

Many contemporary New Testament exegetes and many historians of the early church would agree that if "church" names the institutions most of us are familiar with in our own lives, their origins are not to be found in an explicit, founding consciousness in the historical Jesus. There is no indication that Jesus steps outside of his Jewish faith and Jewish institutions to say what he does or to be who he is. The early communities as well locate themselves within Judaism even as they also break bread together as followers of Jesus. This is not to deny the tensions that exist. In the categories of Victor Turner, we do indeed find elements of antistructure in the communities of Jesus' disciples, both in his life time and after his death and resurrection.

For me the saying of these things does not contradict that church is founded in Jesus, or in "the Christ-event," as we sometimes say, to catch up the life

---

32. Cited by Bernard Loomer in Bretall, *Empirical Theology*, p. 394.

33. Dermot A. Lane, *Foundations for a Social Theology: Praxis, Process and Salvation* (New York: Paulist, 1984), p. 13. Lane has been influenced by process modes of thought and commits a chapter in this book to "Social Analysis and Process Thought Serving Praxis," pp. 83-109.

and teaching and historical activity of Jesus, his death and resurrection, and the communities after Jesus' historical life that Paul unabashedly calls Christ as well.

If Jesus does intentionally call a gathering into existence, a *qahal*, I believe that its nature is *communitas* and not *societas* at that juncture. *Communitas* is the form of the gatherings in the proximate post-Easter years. Today we sometimes call these communities house churches, or households of faith. This is the normative expression of church life until well into the fourth century, and it is the basic unit of church life.

The "household" needs to be defined because it names a social reality that is not familiar to us today in Western culture. In the Hellenized Mediterranean first century CE world, there is frequently a wider web of relationships that centers some of its significant life in the home of a middle-class family. This social unit has been amply described in recent scholarship on church beginnings.[35] Servants are included, sometimes business connections, friends, etc. Something again strange to contemporary Western culture is that there is sufficient organic cohesiveness in these households that individuals would not think of having different religious allegiances than the rest of the members. Stephanus and the entire household were baptized, also Cornelius and the entire household.

When Paul addresses "the church" he sometimes adds the person's name whose household is the place of gathering. He also speaks of "churches" in the plural, e.g., the churches in Galatia, or the churches in Macedonia, meaning the network of house churches in those geographic areas. I have addressed this in more detail elsewhere but enough here perhaps to indicate that "the house church appears to have been the basic unit of ecclesial life in the early centuries, indeed into the fourth century when Christianity became the state religion and could function properly.[36] Once this occurs, institutionalization takes a quantum leap, and *societas* rather than *communitas* begins to dominate how the nature of church is interpreted.

In the rest of this section I will address two issues around the experience of the small ecclesial community. In the first, I want to make a case for the retrieval of *communitas* as the basic unit of church. In the second, I want to note the critical importance of basic Christian communities to the public, political life of church.

34. Ibid., p. 125.

35. There is an abundance of solid work on the house churches, e.g., Robert Banks, *Paul's Idea of Community: The Early House Churches in Their Historical Setting* (Grand Rapids, Mich.: Eerdmans, 1980). Abraham Malherbe, *Social Aspects of Early Christianity* (Philadelphia: Fortress, 1983), esp. Chapter 3, "House Churches and Their Problems." Wayne Meeks, *The First Urban Christians: The Social World of the Apostle Paul* (New Haven: Yale University Press, 1983).

36. Bernard Lee and Michael Cowan, *Dangerous Memories: House Churches and Our American Story* (Kansas City: Sheed & Ward, 1986), p. 23.

I want to say that empirically the Christian *communitas* is the smallest building block of ecclesial reality. The *communitas* and other *communitates* build up into church as *societas*. In the Roman Catholic tradition, the *communitas*, if it exists, is usually interpreted as an administrative unit within the parish. Parish is commonly thought to be the smallest ecclesial unit. The parish is often treated as an administrative unit of the diocese and the diocese as an administrative unit of the universal church. This is not the language used, but the behavior. However, comportment, as Maurice Merleau-Ponty was wont to point out, is a primal mode of thought. While not identical, there are other churches in the Christian tradition with versions of this experience. The failure of the free churches is often in the opposite direction: *communitas* that never locates itself within the nurturing texture of *societas*.

A case can be made for the ontological primacy of *communitas* in ecclesiology by a contrast between Platonic idealism and Aristotelian realism. For Plato, the idea pre-exists any concrete instance of it. The finite, particular instance is always a more or less imperfect expression of the ideal. In *Categoriae* c. 5 Aristotle calls the individual, concrete entity the "first substance" [*prote ousia*]. The "nature" of the individual is "second" substance [*deutera ousia*]. The second substance does not exist if there is no first substance. There is no such thing for Aristotle as an uninstanced "nature." The reality of the universal arises from the reality of the first substances whose natures are "second substances."

On this analogy, I am suggesting that the *communitas*, a small enough, active enough, coherent enough group to be a primary formation "place" for faith, is the smallest unit of church.

It is important to distinguish between a small group and a small community. I am taking up again the notion of a hybrid group presented earlier. Some small groups of Christians are primary groups. Others are secondary groups. Both are necessary. Being an ecclesial Christian community requires some aspects of both the primary and the secondary group, i.e., a hybrid group which builds up within the group and reaches out into world-making beyond the small group (has a mission related to God's reign in history).

I believe that small ecclesial units can be further described. In those communities that understand themselves to be ecclesial units, the following four characteristics are regularly there in some form or another. I want to be clear that I am speaking descriptively and not prescriptively.

1. *Koinonia*. People experience that they participate constitutively in each other's lives. Who they are in great part emerges out of these privileged relationships. For this Paul often uses the Greek word *koinonia*, frequently translated as community. One of the best ways to assess the early community's awareness of *koinonia* is to track down all the instances of the Greek reciprocal word *allelon*: one another. Gerhard Lohfink points out that Kittel did not find the word important enough to have an entry for it in *The Theological Dictionary of the New Testament*.

This one-another-koinonia is analogous to, though not identical with, the sociological category of primary group.

2. *Diakonia.* This is a wide word. Sometimes it is used to name any genuine ministry. Sometimes it is used to name a community's service beyond its own immediate internal needs. That is the specialized meaning to which I draw attention. When the prophet Agabus predicted to the community at Antioch that there would be a great famine, which in fact occurred before the end of Claudius' reign, community members decided as their service (*eis diakonian*) to send whatever they could to their brothers and sisters in need (Acts 11:28-30). Any ecclesial community is in service beyond itself.

3. *Kerygma.* There are other communities in the world than Christian communities who are noted for both community mutuality and committed outreach. What *kerygma* names is that Christian *koinonia* and *diakonia* are storied in the Good News of Jesus Christ. The relentless proclamation of this message or *kerygma* grounds *koinonia* and *diakonia*. *Kerygma* is the why and the wherefore of a Christian community's mutual care and generous outreach.

4. *Leitourgia.* Liturgy is public community ritual. Communities that endure do so because they have created a culture. They have shared understanding, shared values, approved behaviors, and symbols that both carry and transmit meaning to live by. Ecclesial Christian communities have a shared public prayer life of one kind or another—but with forms that reach into the wealthy symbolic store of the tradition.

The two most common forms of Christian *leitourgia* are: liturgy of the Word, with roots that go back to the synagogue; and Eucharist, or the Table of the Lord, which also has roots in both the ancient Passover meal and the *haveroth* of the Pharisees.

Sound liturgy must never be so particular to a *communitas* that the *societas* does not locate its reality there too, nor so generic to *societas* that the *communitas* does not find its particular life celebrated there.

When all four of these features—*koinonia, diakona, kerygma* and *leitourgia*—are present in a community's regular life we know that we are in the arena of churchhood.

The universal church is not merely an arithmetic sum of all the ecclesial *communitates*. It is commonplace to observe that the whole is more than the sum of its parts. Church as *societas* or second substance has meaning loaded into it from every *communitas*, every instance of primary substance. The nature of church as *societas* is more complex than any *communitas* largely because it "holds" them all, and its "holding" needs a far different structure than does the *communitas*. It contains multitudes.

What I have laid out here is an insufficient treatment of churchhood in its universal character. What I have tried to do is rehabilitate the basic ecclesial *communitas* as the building block of church, since that has generally been under-understood. In any larger development I would stress the fretful and/or

friendly dialectic between *communitates* and *societas*. The dialectic is more
fretful during liminal times, more friendly during settled times. The dialectic, however, is never absent, unless the church be without prophets.

There is a worldwide movement of small Christian communities known
by many names: basic Christian communities, base communities, basic
ecclesial communities, intentional Christian communities, house churches,
etc. Maryknoll theologian and missionary Joseph Healy has counted over a
thousand different ways these efforts have been named in print in recent
years. The existence of so many names indicates the size of the preoccupation with the reality of these groups and also their variety and elusiveness. The
word "basic" is especially helpful for what it tries to say. The communities
are basic units of church. They deal with basic life issues. They are called into
existence by basic people, i.e., grassroots people.

I was an American representative at the Fourth European Congress of
Basic Christian Communities in Paris in July, 1991. Nearly a thousand people were in attendance. Interest in this movement is strong among Catholics,
but it is not exclusively Catholic. One of the stronger and older communities
in Europe is a Presbyterian effort in Scotland. The movement in the
Netherlands is very ecumenical, and the network strong and visible enough
to have a membership in the National Council of Churches.

Three things impressed me greatly from the gathering in Europe. The
first is that it is a lay movement, and attracts young people as well as traditional church goers looking for more viable options. While the movement is
largely lay led and lay inspired, is does not exclude members of religious
orders or ordained persons. Second, the tenor of communities varies greatly from country to country, reflecting both pastoral need and cultural temperament. Third, Christian churches in Western Europe are finding organized religion almost without either personal or social impact.

Basic Christian communities are not an alternative to the institution but an
alternative form of institutionalization, which early history makes clear.
They facilitate animated conversation between faith and culture and are
committed to the double program of personal conversion and systemic transformation. The agenda for the European Congress was generated by the
communities themselves. The fourteen topics were largely concerned with
social issues: economics, ecology, the women's movement, etc. The reconstruction of Eastern Europe and the burgeoning European Economic
Community provided backdrop for much of the discussion at the Congress.

There is no question about whether these basic Christian communities
in Europe consider themselves to be units of church. They very clearly do.

Basic Christian communities (BCCs) were first named that way in Latin
America, and especially in Brazil where it is estimated that there are between
80,000 and 100,000 of them. About two decades ago they began to use the
expression "basic ecclesial communities" (BECs) to make an explicit claim
for their churchhood. In Latin America as in Europe, the character of these

communities varies significantly from country to country.

In December of 1991 I had the honor of being a theologian-in-residence to the First International Consultation on Basic Christian Communities, sponsored by the Institute for Pastoral and Social Ministry at the University of Notre Dame. As a consultation, there was representation rather than broad general attendance (as at the European meeting). Each continent had a half day to present its experience.

When the members of the Brazilian communities presented their experience, they had laid out on the floor in the center of the circle (before our arrival in the room) a cross about ten feet long with eight foot cross arms. It was made out of photographs placed side by side of men and women members of BEC's across Latin American who had lost their lives as they challenged the structures that enforced marginalization and poverty upon them.

Sometimes members of BEC's talk symbolically about their gatherings as meeting after the sun goes down to reflect upon their activity in the world while the sun was high. Another image is that of moving through life with a Bible in one hand and a newspaper in the other. Liberation theology has not caused them. Liberation theology is rather the reflection upon the BEC experience.

The fact is that these BECs or BCCs or SCCs or House Churches are a small minority of the religious population. I think they will not become more than that. But they are a vigorous enough minority to be a critical mass that is helping to redefine gospel, churchhood, and the mutual dialectic between faith and culture, not just for their *communitates* but as well for the ecclesial *societas* (which, let it be said, often gets dragged kicking and screaming to its own reconstruction). Their belief that God is calling for a different way of being world, i.e., the reign of God in human history, has brought back into the church an eschatology that it has too long been without.

The Brazilian theologian Leonardo Boff once commented that it may well be the mission of the Third World to evangelize the First World. What I know from reading and from contacts with Third World BCCs is the profound involvement of U.S. economic exploitation in the poverty and marginalization of people in the Third World. Brazil pays $260,000,000 annually in debt interest (without remission of capital), enough for schools for 60 million children of housing for 30 million Brazilians. U.S. missionaries often return from Third World countries radically aware of the need to evangelize economic systems at home. They, like us at home, feel (with good reason) impotent to have significant effects upon megastructures.

Henry Nelson Wieman insisted that redemptive grace has to operate in the human systems that constitute our meaning structures. That is very, very difficult in U.S. culture. Walter Brueggemann's vast body of work has helped call attention to the difference between royal consciousness and prophetic consciousness. Royal consciousness is the perspective of those in power and is protective of their vested interests. Prophetic consciousness emerges from the experience of people on the underside of history, representing their perspective and their vested interests.

In U.S. culture, one function of the theory of separation of church and state (completely alien to the Constitutional intention of preventing official state religion) is to create and maintain an effective barrier between prophetic consciousness and royal consciousness. The dialectic between king and prophet, so crucial to biblical religion and so corrective of both, cannot effectively occur in U.S. culture. The enforcer of the barrier is religious tax exemption, which is lost if religion critiques the body politic, at least if the critique comes from the left. Articulate, fundamentalist *support* from the right has caused no case! The relative silence of churches recently in my home state, with David Duke—ex-Nazi and Klansman—running for Governor is, I opine, an effect of the formidable fiscal wedge between prophetic and royal consciousness.

I can only hint at directions in the U.S. church for BCCs, but an outline of the agenda is not hard to come by if we keep the Bible in one hand and the newspaper in the other.

The church contours of biblical faith have already been sketched, and the justice of God is at the center of God's intentionality for history. It's the newspaper in the other hand upon which I wish to dwell.

In 1990 the 20 percent wealthiest families received about 47 percent of total income, while the bottom 20 percent received 4 percent of total income. That's the largest cut and smallest cut respectively in U.S. history. This is not an isolated year.

In *The Politics of Rich and Poor*, Kevin Phillips looks at a decade (1978-1988) of income statistics, adjusted to real 1987 dollars. The lowest decile lost 14.8 percent, dropping from $4,133 to $3,504. As a matter of fact, there is decline in average family income in every decile in the bottom 80 percent. Average income in the tenth decile increased from $102,722 to $119,635. For the top 5 percent, average income increased from $134,543 to $166,016 (23.4 percent). For the top 1 percent, average family income increased from $270,053 to $404,566 (49.8 percent). There are no signs of trickle down.[37]

Harvard economist Robert Reich says that what's happening in the top 20 percent amounts to a secession of the successful. Philanthropy in that group is significant but tends to be directed to colleges and universities, symphonies, museums, and the like. The money tends to stay in the fiscal loop where it originated. Reich's far-reaching economic analysis for the twenty-first century is a good candidate for the newspaper in the hands of BCC members.[38]

---

37. Kevin Phillips, *The Politics of Rich and Poor: Wealth and the American Electorate in the Reagan Aftermath* (New York: Random House, 1990), p. 17.

38. Robert B. Reich, *The Work of Nations: Preparing Ourselves for 21st Century Capitalism* (New York: Knopf, 1991).

I have indicated the most recent year for which we have statistics on average family income and a brief summary of a recent decade of experience. The pattern is one of the relocation of resources out of the bottom *and* the middle. But this has been documented as well as a two-century-long pattern. At the time of the American Revolution the top 20 percent held 68 percent of total wealth, and two centuries later increased the holding to 84.6 percent. The middle 50 percent had a 30 percent share at the time of the revolution, and two centuries later had 15.4 percent. The bottom 30 percent lost the 2 percent they once had.

It is hard to avoid the judgment that the U.S. system of free market economy has a pattern of distribution that systematically deepens poverty at the bottom and just as surely disempowers the middle. The right to private ownership originally protected the rights of individuals to own property and tended to favor the distribution of resources. When applied instead to giant corporations, it concentrates rather than distributes resources.

Individuals are helpless to restrain such a system. There is little hope except through a power base that can be developed in mediating structures, i.e., through networks and organizations and prophetic consciousness. If the power base for social change in Latin America is largely the poor, in U.S. culture the power base is the large middle class. It is unlikely to get organized, however, until the middle class are informed about their disempowerment. The systemic causes of middle-class disempowerment are identical to those that deepen poverty at the bottom. All the reasons are there for coalitions between the poor and the middle. But pecuniary envy is a dynamic that drives the middle to try to connect upward. When the symbols of upward mobility are purchased, e.g., designer clothes or salad shooters, they have in fact moved downward.

The book *Risking Liberation: Middle Class Powerlessness and Social Heroism* offers a keen social analysis of the issues I am addressing.[39] I do not find the book strong in practical agenda, but the laying out of the case is stunning. I do not think that the Good News of Jesus Christ stands a ghost of a chance of accosting the social systems I am naming without a church rich in *communitas*. The church, a gathering, a social response to the Christ event, has a nature and a mission that requires it to be rich in *communitas*.

CONCLUSION

I have attempted to discuss the nature of the church by saying that nature has everything to do, for better and for worse, with history. I mean the history of the Christ-event itself and the definition it imposes, and with socio-historical responses of people across the centuries, and the definitions they

---

39. Paul G. King, Kent Maynard, and David Woodyard, *Risking Liberation: Middle Class Powerlessness and Social Heroism* (Atlanta: John Knox, 1988).

impose. I have chosen to direct attention to very early history, a period with less institutionalization where the charismatic and prophetic features are in clearer relief and have suggested that many of these recollections are dangerous memories, "dangerous" to our settled instincts, but emancipatory for the very same reasons. Dangerous memories free church to consider new appropriations for new circumstances.

I have dwelled upon the vital interaction between faith and culture, since the living word of God is always an address to us where we are. The justice of God appears not as one of the issues on the church's horizon, not even the most important issue, but is rather the horizon itself. We have seen that while justice does not replace charity, it moves beyond charity as a political energy that addresses social systems in need of transformation. We have affirmed the relationship between faith and culture as mutually critical, since the truth of each must often address the distortion of the other, and it goes both ways. Finally, I have placed great stress upon the *communitas*, the smallest units of ecclesial life but have insisted that it needs a dynamic *societas* just as sure as *societas* atrophies without being exercised by *communitas*. And I have expressed my hope in a future for my own culture and my own faith if the movement of basic ecclesial communities can grab the conscience of religion in America.

CHAPTER TEN

Ecstatic Naturalism and the
Transfiguration of the Good

ROBERT S. CORRINGTON

INTRODUCTION

Naturalism and empiricism have had a long history of cohabitation in the same conceptual space. The inner dynamics of naturalism have been such as to compel continual methodological changes that come to honor the fitful and vast structures of an indifferent nature. While American naturalism has moved in several distinctive directions, empirical method has been stretched and regrounded, often in dialogue with phenomenology, to correspond to the depth logic of naturalism.[1] Value theory has also been transformed so that the emergence of value in time is intimately tied to an evolutionary and creative nature that provides a finite place for concrete value within the vast network of causal events. Empirical method, however envisioned, works in consort with naturalism to find and secure specific values within human communities. Empirical theology, as but one moment within the history of an emergent naturalism, struggles to express the relation between the divine natures and nature as a whole while showing how value is a creative good within the world.

In what follows I will trace out a history of naturalism that moves through four distinct stages. This will prepare the way for an analysis of empirical methods as they themselves correspond to each stage of naturalism. The

---

1. On the correlation of empiricism and phenomenology and the relation of both to naturalism, see, *Pragmatism Considers Phenomenology*, ed. Robert S. Corrington, Carl R. Hausman, and Thomas Seebohm (Lanham, Md.: Center for Advanced Research in Phenomenology and The University Press of America, 1987).

203

status and nature of the good will be redefined in the light of the consummatory phase of naturalism, that of ecstatic naturalism, which has its own unique and combined forms of empirical method and its own conception of the relation between the divine natures and human good. Put in other terms, ecstatic naturalism locates the ethical spheres within a vast metaphysical structure that honors both the sheer indifference of nature and nature's self-transcending potencies.

It is impossible to line up the four stages of naturalism as if they have a clear-cut trajectory and as if there are pure species that have precise outlines and definitions. Like Peirce when he describes the structures of signs, the historian of naturalism must engage in a process of "prescinding" in which certain regnant features are isolated out for analysis while the conflicting or deeply ambiguous features are temporarily muted. No form of naturalism comes "pure" and no one form has historical priority over the others. Rather, each form represents a tendency within naturalism as a whole that needs to be clarified in the light of the other key possibilities.

It should be noted at the outset that each form of naturalism insists that there can be no special realm of the supernatural that somehow remains disconnected from nature itself. Insofar as the supernatural is still affirmed it is done so as one dimension within nature that has its own inner logic and its own forms of interaction with the rest of nature.[2] The connecting link among the various forms of naturalism is not materialism (a common misconception) but the denial that there is any realm totally incommensurate with the world. Materialism is but one conceptual option within naturalism and should never be confused with naturalism itself, which has a much deeper and richer conceptual structure than any materialism that would appear within it. As we will see, some forms of naturalism affirm final and formal cause in such a way as to put pressure on most forms of materialism.

"DESCRIPTIVE" NATURALISM

The first form of naturalism that can be identified is what I shall call the "descriptive" form. This form stresses the primacy of material and efficient cause within a vast cosmic structure that is indifferent to human aspiration, even if it allows for the growth of the good within fragmented human communities. While the history of descriptive naturalism can be traced back to the categorial descriptions of Aristotle and the transformed atomism of Lucretius, its contemporary manifestation can be seen in the writings of Santayana, Dewey, and Buchler, each of whom, it should be noted, were friendly to some aspects of Greco-Roman forms of naturalism. The empha-

---

2. For a thorough study of the religious dimension of naturalism and its rejection of a special realm of the supernatural see, William M. Shea, *The Naturalists and the Supernatural* (Macon, Ga.: Mercer University Press, 1984).

sis of descriptive naturalism is on the finite and instrumental character of the human process as it struggles to stabilize some goods against an indifferent nature.

For Santayana, the human creature is tethered to a particular place and has no sense of a center or circumference for nature as a whole. The ultimate upshot and value of the human process is unknown and there can be no extranatural salvation for the self that is caught in the whirling eddies of an indifferent cosmos. Santayana takes Dewey to task for failing to push his own naturalism past the foreground and the industrial structures of American capitalism. He sees Dewey as working out of an incomplete naturalism that refuses to look nature squarely in the face and thus fails to grasp just how unconcerned nature is with one of its most complex products, the human self.

Dewey, of course, insists that nature is itself instrumental and that human forms of inquiry are themselves products of evolution that have made it possible for the self to find some momentary forms of stability among the precarious features of a changing nature. Dewey hints in the direction of a process naturalism when he argues that so-called structures are actually events with an especially long-term unfolding that serves to mask their event character.[3] Unlike Santayana, Dewey is willing to find a place for final cause within nature provided that such causes are understood to be located within the needs and dynamics of the human process. Material and efficient cause remain central to Dewey's form of descriptive naturalism with his emphasis on the brute and unintelligent qualities of interaction.

Of more recent vintage is the austere and minimalist naturalism of Justus Buchler who was in many respects an heir to Dewey.[4] What Buchler calls "ordinal naturalism" is actually a species of descriptive naturalism because of its focus on a vast and often indifferent nature that yet remains amenable to some forms of instrumental control. The human animal is unique in using several forms of judgment (making, doing, and saying) to transform natural orders into complexes amenable to human need. Yet the sense remains that nature is far too vast and complex to be circumscribed by finite forms of human query. For Buchler, the self is born into a state of "natural debt" that cannot be canceled by instrumental control any more than it can be overcome by divine agency. Nature has no contour and cannot be mapped from a point outside of itself.[5]

---

3. Dewey works out the foundations of his event ontology in *Experience and Nature* (New York: Dover, 1958). The most important chapter is the second, "Existence as Precarious and as Stable."

4. On the development of naturalism from Dewey to Buchler see Robert S. Corrington, "Naturalism, Measure, and the Ontological Difference," *The Southern Journal of Philosophy* 23:1 (1985), pp. 19-32.

5. Buchler's unique naturalist metaphysics is best seen in his *Metaphysics of Natural Complexes*, 2nd expanded ed., ed. Kathleen Wallace, Armen Marsoobian, and Robert S. Corrington (Albany: SUNY Press, 1989).

Descriptive naturalism thus emphasizes material and efficient cause while locating the finite human process within an indifferent nature that allows for the growth of value but doesn't have its own mechanisms for the creation and preservation of the good. All goods are human goods and they remain precariously perched on top of a world that has made no special provisions for their survival. At the same time, descriptive naturalism remains reticent to assign an honored place to the spirit or to the divine natures. For Dewey, the divine can be best seen in terms of the ultimate unifying good that sustains a community of inquiry in search of lasting human values. There can be no extranatural realm of the spirit any more than there can be an extranatural or supernatural divine agent.

"Honorific" Naturalism

Contrasted to descriptive naturalism is what I shall call "honorific" naturalism that places special priority on the role of the spirit in either creating nature or in quickening natural possibilities toward an ideal consummation. Honorific naturalism remains naturalism insofar as the spirit is in and of nature even if it may have been responsible for the creation of nature in the past. The central figure in the history of honorific naturalism is Emerson who struggled to find a clear locus for the spirit within a complex and interweaved nature.

Honorific naturalism has a place for material and efficient cause but privileges formal and final cause. Nature's spirit is purposive and is concresced in forms that have their own spiritual power and momentum. Emerson was deeply sensitive to the locations of spirit and clothed each appearance in a metaphor that gathered together the unique features of the particular order seized by his vision. Nature itself was "saltatory" and exploded with the power of the spirit, moving in fits and starts toward a reintegration. As Emerson's vision darkened in the 1840s this sense of the presence of the spirit faded somewhat from view as his own vision moved toward a more descriptive naturalism. Yet even in his later writings, his honorific naturalism breaks through as he still finds a place for the emergent spirit within a cruel and vast cosmos that seems to mock the poet's hunger for transfiguration.

Of more recent vintage are the later essays of Heidegger where the Emersonian sense of the power of language to evoke and transform the world comes to the fore. For Heidegger, whose naturalism (as manifest in his concern with "worldhood") is clearly of the honorific or even eulogistic variety, language is the "house of Being" that makes it possible for nature to shine forth in all of its plenitude. It is not customary to place Heidegger within the history of naturalism, but I believe this comes from a confusion about the conceptual and experiential possibilities actually prevalent *within* naturalism. Insofar as Heidegger speaks of our alienation from the earth and our need to sustain a world horizon in which the holy can once again return to guide the self toward a primal transformation, he belongs to those for whom philosophy is indeed a return from epistemology to the realms of a healing nature. And, like Emerson before him, Heidegger insists that only a return of a centering power, as emergent from the history of Being (*Seinsgeschichte*) can rescue us from our sheer drift and fallenness within a darkening world.

Honorific forms of naturalism tend to be monolithic in the sense that they envision spirit (or Being) as a single source for the unity of power and meaning within the world. Such naturalists often write as if nature or history has one purpose or one trajectory and that the spirit is an agency with a fairly clear-cut momentum that can be mapped. It might seem strange to call a perspective focusing on spirit a form of naturalism until it is remembered that the spirit, whatever its quasi-imperial intent, is always part and parcel of nature and can only be effective within natural orders of interaction.

PROCESS NATURALISM

A cousin of the honorific view is "process naturalism" where the focus is less on a ubiquitous and omnivorous spirit and more on plural centers of power and awareness that interact to sustain an evolutionary cosmos. Process naturalisms are thus evolutionary and pluralistic and often imply a form of panpsychism, or, in Peirce's terms, the notion that "matter is effete mind." For a theologian like Cobb, the better descriptive term for the process perspective is "panexperientialism" where the emphasis is on the centrality of some form of experience, however primitive, within all orders of relevance. Empirical theology, particularly as manifest in the writings of Wieman, struggles to honor the process account of creative advance while retaining aspects of Dewey's more descriptive naturalism.

Wieman's case is especially instructive because he works out of the tensions between the descriptive and process versions of naturalism. The descriptive dimension is evident when he backs away from some of the more robust conceptual innovations of Whitehead where the plenitude of a primordial god is described. For Wieman, the correlation of the divine and the creative advance of the good is still an event firmly within a causally structured nature. In the following passage, Wieman uses language that points toward the two forms of naturalism just mentioned:

> We shall try to demonstrate that there is a creative process working in our midst which transforms the human mind and the world relative to the human mind. We shall then show how transformation by this process is always in the direction of greater good. The human good thus created includes goods, satisfaction of human wants, richness of quality, and power of man to control the course of events. . . . Throughout the writing

that follows we shall take as our guide the creative event, which produces qualitative meaning.[6]

The process dimension lies in his affirmation that the creative process is somehow larger than the human and that the self participates in something that is not a mere cultural product. The descriptive element lies in the focus on concrete human wants and the control of nature that can bring about a transformation of wants into satisfactions. Where Whitehead and Hartshorne part company from this form of empirical theology is in a stronger focus on the modal and ontological properties of the divine natures themselves. Where Wieman parts company from Dewey, whom he otherwise honors, is in the stress on the metaphysical reality of creative process within nature. That is, creative advance is something "done" by the universe itself and not solely by human beings in search of periodic stabilities within an indifferent nature.

As noted, no form of naturalism comes pure and Wieman's blend of the descriptive and process versions is a perfect example of the native flexibility of naturalism as it struggles beyond its antecedent possibilities toward new innovations. Thus far we have seen that descriptive naturalism stresses material and efficient cause and insists on the indifference of nature to the needs of the human process. It does not follow from this that the self cannot transform nature in small ways to satisfy its needs. Honorific naturalism is monistic in the sense that it envisions a single spirit (or history of Being) that overarches nature and provides the measure for natural forms of interaction. This version of naturalism privileges formal and final cause. Process naturalism pluralizes the spirit and prefers instead to speak of centers of awareness that become aware of each other through a kind of final cause, namely, the feeling of feeling in which an event "chooses" to let another event, now objectified, become relevant to it. At the same time, process naturalism is fully evolutionary and sees the power of creativity throughout the universe. Honorific forms of naturalism need not be evolutionary but process forms must be.

A version of process naturalism can be seen in William Dean's "naturalistic historicism" where the emphasis is on how signs and their objects belong to a historical world in which there are innumerable semiotic chains forming the connecting links of history. Dean, like Cobb before him, insists that the process and historical versions of naturalism are compatible with postmodernist denials of a transcendent realm of signification and are thus sensitive to the explosion of contingency and difference lying at the heart of nature. I call Dean's naturalism a version of process naturalism precisely because it rejects the monolithic structures of honorific naturalism while

---

6. Henry N. Wieman, *The Source of the Human Good* (Carbondale: Southern Illinois University Press, 1946), p. 17.

insisting on the presence of final cause within an otherwise chaotic nature. It privileges history over nature and thereby distances itself from a descriptive naturalism that would see history as a mere species within the vast realms of nature. At the same time, it places religious experience right at the heart of human communities and sees value as emergent from the fitful and fragmented conditions of social and natural life.[7]

ECSTATIC NATURALISM

The fourth and final form of naturalism is that of "ecstatic naturalism" that combines several of the elements of the previous three forms but that transforms all of them by its radical insistence on a fundamental division within nature itself. The most basic division affirmed by ecstatic naturalism is that between nature naturing (*natura naturans*) and nature natured (*natura naturata*). Nature naturing is here defined as the unlimited realm of the potencies. These potencies are not yet possibilities because possibilities can only arise within and among actualities, that is, within the orders of the world (nature natured). Nature natured is the created orders of the world; that is, the manifest orders within which the human process finds itself. There are no bridging metaphors or ontological links between the innumerable potencies of nature naturing and the innumerable orders of the world as manifest. The difference between nature naturing and nature natured is the fundamental divide *within* nature itself. That is, this divide does not separate off nature from some alleged realm of the non- or super-natural but lives out of the heart of a self-transforming nature.

Ecstatic naturalism affirms with descriptive naturalism that nature is often indifferent to the aspirations of the human process. Along with Santayana it insists that there can be no ultimate center or circumference for nature any more than there can be an ultimate foreground or background. Nature has no outer shape or contour. With honorific naturalism it affirms the presence of spirit within nature even while denying that it is an imperial presence. The great divide between nature naturing and nature natured is akin to the ontological difference as disclosed by Heidegger when he speaks of the difference between Being and a being. With process forms of naturalism it affirms the role of creativity within at least some orders of interaction and provides a place for final cause within particular orders. At the same time, ecstatic naturalism works within the evolutionary perspective.

The potencies of nature are preformal and are not yet orders in their own right. Historically, this notion of the potencies can be traced back to Schelling

---

7. Dean's two recent books are of special importance, *American Religious Empiricism* (1986), and *History Making History: The New Historicism in American Religious Thought* (1988) (Albany: SUNY Press). See my review of these books in *The Journal of Speculative Philosophy: New Series* 3:3 (1989), pp. 223-230.

with his concern for regrounding the sciences of nature within an understanding of the creative and ejective power of an organic nature. Tillich
transformed the concept of the potencies in the light of his own understanding of the power of Being as particularly manifest in the New Being of
Jesus as the Christ. In what follows, echoes of Tillich's transformation of the
potencies will be heard.

Ecstatic naturalism thus honors the finite locations of the spirit within
an evolving universe but lives out of the stark recognition that nature itself
is reft into two halves only one of which is directly manifest to the human process. The innumerable potencies of nature naturing are only indirectly available to the self through their manifestations within the spirit that hovers
between and among orders of relevance. As we will see, the concept of the
good itself hovers precariously between these two dimensions of a self-
transfiguring nature.

EMPIRICISM AND NATURALISM

Empirical method works hand in hand with naturalism to insure that
thought remains fully embedded in nonhuman orders of relevance.
Empiricism is not so much a doctrine about the "what" of experience, a mistake made by Hume, but an insistence that experience remains attuned to
the environing conditions of its life. As noted by Dewey, experience is in and
of nature and does not exist in a detached realm outside of its evolutionary
enabling conditions. It follows that empirical theology is not so much a theory about the "what" of religious experience, although it will draw some
conclusions about the referent of experience, as it is an attempt to honor the
ways in which nature enters into the human process and deposits its shapes
in the self. Put differently, empiricism lets the self become permeable to the
not-self so that the orders of nature natured can become deeply relevant to the
self in process.

Each form of naturalism has its own distinctive type of empirical method.
We can trace these through more quickly because their ontological conditions
have already been laid out. Descriptive naturalism uses an empiricism that
remains attuned to antecedent causal conditions and that makes tentative
inductive leaps beyond the immediacies of the given to class or genus specific conclusions. This form of empiricism remains reticent to impose final
cause onto efficient cause even though it will certainly acknowledge the fitful and fragmented presence of purpose within the human order.

Honorific naturalism relies on the primacy of the given in an immediate
intuition that does not admit of comparison or inductive analysis. For
Emerson, empiricism, insofar as he could use such a term, entailed the intrusion of a self-transcending nature into the poetic consciousness. The self
has an immediate and complete awareness of the depth dimension of nature
but is not in a position to compare this experience with that of other selves

nor can the Emersonian self participate in the cumulative method of a scientific community. By the same token, Heidegger's concept of experience does not allow for symmetrical communication among equal selves but can only function within private and highly privileged forms of primal immediacy. Honorific naturalism thus has an empiricism (or concept of experience) without a method.

Process naturalisms, whether fully historicist or not, also fall short on method while denying anything like a primal form of immediacy. Put differently, process naturalism has the hermeneutic sophistication to recognize that prehension (feeling of feeling) is always context dependent and fully perspectival. No prehension is unmediated or pure even if the ingression of relevant material is done "at once" and whole. Insofar as a method *can* be assigned to process forms of naturalism, it would be the method of abstractive generalization where the demands of a generically inclusive vision would remain in tension with the series of actual prehensions available to the naturalist at any given time. Postmodernist versions of process naturalism would place less stress on generalization even while using such strategies to make the claims of radical pluralism viable. This irony should not go without notice. Naturalism in any guise is struggling to become as encompassing as nature itself. While this is a vain attempt, it is not out of keeping with the basic piety of naturalism that wishes to honor a nature that is infinitely vaster than any categorical scheme.

Ecstatic naturalism combines the methodological and premethodological dimensions of the other versions of naturalism but attunes them all to the fundamental abyss within nature, namely that between the innumerable potencies of nature naturing and the innumerable orders manifest as nature natured. Like descriptive naturalism, the ecstatic variety uses induction to locate and grasp the contours emergent from efficient and material cause. Such inductive generalizations are tentative and subject to self-control in the long run. Like Peirce, the ecstatic naturalist locates method within the community of inquiry as it struggles against the opacity and recalcitrance of alien orders of interaction. On a larger scale, the community of interpreters works with this inductive material to shape a conception of an evolving and fragmentary world.[8]

The sense of empirical immediacy found in honorific naturalism is transformed in terms of the potencies of nature naturing that are manifest "on the edges" of the world's orders. For ecstatic naturalism there can be an immediate intrusion of the potencies, but the actual shape of any given potency remains shrouded in mystery. The immediacy is thus located in the impact rather than in any "message" conveyed. Postmodernists prefer to use the concept of "traces" to deal with the realms of the presemiotic. Such

---

8. I have worked out the basic structures of the hermeneutic community in my *The Community of Interpreters* (Macon, Ga.: Mercer University Press, 1987).

language is not inappropriate provided that it is recognized that a given potency will have a "presence" that compels the self to participate in the depth dimension of an ecstatically self-transforming nature.

Like the process naturalist, the ecstatic naturalist will honor the plural ways in which the orders of the world become manifest. If the potencies are felt in terms of their immediate impact, the manifest orders of the world are encountered through the innumerable shocks and separations that continue to alter the direction of the self in process. These shocks are "felt" and have their own vector force moving the self in specifiable trajectories that can be mapped in retrospect if not during their actual manifestation. Abstractive generalization enhances the scope of understanding so that it can grasp, in however tentative a fashion, the upshot of these innumerable causes, both efficient and final, as they shape the self in time.

MUSEMENT

On a higher level of sophistication, ecstatic naturalism uses the methods of abduction and interpretive musement as originally delineated by Peirce. Abduction moves in the opposite direction from induction. If induction moves from case to case in order to generate a claim about a class of objects or events, abduction moves from a general hypothesis (rule) and applies it "backward," as it were, to a given case. The creation of novel and rich hypotheses makes it possible to leap beyond the immediate inductive possibilities so that a more pervasive statistical law can be isolated and articulated. Musement is a species of abduction that works in an even less direct fashion to enhance our grasp of pervasive features. The attitude of interpretive musement is fairly common in the human process but is rarely spelled out in detail. For Peirce, musement occurs after induction, deduction, and abduction (rule to case) have exhausted their possibilities. The semiotic world of empirical knowledge becomes open to novel possibilities when musement works in its seemingly random fashion to let complex and different signs interact in ways that could not have been possible for the other more restricted forms of method. Interpretive musement opens up a free semiotic zone in which the self is actually brought into interaction with the depth structures of nature. Musement thus takes place after instrumental and goal-directed methods have exhausted their potential to render a situation intelligible.

Musement thus becomes one of the key methods of ecstatic naturalism. There is a striking sense in which interpretive musement participates in both sides of the naturing/natured divide. Insofar as musement feels the direct impact of the presemiotic potencies, and has its own momentum altered and transfigured, it lives out of the rhythms of nature naturing. Yet insofar as musement gathers up the traits and features of the orders of the world and hovers over them in creative play it participates in the richness of nature natured.

Thus the method of interpretive musement has the unique distinction of living on both sides of the ontological difference and in providing a means for bringing them together. This fact will have profound implications for our discussion of the good as it emerges from the heart of nature and works its way fitfully into the interpretive communities that surround and support the human process.

Ecstatic naturalism thus uses a variety of methods precisely because it shares certain ontological commitments with the three other forms of naturalism. In spite of some crucial differences among the varieties of naturalism they all share the sense that nature is vast and infinitely complex and that all methods must honor antecedent orders of relevance that determine and alter future possibilities. Possibilities are in and of nature and do not hover outside of the world in some "realm" of the possible. By the same token, actualities are in and of orders of relevance and come and go as these orders change and admit or exclude new possibilities.

THE EMERGENCE OF THE GOOD

The emergence of the good, or of finite goods, is and must be an event within nature. All forms of naturalism concur in the recognition that goods are no more free floating than are possibilities. Goods are in and of nature or not at all. For descriptive naturalisms, goods are secured by human communities that struggle to render the precarious more stable. Santayana would downplay the communal dimension and envision goods in terms of the detached satisfactions of the realm of spirit which has no causal relation to the realm of matter. Be that as it may, all goods are momentary achievements within an indifferent and often hostile nature.

For the honorific naturalist all goods are part of a final consummation that awaits the self in the emergent epiphanies of the spirit. Goods are not exactly eternal, but they are secure against the ravages of chance and an indifferent causal sequence of events. For Heidegger, of course, the good emerges from out of the primal mittances of Being as it gives and withholds itself in the current epoch. Because of their "empiricism" of immediacy, honorific naturalists must see goods as primal givens that stand before the self and promise a transformation of the human process that is more than instrumental.

For process naturalism, the good emerges whenever the universe allows for the creation of more value. Values are themselves products of experience as it becomes more complex and increases the tension between harmony and contrast *within* experience. Intensity is a good in its own right, and many process thinkers argue as if the creation of intensity is the telos of nature itself. Yet as a species of naturalism, the process variety still envisions all goods as being part of nature rather than as being located outside of orders of interaction. The plot thickens when it is remembered that the pri-

mordial mind of God contains all possible generals (eternal objects) in immediacy even if this is not a realm of the compossible, that is, even if God can
allow incompatible traits to coexist within the divine mind at the same
"time." Yet the value and relevance of these eternal objects is only determined
by their full participation in the world of actual occasions that live by allow-
ing eternal entities to become deeply relevant to their own evolving experience.

Ecstatic naturalism, as can be expected, radically redefines the locus of the
good and moves away from antecedent conceptions of how finite goods
operate within the world. The good is not so much a human product, as it
would be in descriptive naturalisms, as it is a precarious product of a self-transfiguring nature. Consequently, ecstatic naturalism rejects Dewey's instrumental view of the good because it is based on an inadequate metaphysics that
in turn ignores the fundamental divide between nature naturing and nature
natured. Dewey's metaphysics is inadequate because it remains, as noted
by Santayana, far too anthropocentric. That is, the human process becomes
nature's center and nature itself is rendered into instrumental terms. By writing the human so large on the face of nature Dewey underestimates the
transformative possibilities within nature. At the same time, his reconstructed
account of experience, while profound and revolutionary in its own right, fails
to understand the depth dimension of both the aesthetic and the religious
dimensions of experience. When he speaks of "quality" as an intensified
ontological integrity that consummates and fulfills human experience, he
comes close to an ecstatic understanding of the human process but remains
cut off from the depth dimension of the spiritual presence that underlies so-
called qualities. By comparison, Tillich's evocative concept of the "gestalt of
grace" moves decisively beyond Dewey's understanding of "quality" and pre-
pares the way for ecstatic naturalism and its conception of the correlation of
goods, both finite and otherwise, and the human process.

An initial road block standing in the way of an ecstatic naturalist conception of the good is the traditional notion, at least since Hume, that it is
impossible to derive an "ought" from an "is." Naturalism is held to be a
framework or perspective deeply attuned to what is the case within nature.
The "ought" is held to be an imperative that may be counter-factual or may
occupy a realm of obligation that cuts across or against nature. One version
of this second view is found in the essays of Kant where he affirms that private maxims are too strongly tied to inclinations, and they must be directed
toward the strictures of the categorical imperative which asks the individual to universalize and reverse given maxims. By attempting to universalize
a maxim (to ask if it applies to all rational beings) and to reverse the same
maxim (to ask if it applies to the individual) the moral agent brings himself
or herself into the position where it is possible to see if the maxim ought to
become binding. If the maxim passes both tests then it can be imposed on the
inclinations that might favor a less general maxim. Kantian dualism is thus

antinaturalist in the sense that it posits an unbridgeable gulf within the self (phenomenal and noumenal orders) that can only be dealt with by an appeal to the non-natural.

Naturalism, of whatever stripe, cannot accept the concept that the "ought" is falsely derived from the "is" any more than it can appeal to a special realm of the "ought" as the locus of finite goods. Ecstatic naturalism, in particular, affirms that the good is not so much derived from the world of actuality as it is one of the more complex and unstable products of a self-transfiguring nature. The debate hinges on the problem of "derivability." If by "derive" one means a clear deduction in which the consequent is prefigured in the antecedent assertions, then it is clear that an "ought" cannot be derived from the "is." If, however, the concept of "derivation" can take on a larger sense to include the concept of "emergence" then it is indeed possible to "derive" an "ought" from an "is." The concept of emergence is thus crucial to any naturalism that wishes to find a proper locus for finite goods within nature.

THE GOOD

Any good is what it is precisely because it has value for the human process and has this value within the context of a community of interpreters for whom all good must emerge in a public way so that they can enhance the share of power and meaning within the community. This is not to say that there are no private goods but to affirm that the so-called private realm derives its own sense of validation from the emancipatory structures of the emergent public good. Goods are never "pure" any more than they are free from the ambiguity of emergence and interaction. The current perspective equates goods with the realm of the "ought" in that such oughts are themselves what they are because of the inner wisdom of the community of interpreters. Put differently, all goods are emergent products of nature that must be assessed by the community. The individual self is a community in its own right (a reflexive community) and uses the same cumulative methodologies as the larger community of interpreters. In assessing these goods the community feels the lure of given goods and is thus bound to enhance their furtherance within the community. Goods in this sense obligate by their very being.

To be a good within nature is, among other things, to be available to human and pre-human organisms as they struggle for security and transcendence within the world. Goods render an organism secure insofar as they insure momentary stabilities against internal and external threats. Goods make transcendence possible insofar as they goad the organism into an enhanced assimilation of signs and values and open the organism to the depth rhythms of nature. A good is thus an ought in that it stands as a call or an obligation moving the organism toward an augmented form of interaction.

Goods stand before the organism and demand a response. Goods are thus not mere products of the self or the organism but are ejective products of a nature that spawns goods without "counting" them or rendering them all coherent or self-consistent. Thus, of course, there can be competing goods and competing obligations.

When the concept of "the good" or of "goods" is invoked it is assumed that one is dealing with orders that can be morally appraised. This issue is deeply problematic and must be addressed from the standpoint of the ontological difference. Can the potencies of nature, which remain hidden to the human process, be morally appraised? The answer must be that they cannot be. Ecstatic naturalism assumes that only manifest orders of relevance can be the subject of moral appraisal. The potencies of nature naturing enter into the human process in unpredictable ways and have no direct relevance to the moral transformation of life. Put in different terms, nature's potencies are "beyond good and evil." They make all orders of relevance possible and they support the human process but they exert no cumulative directionality nor do they have a clear and accessible manifestation. The locus of the good cannot be "within" the realm of nature naturing.

It follows that the "closer" side of the ontological difference, namely, the orders of the manifest world, must be the locus of the good. Yet, this obvious conclusion is not as obvious as it looks. It *is* clear that the world contains orders that can be morally appraised. While no community will have a list of necessary and sufficient conditions for locating and defining the good, some form of consensus will guide cumulative forms of appraisal. Given orders can be ranked in terms of their overall value for the self in process while others can be critiqued in terms of their anti-emancipatory power within a community. The question remains: Are these goods part of the world as manifest or do they come from a deeper source? To answer this question properly it is necessary to make a distinction that will separate off one type of good from another.

Finite goods, such as physical well-being, are indeed within and among the orders of relevance that constitute the world. Nature is replete with such goods even if no one of them is available in an unambiguous way. All finite goods are thus part and parcel of nature natured and remain in flux within nature. Human communities work to enhance the strength and scope of these natural goods so that the human process can increase its semiotic and physical fecundity. These goods thus stand before the community as imperatives for transformation. Ecstatic naturalism thus affirms with the other forms of naturalism that finite goods are in and of nature.

THE NOT YET

Yet do finite goods exhaust the class of all goods? Can we even speak of a nonfinite good or of an infinite good? Is such language in any way compatible with the naturalism which stresses finite conditions of interaction? For ecstatic naturalism the contrast to finite goods is not an infinite good or an eternal Platonic form but a "dynamic good" that lives out of the not yet.[9] The concept of the "not yet" (*noch nicht sein*) comes from Ernst Bloch who radically redefined natural law so that it could be understood as an emergent force coming to the community from an emancipatory future. The "not yet Being" of the dynamic good is a higher "ought" in the sense that it calls the human process forward to a new and transfigured reality that cannot be prefigured in antecedent conditions. Finite goods are available as they are within the present and are located in specific orders of interaction. Dynamic goods, on the other hand, are not spatially or temporally located in the same sense. They hover before the self and its communities in the unique space of the not yet that is not an order within the world. This unique space is actually that of the spirit that is neither a potency of nature nor a specific order of relevance. The spirit lives out of the draft held open by the not yet and is the locus for dynamic goods that stand before the self as it struggles for transfiguration.

Process naturalism well understands the idea of emergent goods and can grasp the idea that all goods are imperatives that call forth a choice on the part of the experiencing actual occasion. That is, a good (value) stands before the occasion and "recommends" itself to the evolving experience so that it can become internally related to the occasion as it moves toward concrescence. In an analogous way, ecstatic naturalism affirms that dynamic goods are located outside of selves and in turn "recommend" themselves to the self in process as it moves toward transfiguration. Finite goods do not radically transform the self. They merely augment those properties that link the self to the orders of the world. The individual can have more health, more comfort, more creativity, or more pleasure, but these finite goods, no matter how accumulated, do not alter the depth dimension of the self. Only dynamic goods, which speak out of the not yet of the spirit, can enter into the depth dimension of the self and bring about a transfiguration.

DYNAMIC GOODS

The new Adam and the new Eve cannot emerge from finite goods within nature natured. Finite goods remain strictly anthropological, no matter how essential they are and no matter how treasured by the human process. Dynamic goods, on the other hand, are eschatological because they emerge from the not yet Being of the spirit. They speak from out of a different time and space than do finite goods. Until naturalism opened out the ontological

---

9. The concept of "dynamic good" points in the direction of Peirce's concept of the "dynamic object." Unlike Kant's "thing-in-itself," the dynamic object moves closer to the interpreter through time as the more available "immediate object" responds to the pressure of the dynamic object that lives within it.

difference it was unable to find the true location for dynamic goods and to contrast them to finite goods. Dewey fully understood the status and location of finite goods within nature but had only the briefest glimpse into the depth dimension of dynamic goods. When he speaks of "quality" he moves toward an understanding of the ontological difference but his conceptual commitments held him back from the ultimate abyss animating thought. It is clear that Dewey saw qualities as being in some sense more real or more vital than the things having them but he could not grasp the originating power of dynamic quality within the not yet Being of the spirit. Put differently, Dewey's "qualities" are immediate finite goods that have a dynamic quality pointing toward the depth dimensions of the good.

Dynamic goods are emergent from the eternal strife between nature naturing and nature natured. For Heidegger, this primal strife is that between "earth" and "world" as they wrestle each other into the clearing of human awareness. Heidegger's rather romantic and even eulogistic language clouds the depth logic of the ontological difference but points in the direction of ecstatic naturalism. Dynamic goods emerge out of this primal strife and live in the between that makes it possible for the ontological difference to obtain at all. Finite goods are clearly emergent on one side of the ontological difference, the side that Heidegger calls "world" and that ecstatic naturalism calls "nature natured." Instrumental methods are appropriate when dealing with such finite goods. The inner logic of dynamic goods makes them elusive and recalcitrant to instrumental control or appraisal.

The unique nature of betweenness can only be understood in an ecstatically transfigured naturalism that derives its own categorial momentum from its response to the eternal rift opened out by the ontological difference. Betweenness is an enabling condition that provides the energized and mobile space within which dynamic goods can emerge for the human process. Dynamic goods only appear elliptically to the self in time and announce their presence through the unsettling rhythms of the spirit. It is easy to give examples of finite goods: health, comfort, intensity of experience, pleasure, self-control, etc., but it is extremely difficult to give examples of dynamic goods. By definition, all examples fall within a genus and represent a variable or value within the genus. Dynamic goods do not belong to a genus but live outside of the genera as traditionally understood. In their depth dimension dynamic goods participate in the divine natures that are themselves only available in an elliptical fashion.

As noted, finite goods augment the self yet fail to propel it outside of its anthropocentric structure. Dynamic goods, by contrast, live on the "other side" of anthropological structures and live out of the spirit of nature. Nature's spirit is neither an imperial self-consciousness (in the sense meant by Hegel) nor a body of attained meanings. Rather, the spirit is a transforming rhythm that combines power and meaning in such a way as radically to transform the self so that it can break free from its own anthropology. Dynamic goods are the manifest dimension of the spirit as it cleaves to the human process. Yet their particular form of manifestation is indirect and elusive.

Wieman comes close to an understanding of dynamic goods when he speaks of the power of "creative events" to go beyond a mere augmentation of the human process. Creative events, like dynamic goods, are deeply transforming and recast the very terms in which the self, the world, and the divine natures are correlated:

> The creative event is one that brings forth in the human animal, in society and history, and in the appreciable world a new structure of interrelatedness, whereby events are discriminated and related in a manner not before possible. It is a structure whereby some events derive from other events, through meaningful connection with them, an abundance of quality that events could not have had without this new creation.[10]

This new abundance comes from a source outside of the human process and, so I would argue, outside of the orders of the world. Creative events emerge from the realm between nature's potencies and the innumerable orders of relevance that constitute manifest nature. Wieman combines, as noted, several features of descriptive and process forms of naturalism. His evocative portrayal of human goods and creative events brings him close to the categorial commitments of ecstatic naturalism. Had he probed more fully into the depth dimension of the ontological difference he might have moved more decisively in the direction of a transfigured naturalism.

Dynamic goods live in the not yet of the spirit and hover around the human process compelling it to acknowledge an elusive presence that can give it a new sense of measure. The new Adam and Eve are themselves products of the spirit and thus of the realm between the potencies and the created orders. On the other side of an augmented or enhanced anthropology is a transfigured eschatology that gives the self over to nature and lifts it out of its own illusory plenitude. Dynamic goods are not human products but are gifts of nature's spirit as it fills the self with the deeper restlessness of the not yet. Eschatology is the measure for anthropology. As argued by Ernst Bloch, nature is itself eschatological through and through as it moves toward a transfiguration of its own possibilities.

INTERPRETATIVE MUSEMENT AND ECSTATIC NATURALISM

The method adopted by ecstatic naturalism for probing into the dynamic goods of nature is that of interpretive musement. This method, which is actually postmethodic in its operation, derives its own momentum from the realm between nature naturing and nature natured. The free play of signs

---

10. Wieman, *Source of Human Good*, p. 65.

and semiotic possibilities responds to the deeper play within nature itself. The movement of the potencies toward manifestation is felt by the sign systems of the musing self. On the other side of abduction, which moves carefully from general rules to specific cases within the world, is the musement that opens out the tensions within the ontological difference. Abduction and induction are appropriate methods when dealing with finite and intraworldly goods. They serve to stabilize and enhance goods so that they can be assimilated and manipulated by the community of interpreters. Musement, on the other hand, is responsive to dynamic goods that live in the between which is the home of the spirit.

Put differently, musement lives out of natural grace and is the manifest side of that grace as it interacts with the semiotic material of the human process. Peirce speculated that nature itself may be the muser and that the human process (our "glassy essence") is the "place" where this musement occurs. Ecstatic naturalism affirms and strengthens this speculation and redefines the depth dimension of the human process in terms of nature's own forms of interpretive musement. Dynamic goods are manifest in an elliptical fashion on the nether side of all of our finite goods and can only appear to us through the clearing provided by musement. Yet their appearance is through a "gestalt of grace" that is more than a mere qualitative or creative enhancement of the self in process.

Finite goods can be grasped and shaped by the individual and by the larger community of interpreters. Dynamic goods, on the other hand, grasp the self and transform the structures of interaction in such a way as to create a new person on the other side of our attained and static anthropology. To be gathered up into nature's musement is to be gathered up into the eschatological transfiguration of the self and to leave behind the old self of mere autonomy. In this fundamental transformation finite goods are not left behind but become revalued in the light of dynamic goods. The goods of the world and the goods of the spirit work in consort both to enrich and to transform the human process so that it can lie fully out of the between opened up by the not yet.

Ecstatic naturalism reaches back historically to the fundamental insight of St. Paul:

> For the creation was subjected to futility, not of its own will but by the will of one who subjected it, in hope that the creation itself will be set free from its bondage to decay and will obtain the freedom of the glory of the children of God. We know that the whole creation has been groaning in labor pains until now; and we ourselves, who have the first fruits of the Spirit, groan inwardly while we wait for adoption, the redemption of our bodies (Rom 8:20-23, NRSV).

We are adopted by the spirit that lives out of the heart of the ontological difference. Naturalism has evolved beyond its earlier stages to a point where it can more adequately locate the spirit in the realm between nature natured and nature naturing. Nature's "groaning" is its movement toward the between that animates all created orders. The spirit gives birth to transfigured and dynamic goods that overcome the "futility" of a subjected nature. To be adopted by the spirit is to go beyond ethics with its own categorical structures to a realm of empowerment that actually brings dynamic goods into inter-section with the human process. Ecstatic naturalism is not so much a per-spective *within* philosophy and theology as a way of honoring the presence of the spirit on the edges of a self-transforming nature. The basic piety of nat-uralism is itself a gift of the spirit as it adopts the human process and brings it closer to the depth rhythms of nature's elusive potencies.

CHAPTER ELEVEN

The Integrity of Creation

FREDERICK FERRÉ

The record of twentieth-century empirical theology—in step with Christian theology as a whole—has been uneven when dealing with the integrity of creation. The possible joining of strands within empirical theology, however, now offers Christianity its best opportunity in centuries for self-reform in its approach to nature. If the organismic insights of one branch of empirical theology can be grafted to other, more human-centered branches, we may find at last the basis for a balanced environmental theology, well-grounded in reason and experience, that can nourish both a sustainable environment and a just human society.

Two of the three branches of empirical theology to be discussed in this chapter will be familiar to readers of this book. These are naturalism and organicism (usually named "process" thought, despite Whitehead's own use of "philosophy of organism" for his position). Another branch, however, deserves to be discussed in the context of twentieth-century, experience-based, reason-oriented theology. This is the empirical theology of personalism, or "Boston Personalism," as it is often called in contrast to the "Chicago School" of theological naturalism. The main figures of personalism were Borden Parker Bowne, Edgar Sheffield Brightman, and Peter Anthony Bertocci—all Boston University professors engaged both with the department of philosophy and, in one way or another, with the Boston University School of Theology. Brightman was Bowne's student and successor, the first holder of the Borden Parker Bowne chair; Bertocci was Brightman's student and successor as second (and, to date, last) Bowne Professor.

What all three, personalism, naturalism, and organicism, have in common is dedication to reason and experience as final arbiters of theological—no less than any other—truth. The three appeal to human reason rather than to any other authority or "revelation." What is "revealed" is just what is experienced in normal human life. To different degrees, each of the three accepts the legitimacy of rational extrapolation from what is regularly found in experience, moving by inference to intellectual constructs taken as explanatory of (or as presupposed by) such experience. Further, all three agree that "experience" does not begin and end with sense experience, as Hume and the positivist tradition assumed. All agree that "experience" instead is a rich, complex phenomenon, containing value-elements as well as sheer facts, often shading off into vague, half-lighted zones where dreaming and waking are hard to distinguish.

It is from this rich domain of human experience that all three branches of empirical theology take their start, since (they agree) without the givens of experience—however resistant they may be to classification and however open to alternative interpretation—reason, emphatically including theological reason, would lack substantive content.

We shall see in what follows that each branch starts with a different emphasis on features within experience. Thus they come to different positions on the nature of God and on the character and value of creation, as we shall also see; but in method these thinkers are all rational empiricists, open in principle to all evidence, whatever it may be, and to following their argument, wherever it may lead. Therefore the possibility of a synthesis, or at least a convergence leading toward complementarity, among the three branches of empirical theology cannot be dismissed.

EXPERIENCE

Personalism is grounded in the experience of the integrated self. The classical "I think" of Descartes starts in the right direction, from the experiencing ego, but is too narrowly focused on the intellect. Personalism prefers to begin with what Bertocci called the "extended *cogito*": that is, in addition to "I think," one can also say, "I will," or, "I feel," or, "I value." And all of these experiences are those of a single whole self in which various functions and activities blend and interact, to be distinguished only later by reflective analysis.

All experience, of course, is mental—that is, experience is necessarily experience of or within some *mind*. Boston personalism's historical associations with forms of idealism deserve emphasis. Borden Parker Bowne was deeply influenced by Lotze and Hegel. Edgar Brightman found the pluralistic idealism of Bishop Berkeley, in contrast, more flexible and adequate to the irreducible variety of entities constituting the world. Peter Bertocci accepted the label of "personalistic idealism" but was in general less concerned for metaphysical issues (except for the existence and character of God) than for the psychological and ethical questions raised by worldviews in conflict. Throughout, however, personalism's approach to experience remains within an idealistic context: To be empirical is to think within the limits of experience, but experience always entails mind. Nothing in experience gives us access to alleged "nonmental" realities. Whatever is real, therefore, is in some essential way mental.

But one need not remain so vague. The only clear case of mentality accessible to our investigation is our own, through the "extended *cogito*" experience of personal being. Thinking, feeling, willing, appreciating, "oughting" experiences, inextricably intertwined, make up the fabric of what we know most intimately to constitute the real. Moreover, we must admit, if we are modest empiricists, that we can have such direct access to nothing else, or at least to nothing that is essentially different—different in kind—from personality. It is within these personal categories, therefore, that theology must forge its doctrines, whether of God or of nature, since there are no other categories intelligible to persons.

The approach to experience taken in Henry Nelson Wieman's naturalism is quite different. He does not start within the Cartesian ego-experience, even in an "expanded *cogito*," but finds the paradigm for experience, instead, in the interpersonal transactions of human social life. From the earliest transactions between an infant and the family, in which mutual interests and needs begin to be communicated and accommodated, to intricate negotiations among national and international structures of civilization, from labor union contracts to international treaties aimed at creating wider good for all concerned, human experience is characterized most deeply by dialogue, fruitful conflict, and creative interchange.

The historical roots of Wieman's naturalism, too, are quite different. Far from the traditions of idealism that shaped personalism's interpretation of experience, Wieman's heritage lay with American pragmatism, particularly the anti-metaphysical, anti-idealist naturalistic pragmatism of John Dewey. Therefore experience, though inevitably structured by human minds, is for him not merely of mentality but of an objective world not sharing the traits of mentality at all. Human mentality is the product of a long sequence of creative events in evolutionary history. For naturalism, theology's main task is to take seriously the structure of such creative events in the universe, whether in searching for an empirical doctrine of God as the source of human good or in attempting to define the appropriate status of nature itself.

Whiteheadian organicism takes a third approach to paradigmatic experience. It is to be found neither in the mature, wakeful, human person, however rich and complex such private personal experiences may be; nor is it to be found in social transactions between humans in creative dialogue, though this, being social, is closer to organicism's starting point. Instead, something much less clear and cognitive is taken as the key to experience at its most fundamental: It is the general awareness of a world impinging, with its vague but unavoidable weight of causal determinacy, its many actual values, its possibilities, and its tendency toward something not yet actualized but in the making. It is an "undifferentiated multiplicity" of feeling that counts as basic experience, and Whitehead acknowledged his debt to the absolute idealist, F.H. Bradley, for this foundational insight.[1]

The main historical vectors operative in organicism's approach to experience, however, are not set by idealism, despite the importance to Whitehead of Bradley and Leibniz, but by the early twentieth-century work of emergentists and vitalists, particularly Samuel Alexander[2] and Henri Bergson.[3] Recognizing fundamental continuity between levels of existence, rather than emphasizing the apparent "specialness" of uniquely human experiences like cognition, moral obligation, and the like, means that the philosophically most important features of experience are those that may be shared, in one degree or another, by all types of organisms. Feeling a world and responding to it is just such a basic feature. It is through the rational unpacking what is implicit in that pervasive experience that organismic theology develops its doctrines of God and nature.

GOD

The empirical starting point for each of these three traditions within twentieth-century American theology gives a distinctive turn to the doctrine of God that each constructs. For each, of course, the developed concept of God must be a matter of inference. God may, indeed, be among the data of experience; but such a claim itself requires articulation and defense within a network of concepts, many of which may be only indirectly related to experience. Still, for each form of empirical theology, experience is basic, and the sorts of theological inferences made will be grounded, in each case, by its prior understanding of experience.

Personalism makes the inference, from its analysis of normative experience as richly personal, that God is best understood as finite person. Not all personalists hold to the finitude of God. Borden Parker Bowne did not. But empirical honesty in the face of unaccountable, "surd," evil in the world, led Brightman and Bertocci to conclude that a perfectly good and all-powerful person would not voluntarily allow the world to be as we find it. Arguing further that the goodness of God is the essential religious quality by virtue of which alone God can rightly be deemed worthy of worship, the personalists followed this argument to its conclusion and abandoned the traditional view of God's omnipotence.

Struck by the incomparable worth of personal traits, like the capacity to

---

1. Alfred North Whitehead, *Process and Reality: An Essay in Cosmology*, corrected ed., ed. David Ray Griffin and Donald W. Sherburne (New York: Free Press, 1978), p. xiii.

2. Samuel Alexander, *Space, Time, and Deity* (New York: Humanities Press, 1920).

3. Henri Bergson, *Creative Evolution* (New York: Henry Holt, 1911).

know, to love, to act morally, and to appreciate beauty, personalism understands the Most High in terms of these values. God is far beyond us in the intensity and quality of achieved personal values but is not to be considered "Wholly Other," as some theologians insist. On the contrary, if God were "Wholly Other," such a being could not be "considered" at all, since the only intelligible categories for our thought are those rooted in our experience as finite persons.

If the only intelligible reality is personal reality, God must be considered a person on a personal continuum with us. God is vastly, indescribably, beyond us in personal integration, wisdom, goodness, and power. But since (measuring the world's surplus of evil by the highest personal moral standards we know) God suffers limits even to huge divine powers, God, too, is not without personal problems. God's aims, as Cosmic Person, must be to enhance personal values wherever they exist, but volcanoes and floods, typhoons and plagues, chance mutations and birth defects, obstruct and defeat these purposes. Still, no sense can be made of the notion of a mind—much less the mind of God—being limited or defeated by nonmental entities. "Nonmental entity," as we saw, is an unintelligible contradiction. Thus, Brightman concludes, the limitations on God's purposes must be found within the divine nature: a "Given" in God.[4] This, too, is an inference based on our own personal experience, in which irrational mental tendencies within our character rise unbidden to challenge our considered aims, forcing us to wrestle with them and sometimes defeating our moral purposes. In the same way, God wrestles with the irrational internal Given and calls on us to help, sometimes to forestall, sometimes to mitigate, disaster.

The markedly different understanding of experience represented by Wieman's naturalism grounds a sharply different set of inferences about what might appropriately be called by the ancient name of "God." The word itself carries so many unfortunate associations, from naturalism's point of view, that it might better be retired from service. But if it must have a place on empirical theology's conceptual map, it should designate the wonderful but natural process which we experience in creative interchange. Creativity, the coming into being of a new good, is never merely the work of human beings alone. The creative event has a structure that goes beyond our cleverness and planning. Circumstances must be right; means must be available; a creative challenge must be felt. To these must be added human readiness to make a creative, dangerous response, to leave the security of "created good" for the adventure of "creative good." The first (senior) "partner" in this dialogue is superhuman (though not supernatural), i.e., the natural universe functioning in dialogue with humans as source of human good; the second (junior) partner is the ben-

4. Edgar Sheffield Brightman, *A Philosophy of Religion* (New York: Prentice-Hall, 1940), see especially Chapter X, "Is God Finite?"

eficiary—though not a passive beneficiary—of the creative event.

"God" is a natural process, the normal, though unpredictable, invitation to creativity in a world of entropy, an invitation-event with an identifiable, recognizable structure. To be an entity is nothing but to be a structured process. Therefore this creativity—God—is a "distinct entity,"[5] if that is important, but this entity is not a person nor a purposive mind. Wieman chides personalism for trying to hang on to traditional doctrines, like creation *ex nihilo*, while claiming to remain empirical. Introducing any characteristics into God's essential nature that are not also essential to human persons, he argues, is to introduce a contradiction into the concept of "person" itself: It would then be both P and more-than-P at the same time, which cannot be. On the other hand, the natural but superhuman source of human good is of transcendent value, worthy of the highest religious dedication, above commitment to any past achievement, institution, or created good, all of which it calls into question, pointing instead to the endless venture beyond.

Organicism's empirical starting-point, defining archetypical experience as precognitive whole-responsiveness to a world felt as constituting us and being constituted by us, offers still a third perspective on God. Like the God-concept of naturalism, this third perspective will be essentially social and interactive, since experience itself is initially described in these terms. Although the word "social" and its derivatives are heavily used by organicist thinkers from Whitehead to Cobb, their sense of the term is much stronger than Wieman's language of "mutuality" and "negotiation" can convey. Those terms, drawn from political contexts where interests are clearly defined and negotiating partners well-distinguished, suggest that an individual self first exists independently, then increases its own and others' good through the interactions it undertakes. For organicism, elements of the world itself are from the beginning and throughout literally ingredient in experience, and the experiencing entity is what it is mainly thanks to its relations to its environment. Internal relations are of the essence to an organism. A cell in a living body is not the same cell it was after it is removed to a test tube. The environment matters to an organism in the way it does not (so much), for example, to a gear or a cog.

"God," for such a vision, is the appropriate name for the ultimate environment of all environments. First, the dynamic, self-creating world of experience requires a primordial environment of permanent possibilities; and, second, the universe of indefinitely many lesser environments requires—if it is to be a cosmos, not a chaos—completion in a single coherent experience of integration into which all its variety is ingredient. God, for organicism, pro-

---

5. Henry Nelson Wieman, *Seeking A Faith for A New Age*, edited and introduced by Cedric L. Hepler (Metuchen, N.J.: Scarecrow Press, 1975), p. 244. Originally published as "Co-operative Functions of Science and Religion," *Zygon—Journal of Religion and Science* 3:1 (March 1968), pp. 32-58.

vides both these environments. Since the complexity and intensity of God's experiential integrations must, on this hypothesis, be great beyond all that we can imagine, we cannot but acknowledge God as conscious, on this aspect of the divine nature, to a superlative degree. This side of God is relational to the highest order: In small part we contribute to making God what God is by what we make of ourselves. But since, in contrast, the well of permanent possibilities in God is bottomless and eternal, this other (unconscious) side of God is absolute. From this abstract store of permanent possibilities, however, God's organic relatedness to us is expressed every moment in offering us— luring us toward—relevant possibilities for concrete, creative novelty. Just as God is who God is in part because of what we make of ourselves, so we become who we are in part because of God's ingredience in our experience of what we might be.

There are many other important elements of organicism's doctrine of God. For example, it is, theoretically speaking, wholly arbitrary why this experienced cosmos of ours has, out of all the infinite alternative possibilities, just the natural laws that it does have rather than some others. God's choice serves as the "principle of arbitrariness" when theoretical explanation is exhausted. This chapter, however, is no place to attempt an explication, for any of these strands of empirical theology, of their full doctrines of God. It is enough for our purposes to sketch the main lines along which each tradition thinks about the ultimate and to connect these lines with the way each empirical starting point treats basic experience.

CREATION

It is an irony of our topic that the traditional language of "creation," in which the title of this chapter is couched, is usable only with qualifications and apologies in connection with the empirical theologians of the twentieth century. "Creation" always implies "Creator"; but it should be clear from the previous section that none of the empirical traditions can agree to the unambiguous application of such a traditional, omnipotent-transcendent, theistic concept to the God they envision. It would doubtless be better from a cautious philosophical point of view to use the word "nature" in place of "creation," but the full theological resonance is not quite captured in the more neutral term. In any case, the following discussion will outline three empirical theologies of the "sub-human" part of the world we experience. These theologies are inseparable from their respective doctrines of experience and God which we have now sketched. They will also lead, as we shall see when we turn toward more practical issues, to important consequences for environmental ethics and for a just and sustainable world.

Personalism has a good deal of trouble with its doctrine of nature, if establishing some "integrity" for nature is the aim. The traces of absolute idealism in Borden Parker Bowne, for example, led him to dismiss nature as mere stage-setting for the drama of mind. Nature has no causality at all, he claimed:

> Nature as an order of law . . . has only phenomenal existence; and the explanations within the order have only phenomenal application. They have no causality in them, and they do not penetrate to the seat of power.[6]

Nature is nothing at all in or for itself:

> The world of space objects which we call nature is no substantial existence by itself, and still less a self-running system apart from intelligence, but only the flowing expression and means of communication of those personal beings. It is throughout dependent, instrumental, and phenomenal.[7]

But if this is so, then nature has no "integrity" at all. Animals, birds, trees, and mountains are only the appearances to persons of an invisible, cosmic Personal Purposer.

Brightman, as we shall see, moved a long distance from Bowne, his mentor, in his own search for an adequate personalist doctrine of nature, but his departure-point remained still firmly grounded in the experience of personal selfhood as the clue to all reality:

> To say that this is a universe of purpose means that everything that is is in some sense controlled by purpose, that nothing is real save purposing beings, namely, persons. In such a universe there is a Supreme Person and such other persons as his purpose may will to exist; physical nature is real only as the concrete functioning of the purpose of the Supreme Person.[8]

The great difference from Bowne is in Brightman's readiness to extend the concept of "person" far beyond human beings. Just as God's personhood, though finite in power, is at an immensely higher qualitative level than our own, so the scale of persons may be extended downward, as well. Where to stop is not so clear. He writes:

> Person is defined as a complex unity of self-consciousness that is able to develop ideal values and to act in itself and to interact with others. This definition itself allows degrees of personality. A moron, for example, is a person; he may be both kind and loyal to a high degree. It may be

6. Borden P. Bowne, *Metaphysics* (New York: Harper & Brothers, 1882), rev. ed. (Boston: Boston University Press, 1943), p. 260.

7. Ibid., p. 278.

8. Edgar Sheffield Brightman, *An Introduction to Philosophy*, rev. ed. (New York: Henry Holt, 1951), p. 262.

debatable whether some of the higher animals are persons, but it seems more reasonable to ascribe a low degree of personality to them than to deny it. But when it comes to the mosquito or the amoeba, personality is more dubious. Whether there is ideal value in the mere thirst for blood or other food, or whether there are values unknown to us experienced by such beings are points on which significant speculation is more than dubious. It seems from their behavior patterns that the mosquito and the amoeba are conscious selves with a very low range of potentialities. Their degree of personality is so low that they are not persons at all in the full sense; yet there is every reason to view them as conscious selves or unities of mental activity.[9]

The point remains firm, for Brightman, that wherever one draws the line the only significant holders of reality or value are persons of one sort or another. All true substances, as we have seen, must be minds, but minds may vary greatly in their degrees of complexity and "wholeness."

A substance may be a relatively simple or a highly complex whole. If a hydrogen atom be a substance (which a personalist would not grant), it possesses a lower degree of complexity than a uranium atom. Or if a grasshopper's mind be a substance (as a personalist would grant), it is a far less complex whole, both actually and potentially, than a human moron's mind; and a moron's mind has a lower degree of complexity than a mathematician's. A supreme Person, a God, would have the highest degree of complexity combined with the highest degree of unity.[10]

Thus personalism acknowledges value and reality in nature only to the degree that degrees of mental complexity can be found or attributed. Granted, one may start to worry at the point where grasshoppers' minds are measured for complexity, or where amoebae are candidates for quasipersonhood, that language is being forced; but this may be uncharitable and may miss the main point. Such positions on the subhuman world have been taken up mainly for systematic reasons: the great extensions of the word, "person," are made to allow personalists to continue maintaining that personality and only personality matters. The central point—the incomparable value of personal experience—is important enough to make worthwhile what Brightman himself acknowledges is "a terminological, but not a real, difficulty."[11]

The naturalism of Henry Nelson Wieman also has problems, for different

9. Edgar Sheffield Brightman, *Person and Reality*, ed. Peter Anthony Bertocci in collaboration with Jannette Elthina Newhall and Robert Sheffield Brightman (New York: Ronald Press, 1958), p. 201.

10. Ibid., pp. 200-201.

11. Ibid., p. 201.

reasons, with a coherent doctrine on the subhuman world. It is true that naturalism is by heritage deeply aware of the massive realities in a universe to which human persons are relative newcomers. At times Wieman writes feelingly of the importance of the natural order on which human intellect floats, like an oil slick, on the deep oceans of prehuman achievement:

> The thin layer of structure characterizing events knowable to the human mind by way of linguistic specification is very thin indeed compared to that massive, infinitely complex structure of events, rich with quality, discriminated by the noncognitive feeling-reactions of associated organisms human and nonhuman. This infinitely complex structure of events composing this vast society of interacting organisms and their sustaining or destructive environment is like an ocean on which floats the thin layer of oil representing the structures man can know through intellectual formulation.[12]

In this mood, he is ready to acknowledge that these are achievements of creativity worthy of respect in themselves.

> The subhuman organism and the human organism at the submental level can have creative interaction with environment. This creative interaction which underlies the creativity of linguistic communication is 1) emerging awareness of a new structure of interrelatedness pertaining to events through a new way of interacting between the organism and its material situation; 2) integrating of this newly emergent structure with ways of distinguishing and relating events that had previously been acquired by the organism, thus achieving a more complex system of habits; and 3) consequent expanding and enrichment of the world of events having quality relative to the discriminating feeling-reactions of the organisms.[13]

But in a different and increasingly dominant mood, Wieman treats all this as above all—perhaps entirely all-important for its instrumental contribution to the quality of human experience. His appreciation of the subhuman is emphatic. He goes so far as to say that human experiences can have depth and richness of quality "only if they continue conjunct and integral with this deep complex structure of quality built up through countless ages before even the human mind appeared."[14] At the same time, when Wieman refers to "the organism," through which these depths are transmitted, he almost always has in mind the human organism, at what he calls its "submental" levels.

---

12. Henry N. Wieman, *The Source of Human Good* (Chicago: University of Chicago Press, 1946), p. 66.
13. Ibid.
14. Ibid.

232   FREDERICK FERRÉ

For example, he declares:

> Any meaning loses depth and richness of quality derived from this
> unknown depth of structured events with quality determined by noncog-
> nitive feeling-reactions of the organism, when it is treated as an end
> instead of as a servant to creativity and all that creativity may produce
> below the level of human cognition.[15]

Thus subhuman nature, even here, serves an instrumental function for human
fulfillment.

> Man can use his knowledge and the truth he seeks to know to serve this
> creativity. Also he can so live as to keep his achieved meanings closely
> bound to the rich matrix of qualified events that cannot be known in their
> specific detail. When he does live thus, he experiences an uncompre-
> hended depth and richness which give content to the abstractions of ratio-
> nally comprehended structures. When he does not, life loses quality and
> value.[16]

This drift toward anthropocentric emphasis, seen here even in one of the
few passages where Wieman discusses creative interaction at the subhuman
level, becomes still more intense in his later works. Nature is and should
be plastic to human intelligence. God is the source of *human* good. Though
creative interaction may occur below the human level, as we have seen, and
though this creative process on the biological level may be traced "far down
the animal scale,"[17] it is only the increase of human good that is our responsibility and only with human existence that we can identify.

> Only by way of illusion can a human being identify himself with any-
> thing except the potentialities of human existence. He can identify him-
> self with the destructive potentialities or with the constructive potential-
> ities or with some mixture of these. But it would seem to be a
> self-contradiction to say that he can without illusion identify with anything
> that is not the potentiality of human existence.[18]

To make certain that the point is not lost, Wieman adds, "This excludes the
subhuman cosmos except as it supports human existence."[19]

Organicism alone, of the three traditions of American empirical theology,

---

15. Ibid., pp. 66-67.
16. Ibid., p. 67.
17. Ibid., p. 70.
18. Wieman, *Seeking A Faith for A New Age*, p. 266.
19. Ibid.

has a theology of nature that is clearly nonanthropocentric. Just as paradigmatic experience, for this tradition, is defined in terms of features (like feeling a world) that can be considered applicable to all organic experience, not just to human experience, so the centers of experience that make up organicism's world of entities can be something for themselves quite apart from the existence of human beings.

Charles Birch and John Cobb call this vision of nature the "ecological model"[20] in which all things are connected to, and mutually influenced by, all other things. The environment matters because it is through internal relations that events are constituted. The world is made up, "all the way down," by such events. They point out that

> the model is not restricted in its application to living things. Events in an electro-magnetic field exemplify the ecological model as much as does animal behavior in the wild.[21]

This does not mean that self-consciousness or moral responsibility can be attributed everywhere in nature. On the contrary, these are special features of human experience that should not uncritically be generalized beyond rare and complex societies of organisms with highly developed nervous systems like ourselves. But it does mean that for organicism nature is full of centers of experience that matter—in some degree—to themselves and to God. Mattering to oneself, however vaguely or briefly, expresses what is meant by having some degree of intrinsic value. Mattering to God expresses what is meant by contributing value to the ultimate environment.

ENVIRONMENTAL ETHICS

Out of the past decade's heated discussion concerning the requirements for an adequate environmental ethics, one conclusion seems inescapable: traditional Western ethics, however stretched or recast, does not deserve to be called genuinely "environmental" as long there is no place within it for the defense of nature *against* genuine human interests, at least under some circumstances and to some degree. This is, very simply, because the human species, acting with exclusive concern for its own interests, constitutes by far the largest single threat to the health and integrity of nature as we have inherited it from prehominid eras.

There are of course other opinions. Some would recommend that "environmental ethics" should simply consist in developing a new set of rules specifying the human uses of nature that will be most fruitful, on the whole,

---

20. Charles Birch and John B. Cobb Jr., *The Liberation of Life* (Denton, Tex.: Environmental Ethics Books, 1990), pp. 79 ff.
21. Ibid., p. 89.

for human welfare in the long run.[22] Such a set of rules would, indeed, be an important advance beyond the short-sighted policies of sheer exploitation that have prevailed for much of human history, especially in modern times. Such environmental norms might help to put brakes on the modern technological juggernaut that now, as never before, provides human rapacity with the power to inflict massive and irreversible damage on the natural order. But if there is a difference between counsels of prudence and counsels of morality, such a set of policies, however wise and useful, will not qualify as environmental *ethics*. Prudence advises what actions would be *useful*, to serve my interests; ethics demands actions that are *right*, whether or not my interests are pinched. And in real life we know that self-interest often conflicts with duty. Granted, we generally acknowledge prudence as a virtue; but a life that never rises above calculating interests is hardly a fully virtuous life—it lacks depth of commitment to anything higher or broader than maximum self-satisfaction. In sum it lacks the disinterested concern for the right or the wider good that essentially marks the "moral point of view."[23]

Our civilization is so far from thinking or acting with an adequate environmental ethics that even rules of prudence concerning our human relationships to nature sometimes seem impossibly high ideals. But environmental ethics, properly speaking, calls for something still higher. At a minimum, a genuine environmental ethics must be capable of disinterested moral evaluation of human interests, even genuinely urgent ones, vis-à-vis threats to the stability and integrity of other parts of creation.

There is no doubt that at the present time there are genuine threats of this sort. They are the constant subject of anxious news reports, e.g., about the shrinking rain forests of the Amazon region, where (literally) uncounted species of plants and animals are being forever extinguished by human hands, where for short-term gains land is being ravaged and made permanently useless by the destruction of delicate forest ecosystems, and where a large proportion of the world's precious capacity to absorb climate-warming carbon dioxide—and to replace it with vital oxygen—is being laid waste at horrifying rates. But these things are not being done for sheer wickedness. The poverty of native peoples, and their interest in sheer survival, combines with the interests of wealthy human enterprises to turn "unimproved" nature into human resources. Here is a tragic case of conflict between the "integrity" of nature and urgent human interests. An environmental ethics should be able to help us make moral judgments about what is right, not simply for humans but in the larger context of humans-in-nature, under such circumstances.

Similar cases abound. It is not only in the developed world, for exam-

---

22. For example, see John Passmore, *Man's Responsibility for Nature: Ecological Problems and Western Traditions* (New York: Scribner's, 1974).

23. See William K. Frankena, *Ethics*, 2nd ed. (Englewood Cliffs, N.J.: Prentice-Hall, 1973), p. 113.

ple, that energy supplies are a problem. In fact, the so-called "energy crisis" for the developed nations, real though the problem is of making a smooth transition from petroleum-based energy to sustainable and nonpoisonous forms (like solar), is far less immediate and painful at the moment of this writing than the severe energy crisis today facing millions of people dependent on firewood for their heating and cooking needs. In Nairobi, *The Standard* for July 24, 1991, reports:

> Ninety percent of Africa's energy needs are supplied by tree products—firewood and charcoal. For millions of rural and urban Africans, the energy crisis is real and immediate. In Kenya the current annual supply of woodfuel is estimated to be 18.7 million tonnes. But due to growing population and slow rates of re-afforestation, this demand by far exceeds supply, thereby leading to rapid depletion of forests and a critical "fuel gap."[24]

Around the world, women (for it is they who bear the brunt of the current crisis) are required to walk farther and farther to find the shrinking forests on which they depend. The ravaging of the forest areas, in turn, is destroying not only the trees themselves but also the habitat in which many endangered species perilously hang on—or go extinct. Again, real conflict emerges between human interests and the "integrity" of creation. Environmental maxims that automatically take the side of human interests are merely instruments of prudence, outside the "moral point of view." What can empirical theology, as we have surveyed its main branches, contribute to a genuine environmental ethics?

There can be little question, for those who have followed the argument this far, that empirical theology's best promise for an adequate environmental ethics is from the branch we have been calling organicism. This still-developing tradition is in the most favorable position to acknowledge values and claims outside the circle of distinctive human culture or personality. Starting with an understanding of "experience" that is in principle not limited to high-order, wakeful human self-consciousness, organicism has a basis for acknowledging, without stress or stretching, that natural entities of many sorts besides the human enjoy experience in various degrees of richness and complexity: that is, that there are many nonhuman centers of experience that matter to themselves. But "mattering to oneself," as we saw above, is what theological organicism means by having some degree of intrinsic value. Thus there is a natural basis in theological organicism for grounding an ethics that can make sense of nonhuman entities having "standing" alongside, and quite possibly in competition with, human claims and interests. Organicism can lead to an ethics not dominated by the anthropocentric

---

24. *The Standard*, Nairobi, Kenya (July 24, 1991), p. 19.

assumptions of most Western thought. There is an important place on this conceptual map for respecting the unfettered integrity of creation: i.e., understanding the worth and dignity of natural processes allowed to work on their own and in their own way.[25]

In addition, organicism's key categories of internal relatedness and holistic fulfillment—fulfillment, in the end, achieved by every finite center of experience contributing its own achievements of value to the experience of the ultimate environment, God—offer refreshing alternatives to the atomistic models of reality that have dominated Western metaphysics and ethics in recent centuries. Society, interconnectedness, mutuality, are essential to organicism, not accidental. Thus the exaggerated individualism of capitalist-liberal ideology can be resisted with the authority of healthy organic life itself.

At the same time, there are problems for theological organicism, if it presses its organic model too far, or too exclusively.[26] The first and most obvious ethical problem is posed by the massive wastefulness of organic life. Life is characterized by superabundance. Organic creativity burgeons far beyond the possibility of all living individuals to survive, much less to thrive. Jay McDaniel, from within the tradition of theological organicism, takes this problem with utmost seriousness in his book, *Of God and Pelicans*.[27] McDaniel considers the problem from the point of view of theodicy: How can the God of organicism be worshiped if organic life itself requires the systematic sacrifice to neglect and suffering of the pelican's second-hatched offspring? We might equally well ask the related question for ethics: How can the model of organic life be taken as normative for ethical theory if the well-being of individual centers of experience seems to count for so little?

The success of evolutionary process, too, depends upon ruthless selection, which amounts to the massive weeding out of genetically less well-equipped individuals, by the countless millions, for the sake of bringing forth organic novelty that will be responsive to and supportable by ever-changing environmental conditions. Some, not only the nineteenth-century Social Darwinists, have taken this as normative, as well, for human life. Currently, on an "ecological model" taken literally as a guide for what he calls a "Promethean" (forward-looking) ethics, Garrett Hardin recommends forcefully against feeding the starving in the Third World and also against "excessive charity," through Social Security or other public "safe-

25. For a passionate development of this theme, see Bill McKibben, *The End of Nature* (New York: Random House, 1989).

26. The actual theological organicists we have been quoting, like Charles Birch and John Cobb, take pains to avoid the following consequences of unmitigated organicism. It should be stressed that they are fully aware of the need to supplement the sheerly ecological model with other principles also found among Whitehead's insights.

27. Jay McDaniel, *Of God and Pelicans: A Theology of Reverence for Life* (Louisville: Westminster/John Knox, 1989).

ty net" programs, in the developed world.[28] Since these ethical consequences are not intended by theological organicists,[29] and since a description of how nature *does in fact* treat polliwogs or pelicans does not fit
most Christian moral intuitions of how we *should in principle* treat persons
(or pets), it is clear that sheerly organic categories need supplementation
with something else.

A related problem rises in connection not simply with the wastefulness but
also with the holism, or internal relatedness, of organic life. Just as individuals do not seem to rate very high in importance relative to their species,
so, it may be argued, for organicism individuals cannot count for much in
comparison with the higher social orders through which they are granted
their identity and find their existence. The cell lives for its organ; the organ
lives for its organism; the organism lives for its society. This is the logic of
unmitigated organic thinking, and it is clear that in human political terms such
logic has led the way to totalitarianism. The sacrifice of the individual to
the well-being of the state (or of the corporation or other "higher" unit) has
been the hallmark of some of the most horrifying episodes of human history, ancient and recent.

In practical terms, the ethics of unmitigated holism, even apart from the
general tendency toward fascism, leads one to look with new concern at
such issues as infanticide, euthanasia, involuntary eugenics, and the like.
The burden of proof seems to be on organicism to show why, for the good of
the whole, the individual—who can at best only have relative value—should
not be sacrificed as a first, rather than a last, resort. Even more obviously, a
defective individual would seem an obvious target for elimination. Are these
the inevitable consequences of adopting organicism's "ecological model"?
Must we pay such a heavy price for the sake of an adequate environmental
ethics?

A JUST AND SUSTAINABLE WORLD

All three branches of empirical theology would be quick to respond to this
dilemma—"should we be arrogantly anthropocentric or, instead, be collec-
tivistically biocentric?"—by rejecting the choice and offering instead alternative proposals for striking a better ethical balance than either extreme can
offer. It is now time to see how each of the three may contribute to a new synthesis supporting both human and transhuman values, both justice to persons
and full ethical responsiveness to the environment.

Personalism, as we have observed, highlights above all else the preser-

---

28. Garrett Hardin, "Lifeboat Ethics: The Case Against Helping the Poor," *Psychology Today* (1974). Also, idem, *Promethean Ethics: Living with Death, Competition, and Triage* (Seattle: University of Washington Press, 1980).

29. This is made eminently clear by Birch and Cobb, *Liberation of Life*, especially in Chapters 5-10.

vation and enhancement of the uniquely personal values. Of the three empirical theological traditions before us, it is in the best position to defend the individual personal self. Nothing is more precious in the universe. God's own self is the prime exemplar of personhood. Personalism will never consent to the wasting of persons, even in a world where life is wasteful. The dangers of collectivist absorption of uniquely valuable persons, too, will be resisted beyond all other threats by personalism.

If only the insights offered by this tradition could be combined coherently with concerns for the integrity of nature, as well, a firm defense for the achievements of the Enlightenment and classical Liberalism might be safely uncoupled from the excesses of anthropocentric domination that have too often in fact been associated with stress on the unique values of humanity. Historically, personalism has had an awkward time in grounding values in nature, as we noted above, but the matter is not hopeless. Edgar Brightman laid the groundwork for such an extension when he showed a willingness to extend the concept of personhood far into the natural order, including, as we saw, even mosquitoes and amoebae in his discussion as "selves" or "unities of mental activity."[30] There seems at least an ontological openness in personalism to the possibility of finding significant intrinsic value in nature, enough to keep hope alive that some synthesis of personalism with organicism may be possible. Further, Brightman showed that he would approve building a cautious environmental ethic on such an expanded ontology. He made that clear in his critique of Hegel's blatantly anthropocentric statement: "nature is for man only the starting point which he is to transform."[31] At best this is a limited truth, Brightman replied:

> What the personalist grants in the statement of Hegel and of the humanists is that human action finds Nature more or less responsive and that, within limits, man can "transform" Nature from a jungle to a garden, from wild profusion to ordered beauty and utility. But what the personalist misses in such humanistic views is a full recognition of the limits imposed on the transformation both by human weakness, ignorance, and sin and by the overwhelming objective power of Nature—that is, by factors not in man's control.[32]

It seems a natural step, given the extension of personhood into nature licensed by Brightman, to add to the limits imposed by the "objective power" of nature some ethical limits required also by the intrinsic values in nature. The prospects for a genuine rapprochement between personalism and organi-

---

30. Brightman, *Person and Reality*, p. 201.
31. As quoted by Brightman, ibid., p. 251.
32. Ibid., p. 251.

cism seem quite good, and the successors of Brightman continue work on these issues.[33]

Naturalism, of the sort we saw propounded by Henry Nelson Wieman, has the strongest basis for demanding social justice and the improvement of human culture. Its original understanding of experience itself assures that creative exchange among socially interactive humans will not give way either to isolated, atomistic catering to mere individuals, on the one hand, or to holistic submerging of individual interests, on the other. In a world desperately in need of creative improvement in human possibilities for life, and no less urgently in need of justice in the distribution of such possibilities among persons, the ethic of creative interchange stands forthrightly for both these ideals.

If only the anthropocentrism of Wieman's various pronouncements could be softened, without losing the essence of his vision, a strong emphasis on human improvement and fair distribution among people could be combined with an expanded moral sense for the transhuman values of the environment. As we have seen, Wieman himself, especially in his later writings, took some explicitly hard-line anthropocentric positions, stating even that it would seem to be "a self-contradiction to say that [we] can without illusion identify with anything that is not the potentiality of human existence."[34] But the situation here, too, is far from hopeless. Wieman is making a logical point about the fact that we are human and that our imaginings and identifyings will inevitably all be done as human beings. At this level we are all fully immersed in what might be called "logical anthropocentrism." No one needs to dispute this as a formal matter; neither personalists nor organicists would attempt to do so. Granting the formal point, what both personalists and organicists would urge, as a substantive addition, is that something like our potentialities for human experiences (of personality, for personalists, of deep relatedness, for organicists) can reasonably be attributed to the order of things beyond our species. With those potentialities we can "identify" both metaphysically and morally, they claim.

For his part, Wieman seems well-positioned to agree, in principle, that such substantive speculations are neither contradictory nor absurd.

At one time, he acknowledges, the only vehicle for creativity was at the level of biological organisms less complex than human beings:

> The existence and reactions of organisms, and these only, can break the continuity of the passage of existence into events. When and if there was ever a time that simple and minute cells of life alone existed in organic form, the only possible events and hence the only possible world were

---

33. See John Lavely, "Personalism Supports the Dignity of Nature," *The Personalist Forum* 2:1 (Spring 1986), pp. 29-37.
34. See note 12, above.

nothing else than the units of reality, discriminated and related by the existence and by the reactions of these organisms. As organisms become more sensitive and more diversely responsive, with more capacity for feeling, the world becomes more ample, more rich with quality, and more meaningful. The creation of such organisms is the creation of the world. This is the work of the creative event at the biological level.[35]

There is no reason in principle, therefore, for naturalism to scoff at the idea that creative events at those biological levels that continue to exist and react, alongside (and sometimes in competition with) human society, continue also to "discriminate" worlds and to create value in and for themselves. On this ontological ground a potential environmental ethic could be founded.

Wieman's ontology does not even exclude the possibility of theological organicism's God, though he is not much interested in this possibility. He writes:

We do not know . . . that vast and complicated organisms may not exist even now in forms quite unimaginable to us. Possibly such organisms react in such a manner as to have a world vaster than our human cosmos because they distinguish and relate events on a scale and with a richness of quality utterly beyond our powers, as our powers in this respect exceed the minute cell. Relative to them we would be minute cells. We may not think there are giants in the earth, or gods, but we mention this speculation to guard against the dogmatism which utterly closes the imagination to unexplored possibilities.[36]

If this mood of openness could be evoked and extended by the present defenders of naturalism, it is hard to imagine where, in principle, there would need to be irreconcilable differences between naturalism and the other more metaphysical branches of empirical theology.

Ethically, once the ontological ground is laid to permit recognition of interests and values beyond human interests and values alone, naturalism could join organicism and extended personalism in affirming the moral importance of defending and expanding the good for the nonhuman as well as the human community. Wieman defines moral conduct in a way that begs for such expansion. He states that "moral conduct, rightly understood, has the aim to expand indefinitely the range of coherent values for all *human beings*."[37] but what is to stop theological naturalists with this widened ontology from aiming to expand "the range of coherent values" for all *beings*

---

35. Wieman, *Source of Human Good*, p. 72.

36. Ibid., pp. 71-72.

37. Henry Nelson Wieman, *Religious Inquiry: Some Explorations*, (Boston: Beacon Press, 1968), p. 120, emphasis added.

capable of values? In such ways an adequate environmental ethic might well be grafted onto the strong stock of social justice represented by Wieman's naturalism.

Organicism excels, as we saw, in offering the basis for a powerful environmental ethics. Does it also have internal resources to recognize the initially quite different insights of personalism and naturalism on the intensely valuable character of individual personhood and social justice, respectively? Without them, organicism's ecological model, attractive though it is for many reasons, poses significant ethical drawbacks for a Christian—or even a humane—worldview.

The answer to this question is unequivocally positive. In addition to the ecological model of reality, which emphasizes the intimate interconnection between various entities internally related to and constituted by one another, theological organicism offers a second, independent normative standard based on the achieved quality of individual centers of experience. That standard, strikingly in harmony with personalism and naturalism, is *richness of experience*. The richer (more complex, more intense) the experience that is attained by an entity, the higher is its intrinsic value. Therefore human personal experience at its best is set apart from the duller, vaguer experiencing of the rest of the natural world. Birch and Cobb write:

> Despite continuity between human beings and other animal species, there are also characteristics of human beings that are lacking in most, if not all, other species. Whereas in animals in general the unified animal experience primarily functions in the service of the body, in human beings it aims at its own richness of experience and frequently subordinates the body to these aims. . . . *Homo sapiens* is a species of animal, but not only that. In human beings consciousness has become conscious of itself. Because of this, human beings are primarily ends and only secondarily means.[38]

In consequence of this second basic standard, grades of intrinsic value are able to be judged within the natural world as well as within different human lives. There is much empirical evidence, for example, that the experience of porpoises, on the whole, is much richer than the experience of sharks. This allows us to conclude "that porpoises as a whole are of much more intrinsic worth than sharks."[39] If we carefully gather evidence about the capacities of various species for richness of experience, we should be able to make wise policies on protection or exploitation of nature with due ethical consideration given. But in all this human beings will have a special place. Even though within human lives there are differences of intrinsic value, "since some human experiences are of vastly more intrinsic value than are oth-

38. Birch and Cobb, *Liberation of Life*, p. 162.
39. Ibid.

ers,"[40] the richness of human experience, and the justice of the distribution of the means to rich human experience, take legitimate priority because of the huge qualitative gap between even the dullest human and the richest non-human existence. But to recognize "the distinctive richness of human experience and its special place in any scale of values,"[41] does not absolve human policy makers, if they are moral, from taking all life into consideration.

> To maximize the richness of experience is to maximize the quality of human life with minimum impact on nonhuman life. Emphasis is put on the quality of human life but not without serious consideration of the cost to other life. . . . The goal then is one in which a large human population learns to live comfortably yet frugally and thereby relaxing pressure on the biosphere as a whole. . . . Every step that could lead either to making room for more people or for more animals, especially wild animals, without lowering the quality of life would be a victory. The balance between human beings and other animals would always be a matter of judgment.[42]

"A matter of judgment" is called for. This, if seriously responded to, would mark a significant advance. Little human thought has been spent, until now in the history of *homo sapiens*, on the relative worth of the claims of our own species when weighted morally against those of others. But what if the judgment must be made between fair claims of justice for human beings and equally fair claims on behalf of the integrity of nature? When legitimate moral claims clash, we find ourselves in the most difficult position of all.

We noted earlier that such apparently conflicting claims—between species dependent on forest habitat and African family firewood needs, for example—are already burning the public conscience. Are there any counsels from empirical theology, as a harmonized whole, that might help to clarify the path to a just *and* sustainable world?

Indeed, by personalism we will be reminded that the millions of actual African persons suffering daily energy shortage constitute the precious centers of personal experience whose needs must be kept vigilantly in focus. We will also be warned to beware of our limited knowledge, power, and virtue in planning our solutions. By naturalism we will be pressed to reckon seriously and creatively with the political and economic structures that currently set conditions for native peoples in developing nations. Above all we will be advised not to allow old structures, however valuable they may have been in the past, to stand in the way of new approaches that may enlarge the total good and avoid the "zero-sum game" aspect of such seemingly

40. Ibid., p. 163.
41. Ibid., p. 172.
42. Ibid., p. 173.

implacable conflicts between humanity and nature. And by organicism we will be asked to consider the problem in its largest context, including (but not limited to) the interactive relationships between poverty, ignorance, nationalism, racism, sexism, anthropocentrism, and the legitimate claims of the nonhuman inhabitants of the threatened forests. Any lasting solutions will need to deal with the elimination of illiteracy, in particular the education of women and men in the importance and methods of reforestation, in family planning and birth control, and the use of new appropriate technology in the family setting.

Above all, we will learn from empirical theology that if a solution is to be *just* it must be *sustainable*, since fairness to future generations of persons will depend upon the long-term fruitfulness of our policies. And we will learn, at the same time, that if a solution is to be *sustainable* it must be *just*, since only the equitable distribution of education, social security, and a decent richness of life-experience for all will permit the wise and self-restrained policies that are needed to protect the long-term integrity of creation[43]

The path to a just and sustainable world will be a long and difficult one, but it is one coherent path, not two incompatible ones. Each of the branches of empirical theology has a share in pointing to features of it. *Persons* must be respected; *structures* must be creatively reformed; the *organic wholeness* of the world we inhabit must be nurtured. Empirical theology of the twentieth century in America has been divided long enough. Perhaps the urgent quest for a just and sustainable world may have the effect of drawing all the divided family back together, in the recognition that the realm of human experience is rich enough to justify all the special emphases of those who begin with it. In the end the integrity of creation may best be sustained by returning to the integrity of experience.

---

43. The mutual requirements of justice and sustainability are beautifully argued in the symposium paper delivered by Robin Attfield at the World Conference of Philosophy, "Philosophy, Man and the Environment," Nairobi, Kenya, July 21-25, 1991. See his "Development and Environmentalism," in the Advanced Volume of Papers and Abstracts, edited by H. Odera Oruka (Nairobi, 1991), pp. 36-45.

PART THREE

"A liberal is one whose blood is growing warmer, whose charity is growing broader, whose vision is growing clearer; who, in the last analysis, is deeply in love with life."

Ray Oakley Miller

CHAPTER TWELVE

Empirical Theology and Pastoral Theology

JOHN B. COBB JR.

Most pastoral theology in the United States has had a strongly empirical character. The problem, often, has been that its theological character has been less clear or developed. That is, much has been written out of the experience of pastors and by those who are sociologically and psychologically trained. Less has been done by professional theologians.

During the neo-orthodox epoch this led to considerable distress. There were efforts to rethink pastoral care from the neo-orthodox perspective. No doubt much of value was said, but the tensions between the pastors' actual experience of damaged and suffering people and doctrines derived from the Bible and tradition were considerable.

The alternative is to relate pastoral care to a theology that is itself empirical. Here "empirical" refers to "radical empiricism," that is, to an empiricism that focuses not on sense experience but on the totality of experience. That means that this theology is not based primarily on what are usually called empirical studies in sociology and psychology, although it is free to use them. It appeals directly to the depths of experience. There is a natural fit between empirical theology in this sense and pastoral care.

Nevertheless, the literature by empirical theologians dealing directly with pastoral ministry is not large. Most of the writings by empirical theologians are oriented to the problems of faith in a changing intellectual context. Its dialogue partners have been philosophy, history, psychology, sociology, and now women's studies, rather than the church. Many empirical theologians have left to church practitioners the task of learning from empirical theology and then developing their practice in its light. On the whole, this has meant that these practitioners have found their major sources in empirical disciplines other than theology.

248 JOHN B. COBB JR.

There have been exceptions. A few empirical theologians have written directly on questions of pastoral care and counseling. And some of those who work professionally in these fields have seen the connections of their work to empirical theology. A few have developed these connections systematically.

Pride of place among empirical theologians who have directly addressed the issues of pastoral care belongs to Daniel Day Williams. In 1961 he wrote *The Minister and the Care of Souls* (New York: Harper & Row). This book is truly written to and for pastors, with sensitive regard to the care of their souls as well as for how they contribute to the care of the souls of others. Indeed, he emphasizes that the quality of the care they provide others is closely connected to the condition of their own souls. This depends in large part on "the minister's self-knowledge." Williams shows that this is not a matter only of psychological understanding. It is also based on the kind of understanding gained through the study of the Christian tradition. One important role of theological education is to assist the minister toward self-knowledge.

Because of Williams' radical empiricist perspective, he is able to draw freely on psychological wisdom without threatening the fully theological character of his writing. For example, he draws on depth psychology in clarifying how the minister can help parishioners. But he argues that "when a broken self finds healing and strength, the healing power belongs neither to the self nor to another who acts as psychiatrist or pastor. It belongs to a power operative in their relationship. That power is God, who as we know him in the Christian faith, is revealed to us in Jesus Christ, the Third Man, who discloses the truth about our humanity in its need and in its hope." (p. 71)

In Section IV the radical empiricist understanding of God underlying this affirmation will be made clearer in the discussion of Henry Nelson Wieman. The same radical empiricism underlies Williams' sensitive discussion of the minister's authority. "The authority of the pastor is not something merely brought into the pastoral relationship but is born out of that relationship. I am taking the view that the authority of the Christian minister, that is, his authority to speak and act as a representative of the gospel of God's forgiveness and his healing power, is given only through the actual exercise of this pastoral office. Real personal authority arises out of the concrete incarnation of the spirit of loving service which by God's help becomes present in the care of souls." (p. 43)

In 1977 I wrote a modest booklet on *Theology and Pastoral Care* (Philadelphia: Fortress Press) for the Creative Pastoral Care and Counseling Series. Since the many other volumes of the series dealt practically with specific areas of pastoral care and counseling, my effort was to display the relevance of theological considerations to decisions made by pastors, especially in their role as counselors. I wanted to show that how one understands the nature of being human and its normative form is a theological question with practical implications, and also that God can be so understood that trust in God becomes a resource of pastoral care and counseling.

The most prolific writer from the perspective of radical empiricism has been Norman Pittenger. He has addressed many topics relevant to pastoral theology, although he has not written a book specifically on this theme. Among his most important relevant contributions are *The Christian Church as Social Process* (Philadelphia: Westminster, 1971), *The Ministry of All Christians: A Theology of Lay Ministry* (Wilton, Conn.: Morehouse-Barlow, 1983), and *The Pilgrim Church and the Easter People* (Wilmington, Del.: Michael Glazier, 1987).

An important ecclesiology written from the radical empiricist perspective is *The Becoming of the Church*, by Bernard Lee (New York: Paulist, 1974). Later Lee teamed up with Harry James Cargas to edit *Religious Experience and Process Theology: The Pastoral Implications of a Major Modern Movement* (New York: Paulist, 1976). This book is a collection of essays by persons in the tradition of empirical theology that have relevance for the Christian community. In most of them, however, the pastoral implications remain largely implicit. Marjorie Suchocki's *God-Christ-Church: A Practical Guide to Process Theology* (New York: Crossroad, 1989 [1982]) has a similar orientation toward the practice of the Christian community.

The literature from the side of practitioners and specialists in pastoral care and counseling has a somewhat different character. Some recognition of the congeniality of the two communities of thought has been widespread. Two persons who have given major leadership in the professionalization of pastoral counseling have had close and friendly relations to empirical theology. I refer to Seward Hiltner and Howard Clinebell.

By far the most sustained treatment of pastoral counseling from the perspective of empirical theology is that by Gordon Jackson in *Pastoral Care and Process Theology* (Washington, D.C.: University Press of America, 1981). This book makes systematic use of the conceptuality of Alfred North Whitehead to explain what does, or can, go on in the counseling situation. It gives extensive attention to God's role in the therapeutic process.

Examples of books that employ empirical theology in dealing with more specialized questions of pastoral care are Archie Smith's *The Relational Self: Ethics and Therapy from a Black Church Perspective* (Nashville: Abingdon Press, 1982) and Robert Kinast's *When a Person Dies: Pastoral Theology in Death Experience* (New York: Crossroad, 1984).

Robert Brizee, a professional therapist who has been a pastor and works closely with pastors, has written a little book, *Where in the World is God?* (Nashville: Upper Room, 1987). Although this is addressed as much to lay people as to pastors, its relevance for pastoral care is evident throughout. Another pastoral counselor, David Roy, organized an Association for Psychotherapy and Process Thought, which, after a period of dormancy, is being revived. At least half of its members are pastoral counselors.

SPIRIT CENTERED WHOLENESS

The congeniality between empirical theology and pastoral counseling is especially clear when we ask about the goals of the latter. These are usually formulated in terms of healing and growth. In the former case the emphasis is on overcoming psychic disturbances and returning people to normal functioning. In the latter case, the emphasis is on the need of all people to go beyond mere normal functioning, to realize more fully what it is possible to be as human beings.

Some theologies define salvation in such a way that these goals of counseling seem only remotely relevant. If salvation is understood in terms of what happens after death or in a final judgment, and if the conditions for salvation are believing particular things or conforming to particular patterns of behavior, then the sort of healing and growth at which counseling aims may appear to be a distraction. Even with this worldly interpretations of salvation the discontinuity can be considerable. For example, if salvation is understood in purely existential terms, the connections with the actual processes and goals of therapy are limited.

But for empirical theologians salvation is defined in terms of empirical changes. Some notion of human well-being or fulfillment functions here much as it does for pastoral counseling. Empirical theologians have the task of describing what the fulfillment or fullness of human life is like, and if they are Christians they will undertake to show a continuity between what they say and some aspects of the Christian tradition.

It is eminently appropriate that the discussions among theologians interact with those among practitioners. Indeed, this is needed if empirical theology is to be truly empirical. And pastoral counselors benefit because it helps them to interact with the tradition of Christian thought in a congenial mode.

Some elements of this praxis orientation are discernible in all of the writings mentioned above. It is most fully developed in the writings of practitioners influenced by empirical theology. They test this theology in daily interaction with real people with real needs. It is important that empirical theologians take the opportunity to test their views of what is normative for human beings in relation to the rich resources offered by those who work with them day after day.

The potential for rich interaction between pastoral counseling and empirical theology is accentuated when the emphasis of the former shifts from the medical model of healing to the growth model. With the medical model of healing the sick, it is easy to take the ability to function effectively in the existing society as the norm of health. Although one may often feel "saved" when a major psychological impediment to such normal functioning is removed, nevertheless, this cannot suffice as a norm for what human beings are to be.

When the task of pastoral care is oriented to human growth, the horizons are vastly expanded. First, they are expanded from counseling alone to the whole of pastoral care and lay ministry besides. Second, the goal shifts from being able to function well in this society to the attainment of a personal wholeness that involves every aspect of existence. Third, personal existence is located in the social and even ecological context, and it is apparent that genuine personal fulfillment is not possible apart from a healed and whole-making world.

In my book mentioned above I wrote of the ideal for human existence in terms of wholeness centered in spirit. The Institute for Religion and Wholeness, founded by Howard Clinebell, organized a conference on Spirit Centered Wholeness. Fortunately, it conceived such wholeness more inclusively than had I, emphasizing institutional and ecological wholeness as well as psychological and personal wholeness. The papers are published in *Spirit Centered Wholeness*, edited by H. Newton Malony, Michele Papen-Daniels and Howard Clinebell (Lewiston/Queenston: Edwin Mellen Press, 1988). These papers help to define what salvation can mean for empirical theologians. This definition can give guidance to pastoral care and counseling as well. From the points of view both of pastoral theology and empirical theology, every such proposal is subject to testing and reformulation both from theoretical points of view and also through practice.

TWELVE POINTS OF LIGHT

One feature of empirical theology is particularly supportive of the effort to broaden the notion of wholeness, healedness, or salvation. This is the doctrine of internal relations. From the perspective of empirical theology, relations constitute us as being who and what we are. At the same time, we are, in each moment, more than these relations. That is, we constitute ourselves as a response to what we receive from others. We are thus both response-able and responsible for how we respond.

This has important implications. First, it means that we cannot seek salvation in a purely individualistic way. For a long time, pastoral counseling, following the general model of psychotherapy, focused on the individual counselee. It dealt chiefly with intrapsychic struggles and problems. Gradually the psychotherapeutic movement has seen the limitations of this approach and has introduced attention to systems, especially family systems. These developments in the wider psychotherapeutic community have encouraged pastoral counselors also to think of their work less individualistically. This move can only be enthusiastically greeted and affirmed from the side of empirical theology, since it conforms to the understanding of the individual person, not as self-enclosed psychophysical organism, but as an interacting participant in community. To whatever extent relations to others make us what we are, we cannot be healed apart from the healing of these relations. And these relations cannot be healed unilaterally by the counselee.

Second, as the limitations of individualistic counseling are recognized, another common move has been to group therapy. This is also to be affirmed from the perspective of empirical theology. It is often easier to learn new modes of relating in a supervised group where discussion of relations and feelings is encouraged than in the established system of the home where habits are hard to break and practical considerations are likely to dominate. Sometimes the newly learned ways of relating can be transferred to other contexts.

Third, however, this attention to systems and group process has sometimes undercut interest in the intrapsychic dynamics within those involved. From the perspective of empirical theology, this is unfortunate. However much individuals are shaped by their relationships with others, still they also decide how to respond. What they become is the result both of their patterns of relationships and of their partly self-determined response. In the examination of these responses, much of what has been learned through more individualistic approaches is valid.

Fourth, empirical theology rejects the deterministic elements likely to emerge in theories both about systems and about the internal dynamics of the psyche. It emphasizes the real causality of past personal experience and also of the larger community, but it insists that there is always something left over for deciding in each moment. It supports pastoral counselors in emphasizing both determination by others and personal responsibility, as well as in trying to discern accurately in each instance where the element of freedom can be found and how it can be expanded.

Fifth, empirical theology rejects the dualism of personal and social concerns. We cannot encourage individualistic self-assertion in counseling and then balance this with the call to social concern in other aspects of the life of the church. The need in counseling and pastoral care generally is to work toward a form of growth that involves the growth of the community as a whole and entails, in principle, the growth of those who are not part of the community. Since we are members one of another, no one can grow far without the growth of the others. Salvation is inclusive.

Sixth, empirical theology insists on the importance, in all of this, of the body. The psyche does not exist apart from the soma. The psyche's health is important for the soma, and the well-being of the soma is important for the psyche. The church has reason to be concerned about hygiene, diet, exercise, and rest, as well as medical care, precisely because it is concerned with salvation. The work of all the healing professions needs to be integrated.

Seventh, wholeness involves not only soma and psyche but also every aspect of the psychic life. The growth of understanding is part of salvation. So is the heightening of the ability to appreciate beauty and the capacity for imagination. It is not enough to concentrate on the emotional life, important as that is. None of this should be separated from growth in relatedness with others in an enlarging community.

Eighth, as the enlargement of community is emphasized, it is important that the wider physical world be given its due place. Community is not of human psyches alone! The bodies of others are included as well as one's own. Furthermore, the pattern of relationships that make us what we are include relations to other creatures as well. The whole biosphere is interrelated with us, and there can be no salvation of human beings while we collectively degrade this biosphere. Even the inanimate world is important to human salvation.

Ninth, a particularly important contribution of our Christian heritage is its encouragement to widen our horizons in another way as well. The worth of other creatures is not only their interconnectedness with us. We are able to recognize that they have worth in themselves, just as we do. We can transcend our own perspectives to recognize how limited and, indeed, distorting they are. We can evaluate our goals, our hopes, our commitments from a more inclusive point of view, one that relativizes them. I call this capacity for transcending ourselves spirit. And I suggest that no image of salvation is Christian, or indeed humanly adequate, that does not give special attention to spirit.

Tenth, the word "spiritual" has other connotations that are also to be affirmed from the perspective of empirical theology. Many empirical theologians have been impressed by what can be learned from other religious traditions that have developed techniques for changing consciousness. Radical empiricists do not disparage ordinary experience, but we know that human beings are normally conscious of very limited aspects of the reality in which we are immersed; that psychic disciplines of various sorts may open us to other aspects of reality is intrinsically plausible and seems to have been demonstrated over thousands of years by those who have engaged in various "spiritual" disciplines. Furthermore, many of the results are highly attractive. Some of the spiritual wisdom we seek is to be found in the Western tradition, but in recent years we have become increasingly aware that in such places as India and China the range of possibilities has been explored far more thoroughly than in the West. Empirical theologians see no reason for rejecting or belittling such experience because it comes to us from alien sources.

If "therapy" means restoring people to normal functioning in society, then most of this discussion has gone far beyond therapy. Pastoral counseling need not be limited to therapy in this narrow sense. But even when pastors do see a person's immediate need in terms of this medical model, and this is often a sound judgment, their way of dealing with the person will be affected by the wider horizon of their own hopes for all their people and for the church community. In other words, the pastor's vision of salvation affects the way she or he seeks to aid a parishioner in overcoming obstacles to participating with others in normal life.

This becomes especially apparent in the eleventh of these points about pastoral care and counseling. Psychotherapy in general has, over the years,

been practiced on women by men. This pattern has been at least equally
true of pastoral counseling. Until very recently almost all the counselors
were men, and far more women than men came to these male pastors in
quest of help. In general women came because of difficulties they experienced
in fitting in to patriarchal society, even if they did not formulate their problems in this way. In general, pastoral counselors, like psychotherapists generally, tried to help the women to fit in—that is, to meet the patriarchal
expectations.

   Given the patriarchal context and the practical options, it may be that the
"help" given was sometimes real. But overall, this was simply a way of
undergirding patriarchy and its values. If, as is now becoming clear, there can
be no salvation for men or women, or for the planet as a whole, without
major changes in basic understanding and behavior, then enabling individuals to fit into the present structures has been at best an ambiguous good. The
way a pastor counsels a woman who is caught in the many binds imposed on
her by patriarchy will be affected by the pastor's understanding of what true
health requires. The pastor who is aware of the need to challenge patriarchy
will offer quite different types of help from traditional psychotherapy. Therapy
in this case, and in others as well, cannot be separated from the vision of
salvation that governs the whole life of the church.

   Twelfth, and finally, empirical theology will be strongly supportive of
the recognition that what makes for true growth is culturally relative. In
some cultures individualistic counseling in a pastor's office will be coun-
terproductive. In others it will require an approach quite different from those
effective in our society. In some cultures the distinction between pastoral
counseling and pastoral care in general will make little sense. Perhaps even
in ours it will have diminishing importance. Empirical theology emphasizes
that all of the church's life is relative to its actual situation and that attempting to impose the patterns of one culture on another, or of one generation on
the next, will often inhibit the salvific process rather than support it.

GRACE AND CREATIVE TRANSFORMATION

   The idea of grace is one on which empirical theologians have much to say.
Traditionally grace is treated in terms of two aspects, and I will follow this
convention. First, "grace" refers to how we receive from others, how they
empower and guide us. Second, it refers to their acceptance of us independent of our deserts. The others from whom grace is received are by no means
limited to God, yet for most Christian theology, the model of divine grace
undergirds what is seen as grace in human relations as well.

   The most important figure in the empirical tradition's discussion of grace
in the first sense is Henry Nelson Wieman. In his greatest work, *The Source
of Human Good* (Chicago: University of Chicago Press, 1946), Wieman
works out in rich detail how human good grows, not by human manage-

ment and control, but as a gift, by "creative transformation." In his words: "The 'grace of God' would then be creative transformation become dominant in the life of" human beings (p. 49).

Wieman's basic point is that the true growth of good in our lives comes when our values and aims are themselves transformed. This means that if we project goals based on our present values and plan procedures for attaining these, we block the working of creative good. Real human good grows as the creative process operates among us and within us. Our need is to trust this process and allow it to achieve for us and with us what we cannot achieve by controlled effort.

Wieman's empirical account of "the grace of God" has never been excelled. He analyzes it into four subevents: "emerging awareness of qualitative meaning derived from other persons through communication; integrating these new meanings with other previously acquired; expanding the richness of quality in the appreciable world by enlarging its meaning; deepening the community among those who participate in this total creative event of intercommunication" (p. 58). Wieman goes on to discuss each of these subevents in some detail.

Wieman's language and mode of analysis fitted more into the philosophy of religion than into Christian theology, despite its obvious and explicit relevance for the latter. Daniel Day Williams employed Wieman's basic understanding of grace in a clearly theological work, *God's Grace and Man's Hope* (New York: Harper and Brothers, 1949). Here Williams showed how understanding God's grace in this way as an actual process transforming human life introduced new alternatives into the ongoing theological discussion of the time.

Williams subsequently wrote *The Spirit and the Forms of Love* (New York: Harper & Row, 1968), a book that remains to this day the best systematic theology written in the tradition of empirical theology. Although the word "grace" is not featured here, the understanding of love is quite close in meaning. There is a shift, however, from Wieman's form of empirical theology to Whitehead's. This leaves intact the basic understanding of grace developed by Wieman, but it introduces a metaphysical background explanatory of what occurs in the world.

Whitehead, like Wieman, sees that growth is not under human control. It comes as a gift, and he calls the giver "God." God provides to every entity, every "occasion" the opportunity to be something more than the mere product of what comes to it from its past. In human beings this can be understood chiefly in terms of the qualitative meaning derived from other persons through communication. The possibility of integrating these meanings and expanding the richness of quality in the appreciable world is given in the possibilities of relevant novelty derived from God. Thus, while Wieman uses "God" to name the process of creative transformation, Whitehead uses "God" to name that transcendent reality whose immanence makes creative transformation both possible and actual.

Jean Lambert has employed this basic model in the interpretation of forgiveness in *The Human Action of Forgiving: A Critical Application of the Metaphysics of Alfred North Whitehead* (Washington, D.C.: University Press of America, 1985). In her analysis "the structure of forgiveness is the structure of action: forgiveness is part of the real world of action; as such it is an approach to the future; it is action in a world where action changes the past in addition to constructing the future" (p. xix). Forgiveness is not to be confused with forgetting, condoning, or pardoning. Forgiveness is needed when a relationship has been broken, and it involves a decision "to trust the original relationship rather than the break or the event that occasioned it" (p. 31).

For Lambert, the structure of forgiveness is the structure of all action. Furthermore, there is an element of forgiveness in all action. And finally, Lambert concludes, forgiveness is the norm for all action.

The empirical character of Lambert's reflection is manifest and explicitly tested in her form of presentation. She interweaves philosophical and theological analysis with case material. And she is satisfied with her theoretical formulations only as they express what occurs in the cases she follows.

Whitehead's metaphysical speculations also introduce the other aspect of grace, grace as divine acceptance. Much of what is distinctive about the theology of Whitehead and Hartshorne in comparison with traditional theism is found in their unqualified insistence that God not only acts on creatures but is acted on by them. This is the apparent meaning of numerous scriptural statements about God, but the Greek influence led to statements by philosophical theologians, from the days of the Church Fathers on, that appear to deny that God can be affected by what happens in the world. Some defenders of the tradition insist that the doctrines of impassibility and immutability are far subtler and more complex and have not really had the meaning that critics ascribe to them—and that is no doubt correct. Nevertheless, the argument from metaphysics itself that God is literally and unqualifiedly affected by all that creatures do and feel is new, and it is central to the challenge of Whitehead and Hartshorne to traditional philosophical theology.

For both Whitehead and Hartshorne the issue is primarily one of the meaningfulness of human existence. The challenge to the meaningfulness of human action is that its results soon fade. Even the memory of the act is quickly lost. So far as the course of events is concerned, it is almost as if it had never occurred. Especially when we consider that in the end all life on this planet will cease, we must acknowledge how ephemeral are all our accomplishments.

Whitehead accentuates this point in his doctrine of "perpetual perishing." Each occasion comes into being in a moment and then perishes. This does not mean that it has no influence on the future. Quite the contrary. But its own subjective immediacy, the locus of its intrinsic value, dies at the moment of its birth. Its immediacy, if not its subjectivity, lives on in its immediate successors, but that too fades quickly. Realizing how quickly immediacy is lost threatens the sense of importance so necessary for creative action.

Whitehead's own categories lead him to speculate that this perishing of immediacy is not the final word. God as the one everlasting entity shares this immediacy with every occasion, and in God it is everlasting. What we do, even what we feel, matters ultimately because it matters to God.

This doctrine lends itself to development in terms of human and divine acceptance. Don S. Browning wrote a book, *Atonement and Psychotherapy* (Philadelphia: Westminster, 1966), in which he employed Hartshorne's doctrine of God's ideal receptivity of worldly events to reflect on the mode of God's acceptance of all that we do and are. He developed the similarity between how God accepts us and how the ideal therapist accepts those who come for help. By grounding such therapy in the divine-human relationship, its rightful place in the life of the church becomes manifest.

Neither God's acceptance of human beings nor the acceptance of the client by the therapist reduces the seriousness of the suffering and sin of those accepted. God accepts us, whatever we do. But God's acceptance of our suffering is a sharing in our suffering. God's acceptance of our sinful thoughts and deeds introduces discord into the divine life, and the suffering our sins cause others—and ourselves—adds to God's suffering. Acceptance intensifies the importance of the character of what is accepted.

THE PASTOR AS PRACTICAL THEOLOGIAN

Empirical theologians have contributed to reflection on the nature of ministry in general. Daniel Day Williams participated with H. Richard Niebuhr and James Gustafson in a major study of ministry. A major motivation of this study was to guide theological seminaries in their task of equipping men and women for the ministerial vocation. It was published in 1955 as *The Advancement of Theological Education* (New York: Harper & Brothers). The conclusion was that the minister's role had come to be that of pastor-director, with counseling and church administration as primary responsibilities.

More recently I participated with Joseph Hough in a much more modest study, this one also guided by an interest in theological education. The resulting book is entitled *Christian Identity and Theological Education* (Chico, Calif.: Scholars Press, 1985). We concluded that the role of the pastor is to be a practical theologian.

The meaning of practical theology for many people is still almost identical with pastoral theology. However, there are others for whom the term has taken on a transformed meaning. Pastoral theology has tended to focus on pastoral care and counseling as in this essay. Practical theology includes atten-

tion to pastoral tasks but views these in the context of the total calling of
the church to minister not only to its members but to the world.

In discussing salvation, above, this wider meaning became apparent.
From the point of view of empirical theology in compartmentalization of
pastoral theology from the whole task of the church in witness to society is
artificial and dangerous. On the other hand, the rootage of practical theology in pastoral theology is important. It is precisely in pastoral theology that
the emphasis on praxis has been most important. For example, it is pastoral
counselors who have most insisted on doing their theoretical work in close
relation with actual cases. They have been the ones most resistant to the
acceptance of traditional ideas on authority when they do not help in dealing
with empirical reality. Practical theology calls for the generalization of this
spirit to the whole of the church's life.

This development of pastoral theology into practical theology has been
largely under the impact of liberation theologies. If individual salvation cannot take place apart from the inclusive salvation of the planet, then pastoral
theology must understand itself within this larger context. It cannot be simply the honing of skills in the attainment of delimited tasks. It must reflect on
how the fulfillment of those tasks affects the work of inclusive salvation.

Don Browning has given major leadership in this country in the development of practical theology in the inclusive sense. Thinkers in the empirical tradition have been conspicuous in their support. Robert Kinast is co-
founder of the Center for the Care of Society, a research, education and
consulting service to promote the integration of theological reflection and
social action. He has written *Caring for Society: A Theological Interpretation
of Lay Ministry* (Chicago: Thomas More Press, 1985).

Others in the empirical theological tradition who have given support and
leadership are David Polk and James Poling. Poling is co-author with Donald
Miller of the first full-length treatment of the broader understanding of practical theology with the tasks of ministry specifically in view. This is
Foundations for a Practical Theology of Ministry (Nashville: Abingdon,
1985). Poling and Miller define practical theology as reflection about experience within the Christian community for the sake of "the formation of persons and communities of faith for the mission of Jesus Christ" (p. 98). They
describe six types of practical theology all of which relate the church to
society. It is in the discussion of the method of practical theology that their
commitment to American empirical theology is most explicit (p. 67).

Practical theology begins with a description of lived experience within its
social and historical context. The second step is self-criticism in terms of
the particularity of interests and perspectives that affect the experience and
its interpretation. Next, the community relates its interpretation of its own tradition to modes of interpretation operative in the larger society derived from
the natural or social sciences or from philosophy. The fourth step, building
on the first three, is critical interpretation of the meaning of the community's

experience as a "testimony to the present activity of God" (p. 91). This is followed by a threefold questioning of this interpretation. Is it relevant to people at all levels of personal development? Is it liberating both within the
church and outside? Does it symbolize life richly enough? Finally, practical
theology articulates procedures for implementing what is believed in the
actual life of the church.

MAKING BELIEF IN GOD RELEVANT

The claims of empirical theology to support both pastoral theology and
practical theology are many-sided. But perhaps the most daring of these
claims is that it can make belief in God genuinely relevant to the way the pastor goes about her or his business. This has been suggested at several points
above, but I will conclude by dealing more directly and practically with this
claim.

To highlight the contribution that can be made by empirical theology it is
necessary to describe the weakness of most other theological positions. This
involves presenting them in somewhat caricatured form. In fact, elements of
these positions can be integrated with attention to empirical fact in ways
that approximate what empirical theology can offer. Indeed, the common
sense and human sensitivity of most pastors lead them to act in many situations in ways that further empirical growth in their parishioners. Nevertheless,
many of their beliefs do not encourage this appropriate behavior.

As heirs of the modern world, many pastors accept the idea that the natural world, including even its psychological component, is essentially self-
enclosed and self-explanatory. That means that although God created it and
established the laws that govern it, no reference to God is needed in the
explanation of natural and psychological phenomena. This assumption controls the university, including much of the seminary curriculum. Given this
assumption, if God plays any role in what happens other than that of creator
and lawgiver, this will be at the end of the course of events or through intervention in it.

This view can lead to preoccupation with the unusual events in which it
may be supposed that God is intervening or with eschatological hopes and
fears. More often it leads to a practical neglect of God as one goes about
one's daily business. Prayer does not really make much sense, except perhaps
praise of God for the greatness of creation. The task of serving people is
carried out best as the wisdom of the secular world is appropriated. Pastoral
counseling draws on the wisdom of secular psychotherapy. Church administration draws on the wisdom of secular management theory. Everything
depends on human action, and that action is understood to be fully
autonomous. God's grace plays no role.

The situation is not greatly changed if God is thought of as the Ground of
Being rather than as the external Creator. If God is understood as the being

of everything that is, this does give a sense of God's immediate role in each being or event. But since God's role in each case is simply to give being, this belief in God has little effect on pastoral functions. This judgment is unfair if it is taken to apply to the whole of the theology of Tillich. With his idea of the New Being, Tillich did provide some general guidance and direction, much of it profound and original. But this does not integrally follow with any necessity from his view God as Being Itself.

There are others whose worldview is more fully biblical. For them the intellectual history of the West does not block a sense that God is very much involved in what happens in the world. The problem here is that their reading of events tends to be uncritical. Where they locate God's role in current events differs from person to person. Many of the decisions appear arbitrary and even willful to others. The results are to absolutize certain events and movements in ways that are idolatrous.

Empirical theology offers a way of thinking of God's working in the world that has far more objectivity and integrity. It begins with the assumption that to speak of God is to speak of that which is wholly worthy of human trust and devotion. What is wholly worthy of trust and devotion must be that which makes for good in the world. Wieman's limitation of the "good" to human good can be overcome without greatly changing what he has said.

Of course, there is no way of gaining complete agreement as to what the good is. But empirical theology can, following Wieman, emphasize that there can be considerable agreement as to the kinds of changes that are desirable. For example, the expansion of awareness and of the ability to appreciate is widely valued even among persons with diverse theories of ethics and value. Indeed, in the interaction of such persons, this expansion of awareness and appreciation can take place to the acknowledged gain of all.

In Wieman's terms, there can be agreement about the creative good without agreement about the exact nature of the created good. And for the purposes of ministry this suffices. The pastor can seek to serve the creative good and to draw others into that service. This service *is* the service of God.

To understand the service of God in this way does not call for actions wholly different from those of pastors who think of God in quite different ways. On the contrary, much of the work of most pastors does serve the creative good. But that is not to say that it makes no difference how pastors understand God's working in the world.

Pastors who think of God primarily as lawgiver and judge or as requiring particular beliefs in order that one be saved will continue to interact with people in some ways that make creative transformation possible. But they will focus on trying to get their people to act in certain ways and to believe certain things. Their focus will thus inhibit the working of creative transformation. Those who understand that God's work is that of creative transformation will seek to encourage openness to that working. That would involve suggesting to people new ways of thinking about their lives and new beliefs about God and the world. But these would be suggested for the purpose of encouraging people to think for themselves rather than to accept any suggestions simply on authority.

This openness to the creative process is likely to be at its greatest in the context of counseling. Yet even here the attitudes and expectations of the past make a difference. One who believes that God is at work in the interaction between pastor and parishioner will feel less tempted to try to determine what the outcome will be in the parishioner's life. Genuinely listening to the hurting person will be experienced as real ministry along with finding ways to speak that can also genuinely be heard.

A church that trusts the process of creative transformation will be one in which people are encouraged to express their real convictions as well as to listen to those of others. Trust in the process means willingness to recognize that one's own convictions may not exhaust the truth, that interaction with others may modify them in unforeseeable ways. One believes that such modification will be growth even though one does not know in what direction the change will be.

Wieman developed his empirical theology partly in reaction to the socio-historical theology that had been dominant at Chicago when he arrived. His strong commitment was to a realistic understanding of God that could give real guidance to living. But in the process he downgraded history, and as a result his own ways of connecting his empirical theology to Christian tradition were not convincing. However, in the ongoing movement of empirical theology others, beginning with Daniel Day Williams, have reintroduced an emphasis on history.

Williams stressed that all knowing and all experience are perspectival. That means that we should acknowledge the perspective from which we feel and think, and for Christians this is to confess the role of the Christian community in making us what we are. In this way, the particularity of the Christian community and the way in which creative transformation operates within it can be made clear.

Radical empiricism affirms that human experience is constituted by relationships much deeper than sense experience. These relationships include those to our personal past and through that personal past to the past of our communities. We are, thus, constituted as historical beings through and through. To be a Christian is, first, to be formed by the Christian tradition through the Christian community.

But we are not merely determined to be the product of our traditions and communities. We also have an element of freedom. That enables us to criticize our traditions and to reject them. It also enables us to affirm our involvement in a community and to assume some responsibility for transmitting its tradition. To be a Christian is to take this second position, willingly to identify with the Christian community and its traditions.

Third, identification with the tradition does not involve treating any form it has ever taken as absolute or final. On the contrary, as the socio-historical theologians of Chicago made very clear, it is participation in repentance for what is wrong with the tradition and in its creative transformation. The Christian tradition is a living one. When it tries to become static, it withers and ultimately dies.

This means that the task of the minister is not simply to encourage the expression of whatever convictions happen to be around. That is important. But in the church the community shares the Christian tradition. It is the creative transformation of that tradition, in faithfulness to that tradition, that is the goal of ministry. That entails, of course, the creative transformation of the community that bears that tradition and lives from it. And that in turn involves the creative transformation of the members of that community.

The teaching and preaching of the church will not, therefore, be general discourses about whatever matters are of topical interest. The focus will be on the tradition. What can be learned about these matters from the past forms of the tradition, especially those that the community has canonized? In what ways does the tradition need to change in light of what we, as a Christian community, are now coming to understand? What does that mean for us as a community and as individuals?

Empirical theology must acknowledge that this free inquiry and discussion is an ideal, and that many people look to the church for security and authority rather than for creative transformation. Pastoral care informed by empirical theology cannot ignore the empirical reality of the desires and needs of the members! These are real needs of real people. Confronting such people with the limitation of their understanding of Christian faith may only drive them into greater defensiveness and rigidity.

But this does not mean that the church should simply acquiesce in this understanding of its role. The goal must be to help those with strong needs for authority to grow to the point that they can become more open to taking responsibility for themselves and participating in an interactive community. The church must confess that it shares in the responsibility of having encouraged the immaturity that now hampers its faithfulness to God and to the tradition. It should strive to become in the future a far better servant of the process.

EMPIRICISM AND SPECULATION

The claim of empirical theology is that what it affirms theologically is what is called for by the evidence. To justify that claim, the evidence must be viewed inclusively. It cannot be limited to what is seen and touched. Indeed, it subordinates this kind of evidence to that which is found in a fuller and deeper description of experience.

Some empirical theologians want to remain very close to the description itself. Among these theologians, I have selected Henry Nelson Wieman for primary attention. Others believe that speculation based on this evidence can be fruitful in two ways. First it can lead to ways of thinking of God and the world that are intrinsically satisfying and religiously important. Second, it can suggest hypotheses for further empirical study. Alfred North Whitehead is the great representative of this kind of empirical theology. In this essay Daniel Day Williams and his student, Jean Lambert, have been given most attention among those who follow Whitehead.

But what is striking is that as long as attention is focused on experience as such, these two groups within the radical empirical community generally support one another in their understanding of pastoral ministry. For the sake of pastoral ministry, the task is not so much to decide the methodological issues between the two groups as to pursue the model so well developed by Jean Lambert. That is, theologians need to test their empirical theology against case material that exposes the empirical situation of real human beings. This is implicit in the program of empirical theologians, and as this is done, the promise of empirical theology for expressing itself as pastoral theology will be fulfilled.

CHAPTER THIRTEEN

Empirical Theology
in the Local Congregation

RANDOLPH CRUMP MILLER

The ultimate pragmatic test of empirical theology is how it works in local congregations and among lay people.

Empiricism begins with observation. This chapter provides a description of what a congregation does. There is particular attention to worship, liturgy, preaching, and religious education (pastoral care has already been interpreted in the previous chapter). We take for granted the assumptions, concepts, and verification established in the other chapters, recognizing the variety of conclusions and the centrality of God in empirical theology. Therefore, "we can be sure about God; but we must be tentative in theology."[1]

In the New Testament, the church is described as the people of God in a covenant relationship with God and others, as a fellowship of believers who participate in the life of the community, as followers of "the Way," which is a lifestyle committed to certain ideals ascribed to the teaching of Jesus.

The church soon developed into an institution in which people are exposed to the tradition by those whom they trust. The first stage of membership is a period in which there is acceptance of whatever is taught. A second stage leads to questioning the teachings, others in the community, and oneself. This leads to a third stage in which there is cultivation of the inner life, of creative transformation of the self and one's goals, and a deepening of relationships not only in the church community but also in the family, and this may lead to concern for moral, social, and political issues. One may develop a sense of the divine mystery at the center of one's life without being able to describe it.

---

1. Ian T. Ramsey, *Christian Discourse* (London: Oxford University Press, 1965), p. 89; also, Ramsey, *On Being Sure in Religion* (London: Athlone Press, 1963), p. 16.

Commitment is at the center of the believer's life in the church. It may be present to a greater or a lesser degree, but it is still present. Bernard Meland describes what seems most important empirically to him:

> Two basic facts provide the basis for my religious commitment. One is that I am a creature of earth processes. The other is that the universe is such that I, as an earth creature, can set up relations with certain aspects of its life, and thus fulfill my own life process. . . . It is to pass from the state of maladjustment to an organic situation in which full adjustment is possible. Becoming aware of these elemental facts, then, is the basic religious experience. It gives me the sense of being at home in the universe and belonging to the life of earth.[2]

This kind of experience is paralleled by those who stress experiences of solitariness, of the right religious adjustment, and of the sense of history in which there are forces at work which may be called "God." William Dean suggests that empirical theologians are also interpretive historians who recognize the power of the past to limit the possibilities of the present and future.[3]

What emerges from these experiences is the discovery that life is social and that living together with others may be harmonious and mutually enriching, with friendship as the result of social interaction. One reaches what Meland calls "the appreciative level" which turns one away from self to "more-than-self." It opens up the vast world of music, art, literature, history, and the capacity to enjoy all of life in spite of its ambiguities and evil. The appreciative level reaches beyond these aspects of life and points to the cosmic mystery. Our response to mystery leads to worship and a sense of communion with God. In turn, the experience of the aesthetic and of worship enrich all the lower forms of earthly existence so that there is a deepening of the meaning of life.

Like the early church, local congregations develop their own oral traditions. No Sunday school in the summer or after the eighth grade, say some congregations. Lay people stay quiet during the worship service and the choir does all the singing, say others. Or, at the other end of the spectrum, lay people share in all the worship except that reserved for the clergy, with singing by the congregation and no choir (especially in the summer). Biblical sermons may explain the text without applying it to the life of the people; or

---

2. Bernard Eugene Meland, *Modern Man's Worship* (New York: Harper & Brothers, 1934), p. 299. See Larry Axel, "Religious Creaturalism and a New Agenda for Theology," in *God, Values and Empiricism*, ed. Creighton Peden and Larry E. Axel (Macon, Ga.: Mercer University Press, 1989), pp. 1-8.

3. See William Dean, *American Religious Empiricism* (Albany: State University of New York Press, 1986), pp. 36-39, 114-118; also, William Dean, "Humanistic Historicism and Naturalistic Historicism," in *Theology at the End of Modernity*, ed. Sheila Greeve Davaney (Philadelphia: Trinity Press International, 1991), pp. 41-59.

sermons may appeal primarily to the emotions and building excitement, or sermons may fit the oral traditions of the congregation but do not stimulate growth in believing or acting.

Tradition is a process, developing from earliest times and changing through the centuries. The Bible does not mention many traditions, such as making the sign of the cross, blessing the water in baptism, using oil in chrism, or even the repeating of the words of Jesus in the consecration of the elements in the communion service. Some congregations today are recovering the early tradition of the passing of the peace, which they see as an expression of the belongingness of every member in the congregation.

Traditions tend to become hardened. People resist changes even when they have forgotten the original meaning of the traditional actions or words. They resist new hymnals and revised liturgies and object to theologically advanced teachings and sermons. But traditions can and do change, as do doctrines, so that the problem is to relate newer concepts and practices to the older ones, maintaining continuity with the older ones to the developing ones, and thus providing relevance to the world of today. Empirical theology, as developed in this volume, offers one way of understanding how a local congregation can deal with these issues.

Henry Nelson Wieman looked at the church as an institution within the larger society and insisted that there must be some correspondence between the lives of those in the institution and those in the broader society. This means that "the ultimate religious commitment be interpreted in such a way that it obviously and directly applies to the entire process of social living."[4] The mission of the church, for Wieman, is to evangelize humanity in the dual commitment to accept the best knowledge attainable and to recognize that the mystery on which people rely can never be completely known.

The church has its own language and every congregation is a community of language. The sources are found in the vocabulary of the Bible and the liturgies, plus the oral traditions. They point to the knowledge that has accumulated and to the mystery that is at the center. At their best they are open to the future. There is a process by which to achieve the goals of accepting the best knowledge we can attain and to accept the mystery that lies beyond our ken. First, according to Wieman, are the rituals and symbols which enrich our personalities and direct them to that reality which sustains, saves, and transforms us. This leads to self-examination, so that we can discover where we have failed. This is a complicated process, hindered by our own deceptions and rationalizations. The congregation offers us the opportunity for such self-examination and provides the social reinforcement to accept forgiveness and to renew our commitment. To understand this process, the church provides instruction and understanding

---

4. Henry Nelson Wieman, *Man's Ultimate Commitment* (Carbondale, Ill.: Southern Illinois University Press, 1958), p. 166.

through education, preaching, Bible study, and prayer.[5]

Anne Rowthorn in *The Liberation of the Laity* suggests that in congregations dominated by the clergy, the above outcome is unlikely, but where the laity have been liberated to fulfill their ministries in the world, social and political developments are likely to occur. She writes that the church is in the world through its laity and that the church has produced a number of saints.[6] In his remarkable chapters on "Saintliness," William James uses his empiricism to describe the many aspects of saintliness:

> If things are ever to move upward, someone must be ready to take the first step and assume the risk of it. No one who is not willing to try charity, to try nonresistance as the saint is always willing, can tell whether these methods will or will not succeed. When they do succeed, they are far more powerfully successful than force or worldly prudence. Force destroys enemies; and the best that can be said of prudence is that it keeps what we already have in safety. But nonresistance, when successful, turns enemies into friends; and charity regenerates its objects. . . . This practical proof that worldly wisdom may be safely transcended is the saint's magic gift.[7]

The congregation is a mixture of saints and sinners, with most people in between, even the leaders. Wieman suggests that leadership has an area of competence. Leaders should know how God works as a creative power and relate this knowledge to what "God demands in the home, in the industrial plant, in the relations of races and nations to one another, and in other human situations."[8] But the leaders should know where their competence ends and where they would be wise to accept the counsel of experts.

WORSHIP

Whitehead speaks of the religious vision, which is empirically based. This vision is complex and full of possible meanings.

The immediate reaction of human nature to the religious vision is worship. . . . The vision claims nothing but worship; and worship is a surrender to

---

5. Ibid., pp. 172-175.

6. See Anne Rowthorn, *The Liberation of the Laity* (Wilton, Conn.: Morehouse-Gorham, 1986), pp. 60-79. For the significance of basic Christian communities, see Bernard Lee's chapter on "The Nature of the Church" (above).

7. William James, *The Varieties of Religious Experience* (New York: Longmans, Green, 1902), pp. 358-359.

8. Henry Nelson Wieman, *The Source of Human Good* (Chicago: University of Chicago Press, 1946), p. 292.

the claim for assimilation, urged with the motive force of mutual love. .
. . The power of God is the worship [God] inspires.[9]

Is this vision empirically grounded? Whitehead would claim that it is,
and for support we can turn to William James' *The Varieties of Religious
Experience*, in which case after case indicates some level of vision. We find
support also in the writings of Douglas Clyde Macintosh and Henry Nelson
Wieman. For some empirical theologians, it is the starting point for interpretation. The response to this vision is worship and thus what was a private
experience becomes a public one.

The experience of worship is crucial for a parish that makes use of empirical theology. Ian Ramsey believed that all theology needs an empirical
anchor for "without such empirical anchorage all theological thinking is
vain, and where there is controversy and argument we are to look for their resolution where they are fulfilled: in worship."[10] The vitality of worship in
the life of the congregation is a measuring rod for the health of the people of
God. Whitehead makes this clear:

> That religion is strong which in its ritual and its modes of thought evokes
> an apprehension of the commanding vision. The worship of God is not a
> rule of safety— it is an adventure of the spirit, a flight after the unob-
> tainable. The death of religion comes with the repression of the high hope
> of adventure.[11]

Corporate worship, to be meaningful, depends on a common ground of
belief and religious language that expresses these beliefs. An empirical theology has a rich vocabulary to point to the reality of God, but it lacks liturgical adaptability. Not many congregations would respond to a prayer that
began "O principle of concretion that is prehended in every flower."

When empirical and process theologians speak of God, their interpretation
of current and historical experience leads to a God who loves us and therefore shares our joys and suffering and through persuasion acts to transform
our lives and restore our spiritual wholeness. They interpret the working of
God as active in history and in the cosmos as well as among human beings.
Human beings respond to the presence of God with reverence and awe before
mystery and thus renew their commitment both to God and to the community of human beings and nature. But some reject such claims on them and
operate free from any such commitment.

Worship, then, is more than a response to a vision. It is being in the presence of an actual entity who or which is worthy of worship. Traditionally this

---

9. Alfred North Whitehead, *Science and the Modern World* (New York: Macmillan,
1925), pp. 275-276.

10. Ian T. Ramsey, *Religious Language* (London: SCM Press, 1957), p. 89.

11. Whitehead, *Science and the Modern World*, p. 276.

has led to the concept of an all-powerful deity who is also absolutely good. Those who are sensitive to the problem of evil find that they are caught up in a contradiction, and they question either the power or the goodness of God, for if God is all-powerful and all-good and evil is genuine, then God is not worthy of worship. Charles Hartshorne has made this clear in his *Omnipotence and Other Theological Mistakes*.[12] We need to analyze the meaning of perfection and to take account of the empirical evidence for freedom, chance, and pluralism in the world. This takes us away from the traditional concept of deity. With William James, we see God as acting within a pluralistic world, within an environment that limits God. Then we can conceive God as good and evil as real.

Most empirical theologians would agree that in worship we are in God's presence, although we also see God in history and meet God in every experience. In church or synagogue or mosque, we meet with others who share our expectations. We become aware that we are in a congregation seeking God together and at least unconsciously entering into the lives of those others in a shared experience. These simultaneous experiences enrich and strengthen all the members in a way similar to what happens to a crowd at a football game or a political rally, except that the focus is on God. This common focus of the congregation increases the depth of devotion to values and the common aim is to align our aims with God's aims as we understand them, leading to moral, social, and political action.

Evelyn Underhill, in her book on *Worship*, although she is not an empiricist, writes of the centrality of the senses in worship:

> Indeed, since we can only think, will, and feel in and with the physical body, and it is always in close connection with sense-impressions received through that body that our religious consciousness is stirred and sustained, it follows that we can hardly dispense with some ritual act, some sensible image, some material offering, as an element in the total act of worship, if that act of worship is to turn our humanity in its wholeness toward God. The mysterious feeding of spirit upon Spirit is made more not less real by the ritual meal which drives home the practical truth of our creaturely dependence.[13]

Sharon Parks makes clear that food plays many roles in human life. Eating together may establish friendship, become symbolic in memory, restore relationships, and be the center of the ritual of Holy Communion. In earlier times, if food was offered, the host became a protector; if no food was offered, the guest might end up with a slit throat. Sharon Parks writes:

---

12. See Charles Hartshorne, *Omnipotence and Other Theological Mistakes* (Albany: SUNY Press, 1984), pp. 1-49.

13. Evelyn Underhill, *Worship* (New York: Harper & Brothers, 1937), p. 25.

Our need to eat is a vulnerability directly related to our vulnerability to love. We need each other in order to survive. We cannot separate the fact "Because I was loved, I am" from the reality "Because I was fed, I am." We are physical beings made in and for relation, and our word *companion* means "one with whom we share bread."[14]

How many realize that they are companions at the altar rail?

Worship incorporates a dual basis. There is the individual who has some experience that is related to deity. The validation of this experience is found in community, especially in worship. The individual in community is aware of the presence of God and of God's awareness of the individual, and the individual is aware of other worshipers as they are aware of God's presence in their midst and of each other. It is a complex and intricate experience, multidimensional in nature and often only actual in the subconscious. The worshiper may be only partly aware of the others and their experience, but it touches the appreciative consciousness and the affective realm.

We forget sometimes that God is present to us not only in worship but in daily life. Whitehead reminds us of this in a remarkable statement:

God is *in* the world, or nowhere, creating continually in us and around us. This creative principle is everywhere, in animate and so-called inanimate matter, in ether, water, earth, human hearts. But this creation is a continuing process, and "the process is itself the actuality," since no sooner do you arrive than you start on a fresh journey. Insofar as man partakes of this creative process does he partake of the divine, of God, and that participation is his immortality, reducing the question of whether his individuality survives death of the body to the state of an irrelevancy. His true destiny as co-creator in the universe is his dignity and his grandeur.[15]

The result of this kind of thinking is the realization of human worth. It emerges early in life but is hard to put into words. The child has a dignity that is totally unselfconscious. There is always a seed of the sense of worth in the most oppressed people, and this provides a basis for their hope. It transcends the sense of sin, for whenever the sense of sin obscures the sense of personal worth, the damage to the psyche is great, "the worst blight that ever fell on man."[16]

Worship reinforces the sense of worth. If the worshipers feel unworthy, and often they do, the promise of forgiveness and reconciliation restores the

---

14. Sharon Parks, "The Meaning of Eating and the Home as Ritual Space," in *Sacred Dimensions of Women's Experience*, ed. Elizabeth Dodson Gray (Wellesley: Round Table Press, 1988), p. 186.

15. *Dialogues of Alfred North Whitehead*, as recorded by Lucien Price (Boston: Little, Brown, 1954), pp. 370-371.

16. Whitehead, *Science and the Modern World*, p. 275.

sense of worth. If the worshipers, feeling the presence of God, have some goal in mind, reinforcement of the value of their selves occurs. But the matter is more complicated. We are assured that God is good, but we remain aware that evil, horror and sinfulness abound. There is an uneasiness and sometimes dread of being in the presence of a deity who is loving and holy. But there are some who are unresponsive to the promise of reconciliation, and the redemptive forces cannot reach such a person.

The sense of sin and denial of human worth are reflected in traditional liturgies. For example, "We are not worthy so much as to gather up the crumbs under thy table." Compare this with the woman who says, "Yes, Lord, yet even the dogs eat the crumbs that fall from their master's table" (Mt 15:27, NRSV). If human beings have less value than dogs, this would indeed be a blight, but we are told that "you are of more value than many sparrows" (Mt 10: 31b, NRSV). "For it is from within, from the human heart, that evil inventions come: fornication, theft, murder, adultery, avarice, wickedness, deceit, licentiousness, envy, slander, pride, folly. All these things come from within, and they defile a person" (Mk 7:21-22, NRSV). So human beings do not have a sinful nature and have a sense of worth, and yet they sin. "If we say that we have no sin, we deceive ourselves, and the truth is not in us. But if we confess our sins, [God], who is faithful and just, will forgive our sins and cleanse us of all unrighteousness" (1 Jn 1:8-9, NRSV). The experience of separation and reunion, of sin and forgiveness, of death and new life, of becoming and perishing, is verified in empirical theology.

If we take seriously what William James wrote about a "mystical germ," which in his case was an explanation of why he responded to the claims of religious experience, it may be that this dimly felt response explains what happens to the worshiper. In and through worship, with its powerful symbols, stories, and ritual, the mystical germ in each of us responds. This means that only as at least a minimum representation of this atmosphere is present does worship seem real. It also explains why some people are cut off from a sense of the presence of God in worship because their mystical germ is not aroused.

In worship, memory and hope are brought together. The past which has perished is brought into the present and enriches it. The present provides emerging novelty, unpredictable change, and new opportunities, and thus there are new goals for which we are responsible. We recite the biblical stories leading to the coming of the church, and by centering on the life of Jesus we recall the reconciling work of God in history and today and express our hope for the future. Both memory and hope are held together in our worship. The memory of the baptism of Jesus by John the Baptist is related to the hope for the future of all people through the sacrament of baptism. The recalling of the Last Supper provides a memorial of that event and a celebration of God's current activity through us and in creation. The metaphor of the cross and resurrection becomes the motif for understanding how the lost may be found, the alienated may be reconciled, and the dead alive again to each other and to God. Daniel Day Williams reminds us that "the suffering, atoning, and redeeming love of God is remembered and represented ever anew when the sacrament is celebrated and, we most certainly add, when it is received in faith."[17]

The symbols, language, and rituals of worship tend to become ossified and thus lose their relevance to the experience of the worshipers. The stained glass windows of ancient cathedrals, for example, no longer have an obvious meaning for many people. The language of the liturgy becomes outdated, as in the use of the Latin Mass or archaic English in many liturgies. The Bible has gone through numerous revisions, often at the expense of offending many believers. From the standpoint of empirical theology such revisions are long overdue; yet there is always resistance to change, sometimes powerful enough to result in schisms. Thus, the congregation suffers from tensions that are often disastrous. But unless there is continuing change the congregation will continue to shrink. Thus the symbols that are ritualized provide both continuing strength to the congregation and the risk of disintegration.

Revision, then, is inevitable, and because liturgical language has not kept up with changing beliefs, more radical changes are needed. Eliminating language that emphasizes the masculine elements in our references to God, eliminating pronouns in certain of our prayers, adding more ecologically relevant references to the relation of human beings to animals and to the natural world, adding images that include all races, and focusing more on the need for justice and peace, would be just a beginning of the changes necessary for today's world.

No longer would God be conceived as all-powerful, changeless and unfeeling, or as one who predestines people to heaven or hell, or as one who is responsible for genuine evil. The images of king, dictator, lord, clockmaker, or an avenger would no longer be used. Rather, God would be thought of as always present, as persuasive love, as the source of forgiveness and reconciliation, as creativity, as the source of novelty, and as the root of judgment. For such insights we need new models.

Sallie McFague has suggested that we need both personal and cosmic models. In worship we are addressing God, not describing deity. We know that the models we use cannot be taken literally, but they point to reality and they provide a focus for prayer, for celebration, and for response in terms of ethics and social responsibility. She suggests the following:

When we address God as mother, father, lover, friend, or as judge, healer, liberator, companion, or yet again as sun, ocean, fortress, shield, or even as creator, redeemer, and sustainer, we know that these terms are not descriptions of God. When we speak to God we are most conscious of

---

17. Daniel Day Williams, *The Spirit and Forms of Love* (New York: Harper & Row, 1968), p. 190.

how inadequate our language is for God, something we more easily forget when we speak about God—that is, when we are doing theology.[18]

We may believe there is no vision of a personal God and all we can say is that there is a "more" (James) or a "divine value-producing factor" (Macintosh) or even a "fellow sufferer who understands" (Whitehead), but we are like Theodore Parker, the Boston preacher, of whom his biographer wrote, "In his *theology* God was neither personal nor impersonal, but as a reality transcending these distinctions, in his *devotions* God was as personal as his own father or mother. And he prayed to him as such, daringly indifferent to the anthropomorphisms of his unfettered speech."[19]

This underscores two points: our models for God must be consistent with our empirical findings, and our language of prayer and worship must have the warmth of full personality and the reality of cosmic influence by God. This leads to the need for worship to be so formulated that it appeals to the congregations's sense of reverence and awe and also appeals to their emotions.

All theologies and dogmas are rooted in emotional experiences. The study of primitive religion, with the emphasis on magic, wonder, awe, and fear, turns on the emotions aroused. Worship, to be valid, is associated with feeling. Bernard Meland suggests that "theologians must be worshipers, first, and interpreters second. . . . An intellectualism that repudiates emotion is bound, in time, to become sterile, because lacking in emotional resources to stir the intellect toward greater insight."[20]

John Dewey was critical of religion based on the supernatural, but his empiricism also led him to a naturalism that was lacking in emotion, and he lamented, "Were men and women actuated throughout the length and breadth of human relations with the faith and ardor that have at times marked historic religions the consequences would be incalculable."[21] Dewey wanted "passionate intelligence," which is exactly what empirical theology needs.

When the traditional concept of deity is dead in the psychology of many people, we find that we are suspended between an impossible ideal and an attractive one. David Griffin deals with this in the final chapter of *Evil Revisited*. He reminds us of the tender elements in the original gospel, and how over the years they were lost sight of in the theologies influenced by the model of the all-powerful monarch, the dictator who governed all things. He states the challenge as follows: "The goal is to bring about a transformation such that the idea of God that intelligently seems *worthy* of worship will

---

18. Reprinted from Sallie McFague, *Models of God* (Philadelphia: Fortress, 1987), p. 181. Used by permission of Augsburg Fortress.

19. Harry Emerson Fosdick, *The Meaning of Being a Christian* (New York: Association Press, 1964), p. 62.

20. Meland, *Modern Man's Worship*, pp. 264-265.

21. John Dewey, *A Common Faith* (New Haven: Yale University Press, 1934), pp. 80-81.

actually *evoke* worship."[22] There are resources in the tradition of worship through the ages that point strongly in this direction. The empiricist will make selections from this treasure with an awareness of what models still have significance and will choose Bible readings, hymns, and prayers as parts of the new liturgy for the congregation.

The problem before us is this: How can worship be sound from the point of view of empirical theology and also appeal to the emotional side of the worshipers? Empiricism appeals to the rational side of the interpretation of experience and lacks the language that stirs one's feelings and therefore is in danger of becoming sterile. Traditional theology provides outworn theological claims and an equally ineffective vocabulary due to overfamiliarity. At the other end of the equation, there are activities and preaching styles that arouse the emotions and manipulate them without being grounded in a sound theology.

If, as Whitehead has written, God "is the lure for feeling, the eternal urge of desire,"[23] we relate to God who provides the initial phase of our purpose in life. Worship becomes theocentric, not anthropocentric. The worshiper's feelings are activated. What Bernard Meland calls "the appreciative consciousness" works in conjunction with what he calls the moral and rational ones as the whole person responds in worship to the presence of God. But there is a simultaneous focusing on the past and future as felt in the present moment. The "not yet" is not known (even to God) and the past and present are influential on the future in ways that cannot be deduced. Worship is again seen as a mixture of memory and hope, and the appreciative consciousness works with the rational and moral to provide stability as the advance into novelty is experienced.[24]

At work here is what William James called "the fringe of consciousness":

> In itself, a blurred thing is just as particular as a sharp thing; and the generic character of either sharp image or blurred image depends on its being felt *with its representative function*. This function is the mysterious *plus*, the understood meaning. . . . It is just that staining, fringe, or halo of obscurely felt relation to masses of other imagery about to come, but not yet distinctly in focus . . . The difference between thought and feeling thus reduces itself, in the last subjective analysis, to the presence or absence of "fringe.". . . . From the cognitive point of view, all mental facts are intellections. From the subjective point of view all are feelings. Once admit that the passing and evanescent are as real parts of the stream

---

22. David Ray Griffin, *Evil Revisited* (Albany: SUNY Press, 1991), p. 212.

23. Alfred North Whitehead, *Process and Reality*, corrected ed., ed. David Ray Griffin and Donald W. Sherburne (New York: Free Press, 1978), p. 344.

24. Bernard Eugene Meland, *Higher Education and the Human Spirit* (Chicago: University of Chicago Press, 1953), pp. 48-78.

as the distinct and comparatively abiding: once allow that fringes and halos, inarticulate perceptions, whereof the objects are as yet unnamed, mere nascences of cognition, premonitions, awareness of direction, are thoughts *sui generis*, as much as articulate meanings and propositions are; once restore, I say, the vague to its psychological rights, and the matter presents no further difficulty. . . . The representation, as such, of the universal object is as particular as that of an object about which we know so little that the interjection 'Ha' is all it can evoke from us by way of speech. Both should be weighed on the same scales and have the same measure meted out to them, whether of worship or contempt.[25]

F.S.C. Northrop has coined a phrase which some people have found helpful. He speaks of "the undifferentiated aesthetic continuum" as opening up the understanding of the awareness of God. William James would agree with this concept of an undifferentiated experience, noting that is becomes differentiated at what he called "the focus of attention."[26]

The positive results of worship are found in the renewal of the urge toward moral and social action. The service may end with the admonition, "Let us go forth to love and serve God."

LITURGY FOR LIVING

Both words, *worship* and *liturgy*, are derived from their original secular use. Worship usually referred to persons of worth, who were addressed as "your worship." Liturgy meant the relation of people to their work. Today, worship is the honoring of God and liturgy is the work of the people in relation to God.

The traditional services have emerged through almost two thousand years of use and change, from informal beginnings to elaborate rituals and formal practices. As there has been variety in these developments, so there is a multitude of types of services, ritual practices, forms of prayer, and the propagation of the gospel message. There have been borrowings from one denomination to another. There is a rich and varied mine of tradition that needs constant evaluation and revision to meet the challenges to worship for today.[27]

The great virtue of the ancient forms of prayer is that they reflect universal human needs and truly catholic aspirations. Their very survival

25. William James, *The Principles of Psychology*, Vol. I (Boston: Henry Holt, 1903; New York: Dover, 1950), pp. 478-479, note.
26. See F.S.C. Northrop, *Man, Nature and God* (New York: Pocket Books, 1962), pp. 186-191.
27. See Marion J. Hatchett, *Commentary on the American Prayer Book* (New York: Seabury, 1980), pp. 1-13; George Hedley, *Christian Worship* (New York: Macmillan, 1953), pp. 10-17.

through the centuries attests their power in helping to make the Christian's prayer real, and their wide acceptance and use reflect their validity as expressions of authentic Christian faith. To substitute for them the extempore outpourings of one individual, in one limited situation, is to endanger at once orthodoxy and catholicity.[28]

So-called "wild cat" prayers are rarely suitable in corporate worship, but new prayers may be written that fit the newer theological insights and the changing world, something never anticipated by ancient writers. New prayers may have the same beauty of form and words.

The basic form of prayer is the collect. Many such brief prayers are available in the tradition and new ones are being written for new occasions. "A collect," according to Parsons and Jones, "is as exacting an art-form as a sonnet. It is free poetry, where thoughts, instead of words, rhyme in definite strophe-patterns. It has underlying principles of prose rhythms."[29] They are meant to be read aloud in the context of a congregation.

Many such prayers, with slight alterations in the address to deity, may prove useful for those who hold to an empirical theology. For example:

[Almighty] God, to you all hearts are open, all desires known, and from you no secrets are hid; cleanse the thoughts of our hearts by the inspiration of your holy spirit, that we may perfectly love you, and worthily magnify your holy name.

[O heavenly] Father, who has filled the world with beauty; open our eyes to behold your gracious hand in all your works; that rejoicing in your whole creation, we may learn to serve you with gladness; for the sake of [him through whom all things were made] your son Jesus Christ [our Lord].

[Almighty God and heavenly] Father, guide the nations of the world into the way of justice and truth, and establish among them that peace which is the fruit of righteousness, that they may become the kingdom of our [Lord and] savior Jesus Christ.

Look with compassion, [O heavenly Father], upon the people in this land (and all lands), who live with injustice, terror, disease, and death as their constant companions. Have mercy upon us. Help us to eliminate our cru-

28. Hedley, *Christian Worship*, p. 140; see John N. Wall, "History, Culture and the Changing Language of Worship," *Anglican Theological Review* (Fall 1991), pp. 403-429.

29. Edward Lambe Parsons and Bayard Hale Jones, *The American Prayer Book* (New York: Scribner's, 1937), p. 144.

elty to these our neighbors. Strengthen those who spend their lives establishing equal protection of the law and equal opportunities for all. And grant that every one of us may enjoy a fair portion of the riches of this (the) land; through Jesus Christ [our Lord].

The above samples come from existing liturgical sources. It is possible also to compose collects from other sources:

God, who has lured us by your persuasive love to align our wills with yours, grant that we may be inspired to use our freedom to create novelty for ourselves and others in the harmony of your kingdom. Save us from merely trivial meanderings. Keep us from weak resignation in the face of evil, and give us the patience to accept the inevitable; in the name of Jesus Christ. (From Alfred North Whitehead).

Eternal God, in these times of stress and calamity, when life seems hard to maintain and cheap to lose, and innocence seems a poor protection and human policies insane imaginations, and passion is spent and peace not won; lead us, we pray, to deal with the world as we inherit it, so to value humanity that we shall find you, so to strive after peace and righteousness as to enter your kingdom of peace; in the name of Jesus Christ. (From John Oman).

O God, grant that we may enjoy living together with other people, discover the giving and receiving of friendship, and enter into the world of music, art, and literature; and in so doing experience the profound joy of your presence, the fulfillment of our lives through the refreshment of your spirit, and thank you for your gracious and loving kindness, manifest in Jesus Christ. (From Bernard Meland.)

O God, grant us a pure heart that we may see you, a humble heart that we may hear you, a heart to love that we may serve you, a heart of faith that we may live in and with you. (From Dag Hammarsjöld).

Longer prayers are often suitable. There are pastoral prayers that sum up the concerns of the congregation. John Suter has written one such prayer dealing with daily anxieties:

Regard, O [Lord] God, with your fatherly compassion, all who are disquieted or tense, who cannot lose themselves either in happy work or in restful sleep, who looking within do not know themselves or looking to you do not find you. Lead them, we pray, out of clangor into quietude, out of futility into usefulness, out of despair into the sure serenity of truth. Teach them to believe that you are faithful, and that your love hopes all things and endures all things; that all the darkness of the world, even the inner blackness of the soul, cannot quench one small candle of your fidelity. Give them of your perspective, your humor, your gift of tranquility and poise. Be so patient with them that they may learn to be patient with themselves; so firm, that they may lean on you; so persistent in leading, that they may venture out and find pasture in the sunny fields of your kingdom, where all who follow your shepherding may find gladness and delight; in the name of earth's most calm and daring son, word of God, and master of us all, our savior Jesus Christ.[30]

Ian Barbour examines one of the new prayers in the 1979 *Book of Common Prayer*, which, he says, "could not have been written before the space age, yet they express traditional themes. The celebrant (C) is at the altar and the people respond (P):

C: God of [all] power, ruler of the universe, you are worthy of glory and praise.
P: Glory to you for ever and ever.
C: At your command all things came to be: the vast expanse of interstellar space, galaxies, suns, the planets in their courses, and this fragile earth, our island home.
P: By your will they were created and have their being.
C: From the primal elements you brought forth the human race, and blessed us with memory, reason, and skill. You made us the rulers of creation. But we turned against you and betrayed your trust; and we turned against one another.
P: Have mercy, Lord, for we are sinners in your sight.

Here again the focus is on the significance of human life in relation to God and the world. This is what is important religiously."[31]

Traditional hymns reflect many images and models which are consistent with empirical and process theology. Some reflect an early tradition and are translations from the Latin, but the popular use of hymns as part of worship began in the eighteen century and really took hold in the nineteenth. One of the earliest is taken from the *Epistle to Diognetus*, dated about 150 C.E.

> The great creator of the worlds. . . .
> He came as Savior to his own,
> the way of love he trod;

---

30. John Wallace Suter, *Prayers of the Spirit* (New York: Harper & Brothers, 1943), pp. 27-28.

31. Ian Barbour, *Religion in an Age of Science* (San Francisco: Harper & Row, 1990), pp. 134-135.

he came to win us by good will,
for force is not of God.

Not to oppress, but summon all
their truest life to find.
in love God sent his Son to save
not to condemn our kind.[32]

Once to every man and woman
[Once to every man and nation]
Comes the moment to decide,
In the strife of truth with falsehood,
For the good or evil side. . . .
New occasions teach new duties,
Time makes ancient good uncouth;
They must upwards still and onward
Who would keep abreast of truth.[33]

A hymn written originally for children has become popular among adults. It picks up the meaning of "saint" as in Ephesians 4:12: "to equip the saints for the work of ministry."

I sing a song of the saints of God,
patient and brave and true,
who toiled and fought and lived and died
for the Lord they loved and knew. . . .
You can meet them in school, or in lanes, or at sea,
in church, or in trains, or in shops, or at tea,
for the saints of God are just folk like me,
and I mean to be one, too.[34]

There are other aspects of worship that are open to interpretation from an empirical and process point of view. The sacramental life of the church, especially baptism and the Lord's Supper, are central to its worship and to the lives of its members. The sacraments underscore the organic relations of the members to each other and to God. This is incarnational as well as organic and the whole event is multirelational. The ritual and the language need to

---

32. From *The Hymnal* 1982, copyright Church Pension Fund. From the *Epistle to Diognetus*, ca. 150, tr. F. Bland Tucker, #489, vs. 5b-6, alt. Music: *Tallis' Ordinal*, Thomas Tallis. Used by permission.

33. From *The Hymnal* 1940, copyright Church Pension Fund. By James Russell Lowell, 1845. #519, vs. 1a,3b, alt. Music: Thomas John Williams. Used by permission.

34. From *The Hymnal* 1982, copyright Church Pension Fund. By Lesbia Scott. #293. vs. 1a, 3b, alt. Music: John Henry Hopkins. Used by permission.

express this complex relationality. The reintroduction of the passing of the peace is a step in this direction, as is the passing of the bread and wine from one to the other rather than have the celebrant dispense the elements.

There is room in such worship for informality and innovation. The "newspaper litany," which I first saw at a meeting of the World Council of Christian Education in Nairobi in 1967, is especially effective in times of crisis, when key passages from news sources reflecting current events are used with responses by the congregation. Other forms of prayers of the people provide for relevance. The use of folk music and even jazz has proven meaningful, especially with young people. In the use of novelty, creative imagination will arouse the sense of reverence and stimulate both the intellect and the emotions.

When we are dealing with many liturgical and denominational traditions, it is difficult to establish norms for such worship, but the goals are clear. If a service is fitly framed together, as George Hedley writes, it will include the acts of acclamation, confession, forgiveness, listening to scripture, asserting the faith of the church, and thanksgiving, with proclamation in terms of a sermon at the proper time. The response will be tested empirically. Is there an experience of the presence of God? Is there a joyful affirmation of commitment? Is there due sense of sin and the need for compassion and forgiveness? And above all is there a creative transformation of individuals in the congregation? These results may not be immediately evident, but the constant exposure to worship over time should approximate such outcomes. If not, then worship may be reduced to custom, emotional satisfaction, and self-righteousness.

PREACHING

The sermon has been part of the experience of the people since the days of Moses, but it was not connected with a system of worship. The great prophets were critical of the temple and preached as outsiders. As prophets and priests worked together, preaching became centered in the synagogue. The early church, emerging from the synagogue, became the locale for the Christian story. By the end of New Testament times, preaching became restricted to bishops. After the sixth century, however, preaching was ignored except for such orders as the Dominicans and figures such as St. Francis.

With the Reformation, preaching was restored to the center of Christian worship. Because of the ignorance of many of the clergy, homilies were created, but they soon became outdated or ineffective because of constant repetition. The Wesleys had much to do with the revival of preaching both in churches and out of doors. In the United States, at least, there soon was too much emphasis on the sermon, to which any ritual was considered only a footnote.[35]

---

35. See Hedley, *Christian Worship*, pp. 164-171.

A sermon should include story, dialogical engagement, and ethical exhortation, and it may be more than a conventional presentation.

The Word of God is greater than any human words and may choose to come clothed in quite different ways. He who was "veiled in flesh" does not now have to be veiled by human discourse. If the Spirit of God can inspire preachers and writers with the word of life that puts fire in our bones and music in our hearts, so can he inspire dance, drama, music, and art. And if the Spirit can open our ears to hear the truth of God in the Bible and in preaching, so can we be opened to see it in the work of Rembrandt, Mozart, and Milton, or Picasso, Auden, and Britten; or thousands of others.[36]

The Book of Common Prayer suggests: "The proclamation and response may include readings, songs, talk, dance, instrumental music, other art forms, silence. A reading from the gospel is always included."[37]

Preaching must be more than mere discussion of biblical texts, more than so-called homilies. There is need for theological foundations, with a style that includes story, parabolic forms, the performative use of symbols and myths, and the imaginative use of language with unsuspected qualifiers. It cannot be dogmatic and authoritarian but must include the freedom of the hearer to interpret what is said or done. It may have the story of Jesus as its center, but relates whatever is communicated to the lives of the hearers.

As the sermon develops, it should appeal to the emotions. "If that emotion is boredom, the feeling will have little intensity. . . . Interest is not the only important emotion. Ideas and images arouse joy and sorrow, hope and despair, guilt and purgation, attraction and revulsion, love and hostility."[38]

The diversity of hearers challenges the preacher to tailor the message within the capabilities and interests of that particular congregation. Preaching needs to operate in terms of empirical theology, beginning with observation, tales of experimental behavior, and the application of reason. Like William James, the preacher has the rich material of direct experience found

---

36. Charles P. Price and Louis Weil, *Liturgy for Living* (New York: Seabury, 1979), p. 179; see Louis Weil, "Facilitating Growth in Faith Through Liturgical Worship," in *Handbook of Faith*, ed. James Michael Lee (Birmingham, Ala.: Religious Education Press, 1990), pp. 203-220.

37. *Book of Common Prayer* (New York: Church Hymnal Corp. and Seabury, 1977), p. 400. "We have a clear record that Augustine's audience at Hippo participated actively with applause, acclamation, laughter, sighing, waving of arms, and beating of breasts, shouting out in anticipation of his next point, group recitation of scripture passages he alluded to." Quoted by Thomas Groome in *Sharing Faith* (San Francisco: Harper, 1991), p. 524, note 121.

38. William Beardslee and others, *Biblical Preaching on the Death of Christ* (Nashville: Abingdon, 1989), p. 61.

in the lives of the listeners and others, imaginative construction of hypotheses, pragmatic outcomes, and rational inferences. But any suggestions will not be dogmatic or specific. As Whitehead has written, "Simple solutions are bogus solutions," and the congregation does not need simplicity. There is an appeal to what Whitehead called "a vague affective tone" that attracts and stimulates the hearers both to think and to do.

Horace Bushnell claimed that it was wise to use many different words with similar meanings, so that one or more would break the ice and lead to understanding. Ian Ramsey claimed that using many models, suitably qualified, would stimulate the imagination and lead to commitment. The challenge is to develop metaphors and models which evoke some discernment, some insight, and some disclosure of the divine. These attempts are not guaranteed to succeed, but they promise innumerable possibilities. "Generalizing," says Ramsey, "metaphorical expressions occur when two situations strike us in such a way as to reveal what includes them but is no mere combination of both."[39]

Wieman reminds us of the danger of assuming the infallibility of the preacher. Only when fallibility is admitted can the preacher awaken the hearers to "the awareness of [human] destiny and the saving and transforming power by which it is accomplished."[40]

Preaching deals with many aspects of believing and living; it is almost encyclopedic in its scope. It communicates with people of all ages and all cultures, meeting them at their growing edge and leading them to deeper commitment to a deity of persuasive love. Because it is part of the church's worship, it has a framework of ritual, lectionary, hymns, and prayers that must be fitly framed together, so that familiarity and creative novelty work together to evoke discernment and commitment.

RELIGIOUS EDUCATION

Like preaching, the purpose of teaching is "to equip God's people for work in [God's] service" (Eph 4:12, NEB). Thus, "we are no longer to be children, tossed by the waves and whirled about by every fresh gust of teaching, dupes of crafty rogues and their deceitful schemes" (Eph 4:14, NEB). The letter goes on to describe the kind of life and attitude that should be the goal.

Every local congregation has an educational program, even when it does not know it. It may be a meager one or a bad one to which little attention is paid. Most congregations, however, are concerned with the education of the young and often of the adults.

When taken seriously, there are still dangers. There may be too much

---

39. Ian T. Ramsey, *Models and Metaphors* (London: Oxford University Press, 1964), p. 53.

40. Wieman, *Man's Ultimate Commitment*, p. 181.

intellectual analysis and formalized information, at the expense of developing habit formation and concrete application. As Whitehead reminds us, "When you understand all about the sun and all about the atmosphere and all about the rotation of the earth, you may still miss the radiance of the sunset."[41] An empirical approach to education starts with the experience of the student. "In the Garden of Eden Adam saw the animals before he named them; in the traditional system, children named the animals before they saw them."[42]

Teaching emerges from a congregation held together by worship. It leads to education for discernment and commitment, which results from an understanding of one's sense of worth and of the world in which one lives. We live in a culture that stands or falls on the strength of its religious nucleus. We need to take seriously the fact that one cannot teach much about religion when the students are denied the bodily requirements of food, clothing, and shelter. We need to resist the overpowering authority of nation and church in order to keep a balance between order and freedom. We need to recognize that the way of persuasion is the basis for community living and for successful religious education, for it provides the freedom of response and the sense of worth that makes faith and commitment possible. And behind all these aspects is the sense of a persuasive and loving God, toward whom one's reverence increases through the experiences of worship and reflection on all kinds of experience.[43]

The objectives of religious education should include the development of aesthetic apprehension, especially as found in art, music, drama, and, with smaller children, the wonder of the natural world. The mechanical routines of much of modern life can be deadening, especially when replicated in the church. Adjustments to today's life may be threatening, but reassurance comes with the realization that life has always produced new developments which are either benign or evil and frequently ambiguous. They simply take on new and sometimes unexpected forms.

Almost fifty years ago, Edgar Dale formulated a "cone of experience." The most concrete way of learning is through direct experience. Less concrete is observation. Finally there is the process of symbolizing in terms of visual and

---

41. Whitehead, *Science and the Modern World*, p. 286. For Whitehead's theory of education see *The Aims of Education* (New York: Macmillan, 1929; Free Press edition, 1967), pp. 1-41. Also, Randolph Miller, "Process Thought, Worship, and Religious Education," in *Aesthetic Dimensions of Religious Education*, ed. Gloria Durka and Joanmarie Smith (New York: Paulist, 1979), pp. 107-120; "Whitehead and Religious Education," *Religious Education* (May-June 1973), pp. 315-322; "Process Thinking and Religious Education," *Anglican Theological Review* (July 1975), pp. 271-288; "Dewey, Whitehead and Education," *The Living Light* (Fall 1985), pp. 35-44; Robert S. Brumbaugh, *Whitehead, Process Philosophy and Education* (Albany: SUNY Press, 1982).

42. Whitehead, *Science and the Modern World*, p. 285.

43. James Michael Lee, ed., *The Religious Education We Need* (Birmingham, Ala.: Religious Education Press, 1977), pp. 44-45.

verbal symbols. The degrees of abstractness are correlated with the distance from concreteness in the learning process. Students may respond to different levels in this "cone." The teacher needs to distinguish which levels are suitable to the learners, and make use of doing, observing, and symbolizing as ways of approaching a full understanding.[44]

James Michael Lee reminds us that we are concerned with educating the whole person. This involves nine forms or processes: conscious content, product content, process content, cognitive content, affective content, verbal content, nonverbal content, unconscious content, and lifestyle content. When all of these are in some degree of balance involving the whole person of the learner, religious education may take place. This leads to a multidimensional approach to the learners. Lee places experience at the center, which makes his approach appropriate for empirical or process theology.[45]

William James developed an educational philosophy in his *Psychology* and in *Talks to Teachers*. From these sources we can flesh out the beginnings of an approach to religious education. At the conclusion of his *Varieties of Religious Experience,* he writes that one becomes conscious of a *more* to which one may turn. This is an individual experience, probably the product of what he called a mystical germ. Although he was skeptical of the teachings of Christianity, religion was at the center of much of his thinking. If there is a mystical germ in most of us, the pupil needs to recognize it. It may be so vague and unconscious that it is difficult to identify, but the pupil can be led to discern it with proper educational leading. The use of religious language needs constant revision in order to account for such an experience. If we follow James' approach, the theology will be radically different from traditional doctrines. Individuals must do their own thinking and believing, and thus make their own acts of faith. James concludes:

> Don't preach too much to your pupils or abound in good talk in the abstract. Lie in wait rather for the practical opportunities, be prompt to seize them as they pass, and thus at one operation get your pupils both to think, to feel, and to do. The strokes of *behavior* are what give set to the character, and work the good habits into the organic tissue.[46]

---

44. Edgar Dale, *Audio-Visual Methods in Teaching* (New York: Dryden Press, 1946), p. 52; see p. 37-52; see Randolph C. Miller, *Education for Christian Living* (Englewood Cliffs, N.J.: Prentice-Hall, 1955, 1963 ed.), pp. 196-197; James Michael Lee, *The Content of Religious Instruction* (Birmingham, Ala.: Religious Education Press, 1985), pp. 689-690.

45. Lee, *Content of Religious Instruction*, pp. 13-15, 42-48.

46. William James, *Talks to Teachers on Psychology; and to Students on Some of Life's Ideals* (New York: Henry Holt, 1899), p. 71; see Randolph C. Miller, "The Educational Philosophy of William James," *Religious Education* (Fall 1991), pp. 619-634.

Whitehead suggests that wandering has been the stimulus for the upward trend of animals. Animals in the wild constantly wander, or they die. Humankind "has wandered from the trees to the plains, from the plains to the seacoast, from climate to climate, from continent to continent, and from habit of life to habit of life."[47] The human mind has also wandered from superstition to philosophy, from philosophy to religion, from religion to science, and back from science to a religion consistent with a scientific view of the world; it has wandered from supernaturalism to naturalism, from supernaturalistic revelation to empirical naturalism. Today many people are seeking new knowledge which comes from better observation, speculation, imagination, and empirical testing in science and religion.

There is, then, a challenge to develop a reconstructed view of religious education. Teachers are not authority figures with all the answers. Even great scholars, as teachers, function as enablers or equippers or coaches and assist students to develop powers of observation and reason with freedom to wander as continuing learners.

But what makes such education Christian? First, the subject matter to which education as a discipline is applied deals with the biblical and Christian tradition and its interpretation today. Second, the overtones of commitment and loyalty to the deity are studied, so that the personal element enters fully into the picture. Third, a community that is empirically anchored in the worship of God is a significant part of the process. Fourth, the teacher and presumably the students must be, at least potentially, loyal members of the community of believers. These four elements create an atmosphere in which the process of Christian education takes place and commitment is encouraged.[48]

Theology is the clue to educational theory. Sara Little suggests that belief systems should function to help persons

make sense of the world and have a frame of reference for understanding, caring, deciding, and doing . . . to aid a community—in our case, specifically the religious community called the church—to achieve identity and maintain continuity . . . to link human experience and the Christian tradition through an interpretation that internalizes meaning and gives direction to life . . . to link lives of individuals and communities to larger ultimate realities and purposes.[49]

Good education, then, leads to devotion to values and to ethical behavior. God is seen as the giver of values and the source of potential emerging nov-

---

47. Whitehead, *Science and the Modern World*, p.298.
48. See Randolph C. Miller, *The Language Gap and God* (New York: Pilgrim Press, 1970), pp. 38-39.
49. Sara Little, *To Set One's Heart* (Atlanta: John Knox, 1983), pp. 19-21. See Randolph C. Miller, *The Clue to Christian Education* (New York: Scribner's, 1950).

elty. The umbrella value is beauty, and the good and the true are subsumed under the category of the aesthetic. Because God in the primordial nature is pure potentiality, we rely on the consequent nature for our ethical guidance, where God's aims for us may be discerned. Therefore, our best actions are only approximations of God's will. There may be conflicts between two courses of action, both of which seem to be good. It may be simply a matter of emotional preference. Sometimes the choice is abundantly clear. But the tension remains because we can never be sure. Other choices are between good and evil, and we are tempted to choose the evil one. Because we live in an immoral society, many possibilities are relatively evil, and yet we cannot abdicate from society. Finally, there is the choice between two evils, as in the case of war, when one may choose not to defend one's country or to participate in the destruction of the enemy.[50] Good religious education will deal with such issues and seek to lead people to recognize that faith without works is dead. We are to go from church to love and serve God.

When empirical theology is the basis for religious education, there needs to be a discussion of what kinds of evidence are considered empirical and what methods are used to establish basic definitions of God as "the growth of meaning and value" (Wieman), "divine value producing factor" (Macintosh), "the creative passage (Meland), or "principle of concretion" and "primordial and consequent nature" (Whitehead). From there one moves to analogies and models that are recognized as such, so that they are not taken literally. Then we can speak of God as redeemer, reconciler, persuasive love, "the fellow sufferer who understands" (Whitehead). God suffers with us and shares our joys, provides direction for our lives, gives us strength, forgives us, arouses feelings of awe and wonder, and transforms us as we cannot transform ourselves. "The power of God is the worship [God] inspires."[51]

In *Teaching from the Heart*, Mary Elizabeth Mullino Moore has developed an understanding of method from the standpoint of process theology and her perspective as a woman. She has a passion for organic theology and teaching, seeks to bring theory and practice together, and sees the interconnections in the educational enterprise. It is a holistic and empirical view of the process. She categorizes her methods as midwife teaching, integrative teaching, incarnational teaching, relational teaching, liberative teaching, and teaching from the heart. These are a far cry from the more mechanistic models current in educational theory, and they lead to a more wholesome and holistic result. Her book is a justification of this approach to religious education.[52]

---

50. See Randolph C. Miller, *The Theory of Christian Education Practice* (Birmingham, Ala.: Religious Education Press, 1980), pp. 115-152, for a more complete discussion of values and ethics.

51. Whitehead, *Science and the Modern World*, p. 276.

52. Mary Elizabeth Mullino Moore, *Teaching from the Heart* (Minneapolis: Fortress, 1991).

Christians still need to face the question of interpreting such ancient doctrines as the Trinity from an empirical base. Although many people now object to the patriarchal use of "Father" and "Son," these models are part of the tradition and need reinterpretation. We may say that God as Father is the power who is the unchanging source of values; as Father, God is primordial and everlasting, the source of creativity, potentiality, and emerging novelty; it is God's aim to which we should attempt to align ourselves. God as *Logos* and *Sophia* is the Word and Wisdom,[53] that mode through which God is revealed to us in experience. The human personality of Jesus was the point at which the Word and Wisdom became a unique ingredient in the world, so that we can say that Jesus' human aim and the aim of God came freely into union. God as Spirit (*Ruach*) is the indwelling of God as consequent in human nature, giving us both life and hope. This keeps the essential meaning of God as Trinity, for the three aspects of God should be considered as three "faces" or "modes" or "masks." This is to be understood as an analogy and a model and not as literal truth.[54]

H. Richard Niebuhr reminds us that "the enduring contribution of empirical theology, from Schleiermacher to Macintosh, lies in its insistence on the fact that knowledge of God is available only in religious relation to [God]."[55]

There is a warning in *Doctrine in the Church of England*: "It is always to be remembered that the religious value of the incarnation consists primarily in what it declares concerning God rather than what it claims for the historic Jesus, while yet it is *through* faith in Jesus Christ that [believers] were led to the Christian's knowledge of God. They saw 'the light of the knowledge of the glory of God in the face of Jesus Christ.'"[56]

Seen in this light, it is possible for an empiricist to be a Christian and for a Christian to be an empiricist. And it is possible for a congregation to embrace an empirically based Christianity in their worship, their preaching, their religious education, and their pastoral care, resulting in an impact on the social, political, and environmental issues of their daily lives.

---

53. See Charles Melchert, "Wisdom Is Vindicated by Her Deeds," *Religious Education* (Winter 1992), pp. 127-151.

54. See Randolph C. Miller, *This We Can Believe* (New York: Hawthorn/Seabury, 1976), p. 98; Marjorie Suchocki, *God-Christ-Church* (New York: Crossroad, 1982), pp. 213-223; William Temple, *Nature, Man and God* (New York: Macmillan, 1934), p. 259; John Cobb Jr., *Can Christ Become Good News Again?* (St. Louis: Chalice Press, 1991), pp. 48-50.

55. Julius Seelye Bixler, Robert Lowry Calhoun, Helmut Richard Niebuhr, eds., *The Nature of Religious Experience* (New York: Harper & Brothers, 1937), p. 112.

56. William Temple, chairman, *Doctrine in the Church of England* (New York: Macmillan, 1938), p. 76.

Contributors

JOHN B. COBB JR. recently retired from the School of Theology at Claremont. He is the publisher of *Process Studies* and the founder of the Center for Process Studies where he continues to serve as a co-director. He teaches now part-time at the Claremont Graduate School. Among his publications are *Christ in a Pluralistic Age, Beyond Dialogue, Process Theology and Political Theology, The Liberation of Life* (with Charles Birch), *For the Common Good* (with Herman Daly), and *Matters of Life and Death.*

ROBERT S. CORRINGTON is Associate Professor of Philosophical Theology in the Graduate and Theological Schools of Drew University. He is the author of *The Community of Interpreters* (1987), and *Nature and Spirit: An Essay in Ecstatic Naturalism* (1992). He is co-editor of *Pragmatism Considers Phenomenology* (1987) and *Nature's Perspectives: Prospects for Ordinal Metaphysics* (1991). His research is in the areas of American philosophy, semiotics, and liberal theology. He is currently at work on a three-volume work entitled *The Signs of the World.* He is on the Executive Board of the Semiotic Society of America and is Past President of the Karl Jaspers Society of North America.

WILLIAM DEAN is Professor of Religion at Gustavus Adolphus College. His writing of the 1970s argued for the centrality of an aesthetic perspective in religious and moral thought, especially in process theology (*Coming To: A Theology of Beauty* [1972]; *Love Before the Fall* [1976]. In the 1980s he demonstrated how empirical theology fits and amplifies religious thought in the American, postmodern context (*American Religious Empiricism* [1986]. *History Making History: The New Historicism in American Religious Thought* [1988]; co-edited with Larry Axel T*he Size of God: The Theology of Bernard Loomer in Context* [1987]). Currently, he is working to develop a historicist concept of God and to show it makes possible a more viable public theology.

FREDERICK FERRÉ was born in Boston in 1933. He studied at Oberlin College, Boston University, Vanderbilt University, and the University of St. Andrews (Ph.D. 1959). His teaching career drew him to Vanderbilt University, Mt. Holyoke College, and Dickinson College prior to his present position as Research Professor of Philosophy at the University of Georgia. His main early interests, centered around philosophy of religion, gradually evolved to include philosophy of technology and environmental ethics. His first book was *Language, Logic and God* (1961); his most recent was *Philosophy of Technology* (1988).

NANCY FRANKENBERRY is Professor of Religion at Dartmouth College in Hanover, New Hampshire. She is a graduate of Marquette University (B.A.) and the Graduate Theological Union (M.A., Ph.D.). Her research interests range widely over the areas of American religious empiricism, Buddhist religious philosophy, and feminist theory. She is the author of *Religion and Radical Empiricism* and numerous articles in scholarly journals. Her next book will assess the contemporary significance of religious naturalism and pragmatism.

TYRON INBODY is Professor of Theology at United Theological Seminary, Dayton, Ohio. His Ph.D. is from the Divinity School of the University of Chicago (1973). He has published numerous articles in books and academic journals, including *Process Studies, Zygon, Encounter, Anglican Theological Review,* and *Theological Studies.* Several of his essays are on religious empiricism and Bernard Meland. He is a founding member of the Highlands Institute for American Religious Thought and is the editor of the *American Journal of Theology and Philosophy* and the *United Theological Seminary Journal of Theology.*

BERNARD J. LEE is Professor of Theology at Loyola University in New Orleans and Director of the Graduate Institute for Ministry. Major interests include: retrieving the Jewishness of Jesus and of Christian origins into contemporary Christian identity; the role of practical theology, both in the faith life of basic Christian communities and in the current evolution of graduate ministry education; and the confluence of process theology, pragmatism, hermeneutics and deconstructionism in theological method. Recent books: *Dangerous Memories: House Churches and Our American Story,* and *The Galilean Jewishness of Jesus.*

RANDOLPH CRUMP MILLER is Horace Bushnell Professor of Christian Nurture, Emeritus, at Yale University Divinity School. He was the editor for twenty years of *Religious Education.* He was born in Fresno, California, and grew up in Los Angeles. From 1936 to 1952 he taught at the Church Divinity School of the Pacific and was in charge of an Episcopal congregation. Among his many books are *The Clue to Christian Education, Education for Christian Living, The Language Gap and God, The American Spirit in Theology, This We Can Believe,* and *The Theory of Christian Education Practice.* He is married to Elizabeth Williams Fowlkes, and they have six children.

KARL E. PETERS is Professor of Philosophy and Religion at Rollins College. From 1979 to 1989 he was editor of *Zygon: Journal of Religion and Science*; he is now co-editor. He is a graduate of Carroll College (B.A.), McCormick Theological Seminary (M. Div.) and Columbia University (Ph.D.); is a leader in the Institute on Religion in an Age of Science and co-chair of the Theology and Science Group of the American Academy of Religion; and has published several articles on science and religion, especially on evolutionary theology, evolutionary epistemology in religion, and humanity's relation to nature.

GERARD STEPHEN SLOYAN is Professor Emeritus of Religion at Temple University where he taught New Testament and early Christianity for twenty-four years. Previously he was on the faculty of The Catholic University of America for seventeen years, and currently he is teaching at St. John's University, Collegeville, MN. He is a priest of the Catholic Diocese of Trenton, N.J. His recent books include *Jesus on Trial, Jesus in Focus,* and *The Jesus Tradition.*

MARJORIE HEWITT SUCHOCKI is Ingraham Professor of Theology at the School of Theology in Claremont. She also serves with John B. Cobb Jr., David Griffin, and Mary Elizabeth Moore as one of the co-directors of the Center for Process Studies. Her most recent books are *God-Christ-Church* and *The End of Evil: Process Eschatology in Historical Context.*

WILLIAM CALLOLEY TREMMEL is a native of Colorado, where he graduated from the University of Denver (B.A.) and the Iliff School of Theology (Th.M., Th.D). He engaged in postdoctoral studies at the University of Southern California and the University of Chicago. Early in his career he engaged actively in the ministry of the United Methodist Church, both in Colorado and Kansas. In Kansas, he accepted professorships at Kansas State Teachers College, Emporia, and at Kansas State University, Manhattan. He then moved to the University of South Florida in Tampa, where he established the Department of Religious Studies—a department he chaired for twenty-two years. He is author of numerous articles and of nine monographs and books. Four of his books are currently in print—*Religion: What Is It?; Dark Side: The Satan Story; Running on the Bias;* and *The Jesus Story in the Twenty-Seven Books.*

Index of Names

(The most important references are in **boldface** type)

Index of Subjects

(The most important references are in **boldface** type)

Abba, 187
abduction, 71, 212, 220
abortion, 80
absolute idealism, 228-229
abstraction, abstractions, 125-126
actual entities, 39
Acts, 180
Advancement of Theological Education,
 The (Niebuhr, et al.), 257
Adventures of Ideas (Whitehead), 140
aesthetic experience, 127
aesthetic order, 41
aesthetic sensibilities, 29
aesthetic value, 34, 35
aestheticism, 126
affirming the opposite, 71-73
Africans, 235
allegory, 85
allelon, 196
Amazon, 234
ambiguity, 6, 7, 27, 48, **49**, 94, **101-104**,
 110, **125-127**
American Academy of Religion, 35
American God, 112
American history, 108, 109
American Journal of Theology and
 Philosophy, 35
American perspective, 7, 107
American theology, 109
Americans, 110-111
analogy, analogies, 71-73, 75, 286, 287

angst, 163
animals, 8, 157, 161, 162, 230, 241, 272,
 285
anti-realism, **47-48**
appreciative awareness, 127
appreciative consciousness, 29, 141, 274 ˙
appreciative level, 10, 265
appreciative openness, 123
Atonement and Psychotherapy
 (Browning), 257
authority, 60-61, 87, 248
autonomy, 51

baptism, 271
basic Christian communities, 8, 180, 184,
 194-202
beauty, 69, 127, 286
becoming, 37, 127, 286
Becoming of the Church, The (Lee),
 249
being, 52, 206-207, 209, 213
Ben Sira, 143
Bible, 247, 266, 272
Big Bang, 156, 157
biosphere, 155, 157, 242, 253
birth control, 243
bishops, 85, 280
bodily feelings, 12
body, 38, 241, 252, 269
Body of Christ, 151, 183
boredom, 281

296